WORKING THE

Also by Geoff Dyer

WORKING THE ROOM

Essays and Reviews: 1999–2010

GEOFF DYER

CANONGATE
Edinburgh · London

Published by Canongate Books in 2015

1

For a list of illustrations, please see page viii
For acknowledgements, please see page 389

First published in Great Britain in 2010 by Canongate Books Ltd, 14 High Street,
Edinburgh EH1 1TE

www.canongate.tv

British Library Cataloguing-in-Publication Data
A catalogue record for this book is available on
request from the British Library

ISBN 978 1 78211 511 3

Typeset in Berkeley by Palimpsest Book Production Limited,
Falkirk, Stirlingshire

Printed and bound in Great Britain by Clays Ltd, St Ives plc

For my mum and dad

'There are writers for whom no forms exist: too clever for novels, too sceptical for poetry, too verbose for the aphorism, all that is left to them is the essay – the least appropriate medium for the foiled.'

Don Paterson

Contents

Verbals

Variables

Personals

Contents

List of Illustrations

Colour plates

Introduction

This collection of essays and reviews follows right on from *Anglo-English Attitudes*. The last piece in that book was written in 1999; the earliest one here is from the same year. To be honest, nothing much has changed in the interim. I write about whatever happens to interest me, sometimes accepting commissions from editors, sometimes writing pieces and sending them in on spec. A decade from now, by which time I'll be in my sixties, I hope to have enough new material to bring out a third volume. You see, I've got tenure on this peculiarly vacant chair – or chairs, rather. It's a job for life; more accurately, it *is* a life, and hardly a day goes by without my marvelling that it is somehow feasible to lead it. As in the earlier collection, there's no area of specialised concern or expertise; on the contrary, the pleasure, hopefully, lies in the pick 'n' mix variety, the way one thing leads to another (often quite different) thing.

Actually, one thing has changed: in the last ten years I've been asked to contribute introductions to quite a few books, either re-issued literary classics or photographic monographs and catalogues. I love doing this and am especially grateful to the editors who somehow got wind of the idea that I was interested in Rebecca West or Richard Avedon or whoever and gave me the chance to get between the covers of a shared volume with them. This seems to me the greatest privilege that can be afforded any reader (even if it slightly undermines the idea of being – as I claim in a piece to be found later in this volume – a gatecrasher).

Booksellers and customers often complain about the difficulty of knowing where to stock or find my books. A similar problem crops up here. There is, inevitably, a fair bit of seepage between the various categories on the contents page – Visuals, Personals etc. – but, overall, this seemed the least unsatisfactory way of organising the material. To make things a little less rigid these category headings are not indicated within the pages of the text itself, so that the very personal piece on ghost bikes is followed, without warning, by the first categorically Personal piece. Like this there are only invisible, ghostly residues of division in the unfolding continuity of the book.

There is also, inevitably, a bit of repetition. I see I keep coming back to Rebecca West or John Cheever or D.H. Lawrence when I'm writing about other people: they constitute the core of my personal canon, the writers I can't do without. The fact that Robert Frank keeps coming up as a point of comparison when I'm talking about other photographers might be a symptom of the author's inadequate frame of reference; or perhaps it shows that there is no getting away from him (I meant Frank but perhaps the same is true of the author).

I originally intended using 'My Life as a Gatecrasher' as the title for the whole collection but discarded it for the reason mentioned above. The current title crops up in the essay on Susan Sontag – 'Critics are always working the room' – but although it was absolutely perfect I couldn't use it because Jonathan Lethem had told me, a couple of years earlier, that he had the phrase laid away as the intended title of a future collection of his critical writings. I dropped him a line anyway and asked if he would consider loaning it to me. He agreed, and I'm extremely grateful to him for that characteristic bit of generosity.

G. D., London, June 2010

WORKING THE ROOM

Jacques Henri Lartigue and
The Discovery of India

'You can hardly expect me to fall in love with a photograph.'
Jawaharlal Nehru

This photograph was taken by Jacques Henri Lartigue on the Cap d'Antibes in 1953. He was almost sixty by then, had been photographing for half a century. The picture is of a woman – I don't know who – propped up on a lilo or lounger on the terrace of some presumably luxurious hotel or villa. She's wearing a swimsuit and one of those fun wigs made of strips of coloured paper that you can buy in party shops. You can't see her eyes, she's wearing a pair of big plastic sunglasses, but there's a hint (and this is the lovely flirty thing about the picture) that she is glancing up at the photographer – which means that she is also glancing up at me, at us – rather than reading the unbelievably serious book in her hands: Nehru's *The Discovery of India*! It looks like it's about 800 pages long and weighs a ton. It wouldn't be anything like the same picture if she was reading *Bridget Jones's Diary* which, obviously, hadn't been published back then – but that's another thing about the picture: it could have been taken yesterday, it could have been taken today (especially now that white sunglasses are in vogue again).

The book is a touch of genius – either the genius of contrivance or of the moment – but, actually, if any element of the picture were removed (the wig, the glasses, the painted nails or lipstick) it would be thoroughly diminished. That's the thing about all great photos, though. Everything in them is essential – even the inessential bits.

It occurs to me that the things that are *not* in the photographs are also important. The inclusion of certain things can not just diminish a photograph but destroy it. In this case – all the more remarkable in a photograph taken in 1953 – the absence of a cigarette (so often considered an accessory of glamour) or ashtray is crucial to its allure and its contemporaneity. A cigarette would 'date' or age the photograph as surely as it ages the faces of the people who smoke them. If there were any evidence of smoking I would have to look away. As it is, I can't tear my eyes away. I can't stop looking at her.

So who is she?

But there I go, forgetting one of my own rules about photography, namely that if you look hard enough a photo will always answer your question – even if that answer comes in the form of further questions. Well, whoever she is, she's beautiful. Actually, I can't really tell if that's true, for the simple reason that I can't see enough of her face. But she must be beautiful, for an equally simple reason: because I'm in love with her. Lartigue, too, I suspect. Now, plenty of men have photographed women they love but this picture depicts the *moment* when you fall in love.

That's why the suggestion that she is looking up, meeting our gaze – the photographer's, mine – is so important: this is the first moment when our eyes meet, the moment that each subsequent meeting of eyes will later contain. If this picture is of a woman Lartigue has been with for ten years it actually proves my point: that look, that meeting of the eyes, still contains the charge of the first unphotographed look from way back when. As for me, since I've only just seen the photo, it's a case of love at first sight. And that, I think, is why Lartigue became a model for so many fashion photographers. The most effective form of subliminal seduction – the best way to sell the dresses or hats featured in photos – is to make men fall in love with the woman wearing them, and photographers are all the time trying to emulate or simulate that feeling. With Lartigue, though, it's for real, and the accessories on offer are what? A daft wig, some zany sunglasses and a hardback of *The Discovery of India*! That's the charm of the picture, its magic.

As I said at the beginning, they're all crucial, these ditzy accessories.

The book lends a hint, at the very least, of the exotic. And the wigs and glasses give the picture its faint but unmistakable touch of the erotic. If you want to see her without the wig and glasses then you are already starting to undress her. Not that there is anything explicitly sexual about this – it's more that you want to see what she really looks like. In other words, you want an answer to the question the picture insistently teases us with: to what extent is it posed, contrived? I'd love to know. It would probably be possible to find out by consulting one of the many books about Lartigue currently available but I prefer a less scholarly, more direct but – I hope – not too intrusive approach. '*Excusez-moi, mademoiselle. J'espère que je ne vous dérange . . .*'

2005

Ruth Orkin's 'VE Day'

Photographs depict a moment but they can *contain* years, decades. Few, however, are as saturated with history as Ruth Orkin's picture of the crowd gathered in Times Square on VE Day, 8 May 1945.

To release this history from the image we need to go back at least to 1914, to the photographs of the 'long uneven lines' of men queuing up to enlist. For Philip Larkin, in his poem 'MCMXIV', the grinning faces make it all look like an 'August Bank Holiday lark'. Photographs like these are complemented by the ones taken in 1919, when an army of the surrogate dead marched past the Cenotaph in London in acknowledgement of the cataclysm that the lark had turned into. In another sense, though, the catastrophe was not complete: the ending of the First World War created the conditions for a Second. The treaty at Versailles merely closed a phase of a war that would last, with rumbling truces, until 1945.

The end of the Second World War left Britain militarily victorious but economically ruined. America, meanwhile, was unequivocally victorious. Power crossed the Atlantic. 'The United States', Churchill conceded, 'stands at this moment at the summit of the world.' That summit would not be attained until victory over Japan but Orkin's picture shows the jubilant future that is now within reach. In her novel *The Great Fire,* Shirley Hazzard paints a dismal picture of London in the immediate post-war period. Even in 1948, 'everything is shabby and sombre as in wartime, and greatly scarred'. When Albert Camus had arrived in New York two years previously, by contrast, his impression was 'of overflowing wealth'. This wealth is conspicuously advertised in Orkin's picture. Churchill was obsessed with maintaining the British Empire but from now on the IMPERIAL march of American branding and merchandising will be unstoppable.

Orkin's picture also contains a certain amount of photographic history. Walker Evans had established street signs and billboards as part of the lexicon of American photography in the 1930s. (Orkin's behind-the-scenes shot of a historic event is also a behind-the-*signs* view that anticipates Robert Frank's 1958 picture of part – OH – of the Hollywood sign or Michael Ormerod's later view of a TEXACO sign.) Edward Steichen and Alfred Stieglitz had both photographed the Flatiron building at the beginning of the century, immediately adding it to the photographic catalogue of New York landmarks. The office block in the middle of Orkin's picture shares the high-prowed magnificence of the Flatiron building to such an extent that it looks, almost, like an ocean liner surging into the future. The name of this ship? Well, the figurehead makes that obvious: the SS *Liberty*! Although we are seeing an actual place, it is as if various geographically dispersed symbols of New York have been compressed into a composite of the city, a concentration of American-ness that is at once mythic and real. There is even something identifiably American about the people on the roof. The body language of the guy in the white shirt and trilby could only be American. Finding something 'peculiarly American' about Gatsby's 'resourcefulness of movement' Scott Fitzgerald wondered if this might be down to 'the absence of lifting work in youth' (which makes *us* wonder how places like Times Square got built in the first place).

The Third Reich had tainted the idea of the crowd. The carefully drilled Nuremberg rallies were frightening demonstrations of the way that a people could abandon the cherished ideals of the Enlightenment and plunge, willingly, into the darkness of the herd-instinct. In Times Square the crowd is not deliberately choreographed but the occasion was arranged in a way that has since become widespread in that its purpose was, partly, to be recorded. Orkin, in this respect, was the perfect person to do the recording. Her most famous picture is of a young American woman walking down a street in Florence, leaving a trail of gawping men in her wake. It's a classic piece of spontaneous street photography – except it was set up in advance by the photographer and a model friend of hers. The lecherous Italians were actually being good sports, were playing themselves.

The Times Square crowd is good-natured, ecstatic. Cleverly, Max Kozloff, editor of the book *New York Capital of Photography* (the title alone is a fine example of the vaulting confidence that pervades America in the post-war period) juxtaposes Orkin's picture with Weegee's of the sardine-crowd on Coney Island on a sweltering day in 1940. Weegee's explanatory caption could be transferred to Orkin's: 'They came early and stayed late' – and, it could be added, they played their part with gusto. In the sixty years since VE Day, news stories and staged media events have become almost impossible to disentangle from each other. In keeping with this Orkin records the event as it is being recorded by CBS.

That logo looks quaintly old-fashioned but something else gives the photo a very contemporary touch: the woman to the right of the picture. The fact that she has gained access to this privileged vantage point is a significant achievement in itself. She could be one of the brainy, ambitious Vassar girls whose lives were chronicled by Mary McCarthy in *The Group*. As such she is a role model for the later masters – mistresses, rather – of discreet reportage such as Joan Didion and Janet Malcolm. Most obviously, though, she can be seen as Orkin's own deputy. Orkin stays in the background, unseen, but as Dorothea Lange, one of the pre-eminent documentary photographers of the 1930s, had recommended, she includes her own representative in the picture: 'a figure who is part of it all, though only watching and watching'. What makes this picture so utterly contemporary, however, is not the woman's presence but her *posture*. What is she doing? Cut her out of this 1945 photo and paste her into a shot of some contemporary news event – Pope X's funeral at St Peter's, for example – and you would swear that she was talking on a cell phone.

Since Orkin's picture shows people documenting an event that occurred partly so that it could be documented I began to wonder if there were photos which showed *this* document – this photo – being made. I found several – or thought I had. The best one, by an uncredited photographer, shows the view from behind Liberty. Exactly as in Weegee's Coney Island photograph the people in the crowd raise their hats and wave to the camera. But even if you know where the HOTEL ASTOR is – or used to be; it has since been demolished – you can't quite make out the sign. And working out exactly where the unknown photographer was standing – finding him within Orkin's field of vision – proved far trickier than expected.

After scrutinising both photos I looked at the cinema just above the O of the hotel in Orkin's picture. It was showing a film called *Salty O*-something, starring Alan Ladd. And that same sign can be seen in its entirety (*Salty O'Rourke*), just above the sea of heads, at the far left-hand side of the other picture. Calibrating the various angles of vision was like trying to trace the trajectory of bullets from the JFK assassination – and the evidence didn't quite match up. I assumed that the shooter was somewhere below the American flags (above the reversed E of HOTEL) but that didn't make sense because the photo was taken to the right – from Orkin's point of view, the left – of Liberty. This meant it had to have been taken somewhere below the IMPERIAL sign. If this was the case why couldn't we see the cinema showing the movies with Cary Grant and Ray Milland? Perhaps the news cameramen were in the way. They are – but glimpsed between the chest of the guy in the white shirt and trilby and his colleague you can *just* make out a few letters – the GRAN of Grant, the LAN of Milland – of this sign. We can now see the event from both sides. It is complete. By obliquely corroborating each other's testimony the two photographs seal us within the moment. But how long does this moment last, how far into the future does it extend?

Orkin depicts a day of boundless euphoria. The ship of Liberty sails into the future but in doing so – unlike the woman photographed by Orkin in Florence – it leaves increasing hostility in its wake. As the American imperium grows so the meaning of its symbols changes, especially in the Arab world. By the 1970s, to the Syrian-born poet Adonis (Ali Ahmad Said),

> New York is a woman
> holding, according to history,
> a rag called liberty with one hand
> and strangling the earth with the other.

Adonis' visionary poem is prophetically entitled 'The Funeral of New York'. A reaction of some kind to the hubris it depicts is inevitable. We live now in the aftermath of that reaction. 'Let statues of liberty crumble,' the poet continues. 'An eastern wind uproots tents and skyscrapers with its wings.' Taken in the middle of New York, Orkin's photograph stands right in the middle of the American century which began with the larking crowds of 1914 and ended with the shocked onlookers gazing in disbelief at the World Trade Center on 11 September 2001.

2005

Richard Avedon

In 1960 Richard Avedon photographed the poet W. H. Auden on St.
Mark's Place, New York, in the middle of a snowstorm. A few passers-
by and buildings are visible to the left of the frame but the blizzard
is in the process of freezing Auden in the midst of what, in the US,
is termed 'a white-out'. Avedon had by then already patented his
signature approach to portraiture, so it is tempting to see this picture
as a God-given endorsement of his habit of isolating people against
a sheer expanse of white, as evidence that his famously severe technique is less a denial of naturalism than its apotheosis.

Auden is shown full-length, bundled up in something that seems
a cross between an old-fashioned English duffle coat and a prototype
of the American anorak. Avedon, in this image, keeps his distance.
More usually his sitters (who are rarely permitted the luxury of a
seat) are subjected to a visual interrogation that quite literally flies
in the face of Auden's ideas of good photographic manners:

> It is very rude to take close-ups and, except
> when enraged, we don't:
> lovers, approaching to kiss,
> instinctively shut their eyes before their faces
> can be reduced to
> anatomical data.

Avedon's critics allege that this is what he did consistently and deliberately: reduced faces to anatomical data. At the very least, as Truman

Capote happily observed, Avedon was interested in 'the mere condition of a face'. If this had the quality of disinterested inquiry others claimed that his impulses were crueller, more manipulative – an opinion that Avedon occasionally confirmed. In 1957 he caught the Duke and Duchess of Windsor recoiling from the world as if it were a perfectly bloody little place. According to Diane Arbus this result was achieved by Avedon explaining that on the way to the shoot his taxi ran over a dog. As the Windsors flinched with sympathetic horror he clicked the shutter.

It has also been suggested that the photographs of crumpled, ageing faces were in some way Avedon's revenge on the fashion and glamour business in which he made his name, an explicit rebuke to the claim that his work was all surface and no depth. This opposition cannot long be sustained. As Avedon rightly insisted, 'The surface is all you've got. You can only get beyond the surface by working with the surface.' And the movement between the two activities, between fashion and portraiture was, in any case, constant and mutually informing.

A little detour, via French street photography, will show how.

Jacques Henri Lartigue's photographs have exactly the unposed, felicitous spontaneity that made Robert Doisneau's later image of a Parisian couple kissing immediately appealing. As is now well known, 'The Kiss' was deliberately choreographed by the photographer. In this transition, from the happy accidents of Lartigue to the premeditated charm of Doisneau, we can see one of the two contradictory but complementary impulses that have also animated the history of *fashion* photography. The unposed becomes the template for a pose; the miracle of the unguarded moment is always being turned into a style and a commodity.

Evidence of the other, contrary, movement is also found throughout the history of fashion photography. An established way of photographing models or clothes becomes too artificial, too static, too posed. Then someone comes along and, through a combination of ambition, daring and vision, injects an element of spontaneity, naturalness. Take any of the famous names in the history of fashion photography and the chances are you will discover that they once offered a liberating alternative to the staid, that they wanted 'to get away from the piss elegance of it all' (not Bailey, *Beaton*!) or felt like 'a street savage surrounded by sophisticates' (Irving Penn!). The peculiar twist of fashion photography is that this 'naturalness' is achieved by – or immediately creates the conditions for – further contrivance. It cannot be otherwise, for the effect the images are ultimately intended to create (a willingness, desire or aspiration to purchase the stuff the models are wearing) precedes and has priority over what is randomly discovered.

This is why any discussion of fashion photography comes, inevitably, back to Avedon, who tirelessly and inventively raised the bar of contrived naturalness. Far from negating this practice his portraits are the most extreme expression of contriving a way of stripping away contrivances. One sees this nakedly in Laura Wilson's photographs of Avedon at work on the portraits of drifters and workers collected in *In the American West*: lights, assistants and blank white paper cut off his subjects from their natural habitat more completely than the bars of a zoo. Thus confined they are granted an anonymous kind of celebrity, ostensibly because Avedon was a photographer with an instantly recognisable style; more subtly, because the cumulative effect of ruthless stripping away is not simply to lay bare. Revelation is also a means of generation.

What, then, is being generated?

In the work of David Octavius Hill and his contemporaries, Walter Benjamin was struck by the way that 'light struggles out of darkness'. Benjamin went on to describe how, from about 1850 to 1880, the client was confronted with a 'a technician of the latest school' whereas the photographer was confronted by a 'member of a rising class equipped with an aura that had seeped into the very folds of the man's frock coat or floppy cravat'. Benjamin was adamant that the aura was not simply the product of primitive technology. Rather, in that early period, subject and technique were 'exactly congruent'. This lasted only a short while, for 'soon advances in optics made instruments available that put darkness entirely to flight and recorded appearances as faithfully as any mirror'. As a result the aura was 'banished from the picture with the rout of darkness through faster and faster lenses'.

With Avedon – 'that wonderful, terrible mirror', as Cocteau called him – the wheel came full circle. Absolute whiteness took the place of the darkness against which the light had struggled to emerge. And in this renewed and reversed congruence of subject and technique, a new aura and order emerged, one based on the reciprocity of fame. A famous photographer takes pictures of famous people (people whose aura has seeped into their cravats – or shirts, or dresses – and whose aura, in the kind of inversion beloved by the Frankfurt school, is often the *product* of the cravats – or shirts, or dresses – which they have been paid to model and which he has been paid to photograph). In the 1960s and '70s, according to Diane Arbus' biographer, Patricia Bosworth, 'everybody who entered Avedon's studio was some kind of star'. Thereafter, even if you weren't famous when you went in, you sort of were when you came out. Either way, a portrait of oneself by Avedon was a highly person-alised status symbol. OK, he might make your face look, as Les Dawson said of his mother-in-law, 'like a bag of spanners', but the photograph had the quality of – in fact was a record of – election. To be photographed by Avedon thus afforded a double means of *recognition*. Consequently people turned up for their session as if for a once-in-a-lifetime oppor-tunity, almost, as the saying goes, for a rendezvous with destiny.

Again this connects Avedon with nineteenth-century photographers such as Julia Margaret Cameron (with whom he felt a special affinity). Back then, according to Benjamin, everything about the elaborate proce-dure of having one's picture taken 'caused the subject to focus his life in the moment rather than hurrying on past it; during the consider-able period of the exposure the subject as it were grew into the picture'. In these pictures, 'the very creases in people's clothes have an air of permanence'. Avedon, of course, worked with split-second exposure times but the results were in some ways even more striking: the creases in people's *faces* have an air of geological permanence. There is the sense, often, of a massive extent of time being compressed into the moment the picture was taken. 'Lately,' he said in 1970, 'I've become interested in the passage of time within a photograph.' So, in one of his most famous portraits, Isak Dinesen looks like she was once the most beautiful woman in the world – about two thousand years ago.

It's a picture which makes one think of the Sybil who asked for immortality while forgetting to ask for eternal youth. For his part Avedon wondered if people came to him in the same way they might go to a fortune-teller. (He was not alone in this: André Breton, Bill Brandt and Diane Arbus also believed the photographer should attempt to conjure a likeness which, in Brandt's words, 'physically and morally predicts the subject's entire future'.) If that's the case then Avedon's prophecies are self-fulfilling and self-revealing. Character is fate. Or maybe that should read character is face. George Orwell famously claimed that by a certain age everyone gets the face they deserve; Martin Amis updated this: nowadays everyone gets the face they can *afford*. In America this might seem like a quaintly British distinction: you deserve what you can afford; as far as Avedon was concerned everyone's face got photographed the same way regardless (we'll return to that word shortly). Fame, face and fate were – give or take a consonant – synonyms. It was a credo that kept faith, simultaneously, with the hierarchy of glamour and the levelling gaze of biological destiny. Looking at his photographs we have the distinct sense that what is being uniquely revealed is, as Milan Kundera puts it in *Immortality*, 'the non-individuality, the impersonality of a face':

> The serial number of a human specimen is the face, that accidental and unrepeatable combination of features. It reflects neither the character nor the soul, nor what we call the self. The face is only the serial number of a specimen.

Hence the impossible contradiction whereby the devastating pictures in which Avedon's dying father seems to be dissolving into – or being reclaimed by – the white radiance of the backdrop show, according to his son, 'what it is to be any one of us'.

It was inevitable that, despite his undimmed energy and enthusiasm, Avedon succumbed to a kind of rote. In his last years, as photographer for *The New Yorker*, he sometimes seemed to be running on empty. He never lost the appetite for discovery but he kept discovering the same thing. The photographer who wished he 'just could work with [his] eyes alone' was so highly regarded that he was able, in a quite literal sense, to carry on regard-*less*. Even so, when he died, the huge swathe of his work, the sheer number of specimens he had scrutinised *over time*, suggested that it was not just an individual who had passed away. An era came to an end, too, the era when – at the risk of being tautologous – it was possible to be photographed by Avedon. At that moment the means of recognition were altered and diminished, permanently.

2007

Larry Burrows

In 1997 Horst Faas and Tim Page published *Requiem*, a homage to the 135 photographers who died while covering the wars in Indochina and Vietnam. The work of Larry Burrows, who photographed the war in Vietnam from 1962 until he died in a helicopter shot down on the border with Laos in 1971, was central to that undertaking. *Vietnam*, a more extensive selection of his work, enables us to see his achievement more extensively and to define it more clearly.

Burrows was born in London in 1926. He left school at sixteen and got a job in *Life* magazine's London bureau, where he printed thousands of pictures by Robert Capa and others. It would be hard to exaggerate the effect of this apprenticeship on his subsequent career. Capa practically invented the genre of combat photography and defined the standards by which it would be judged. If your pictures aren't good enough, he was fond of saying, that's because you're not close enough. Burrows took Capa at his word. In Vietnam a colleague decided that Burrows was either the bravest man in the world or the most short-sighted. Tales of that myopic bravery are legion, and Burrows himself thought 'the best thing that happens . . . is when someone turns around and says, "Well, you've taken your chances with the rest of us."' Like other photographers in Vietnam Burrows fell into the habit of edging right up to death, but whereas Page and Sean Flynn (son of Errol) were swash-buckling, wild, stoned, Burrows was distinguished by his patience and meticulous calm. It is possible to detect these qualities in the formal elegance of the work. While Capa said he would 'rather have a strong image that is technically bad than vice-versa', Burrows was obsessed with making strong, technically perfect images. Looking at his best photos reminds me of some documentary footage I once saw of men coming suddenly under fire in Bosnia. Everyone hit the dirt. It took a while to take in what was so strange and unnerving about this footage. Then I realised that the camera recording it all had remained absolutely steady.

This unflinching quality is seen to dramatic effect in a black-and-white photo-essay published in *Life* in April 1963. Burrows was photographing a Marine helicopter squadron, focusing on James Farley, a fresh-faced twenty-one-year-old gunner. In the course of what was expected to be a routine mission the squad comes under heavy fire. One of the helicopters goes down and Farley's chopper lands nearby, attempting to rescue the crew. By the time they are airborne again two badly wounded men are sprawled on the floor of the helicopter. One of them dies. The resulting photos have all the cramped panic and horror of Snowdon's death in *Catch-22*. But what makes them into a perfect *story* is the shot of Farley back at base, sobbing, aged by more than a decade in the course of a dozen photographs.

That was the luxury of working for *Life*: an absence of deadlines and the freedom to construct a narrative around photographs rather than taking them to illustrate breaking news. Burrows used these freedoms to similar effect in the colour sequence on *Operation Prairie* (1966), which culminates in the famous image of the wounded black sergeant apparently reaching towards his white comrade, also wounded. On the one hand it's an unadulterated image of the chaos, mud and blood of the aftermath of combat. But it is also a classic *Life*-like image in that it is, simultaneously, a statement of fact (this really happened) *and*, precisely by virtue of the unimpeachable quality of its evidence, an illustration of a larger truth (in this case the equality of suffering and tenderness between races) which might not be true at all. What we have, in other words, is a vivid example of the camera's unique capability: not the creation of a myth but its depiction.

It would be a mistake, therefore, to see images like this as proof of the photographer's anti-war stance. At that time, in fact, Burrows was still, in his own words, 'rather a hawk'. It was only later, in 1969, that he attained *A Degree of Disillusion*. That was the title of another photo-essay, belatedly focusing on the impact of the war on the Vietnamese, as Philip Jones Griffiths had done throughout his time there. By then Burrows said the faces all over Vietnam were 'more tired' and 'dazed' than he had ever known. In Roger Mattingly's well-known 1971 portrait that fatigue can be seen in Burrows' own face. He looks exactly like one of the combat-numbed grunts he had so often pictured: a sign of how the gap between photographer and his subjects was shrinking, lethally. This is suggested still more powerfully by Henri Huet's picture in *Requiem* of Burrows helping to carry a wounded soldier, whipped back by a chopper's downdraught. Burrows' thick-framed spectacles make him instantly recognisable, which is slightly odd given that the photo is so like one *by* him, thereby forcing the viewer to concede that a Burrows image is not as instantly recognisable as is often claimed. Indeed, to this observer, Huet's images and Burrows' are often almost interchangeable. Since the two photographers died together on that helicopter flight on the Laos border this is not inappropriate. But the images in the pages of *Vietnam* also have much in common with those in Page's *Nam* (1983). Page was spectacularly high on the 'glamour' of war; according to his epitaph in *Life,* on the other hand, when Burrows looked at war 'what he saw was people'. Except, it turns out, his coverage of 'The Air War' shows Burrows to be just as intoxicated by the psychedelic technology of American firepower as Page was. Two almost identically framed shots, taken at the same moment, in 1969, in Cholon – one in colour by Burrows, the other in black-and-white by Griffiths – of a blood-drenched woman with a soldier kneeling over her, staring nine hundred yards into the distance, crop up in both *Vietnam* and *Vietnam Inc.* (the Welshman's camera can be seen in the bottom right-hand corner of Burrows' picture).*

This is not to diminish Burrows' individual talent or achievement. It is simply to recognise the accuracy of Sontag's judgement from the

---

*Actually, they are even more similar than I thought: although Jones Griffiths' image is printed in black-and-white in *Vietnam Inc.*, it was shot in colour.

'70s, namely that 'the very success of photojournalism lies in the difficulty of distinguishing one superior photographer's work from another, except insofar as he or she has monopolised a particular subject' – and in Vietnam they were all shooting the same subject. Similarly, Burrows has always been praised for his humanity and compassion when, if you think about it, what would really set a photographer apart would be the ability to photograph injury, suffering and death with a lack of compassion, even, possibly, with a touch of glee. No, Burrows is a great photographer less because of what distinguishes him as an artist than because of what he has in common with his colleagues and subjects. And I think that those trademark spectacles of his enable us to view his legend (in the cartographic sense) more clearly.

It's a classic sixth-form debate: whether to take photographs of the injured or to try to help them. Burrows repeatedly took photographs of wounded men being helped by their comrades, even when they were themselves wounded. He was drawn to such scenes because they dramatised that ethical dilemma so clearly as to simultaneously resolve it. Looking at photos like this it is striking how often one or more of the people doing the helping are wearing spectacles like Burrows'. Maybe it's just a coincidence (though that in itself is almost meaningless in a medium that is *about* visual coincidences) but it is difficult not to regard these bespectacled helpers as the active representatives of Burrows's own seared conviction: that showing the wound was also a way of tending to it.

2002

Enrique Metinides

Turns out they could be wrong about suffering after all, the Old Masters. As famously evoked by W. H. Auden, everyone 'turns away / Quite leisurely from the disaster' of the boy falling out of the sky in Brueghel's *Icarus*. As recorded by Enrique Metinides such incidents attract crowds of spectators whose faces reflect our own shocked fascination with carnage.

For almost half a century Enrique Metinides photographed death and disaster in and around his native Mexico City. Stabbings, shootings, suicides, drownings, fires, freak accidents ('A high voltage cable snaps loose and hits a man walking along Tacuba Street . . .'), natural and unnatural disasters – Metinides' work is a crash-course in the diverse ways people get mangled and killed. If something terrible happened, Metinides was there with his camera, recording not just the wreckage but the way such incidents became sites of instant pilgrimage. He spent most of his career working for the mass-circulation Mexican tabloid *La Prensa*. To that extent he pandered to an atrocious appetite for calamity and mishap; such is the single-mindedness with which he pursued this line of work, however, that it does not seem inappropriate to speak of his *devotion* to the subject.

Metinides was born in 1934 and began taking pictures of car accidents when he was twelve. (At the same age, in France, in the early 1900s, another prodigy, Jacques Henri Lartigue, had taken photographs of the idyllic dawn of the automobile era.) The cops let this precocious kid – El Nino, they called him – hang around the precinct, allowed him to take pictures of prisoners in custody, the injured, the dead. The first photographs he'd ever taken were of moments from his favourite movies – snapped while they were being projected on screen – and what happened next was like something from the film *City of God*: while Metinides was photographing a car crash the crime photographer of *La Prensa* approached the boy and hired him as his assistant. Still in his early teens Metinides began to learn his trade in earnest, honing his technique and becoming a regular at the hospitals, crime scenes, morgues and crash sites that would be his stamping ground for the next forty years. Like Weegee, Metinides became a part of the scenes he depicted, especially when – again like Weegee – he began using shortwave radios (up to four at a time) to tune in to police and ambulance frequencies so that he would arrive at the incident alongside the emergency services.

Metinides has continued to keep abreast of the technological potential for tracking disaster. Since 1997, when he stopped taking photographs, he has turned his attention to the moving image, monitoring catastrophes on a bank of TVs in his apartment, compiling the kind of taxonomy of 'crash sequences' itemised by DeLillo in *White Noise*: 'Cars with cars. Cars with trucks. Trucks with buses. Motorcycles with cars. Cars with helicopters. Trucks with trucks.'

To say that his interest in such things is sensationalist or exploitative is to utter a banality along the lines of 'Pain hurts.' But by implicating us in the reciprocity of gawp – onlookers stare blankly at the camera; we stare back, our eyes flicking from them to the mangled cyclist in the foreground – the pictures exempt themselves (and us) from the hypocrisy mercilessly exposed by Thomas Bernhard in his final novel *Extinction*. The narrator's parents have been killed in a car wreck and he is appalled by the 'ruthless cruelty' of the tabloid press and their 'abominable pictures' of the death-scene.

> They even printed a large photograph of my mother's headless body. I gazed at this picture for a long time, though all this time was naturally afraid that someone might come into the kitchen and catch me at it . . . Each paper felt obliged to outdo the next in vulgarity. *Family wiped out*, screamed one headline, under which I read, *Three concert-goers mutilated beyond recognition. Full report and pictures centre pages.* I at once searched for the centre pages,

shamelessly leafing through the paper to find the illustrated report promised on the front page and simultaneously keeping my eye on the kitchen door, fearful of being caught in the act. I mustn't immerse myself entirely in these reports of the accident, I told myself, as I may not notice if someone comes into the kitchen and catches me at it.

Egged on by Bernhard one might as well concede that there is an absurd and, by extension, perversely humorous side to Metinides' work. The gathered crowds often have something in common with the people glimpsed in the background of photos of a fisherman who has had the good fortune to land a record-breaking marlin. In both circumstances spectating becomes a form of vicarious participation. As his fame increased so his presence must have served as an additional inducement to come and have a look – and maybe get photographed in the act of looking. (Occasionally he shows the victims on their own, in the solitude of death. The silence of these pictures – of a woman who killed herself, for example, because her estranged husband took their child away to live with him and his lover – is all the more poignant given the din and jostle that normally surrounds such scenes.) Metinides has said that he has 'photographed everything except a spaceship or submarine collision' but his pictures of upended buses often look like a meteorite has come crashing out of space and landed in Mexico City. And although his pictures are grimly matter-of-fact they often have an other-worldly quality about them. Partly this is because what is so shown is often so strange (a bus is winched out of a lake like a giant fish, a huge truck lands on the roof of a car); partly it is the result of *how* it is shown (he was one of the first photographers to use a flash in daylight). The combination lends the pictures an aura that is both filmic and religious.

The films Metinides saw as a boy – gangster movies, especially – profoundly shaped his signature aesthetic, whereby a sequence of action is reduced to a single image. If the technology were available whole segments of action could be extrapolated and derived from these daylight *noirs* of Metinides. A shot of a shoot-out between cops and robbers in a supermarket reads like a script in super-condensed form. Another photo shows a conflagration at a gas station, started, apparently, by two young men who drove off without paying but *with* the hose still in their petrol tank. Glamorous as a movie star, a blonde woman is smashed by a car and becomes, in death, a broken – and eerily serene – mannequin. It seems possible that pictures like these provided part of the inspiration for the hectic, tragi-comic action of *Amores Perros* by Alejandro González Iñárritu. Often people who are witnesses to – or victims of – a calamity say that it was 'like being in a movie', and many of Metinides' pictures look not so much like film stills as still films. Perhaps this is why, on occasion, they are reminiscent of images by Jeff Wall, who operates in exactly this idiom of artificially enhanced reality. The difference is that while Wall's tableaux are resolutely enigmatic Metinides seeks, always, to elucidate. In this sense, it could be said, he is a reporter rather than an artist. As well as being the source of a peculiar kind of information about the world and its ways, his pictures also offer gory solace – in the form of knowledge. Maybe this is one of the reasons the crowds gaze at the photographer: in the hope that he can provide an answer as to why such terrible things happen. Within the limits of his chosen medium, Metinides does his best to oblige. In this sense, he is a storyteller.

His stories often involve a bus. Whereas many people spend their lives waiting for buses, life, for Metinides, is an accident waiting to happen. Basically, the bus brings the two together with devastating effect. Anyone who has travelled in Mexico will be familiar with the way these buses speed and surge around curving mountain roads. The inkling that your chances of survival are as dependent on the image of the Virgin swaying from the rear-view as they are on the driver or his brakes creates a weird sensation of hope, dread and resignation. The feeling is allied, in this part of the world, to the 'deep conviction' – as Cormac McCarthy puts it – 'that nothing can be proven except that it be made to bleed. Virgins, bulls, men. Ultimately God himself.'

This is why faces of the people in Metinides' photographs have a look of shock or astonishment but never of disbelief. His photographs, in fact, are of *believers*. The catastrophes visited upon them actually confirm people in their belief in the bloody way things are, have been and always will be. If this were not the case then the world would be a truly terrible place – because then there would be no room left for miracles.

The causes of the bleeding obsessively recorded by Metinides are ridiculous as often as they are tragic. By explaining and giving meaning to the permutations of random disaster, the pictures' captions offer the viewer an empirical equivalent of the faith that consoles the people in them. Knowing *what* happened stands in for the need to understand *why* it happened.

Most of the photographs take place *after the fact* – after the stabbing or crash – but the outcome can rarely be assumed. A plane ploughs into a field, killing everyone on board. A plane crash-lands on the Mexico–Puebla highway and no lives are lost. What can we deduce from the forensic-artistic evidence offered by these twinned images of hazard? In Metinides' view an accident is both inevitable and avoidable in the sense that it could have been avoided if it hadn't happened. Out of this emerges the intermingling of chance and logic otherwise known as fate. Metinides shows us not only what it looks like but – and this is the twist of the *artist* – how to recognise it.

2003

Jacob Holdt's America

Artists are part of a tradition even if they are oblivious to it – even if they do not consider themselves artists and are actively hostile to being regarded as such. Photography is a particularly broad and welcoming church in this respect. You don't disqualify yourself by claiming to be interested in the medium only as a lobbying tool, as part of a larger agenda of social activism. By making this plea for exemption, you're actually enlisting in a regiment with a particularly distinguished and proud photographic history. Commit yourself to the wider, non-ideological role of bearing witness and providing visual testimony, and you move still closer to the mainstream of that history. But what if you're a self-proclaimed vagabond, if you not only refuse to consider yourself an artist, but are adamant that you are 'not a photographer' either? Then step inside, please: you will meet many kindred spirits and fellow refuseniks with whom you have much in common.

In 1975, in a bookstore in San Francisco, Jacob Holdt chanced upon – and stole – a copy of *How the Other Half Lives* by Jacob Riis. Holdt was otherwise unaware of – or, at the very least, indifferent to – the fact that he might be treading in the footsteps of earlier photographers, but for anyone with basic photo-forensic skills their prints are easy to find and follow. Temperamentally and technically, Holdt may have nothing in common with Robert Frank but – whether he cares about it or not – both are part of that mini-tradition of Europeans crossing the Atlantic and, to borrow the title of Richard Poirier's book of essays, 'trying it out in America'.

Part of the fascination of what Holdt found and photographed in America lies in its unconscious relation to work that has gone before or that was being made at roughly the same time. A tacit dialogue insists on being – if there is a visual equivalent of overheard – over-*seen*. The black-and-white sign above the gas pumps in Frank's *The Americans* urged us to S A V E; the one snapped by Holdt urges us, red-and-yellowly, to S ELL.

Holdt did not share Frank's devotion or debt to Walker Evans but elements of the America catalogued by Evans form an unavoidable backdrop to Holdt's project. In terms of what they sought to accomplish and how they wished their work to be viewed the two men could not have been more different. Evans wanted his photographs to be seen without any ideological filtering. 'NO POLITICS whatever,' he insisted, though of course this disavowal of political intent did not mean there was no political content. However starkly and unsentimentally Evans recorded the poor sharecroppers of Alabama, his pictures have, over time, acquired a stone-washed glamour of their own. Free of the vulgar trappings of modern poverty, those 1930s shacks now look quaint and clean. Like some high-intensity detergent, black-and-white smartens a place up, gets rid of dirt in a gradual flash. Concerned that his pictures might be doing something similar, Holdt was adamant that his experience of the shacks of the rural African-American poor 'was far, far worse than they appear in photographs. In such pictures you can't *see* the wind which whistles through the many cracks making it impossible to keep warm in winter. You can't see the sagging rotten floors with cracks wide enough for snakes and various vermin to crawl right into the living room.'

This may be true, but few photographers have made the day-to-day poverty of an affluent society – plenty of TVs; a huge fridge, filthy, and crammed with nothing that looks safe to eat – look more *impoverished*. So much so that his photographs of people and their homes look like they were made not in the 1970s but seventy years ago, as if they were a recently exhumed part of the stash of colour pictures taken under the auspices of the FSA – minus the bright, uplifting imperatives encouraged by the organisation's director, Roy Stryker. Like many petitioning photographs, Holdt's depend on an

initial reluctance to accept what they show, to reject what they seek
to prove: surely people could not be living like that in the 1970s, in
America. By then, by the 1970s, Evans' pictures had acquired a
texture and glow that brought about a retrospective improvement to
the lives he had recorded. Roughly the same amount of time has
already passed since Holdt made many of his best-known pictures
and it seems unlikely that they will ever undergo a similar kind of
upgrade. It looks like it might be quite nice to sit on the stoop of
one of Evans' shacks and suck down a cold one with Floyd Burroughs,
but you'd never want to sit on one of the sofas in Holdt's places, let
alone sleep in one of the beds. But that's being too solemn and snooty.
Put it this way: if Holdt was showing us these images as holiday
snaps (which, in a sense, they are) we'd have to say, 'Man, you stayed
in some shitholes!'

There is a qualitative technical difference too between Holdt and
Evans. Made by a man assured of his vocation, Evans' work aimed
at deep permanence. His prints are luminously beautiful. Shot with
cheap film, Holdt's photographs were notes made in passing, 'a kind
of diary' or visual journal of a man who abjured all sense of vocation
and purpose other than hitching a ride or finding a place to sleep.
There's minimal disjuncture between what he was photographing and
the means with which he recorded it.

As with homes and furnishing, so with people. FSA-style photography, especially in the magisterial images by Dorothea Lange, meant
that even when stripped of everything else the Okies retained their
dignity. So much so that the Depression became a form of visual
attrition, stripping people down to their essential dignity. There are
occasional traces of this in Holdt's work. The woman that he finds
in Florida – haven't we seen that deeply lined, dried-out, life-ravaged
face before? We have, of course; it is the stoically defiant face of the
Great Depression, but whereas Lange's 'Migrant Mother' cradled her
children, this woman nurses a cigarette over cans of Budweiser in a
bar; and it's not her helpless children, it's a husband or boyfriend
who is sidling drunkenly up to her. His neck might be red but the
face of the guy Holdt meets in a bar in Mississippi has the battered
charisma of a Johnny Cash song – and his shirt's nice too. Around

the younger women photographed by Holdt there sometimes lingers the possibility, not just of a place to stay but the dangerous allure of cross-racial romance.

The deprivation witnessed by Holdt often robbed people of everything, including their dignity – with the coming of junk food, poverty tended to bloat, physically, rather than erode – but this is balanced by the way his pictures lack the single-minded pride that Evans, Lange and others took in their medium and in their own status within the pantheon of its greatest practitioners. The disconnect between what is recorded and the way in which it is recorded is at its starkest and most blatant in Richard Avedon's photograph 'William Casby, Born a Slave, 1963'. It's a great picture, an unflinching depiction not just of a man's face but of the very thing that obsessed Holdt: the psychological and historical residue of slavery, of internalised powerlessness. Unlike Casby, the picture of him is absolutely confident of its power, of its self-evident right to rub shoulders with works by any of the masters of portraiture from the entire history of art. While Avedon called the shots, as it were, Holdt addressed his subjects – like 'Charles Smith, a former slave' – more modestly, on their own terms and in their own homes. As vagabond and photographer he depends upon and graciously accepts people's hospitality. That's the advantage of the vagabond-artist method: black, white, rich, poor, racists, junkies, hookers, pimps, Klansmen, gun nuts, rednecks – they all extend their kindness and trust to Holdt and, as a result, are seen at their best, at their most *American*.

Unobtrusively, almost incidentally impressive, Holdt's photographs have – as we have seen – ended up in a museum in spite of their maker's declared intentions. It was only recently, after a quarter-century wait, that they took their place alongside the work of his contemporaries and successors. As soon as they did, certain resemblances were so striking, the feeling of kinship so strong, that it was as if a prodigal had finally agreed to show up for a long-postponed get-together. The young, sticker- and badge-festooned Republican photographed by Holdt at a convention in Florida way back in 1972 is reunited with the boy in the straw hat and the Bomb Hanoi badge (as seen by Diane Arbus) on a pro-war parade in 1967. The 87-year-old woman Holdt drove all the way from Alabama to Arizona, the one brandishing the gun in the doorway of her shack, meets up with the old guy sitting on a bed with *his* gun (photographed by William Eggleston) in Morton, Mississippi. Actually, once you make adjustments for some variation in palette, there is evidence of a whole generation of interbreeding between Holdt and Eggleston, especially if we bear in mind the latter's declared intention to photograph 'democratically'.

'Eggleston' has become a kind of shorthand or metonym for colour photography generally and, in Holdt, there are glimpses of the kind of stuff that fascinated another renegade colourist, Stephen Shore, in *American Surfaces*. What Luc Sante said of Nan Goldin – that she was able to 'take the most squalid corner of the worst dump and find colours and textures in it no one else saw' – almost holds true for Holdt. Whereas Goldin finds 'oceanic' blues and 'crepuscular' oranges, Holdt sees the same, unexceptional colours as the rest of us but – like Helen Levitt in her colour work – coaxes an understated harmony from the muted maroons, pale greens and (in one of his best pictures, of a girl on a bed, watching telly) dullish purples, grey mauves. What he shares with Goldin is an absolute lack of distance or inhibition between photographer and subjects. In Goldin's *The Ballad of Sexual Dependency* (which, like Holdt's American pictures, enjoyed its first incarnation as a slide show) we get an hermetic account of a community with a fairly fixed cast of characters within a city at a particular historical moment. The same is true of the grey rush of Larry Clark's *Tulsa* (1971). With Goldin it's transgressives, bohemians and druggies on the Lower East Side; with Clark it's teenage speed freaks shooting up in Oklahoma. Holdt's project is inherently less circumscribed. His readiness to go along with whatever happens and to get along with whoever he happens to run into makes for a sprawling odyssey of serial intimacies and random proximity. Along the way he occasionally gets to watch a bit of TV (there are a lot of them about) or to watch people watching it (or, on one occasion, to watch them stealing it). In the image of Baggie feeding her baby while Nixon is beamed into the room, the political irony is implied silently. In others there is the sense, observed by Lee

Friedlander (in photographs) and later verbally corroborated by Jean Baudrillard, that a television might be broadcasting from 'another planet' or showing 'a video of another world'. In this world, meanwhile, Holdt accidentally witnesses the scenes of violent death sought out by Enrique Metinides, another photographer only recently promoted to gallery status.

That Holdt's pictures did not go knocking on the doors of museums, as it were, did not plead for institutional recognition or art-critical approval is a prime reason why they deserve admission. As more and more people use cameras as a way of gaining acclaim not as photographers but as artists, so the status of this surrogate medium is in danger of becoming somewhat overblown. Literally. The question one asks repeatedly in gallery shows of 6 x 10 prints (feet, I mean, not inches!) is: Does this work earn its size? Would this photograph be able to make the grade as a work of art if it had not been pumped up with the growth hormones of the artist's huge aspirations and ambitions? The paradox is that some of the most artistically valuable contemporary photographs are content with being *photographs*, are not under the same compulsion to pass themselves off – or pimp themselves out – as art. The simple truth is that the best exponents of the art of contemporary photography continue to produce work that fits broadly within the tradition of what Evans termed 'documentary style'.

Obviously it was not intended in this way, but Holdt's photograph of the bearded black guy mowing a lawn in shorts and t-shirt in Saratoga can usefully be seen as a modestly prophetic corrective to Paul Graham and the grandly sublime ambitions expressed by the images of a black guy mowing a lawn in Pittsburgh (2004) from the series *A Shimmer of Possibility*. Unexceptional – and admirably so – Holdt's picture is a persuasive demonstration of how photography might keep itself trim or cut itself down to size.

Holdt's movement from the photographic fringes to the walls of a museum – and the corresponding shift of emphasis in any assessment of his career, from activist to photographer – is not just deserved, it is historically inevitable. Records of moments in time, these photographs have outlived their time in a way that the words surrounding them in the book *American Pictures* have not. Perhaps this conforms to a more general truth about the relative longevity of words and images when paired together in this way, for the same thing happened to *Let Us Now Praise Famous Men* (1941) by Evans and James Agee. Gore Vidal wittily scorned the 'good-hearted, soft-headed admirers of the Saint James (Agee) version of poverty in America' which, over time, has come to seem at odds with the enduring value of Evans' 'austere' photography. Holdt's engaging naivety saves him from the kind of Scandinavian omniscience that becomes wearisome in Sven Lindqvist's later polemical writing, but the text of *American Pictures* would not be reprintable today except as a historical document or exhibit, like one of those mammals found preserved in a glacier. The enduring vitality of the photographs, on the other hand, is evident in two, apparently contradictory, ways.

First, they wouldn't look out of place in Claude Brown's *Manchild in the Promised Land* (1965), a first-hand testament to the problems of addiction, poverty and deprivation that pre-dates Holdt's arrival in America. Second, they could readily be inserted into more recent accounts of the drug-ravaged American ghetto, such as Richard Price's novel *Clockers* (1992) or David Simon and Ed Burns' masterpiece of 'stand-around-and-watch' reportage, *The Corner* (1997). Holdt photographed Ronald Reagan in 1972, 'long before he became president'; Simon and Burns quote him years later, saying that 'we fought a war against poverty and poverty won', a line that could serve as a caption for any number of pictures in this exhibition. The so-called war on drugs, the authors insistently remind us, actually became a war against the poor. Holdt, in this sense, was a combat photographer, embedded in the front line. His experience renders him more, not less, sympathetic to those caught up – or actively engaged – in the conflict, visually affirming Simon and Burns' claim that 'if faith and spirituality and mysticism are the hallmarks of any great church, then addiction is close to qualifying as a religion for the American underclass'.

The issue, as always, is one of precision and detail, which the pictures provide in deliberate and accidental abundance. (Strangely, the hairstyles and clothes date the pictures in the sense of identifying them with a period – Holdt was working at the same time as Garry Winogrand, obviously – without confining their relevance to that time.) There is a good deal of rhetoric in Holdt's writing, almost none in the pictures. This is partly because some of the pictures are not *about* anything; certain moments or events – students on spring break jumping, scarily, from their balcony into the hotel pool – just happened to catch his eye. And partly it is because some are about so much more than what they are ostensibly about.

For a photographer whose interest is primarily documentary or polemical, Holdt's work is surprisingly rich, psychologically. The people in his pictures are never just representatives of the fallen condition in which they find themselves. The stories implied by the photographs are often more subtly individualised than the ones set out by the text of *American Pictures*. As with Eggleston – again – a tacit narrative seems poised to unfold *within* each frame. Some are tense with expectation, like Jeff Wall tableaux, almost, frozen in the act of time. But even off-the-cuff ones condense an unexpected amount of time into the split-second of the photograph's creation.

Take the picture of the woman in the green halter-neck dress, eating a lobster and smoking a cigarette at a lavish dinner in Palm Beach (see plate 1). The photograph is neither caustic nor judgemental – how could it be when the man seated between the woman in green and the fellow in the related green blazer is wearing one of the funnest jackets ever seen? – but its overt message or social meaning has to do with the gluttony or vulgarity of someone eating and smoking at the same time (weirdly, the one thing she does not seem to be doing is *breathing*). The fact that these two activities – eating and smoking – normally occur successively rather than simultaneously suggests that the exposure has taken twenty minutes (i.e. the time it would take to tuck into the lobster and *then* smoke a cigarette) while the guy swigging momentarily from his champagne shows the real speed of time. Perhaps that's why there is a sense that she has slid out of the shared time of the table and into some kind of private trance (technically a result of Holdt's flash?) as if she might actually be one of the undead, the unbreathing, or an alien in human form, some kind of Stepford Wife who found that those two lines of coke before dinner had really put the kibosh on her appetite. When Deckard subjects Rachel to the Voight-Kampff test in *Blade Runner* it takes far longer than usual to establish that she is actually a replicant – because she is under the illusion that she is a human being. Holdt here photographs, or suggests, someone during a moment when she gets an inkling that all the things that make her life humanly meaningful might actually be illusory, false. Or maybe we're being too solemn again: could be she's *really* feeling that coke, so intent on appearing to listen to whatever the (unseen) guy across the table is blahing on about that she's not heard a goddamn word, even though it seems like he's been talking at her since the dawn of time and no punchline is yet in evidence. Either way, the condensation of time in the image means that this moment lasts for both a hundredth of a second (shutter and flash, sip of champagne), twenty minutes (eating and smoking) and, extrapolating from there, a lifetime.

2009

Martin Parr's *Small World*

The tradition of photographing exotic places reaches back almost to the invention of the medium. As the Grand Tour was extended to take in 'the Orient' so, in the 1850s, photographers such as Francis Frith lugged their bulky equipment to the eastern Mediterranean and beyond. Once the resulting pictures of the pyramids and other wonders became widely available the desire to go to these places increased. Such was – such *is* – the allure and promise of photographs that people wanted to see the precise spots shown in the pictures. Part of the motive for travelling was, as it were, to *experience* the photographs on site, for real. Of course there was a lot to see that hadn't been photographed, but the places in the frame served as oases or taverns, nodes that visibly determined one's itinerary. Adventurous travellers naturally wanted to get off this pre-beaten track. By so doing, the places they visited gradually became part of the track. Just as Wordsworth complained about the growing numbers of visitors to the Lake District that his poetry had attracted so travellers to out-of-the-way places began to lament the tourists that came after them.

As travelling has become quicker, easier and cheaper so this problem – or syndrome – has grown more acute. Whereas it once required a considerable effort of will and some ingenuity to get to Egypt, Paul Fussell, in his book *Abroad*, thinks that the coming of efficient, uniform jet travel – which 'began in earnest around 1957' – 'represents an interesting moment in the history of human passivity'. Maybe so but, as Garry Winogrand's airport photographs from the 1960s and '70s attest, it also heralded a great democratic expansion of the opportunity horizon.

The pictures in Martin Parr's *Small World* both sum up this contradictory history and depict what might turn out to be its terminal phase. They show the places photographed by the likes of Frith (the pyramids) and they show how the excitement and promise of Winogrand's pictures has become a source of cramped frustration. When I was seven, in 1965, my parents and I went to London for a week's holiday. One day, as part of this vacation, we took the Tube out to Heathrow, not to fly somewhere, just to see the airport. For us it was not a place of departure but a tourist destination in its own right. With the inconvenience of air travel drastically increased in the wake of 9/11 the average traveller – i.e. anyone not in Business or First – dreads going to the airport. To add insult to injury – or, more exactly, guilt to discomfort – we are now acutely conscious of the cost to the environment, of the way that air travel is contributing to global warming. In this context a stay-at-home like Fernando Pessoa seems almost visionary: 'What is travel and what use is it? All sunsets are sunsets; there is no need to go and see one in Constantinople.'

It's not just the sunsets. When people do travel to Constantinople – or anywhere else for that matter – they can increasingly expect to find many of the things and conveniences taken for granted at home. Back in the 1950s the Swiss tourist Robert Frank travelled through America photographing 'the kind of civilization born here and spreading everywhere'. Frank was right: forty years down the line Parr finds bits and pieces of the American imperium everywhere. (He also records the contrary tendency whereby one no longer has to travel to Egypt – with the attendant threat of terror – to experience the Orient; it can be found in Las Vegas, in the shape of the Luxor.) In order to escape the tentacles of this homogenising 'civilisation' it is necessary to travel further and further afield. And by so doing you drag those tentacles after you. We are all responsible for the ruination we lament. Wherever you travel some kind of industry develops to cater for you – even if it's not the kind of catering you, personally, were hoping for. A couple of years ago my wife and I travelled to Jaisalmer in the desert of Rajasthan, a place she remembered as being almost Calvino-esque in its isolated beauty. In the decade since her first visit, however, it had been incrementally trashed. With every wall festooned with Indo tat – sarongs, knick-knacks, junk – it resembled nothing else so much as a fortified reincarnation of Camden market. In a cruel twist to the familiar story of how the indigenous people of a place ('Indians' as they were referred to throughout the Americas) traded the wealth of their land for a few worthless trinkets, the people of Jaisalmer, having put their heritage in hock, were left selling worthless trinkets that no one wanted – and, as a result, we, the tourists, felt cheated by the commerce that had sprung up to pander to us.

The effects of tourism are, of course, not uniform. Not all places have given themselves over entirely to tourism. But, as Mary McCarthy wrote almost half a century ago, 'there is no use pretending that the tourist Venice is not the real Venice, which is possible with other cities – Rome or Florence or Naples. The tourist Venice *is* Venice . . . Venice is a folding picture-post-card of itself.'

Venice is an extreme case. Even in Rome or Florence, however, visitors feel reassured by the way there are so many others doing, seeing – and photographing – the same things. Off-putting to some, a restaurant offering a 'Tourist Menu' is tempting to many. At the risk of being racist, the Japanese – the 'lens-faced Japanese', in Martin Amis' phrase – seem to take particular comfort in being photographed in places where everyone else is being photographed. People go to places not to see the places but to obtain evidence – photographs of themselves – of having been there. (Actually, this argument has been rehearsed so many times that it's a negative version of the same tendency. By making the point I am effectively making a record of myself standing in front of a cultural edifice signifying superior worth and discernment.)

Parr takes things a logical stage further: photographing people being photographed and taking photographs. In this respect the *Small World* pictures stand comparison with the large-scale images by Thomas Struth, in which we look at visitors looking at famous works of art (which, lest we forget, are also tourist attractions). The difference is that whereas in Struth's photographs the greatness – or aura or whatever you want to call it – of these artworks survives the process of mediation, in Parr's 'place' and visitor work to their mutual diminution. Tacitly – or maybe not even tacitly – he endorses the verdict of the narrator in Don DeLillo's *The Names*:

> Tourism is the march of stupidity. You're expected to be stupid. The entire mechanism of the host country is geared to travellers acting stupidly. You walk around dazed, squinting into fold-out maps. You don't know how to talk to people, how to get anywhere, what the money means, what time it is, what to eat or how to eat it. Being stupid is the pattern, the level and the norm.

Like DeLillo, Parr is not scathing or moralistic about this perceived failing. He enjoys it too much for that. There's too much mileage in it.

It is as hard for photographers to be funny as it is for a critic to explain a joke (this probably has something to do with the medium's defining quality of reproducibility; how many jokes can withstand infinite repetition?) but they *can* be witty. The wittiest photographer was Henri Cartier-Bresson (with Winogrand a close second), who, if he had worked in colour, might have relied on some of the same devices as Parr. Ironically, it was at the opening of *Small World* in Paris in 1995 that Cartier-Bresson told Parr that he must be 'from a different planet'. One sees what he means but one also sees that, at some point in their orbits, their two planets are thrown into unexpected alignment. In the random accidents of colour Parr contrives to find a version of the rhymes and puns that Cartier-Bresson discovered in the fleeting symmetries of pictorial geometry.

Are Parr's visual jokes at the expense of the people depicted? Is he fair? In the context of a world in which war photographers are snatching images of death, maiming, grief and suffering Parr's trespasses are easily forgiven. (Having mentioned war it's worth remembering that, since Parr works in some of the most intensively photographed spots on earth, he can probably claim immunity on the grounds that they are, to use a phrase from Vietnam, free-fire zones.) I suspect, also, that the people in the photographs would recognise themselves and their fellow-travellers. They would agree that, although they have chosen and paid to come to these places, sightseeing in particular and holidaying generally are often the opposite of fun – partly because of all the other *tourists*. (Like car drivers moaning about traffic, the discerning tourist often complains that a place is 'too touristy'.) And the money, even in supposedly cheap places, slips through your fingers like water. Forty years on, my father is still traumatised by the extraordinary price of the choc-ice we almost bought outside Madame Tussaud's during that trip to London. In this respect he has something in common with D.H. Lawrence, who, in *Sea and Sardinia*, is in a state of constant fury about being overcharged: 'I am thoroughly sick to death of the sound of liras . . . Liras – liras – liras – nothing else. Romantic, poetic, cypress-and-orange-tree Italy is gone. Remains an Italy smothered in the filthy smother of innumerable lira notes: ragged, unsavoury paper money so thick upon the air that one breathes it like some greasy fog.'

There is no way round it: to travel, either as backpacker or package tourist, is to be forced into being an incessant consumer. Factor in queues, hassle, jetlag and tummy upsets and it's a wonder, even now, when travel has become so *easy*, that people still want to do it. Philip Larkin certainly didn't want to, but he did consent, every year, to take his mother away for a dismal week somewhere in England (he didn't believe in 'abroad'). The experience led him to develop 'a theory [that] "holidays" evolved from the medieval pilgrimage, and are essentially a kind of penance for being so happy and comfortable in one's daily life'.

That's what the pictures in *Small World* depict: the form and state of modern, faithless pilgrimage. I think, next year, I might try Mecca.

2007

Joel Sternfeld's Utopian Visions

One of the most moving photographs I know is also one of the dullest: an empty, uninteresting-looking room with a brown carpet and beige walls. It comes at the end of Joel Sternfeld's book *On This Site* (1996). On each of the previous recto pages is a colour photo of an ordinary bit of America: a street corner, a rural grocery store (reminiscent of ones photographed by Walker Evans in the 1930s), an urban hotel, a deserted highway. On each of the facing pages a brief text explains that this is, respectively: the place in Queens where a woman was stabbed to death outside her apartment; the store in Mississippi where fourteen-year-old Emmett Till addressed a white woman as 'baby' and, as a result, was kidnapped, tortured and killed; the hotel where presidents of the major tobacco companies decided to begin an aggressive advertising campaign to counter scientific claims that cigarette smoke caused cancer; the road in Oklahoma where Karen Silkwood died after 'crashing' her car. Devoid of obvious 'interest' these apparently random places become freighted with invisible narrative and, as a consequence, are changed, utterly, into sites of hideous violence and atrocious corporate greed. Crucially, the photos are not *of* memorials. The photos *are* memorials which then turn the places *into* memorials.

The picture I referred to at the beginning is a kind of postscript; it comes after the Afterword, after the Acknowledgements etc. The dull room is in the Masjid-Al-Rasul mosque in Watts, where 'members of the Bloods and the Crips, rival Los Angeles gangs, negotiated and signed a truce on April 26, 1992'. In the aftermath of all that has gone before the *promise* of this picture is all the more immense for being tentative, provisional. It offers simple documentary proof of Maxim Gorky's belief that 'Life will always be bad enough for the desire for something better not to be extinguished in men.'

There is something distinctly Russian about progress being negatively affirmed in this way. An American version would reverse the emphasis: however *good* life is it will never be so good that people stop wanting something better. Implicit in the foundation myth of America, the utopian impulse is etched into the country's history and geography. On hearing of the lure of California one of the Polish emigrants in Susan Sontag's *In America* remarks on how American it is, the idea 'that America has its America, its better destination where everyone dreams of going'. Often this ambition operates simply at the level of endlessly mobilising consumer demand. An alternative expression of the same impulse explicitly rejects – or, in the testaments of Emerson and Thoreau, seeks to transcend – a version of satisfaction which generates insatiability. The other key part of the American estate, pragmatism, has sought to make the utopian yearning tangible, not through revolutionary overthrow of the existing order (as advocated by Marx and Engels) but by establishing small 'communities of common purpose'. Some of these have survived into the era of triumphal capitalism that followed the collapse of the Soviet Union. Some . . . Well, we'll come to them in a moment.

Sternfeld identifies three periods in which experimental communities bloomed. The first, in direct response to the dehumanising blight of the factory system, occurred between 1810 and 1860. Thereafter communities were set up sporadically – particularly in California – but it was not until the 1960s and the mushrooming hippie counter-culture that there was another peak in utopian activity. The third phase, under way for about fifteen years, has seen the spread of eco-villages or co-housing communities.

The companion volume to *On This Site*, *Sweet Earth*, deploys the same format. On one page are photographs of the grounds of a community or of one or more of its members. On the facing verso page Sternfeld tells the story of the pictured community. In some instances all that remains are ruins, visible signs of poor planning or corrupted ideals. The stories of the failures are often hilarious. Here is what happened during the terminal phases of Biosphere 2 in Arizona: 'As conditions worsened . . . tensions mounted among the crew. On the first anniversary of the experiment, Jane Goodall visited to observe the inhabitants. Allegations of food hoarding and food stealing abounded, and the Biospherians had splintered into two antagonistic groups. Though most had televisions in their apartments, they reportedly found it too torturous to watch because of McDonald's advertisements.' Where the founding principles are polygamy and free love, jealousy and sexual abuse have a habit of flourishing. At the other end of the spectrum celibacy – popular among the first, religiously inspired wave of settlements – is a mandate for self-extinction.

Many of the places founded in the 1960s fell victim to their own success, attracting people who would lead, ultimately, to their collapse. This is what happened in Drop City, both the real one (or all that's left of it) photographed by Sternfeld in Colorado (see plate 3), and the fictive one imaginatively transplanted to California by T.C. Boyle in his novel of that name. 'Drop City?' says the driver to a hitchhiker who has just announced where he's heading. 'You mean that hippie place? Isn't that where everybody's nude and they just ball and do dope all day?' The Drop is doomed by its allure. As Sternfeld points out, however, every societal enterprise is marked by widespread failure. 'We don't do away with the institution of marriage or corporations simply because there are divorces and bankruptcies.'

In any case, the mistakes, farces and failures make the successes more heartening. Some places – like The Farm in Summertown, Tennessee – have not simply survived but thrived, keeping faith with their own varied ethics – self-reliance, eco-purity etc. – *and* generating wealth. Having learned from the heady excesses of the 1960s and '70s, the current wave of settlement is marked by less radical declarations – no income sharing or cult-like dedication – of shared purpose. The modest ambitions of these eco-villages, Sternfeld suggests, may make them the most durable and viable models of community living.

Along with William Eggleston, Joel Meyerowitz and Stephen Shore, Sternfeld was one of the pioneers of colour photography in the 1970s.

(With a zeal appropriate to *Sweet Earth* he has referred to that time as 'the early Christian era of colour photography'.) First published in 1989 his *American Prospects* is both a benchmark book in its own right and an important chapter in the ongoing tradition of photographers such as Walker Evans (*American Photographs*) and Robert Frank (*The Americans*) making visual records of their road trips through the country.

Few of the individual photographs in *Sweet Earth* have the totalising clarity, the weird quality of hermetic suspense, of those in *American Prospects*. Does the fact that the pictures do not speak for themselves – that they need to be seen in tandem with an accompanying text – diminish the value of the book? In a way it is an impertinence to ask, for this, precisely, was the question posed by Sternfeld himself in *On This Site*. It was we, the viewers, who were being interrogated, forced to answer the most basic of questions: Do you have any idea what you are looking at? The conceptual tension of the book was generated by the gap between the unseen (the words) and the seen (the pictures). Once the freight of invisible narrative was revealed the gap became a bridge.

Sweet Earth continues Sternfeld's formal investigation into what he terms 'knowability', but the result, appropriately enough, is more *accommodating*. A history of endeavour, hope and resilience resides in these places, in these photographs; the texts offer a kind of hospitality, an invitation to step inside, to share in it.

2006

Alec Soth: Riverrun

If I remember my A-level Geography correctly the Mississippi lumbers down through the centre of the United States, picking up a great load of dust and dirt en route, carrying it south until, becoming choked by its own weight, it runs out of steam and starts dumping everything in its southern reaches. As these alluvial deposits build up so the river fans out and detours in its search for the sea, forming a delta in the process.

According to Joseph Brodsky, the Neva, which flows through St Petersburg, provides the city with an abundance of mirrors. 'Reflected every second by thousands of square feet of running silver amalgam, it's as if the city were constantly being filmed by its river, which discharges its footage into the Gulf of Finland which, on a sunny day, looks like a depository of these blinding images.'

I see Alec Soth's visual account of the Mississippi as an amalgam of these two processes, one literal, the other metaphorical.

The various tributaries of American photographic history flow together to constitute a tradition, a meandering history. An important part of that tradition is the trip across – or at least through – country. These expeditions could be said to have started with the photographers who accompanied and documented the pioneering surveys of 1860–85. They flourished again in the 1930s with work undertaken for the Farm Security Administration, the best and most personalised of which was made by Walker Evans. Then there were the post-war, Guggenheim-funded journeys of Robert Frank (in 1955–6) and Garry

Winograd (1964). Most recently and importantly for Soth are the trips made by Stephen Shore and Joel Sternfeld. (It was, apparently, a photo of the *van* that Sternfeld had used on his journeys that first made Soth fall in love with 'the process of taking pictures, with wandering around finding things'.) The work produced in this 'tradition' has become less rigorously systematic, more personal, more serendipitous over time. In the wake of Frank the idea of the arbitrary became elevated to the level of an organising principle in its own right.

The first picture in *Sleeping by the Mississippi* is of a snowbound houseboat in Minnesota, with brightly coloured clothes hung out on a line to dry, like prints in a photographer's studio (see plate 4). In the course of the journey that follows bits and pieces of American photographic history are picked up, taken elsewhere and set down. The accumulated weight of what has gone before obliges Soth to shift sideways, to move forward by drifting laterally. Traces of earlier photographic projects float throughout his work, changed by their journey, but not – as the phrase goes – beyond recognition. Maybe Soth didn't have Evans or Frank in mind when he photographed Jimmie's apartment in Memphis, Tennessee (with a hat propped on the edge of a chair), or the Reverend and Margaret's bedroom in Vicksburg, Mississippi (ditto), but the fact of the matter is that in Evans' picture of a Negro barber shop in Atlanta (1936) a hat is there, waiting for someone to pick it up. In the syntax of photography this needs to be re-phrased slightly as *waiting for someone to pick up on it*. When Frank photographs a hat on the desk of a bank in Houston, Texas, he is doing just that, tacitly nodding towards Evans – tipping his hat to him, if you will. Like the notes left by Arne Saknussemm in *Journey to the Centre of the Earth*, these hats indicate both that someone has been here before and show a possible way ahead. Perhaps these hats even served as unconscious triggers, subtly suggesting to Soth that pictures were there for the taking.

It is, in other words, not just a place that Soth is photographing; it's also, unavoidably, a tradition. A tradition that extends up to the present. That autumnal chair in Sugar's place, Davenport, Iowa, looks as if it is still warm from – still bears the imprint of – Eggleston's sitting in it (photographically speaking). It doesn't matter whether Soth is doing this by design; the point is that there is no getting away from the photographic precedents. (Many of the pictures in *Sleeping by the Mississippi* have photographs in them; the number of photographs glimpsed *in* this series of photographs exceeds the number of photographs *by* Soth.)

Artists have long felt that they are near the end of a tradition, closer to the mouth of the river than its source. Consistent with this, the picture by Soth (born in 1969) of Luxora, Arkansas, is suggestive of a place where the tradition seems to have washed up. Littered with bits and pieces of Americana, it looks like a spot where, over time, all sorts of American photographers have gathered for a picnic and moved on – without bothering to clean up after themselves. (Art history is the opposite of wilderness camping: you're *meant* to leave a trace; that's the point.) It's in such a mess, this spot, you could be forgiven for thinking it had been left that way deliberately. It looks, that is to say, as if one of the photographers who passed through here might have been Jeff Wall.

This is not the only place where the Canadian makes his presence felt. Soth's view of brackish waste land in Hickman, Kentucky, is strongly reminiscent of Wall's 'The Crooked Path'. In the background of Wall's picture is the wall of some kind of food manufacturing place. In the background of Soth's is the river. As the title of Wall's picture suggests, this otherwise nondescript bit of landscape is identified by the path that leads *into it*. In Soth there is no path into the picture but, in the background, there is a way out of it: the river, leading on to the next photo – which happens to be of the walls of a room in Missouri, stuck to which is a picture of a river. The sequence, the flow, is all-important. 'Anyone can take a great picture,' Soth has said, 'but very few people can put together a great collection of pictures. This is my goal.'

Beds play an important part in the rhythm and sequencing of Soth's journey. The penultimate picture in the book is of Venice, Louisiana, 'the furthest south you can travel the Mississippi by car'. It shows a bed frame choked by the abundance of stuff growing around and through it. The bed itself is sleeping in a bed of leaves, of grass. Soth notes that places like this may disappear as, each year, parts of the coast of Louisiana vanish into the Gulf of Mexico. The possibility that, in the wake of Hurricane Katrina, this fear may already have been realised simultaneously raises the value of his work as documentary record (preserving evidence of what was once here) and as its lyrical complement, the reverie (an evocation of something intangible, subjective). 'We all have a memory of life that goes on behind our eyes,' said Frank. 'Since 1974, in my latest photos, I have actually tried to show what was going on behind my eyes.' Soth's title also urges us towards a sense of slumbering subjectivity. These are images not just of places at a particular time, but of a kind of documentary dream-time.

This combination of the oneiric and objective detachment is susceptible, in part, to technical explanation. The cameras used by Frank and Winogrand were so light that they were able to snap pictures as they drove, without stopping. This was a great liberation but ease generated a certain profligacy. Stephen Shore remembers that when he made the trip that resulted in *American Surfaces* he ended up photographing *everything*. Moving to a large-format camera forced him to slow down. Sternfeld – who was one of Soth's teachers – also felt the same. The large-format camera imposes a patience of composition and selectivity that is in keeping with the slow drift of a river. Whereas Frank snatched instants from the rush of time the view camera enfolds itself around a moment. In the course of a discursive trip down another river – the Danube – Claudio Magris remarks that 'Squalor has a mysterious majesty of its own.' The density of information of the large-format negative bathes squalor in its own peculiar majesty; it also lends a hallucinatory or dream-like quality to the most humdrum situation.

Soth's work lacks the gleaming, pristine quality that Brodsky associates with the Neva because the river and the tradition of which it is, in this context, a physical manifestation have been around so long. Like many great rivers the Mississippi is no longer in any hurry to get to the sea (why bother? It's seen it all before); cauterised by its own weight, the river drags its huge memory-belly along like a weary earth-coloured snake. It is too laden with history, with images. What it longs for more than anything, in fact, is to rest. After all this time it can get to the Gulf of Mexico in its sleep.

2006

Michael Ackerman

I first came across Michael Ackerman's photographs in a cinema in 1999. My then girlfriend and I were waiting for the film to start when she pulled out a copy of *The New Yorker* that featured a collage of half a dozen black-and-white pictures of a woman. In five of the six pictures she is in a cramped apartment, naked or in the process of getting dressed, cleaning her teeth, sitting on the toilet; one shows her dressed and out on the street. In the darkness of the cinema it was impossible to see the pictures properly, and I spent the next two hours impatiently waiting for the film to end so I could see this other movie – a whole film in just six frames! – clearly. Even in bright daylight this turned out to be impossible. That, it became clear, when I got to know Ackerman's work better, is the point. By his standards, in fact, these images were razor-sharp. A caption explained that the six photos comprised a detail from a series called *Paris, France, 1999*. The pictures were subtly erotic, incredibly intimate and, as can happen when you are exposed to certain works of art, I felt as if something in me had been *waiting* for them. It was like falling in love.

No, it was more than that: it was like falling in love and moving in with someone, when being able to watch them doing the most ordinary things is touched by rapture, undulled by familiarity. There is what might be called a lavatorial precedent for this kind of thing. In 1920, Jacques Henri Lartigue had photographed his wife Bibi, on their honeymoon, sitting on the toilet. The photograph is a frank and lovely record of a moment. Such frankness had, of course, become obtrusively routine by the late twentieth century. Ackerman does something else, regaining the lost delicacy of Lartigue's image by inflecting it with a tinge of dream, as if what we are seeing is the record not of a moment but the way it lingers in the memory and becomes changed by its association with other moments, other memories.

I was keen to see more of these pictures from Paris but at that time Ackerman's only book, *End Time City*, was of photographs from Varanasi (Benares). The lyricism of the Parisian images here gave way to a glaring intensity. These weren't pictures you went and looked at calmly; they accosted you, came lunging and reeling at you. Some were like the shock of daylight after emerging from a dark lane; others were as impenetrable as a darkened alley after hours spent sight-seeing in bright sun; most somehow contrived to be both simulta-neously. And the felt subjectivity of the Paris photographs – the sense that Ackerman was recording not what he saw but what he was feeling – was even more pronounced. Offering a raw, stunned reac-tion to a place, they were like photos of the inside of his head while he was there. As such they seemed to insist on an equal ferocity of response from anyone looking at them. You could not simply admire or contemplate these pictures; you had either to love or recoil from them – or both.

One of Ackerman's Paris photos was eventually used on the cover of the paperback of my novel, *Paris Trance*. Then, shortly after the book appeared, a strange coincidence took place. In Bangkok I was introduced to a photographer who showed me some examples of his work. After looking through his pictures I said that they reminded me somewhat of Michael Ackerman's work. The photographer – whose name I've forgotten – flicked back through the pile of photos until he came to one of a shaven-headed guy and said, 'That is Michael Ackerman.'

It seemed entirely appropriate that Michael Ackerman should look like an Ackerman photograph – even more so in what was evidently a self-portrait in his next book *Fiction* (2001). A chronology explained that he was born in 1967 in Israel and had moved to New York in 1974, but in the main body of the book dates and places had been entirely obliterated or buried. *Fiction* included the Paris pictures I had already seen but there was nothing, here, to indicate where they had been taken. Now they were just part of an ongoing, unlocatable swirl of images. Faces lurched out of the darkness; bodies writhed in shadow. 'As I see it,' Ackerman said in an interview at the book's conclusion, 'places do not exist. A place is just my idea of it.' The intense subjectivity of the work I had seen earlier had been raised to the level of a solipsistic world-view. Often credited with instigating a move from 'documentary' to more personal photography Robert Frank had clearly been an influence but here the opposition to the idea of photography as documentary record had become nearly pathological. At a certain point Ackerman decided he 'no longer wanted to see any information in [his] pictures'. In photos of the street he wanted to . . . get rid of the street! The sense of dislocation is exacerbated by extremities of contrast, the smudge and slur of printing. As a result it is sometimes almost impossible to see what is going on through the sleet and blur – until, that is, you stop trying to see *through* it and accept that the sleet and blur is precisely what is going on.

There is a considerable and dramatic gain in this approach but there is also a corresponding loss. The effects in the pictures of Benares were a specific and fitting response to a place. In *Fiction* the volume is consistently turned up to a point at which it distorts. Everywhere looks weirded out in the same way, irrespective of what or where it is. Like Francis Bacon, Ackerman himself seems happy to take this risk: 'The pictures that mean something to me always evoke the same thing,' he has said.

After being so fascinated by and curious about Ackerman's work I finally got to meet him in New York in 2003. He arranged a slide show of some of his photographs at his apartment. The intensity of the work had not diminished at all; the same pitch of psychological torsion had been obsessively maintained. Everything in these pictures was melting, dissolving, deranged. Light itself had been turned into a species of darkness. It was as if the camera had been recalibrated in such a way as to preserve not what is there but what had been there a second or two earlier so that the frame is filled with the ghostly aftermath of action, a ghastly residue of gestures. The effect was charged, overwhelming, unrelenting. These were not pictures *of* a world, this *was* a world.

When the screening was over, eager to demonstrate some aware-ness of the technical side of photography (of which I know nothing), I asked Ackerman what he did to achieve the signature blurring and distortion of his images, his world. He looked at me as if the question made no sense at all.

'That's just how it is,' he said.

2004

Trent Parke

I was introduced to the work of Trent Parke (born in Australia in 1971, a member of Magnum since 2007) by a mutual friend, the photographer Matt Stuart. He showed me two books by Parke, both self-published. The first was *The Seventh Wave* (2000), photographs of Australia's beaches, by Parke and his partner – now wife – Narelle Autio. A more intimate and egalitarian collaboration is hard to imagine. Without the list at the end explaining which pictures are by whom it would be impossible to tell them apart. Much of the action takes place in or under the waves. You don't look at this book. You open it and plunge in. *Whoomp!* Immediately, you're immersed, submerged. They're like pictures of being born, of people exploding into life beneath the sea, or bursting through the surface and into being. It's as if evolution has been speeded up and compressed so that the origins of life on the planet turn, in a split-second, to the creation of an individual human life. In the same breath it's mythic and candid – street photography from Atlantis!

The surface of the sea is a film separating two worlds, that of water and that of air. Though absolute, the distinction is perpetually on the brink of dissolving, melting away. People fly through the water as if suspended in a turbulent sky, or float through great clouds of aquatic light. That's what water is for Parke and Autio – *liquid light*. Forms dissolve, blur, swim into and out of focus. Quick and silver, the water is a flash-flood of mercury. Part of the attraction of this undertaking, I'm guessing, is that the conventions of perspective and composition are not so much broken as bent out of shape, temporarily suspended. So completely has perspective been absorbed into our understanding of human perception that its abandonment suggests that we might be sharing a non-human or shark's-eye view. This lurking sense of danger is also a product of association. When a squid is under attack it emits clouds of ink – which is exactly what we get here: huge oil-spills of dense, billowing black, while people dive and bomb through the surface and into the picture frame. They're like human depth charges, or flash-bulbs exploding. As the shockwaves pass through the pictures it's as if they're in the process of being blasted apart – except it's all pretty puny in comparison with the massive force of water, the rips and moon-tugged tides. Life on earth, in some of these pictures, looks like it could be ending as well as beginning.

The other book, *Dream/Life*, was actually published a year earlier. As with *The Seventh Wave* the impact is immediate and jolting. Wow! It's only as you look at it over time that you sense that there is a degree of dues-paying going on. As with certain jazz albums original work is mixed up with a selection of standards – Parke's own take on other photographers' compositions. In *The Seventh Wave* there is what appears to be a version of Martin Munkácsi's 1929 photograph of silhouetted boys charging into Lake Tanganyika. This was the picture that had a profound effect on Henri Cartier-Bresson after he travelled to Africa in 1931: 'that tremendous feeling for plasticity, for life itself, the black, the white, the spray!' He might have been describing Parke's picture. Was this a deliberate allusion and homage on Parke's part? I don't know. But photographers tend to be deeply aware of what has gone before. A picture of white hats, flowing down a street in *Dream/Life*, is surely a response to the call of Tina Modotti's 1926 picture 'Workers' Parade', of sombreros borne along by the tide of history.

The most obvious debt in *Dream/Life* is to Robert Frank. We don't want to get bogged down in the anxiety of photographic influence, but it is possible that, as an artist, Parke became fully himself only after he had thoroughly assimilated the lessons of Frank's vision. One of the animating procedures of modern art in all media is to absorb the work of a master and then take it back to – in this case, turn one's lens on – one's native land. This is not copying because the approach, the lens itself, is changed and recalibrated by what it depicts, and confronts.

In Parke's case the revelation was the transforming power of Australian light. The light is inescapable, tremendous. Technically, the strength of the light meant that some detail could remain illuminated while all else was plunged into a pandemonium of roiling smoke. Darkness visible! The brighter the day the darker it could be made to look.

Dream/Life comes to a premature or arbitrary close in that it signals the impatient ending of a phase, not the completion of a project. It establishes an approach, suggests parameters of style and subject that will characterise – but not limit – Parke's future output. Later works will continue but intensify the *Dream/Life* vision so that, at its most extreme, Sydney becomes a kind of ghost city, in the process of being annihilated by light. A passer-by will be transformed into an accidental super-hero: 'Solar-man', a bleached absence of pure radiance! (Part of the fascination of this picture is of the photographer-as-magician kind: how did he *do* that? The difference between magic and photography is that the spell remains unbroken even when the technical explanation – which, in any case, I cannot recall – is forthcoming.) People on a beach will gaze towards the horizon as if at a nuclear test, source of a light so bright that even the sky becomes a vast shadow.

Photography is a generous, abundant medium and Parke is a voracious photographer. Keeping track of what he's been up to since the publication of these two books can be a little difficult. He is amassing a vast quantity of pictures, working on multiple projects, which are still in the process of being arranged, edited and exhibited. In some of the large format colour photos of billboards and intersections in cities and suburbs it seems as if Jeff Wall has come out of a pub and, confronted by blocks of unyielding colour, become convinced that he has stumbled into an entire world predicated on his idea of artistically heightened reality. I mean, what is that guy *doing* outside the store with the Championship Bay Trophy sign? Is he the only competitor in the 100-metre street-crawl? Or is he the Australian incarnation of one of those Buddhists who make immense pilgrimages to Tibet, on foot, stopping every few yards to prostrate themselves and offer homage – in this case to the liquid god Castlemaine? It's also an emblematic image in that it reveals, in densely concentrated form, a quality shared by much of this colour work: the feeling of a larger emptiness that defines and lies beyond the picture frame. It's as if every Australian city were a franchise of *The Truman Show* – except it's not reality that lies beyond the flimsy construct of the city, it's a nothingness that can never be kept entirely at bay; developers' plans to expand into this emptiness simply present it with new corners to infiltrate.

If the colour and light in these pictures seems artificially height-ened, devoid of subtlety and nuance, that is because they are entirely naturalistic. The light is solid, like walking into a wall. The sky is the opposite of sheltering, as if the long-threatened ozone layer has been completely boiled away. So people stand at street corners, fried by radioactive light so penetrating it's hard to believe there can be such a thing as interior or inner life. No one looks like they're ever going to get anywhere. They stand there like survivors of an army of the undead, entombed by the triple glare of heat, light and camera, going nowhere, stuck there not till the end of but in the *middle* of time.

Then there are the Christmas pictures, provisionally collected under the title *Trent Parke's Family Album*. This is like a slasher movie in stills – in which the murder weapon turns out to be an inflatable toy. Or, to put it the other way around, a fun-for-all-the-family comedy in which something sinister – a slaughtered mouse beneath the stairs – always lurks. Looking at these pictures you wonder if 'Silent Night, Holy Night' might actually be a murder ballad in disguise.

Parke's most ambitious project of the last few years has been *Minutes to Midnight*, exhibited in several museums but not yet published as a book. It is the record of a two-year, 60,000-mile road trip around Australia that Parke and Autio began in 2003. (Once again a prece-dent set by Frank – the mid-1950s trip that led to *The Americans* – springs to mind.) The result is what Parke calls 'a psychological portrait' of Australia in the midst of the worst drought in the country's history – and of the fires that resulted from that drought – and, less tangibly, of the sense of threat that came in the wake of the Bali bombings in which many Australians lost their lives.

Settlement in Australia is centrifugal. Cities cling to the rim of the island-continent. As a result the interior possesses a perpetual and primal allure. An expedition by the Prussian explorer Ludwig Leichhardt (who disappeared in the Australian desert in 1848) provided the inspiration for Patrick White's 1957 novel, *Voss*, about a doomed attempt to cross the continent. 'Every man has a genius,' says Voss at one point. 'Though it is not always discoverable. Least of all when choked by the trivialities of daily existence. But in this disturbing country, so far as I have become acquainted with it already, it is possible more easily to discard the inessential and to attempt the infinite. You will be burnt up most likely . . . but you will realise that genius.' Voss, here, is the mouthpiece for White's sense of his own heroic artistic endeavours – but he might also be commenting on Parke's photographic odyssey.

A simple comparison brings out the scale and clarity of Parke's undertaking. When the Goncourt brothers travelled from Paris to sunny Rome for a few weeks in 1867 they quickly became 'nostalgic for grey'. Of his own trip, Parke has said that no single moment made as deep an impression on him as the protracted experience of not seeing a cloud for three months. 'It felt', he said, 'like we had slid from the face of the earth and ended up in some future world.' This, then, was a journey not to a heart of darkness but to the heart of light. And whereas Voss fails to cross the continent, or to find any sign of the inland sea mythically imagined to lie at the core of any arid country, Parke offers documentary proof that it exists: in the form of a small water tank in the middle of the outback. Someone is diving into the water as if, in some scorched future, this is all that remains of the untamed seas of *The Seventh Wave*.

With their starkness and intense expressivity some of the photographs in *Minutes to Midnight* are reminiscent of work by Michael Ackerman. Like Ackerman, Parke is interested in the emotional or psychological contours of a scene or event. In his recent work Ackerman has pushed further, into the realm of what he terms 'fiction'. The specifics of where he ends up make no difference. Not nearly so solipsistic, Parke is profoundly attached – in his working life – to one place and one place only: Australia. And whereas, for Ackerman, the intensity and distortion in the pictures is less a response to where he finds himself than a default setting, Parke, in the bush, discovered a place where the technical extremes that his work tends towards were demanded by the subject matter. It is as if, in the outback, there is nowhere for life to hide; it is always and constantly exposed, raw. Storms, when they come, are of an intensity that is devastating, biblical.

In the American west contemporary photographers often tread consciously in the wake of illustrious predecessors such as Timothy O'Sullivan, who accompanied the great surveys that set out to map the country. In Australia the early expeditions were undocumented by photographers. What was discovered, in the absence of the picturesque, the spectacular or distinctive, was a daunting extent of emptiness. As a result, these expeditions were largely invisible affairs. Parke, of course, is by no means the first to make good this lack. But his method is one that shares an unlikely affinity with the kind of experience recorded in the journals of those early explorers. The lack of conventional 'sights' or landmarks meant that these journals lacked obvious narrative direction. So, asks the writer Paul Carter in his book *Living in a New Country*, 'What is it that gives the discontinuous aggregation of details its narrative direction?' The answer – but note, first, the concise characterisation of the typical photographic journey à la Frank contained by that question – is that the true subject of these explorer writings is '*historical space* – spatiality as historical experience'. Or, to put it in terms borrowed from the fictional explorer, Voss, infinity as glimpsed at a particular moment in time or history.

At this point it is worth re-emphasising that Parke is a member of Magnum. In some ways the opportunities for photojournalism no longer exist in the way that they did for Robert Capa, W. Eugene Smith or Larry Burrows in the various heydays of *Life* and *Time* magazines. While it is tempting to lament the decline of photojournalism of the sort traditionally associated with Magnum the recruitment of people like Parke, Martin Parr and Alec Soth has been crucial in preventing it from becoming a kind of heritage agency whose members can be relied on to stamp stories with the photographic equivalent of a heraldic seal. Perhaps the most noticeable recent development in photojournalism – a development coupled with the decline of *Life*-like magazines and the subsequent increase in opportunities for the presentation and sale of photography as art – is for more intensely and varied subjective responses to events and places. Needless to say, this complicates but does not undermine the documentary imperative to bear witness, to report back on what one saw at a particular time, in a certain place.

The reportage in *Minutes to Midnight* is of a highly personal and elemental kind: events, people and places as they are chanced upon and as they appear, not in the face of a looming deadline, but in the perma-glare of the outback. Take the well-known picture of Aboriginals hanging out in the street outside the Club Hotel, Wiluna. The hotel sign reads 'Welcome to Paradise'. Plenty of photographers have exploited the ironic gap between the boasts made by billboards or signs and the way that the surrounding reality falls short of those claims. In this sad place irony seems an alien luxury, an exotic import, and the gap is as vast and arid as a desert. And it's not just irony that is lacking. The moment caught in this shot of paradise and the wreckage strewn around it is devoid, also, of the kind of split-second urgency that characterises Capa's famous D-Day photographs. What we get, in this shattered paradise, is the depiction of a state in which what might be expected to be a matter of urgent attention has become a permanent condition of existence, one marked by the complete erosion of any notion of urgency. Like many of Parke's photographs it is beyond news. It looks as if it could have been taken the day after tomorrow, in the aftermath of history.

2008

Miroslav Tichý

Van Gogh's rise to posthumous glory is unsurpassable but, in scale and strangeness, the story of Miroslav Tichý's triumph will take some beating. And, unlike Van Gogh, he is around to enjoy it – sort of. Tichý is eighty-two now, and if he could be persuaded to leave his lair in Kyjov, in the Czech Republic, he would see his name writ large on the banners fluttering outside the Pompidou Centre in Paris, where a retrospective of his work has just opened.

The first things on display are Tichý's cameras and lenses, looking as rusty and old as weapons unearthed from the battlefields of the First World War. Photographers tend to be obsessed by kit, are always trying out new lenses, films and processes. Tichý began photographing with the most basic Russian-made camera – and this was the technological *high*point of his career. Thereafter he became a scavenger, modifying and building his equipment with whatever came to hand: a rewind mechanism made of elastic from a pair of shorts and attached to empty spools of thread; lenses from old spectacles and Plexiglas, polished with sandpaper, toothpaste and cigarette ash. His telephotos were cobbled together from plastic drain pipes and empty food tins. He also made his own enlarger, out of cardboard and planks. Tichý's make-do-and-mend philosophy apparently extends to his own, um, wardrobe. Photographs from the early 1990s show him holding his DIY camera, wearing a filthy sweater, stitched together with what look like dead beetles. These portraits of the artist as an old castaway remind one of John McCarthy's reaction on first seeing long-term hostage Brian Keenan: 'Fuck me, it's Ben Gunn!'

So what did Tichý do, once he was kitted out with his homemade arsenal? Put as simply as possible, he spent the 1960s and '70s perving around Kyjov, photographing women. Ideally he'd catch them topless or in bikinis at the local swimming pool; failing that, he'd settle for a glimpse of a knee or – the limitations of the camera meant the framing was often askew – an ankle. That is the least of the pictures' defects: most are under- or over-exposed as well. Michael Hoppen is currently exhibiting a small selection of Tichýs at his London gallery. I asked him how many really good Tichý pictures there were in total. 'In focus?' he replied, as if that were a personal preference, and not a prerequisite for photographic adequacy. 'Maybe two or three hundred.' In some of these the ostensible subject is all but blanched out of existence by a blaze of intruding light.

We have concentrated, so far, on the most orthodox phase of Tichý's working methods. Once developed and printed the pictures were subjected to a protracted form of editorial hazing: left out in the rain, used as beer mats or to prop up wobbly tables. Where the definition was not sharp enough Tichý would pencil around breasts or hips like an enthusiastic but unqualified cosmetic surgeon. Sometimes he'd frame the pictures with a specially chosen mount: a garbage sack, say, or a bit of squiggled-on card. One of the works at the Pompidou has been gnawed by the rats with whom the artist shares his home. It may be hard to resist the conclusion that Tichý is a few frames short of a roll – but he's shrewd with it: 'If you want to be famous,' he has said, 'you have to be worse at something than everyone else in the world.'

And the eccentricities of Tichý's habits should not blind us to the conventional aspects of his early formation. Enrolled at the Academy of Fine Arts in Prague in 1945, he eagerly embraced the liberationist promise of modernism. This promise was broken when the Communists came to power in 1948, dragging in their wake the social-realist imperatives of heroic representation of proletarian endeavour. After a brief period of military service Tichý responded by retreating to his home town of Kyjov. In 1957, during the cultural thaw ushered in by Stalin's death, Tichý was slated to participate in a group exhibition from which he suddenly withdrew. Gripped by the delusion that his colleagues were part of a fascist conspiracy, he suffered a complete breakdown that led to his being committed to a psychiatric clinic for a year.

From that time on his life assumes the curious combination of neglect and compulsion that will eventually be transformed into the stuff of cultural legend (Nick Cave has written a song about him; Michael Nyman is contemplating an opera based on his life). He abandons everything else and, throughout the fluctuating political climate of the 1960s and '70s – and despite repeated victimisation by the authorities and further incarceration in psychiatric hospitals – burrows away at his new existence as 'a stone-age photographer'.

As often happens, the fairy-tale outcome of his story is largely down to the efforts of a confidant uniquely convinced of the worth of a man assumed to be an unstable outcast or renegade loser. (The film *Round Midnight*, based on the relationship between the alcoholic, tubercular and periodically mad pianist Bud Powell and Francis Paudras, the young Frenchman who saves him from ruin, is archetypal in this respect). In Tichý's case it was the boy next door, Roman Buxbaum, who began collecting and conserving the work that Tichý treated with consummate disdain. (There is a wonderful sequence in Buxbaum's documentary, *Retired Tarzan*, where Tichý flicks through samples of his work before tossing them onto the compost heap of the floor.) Buxbaum wrote the first article about Tichý, which led to a solo exhibition organised by curator Harald Szeemann in Seville in 2004, to the formation of the Tichý Ocean Foundation, and, now, to the Paris show.

It is in the nature of fairy tales of this sort that there is a potential for murkiness or unease. Here is a paranoid old man with a history of mental illness, unmarried, childless, so habituated to austerity that he has no need of money, whose work and legacy have been surrendered to those who find themselves in control of an extremely valuable body of work. The situation is inevitably complicated because the work has only assumed this visibility and value thanks to the efforts of the very custodians who lay themselves open to charges of exploitation and self-advancement. (*Round Midnight* immediately provoked critical blowback from people claiming that Paudras was not quite the selfless devotee portrayed in the film.) The bottom line, in this instance, is that without Buxbaum and the Tichý Ocean Foundation I would never have heard of Tichý and you would not be reading about him.

Tichý's late rehabilitation may be the most extreme in the history of photography but it is not entirely unprecedented. In 2006 Hoppen cleverly paired Tichý and Jacques Henri Lartigue, whose work overlapped in several striking ways. Born into a life of privilege in 1894 Lartigue began photographing when he was a boy. Aged thirteen he suddenly got 'a new idea: that I should go to the park and photograph those women who have the most eccentric or beautiful hats'. A year later he declared that 'everything about [women] fascinates me – their dresses, their scent, the way they walk'. The results of these enthusiastic expeditions were pasted into homemade albums by the adolescent boy who went on to develop ambitions to be a painter. This desire was unfulfilled, but Lartigue continued to take photographs for his own delight and distraction. It is not until 1963, when he is almost seventy, that Lartigue finds himself exhibited at the Museum of Modern Art in New York and retrospectively installed as one of the founding fathers of modern photography.

Then there is E.J. Bellocq, whose photographs – some of them badly damaged – of prostitutes in New Orleans from the 1910s were eventually brought back from a long-forgotten death by Lee Friedlander (who also played a key part in the posthumous revival of William Gedney, another self-sufficient recluse). The difference between Bellocq and Tichý is that the former, evidently, was on close and friendly terms with the women he photographed. Even when Tichý's wonky telephoto enables him to snuggle up deceptively close, his pictures gaze longingly on a world from which he is excluded. Whether the women look at him, berate him or remain oblivious to his approaches, they are absolutely beyond reach. This is formally enhanced by the fence that so often comes between the photographer and the women in the frame. It's just the fence at the local pool but it imparts to the pictures the intensity of a prisoner's peering through the bars of a cell.

Since the show is in Paris a personal anecdote about the city might be relevant at this point. In the summer of 1991 I went to live in

Paris for a while. It was blazing hot, I knew almost no one and was in a torment of loneliness and sexual frustration. My apartment was a pit so I spent the afternoons in the park, looking, hoping, torn between the desire to talk to one of the many women sunbathing and terrified that to do so was a form of harassment. Meanwhile, other men *were* doing exactly what I wanted to do, sitting down, chatting to women – and not always getting told to shove off. I remember being crushed by the way the simple mathematics of desire refused to come out right: there were so many women in the world, how could it be so difficult to find one? The question contains its answer: it's that tormenting and beckoning *one*, the chance in a million which non-mathematicians call love.

Tichý's pictures are like photographs of that summer of longing extended over the course of a lifetime until it assumes a quality of stoic resignation or exile. Some are as erotically and romantically charged as any ever made. If anything that charge is felt even more strongly now, in the era of Internet porn, because, in spite of their abrupt cropping and haphazard framing, they *contain* the plausible context of desire and its frustrations and restraints of which the porno world is temptingly and deceptively devoid.

Not that *all* of Tichý's pictures are of women. He sometimes photographed random objects, stuff he came across on a washing line, for instance. It just happens that the washing line is laden with bras hung out to dry. When Tichý was not on the prowl or lurking round the pool he would photograph women at home, screen-grabbing them from the telly. 'People say I think too much about women,' another artist once remarked. 'Yet after all, what is there more important to think about?' That was Rodin. At times, though, Tichý's one-track mind suggests a kinship with figures lower down the cultural totem pole: Benny Hill, for example. When Tichý comes across a team of women stretching and exercising in a park the resulting image cackles with barely suppressed glee. But the distinction between high and low is not easy to sustain for there is, of course, a Benny Hillish quality about passages in the novels of Tichý's celebrated fellow Czech – and near-contemporary – Milan Kundera. In both, the abundantly erotic – participatory in the novels, entirely voyeuristic in the photographs – is a tacit escape from the deadweight of historical materialism.

Different men tend to be attracted to different physical types of women: thin or voluptuous, blonde or brunette. For Tichý anything in a dress was great – though without a dress was even better. He sees a hefty, middle-aged-looking woman in an unflattering calf-length skirt bending over to talk to someone in a car – yep, that'll do. He would have endorsed, wholeheartedly, the title of Garry Winogrand's 1975 book of street shots, *Women Are Beautiful*. Some of the critical flak aimed at Winogrand might have been dodged if lines written ten years later had been available as a contextualising epigraph. 'Women are beautiful when young, almost all women,' says the elderly female narrator of John Berger's *Once in Europa*. 'Whatever the proportion of a face, whether a body is too skinny or too heavy, at some moment a woman possesses the power of beauty which is given to us as women. Often the moment is brief. Sometimes the moment may come and we may not even know it. Yet traces of it remain.' This is Tichý's equivalent of the decisive moment – a moment which, for all the reasons outlined above, cannot be reliably captured. It's hit and miss. 'When I do something, it has to be precise,' Tichý has said. 'True, the lens was not precise, but maybe that's where the art is.'

That Tichý's art is inseparable from the technical limitations and imperfect state of his pictures is manifest at many levels. At least until the eponymous film came and slightly spoiled things, Bob Dylan's song 'I'm Not There' was the most cherished of all the bootleg recordings – in spite of and because of the lyric being incomplete and, in places, inaudible. The effect is movingly evoked by composer Michael Pisaro: 'It's almost as though he has discovered a language or, better, has heard of a language: heard about some of its vocabulary, its grammar and its sounds, and before he can comprehend it, starts using this set of unformed tools to narrate the most important event of his life.' Or, to translate this back into visual terms, to capture the most important moments in his life on film – but since these moments lack clarity and definition they could, as easily, be any man's or everyman's.

The value of 'I'm Not There' is also a function of its rarity: the song is almost not there, exists only in this incomplete take. The production of images gathered pace throughout the twentieth century and then, with the spread of digital, the idea of scarcity or any economy of production simply disappeared. Tichý's pictures – he seems not to have made multiple prints – have the quality of relics that have survived some kind of visual holocaust, when only these decrepit traces (that Berger word again) remain. They share with the earliest pictures by William Henry Fox Talbot the sense of wonder that a thing such as photography has actually come to pass. Hence the peculiar temporal compression of Tichý's work. It is as if one of the pioneers of photography, instead of taking slow pictures of flowers or statues, was somehow able to snap chicks in bikinis! So they are like premonitions *and* memories. 'Memory has a spottiness,' writes John Updike, 'as if the film was sprinkled with developer instead of immersed in it.' The chemical stains, bleaches and other defects make Tichý's pictures seem like highly personal memories of universal longings – but memories in the process of fading so that they are indistinguishable from desires that may never be realised.

As a species we have remained physically unchanged for millennia. This accounts for the primal pull of Tichý's images. But this biological imperative has been refined, recalibrated, mediated and – at times – challenged by the long history of art. Patched-up equipment notwithstanding, the ageing voyeur and former art student was conscious of the gestures catalogued by this tradition so that his pictures, at their best, have the delicacy and poise of a smutty Vermeer.

Or, to get to the quick of the matter, the indelicacy of a certain Courbet. In 1866, at the request of a Turkish diplomat, Courbet painted a tightly cropped close-up of a woman's stomach and genitals called *The Origin of the World*. The first Tichý photographs on show at the Pompidou are, in representational terms, near-failures. In some you can make out the shape – elusive and suggestive as the constellations – of what may be a woman. Others are just blurs and protoplasms of light emerging from infinite darkness. If you were able to travel back to the dawn of time, as the universe writhed into existence, this, perhaps, is what you might see.

2008

Saving Grace: Todd Hido

It makes sense to talk about Todd Hido's *approach*. *Roaming* shows roads taken and not taken, some peering back into the photographic past (right back, in fact, to the murky dawn of pictorialism), some blurring into obscurity, others hinting at visual possibilities that might lie ahead. *House Hunting* reveals where some of these roads lead, the homes at the end of the street. Occasionally Hido enters the premises and finds signs of discarded life: a stained mattress, a towel on the carpet. But never people. It's as if something is missing from the title. All the vowels are present except the absent 'a', which lurks, unseen, tacitly between the 'h' and the 'u' of *Hunting*. This sense of the pictures being haunted by what is absent is integral to their effect.

These exteriors, with their brightly lit windows, are reminiscent – in a modern, democratic, American way – of the paintings of Victorian mansions at twilight by Atkinson Grimshaw. Grimshaw's work depends on a paradox of domesticity: the best way to appreciate being inside is to imagine what it might seem like from the outside (that's why people leave their curtains open). Step through the doorways of Hido's photographs and any promise of cosiness is broken – as is much of the stuff we see lying around.

The relationship between a particular exterior (which serves as a kind of establishing shot) and a neighbouring interior is suggested but never verified. Instead of confirmation there are further doubts and, as often as not, more doors. The lines from Whitman, used as an epigraph to the catalogue of Walker Evans' 1971 retrospective at MoMA, are hard to avoid: 'I do not doubt interiors have their

interiors, and exteriors have their exteriors, and that the eyesight has
another eyesight . . .'

The inhabitants of the buildings are finally – if fictively – revealed
in *Between the Two*. The threshold we have crossed appears physical
but it is also a subtler one separating documentary record from
psychological construct. The interior in which we find ourselves is
the photographer's head. Put it another way. Stepping inside Hido's
buildings is like finding a drawer, once stuffed full, now empty except
for a photograph that got left behind when everything else was
chucked out (a negative definition of editing, I guess). Inevitably, this
photograph has about it the quality of a secret. Not just any secret
but, specifically, of a sexual secret. What are the defining qualities of
sexual secrets? That, with the odd variation – a preference for one
shade or style of underwear – they are pretty much the same as everyone else's. Another name for such universal secrets is the unconscious.

This is not to diminish the importance individuals attach to
achieving their own peculiar ends. Wear this wig, Hido tells his
models. Put these shoes on. Move your leg over that way. Approach
an ideal I have in my mind. The photos that result simultaneously
record both this ideal and a failed distance from it. The degree of
contrivance required to realise this vision – i.e. to fall short in exactly
the desired way – is considerable: the artificial nature of the set-up
(hired models sort of acting like hookers, in the service not of sex
but of art); location-scouting a hotel because it is redolent of nowhere
in particular; high-end camera with a tripod, large negative and incon-
venient exposure times. The pictures, let's say, have to work over-
time to achieve a heightened idea of the tawdry.

It was almost inevitable that Hido would take things a stage further
(those signature images from *Roaming*, of telegraph poles receding
into the uncertain distance, serve as a visual incitement to do just
that, to keep going) and supplement the large-format, meditative
images of *Between the Two* with pictures snatched with the kind of
camera anyone could use, to replace the careful modulation of natural
light with the unforgiving glare of the on-camera flash. (There are
precedents for this kind of low-spec investigation: the most significant
would be Evans using a Polaroid camera – or 'toy' as he first thought

of it – to make thousands of pictures in the last years of his life.) The results are like accidents that couldn't wait to happen.

The scenario is so familiar, from both the point of view of the women (the models) and the men (the photographers) as to be almost archetypal. The narrator of Lorrie Moore's novel *Anagrams* recalls a number of episodes that could double as captions for pictures like these: 'Three times before, my husband had asked me to pose with various articles of clothing removed. Once in the bedroom wearing only boots and one of his ties. Once in the bathroom with a red towel draped strategically to miss one breast. Once in the kitchen in just my bra. And today. I did this because I loved him, I supposed, but maybe I did it because I'd grown up in a trailer and guessed that *this is what people did in houses, that this is what houses were for*' (italic added).

As far as the men are concerned, the idea is to make your girlfriend or wife look like herself *and* someone else, to fulfil, simultaneously, what a character in Jay McInerney's *Brightness Falls* famously reckons are two of men's basic needs: 'pussy and strange pussy'. The sudden lurch of the flash accomplishes this but, in doing so, it leaves the women stranded – and not just between their actual and assumed identities. Diane Arbus observed a similar tension when she was photographing beauty queens in the early 1960s. What intrigued Arbus was the way that the girls 'continually made the fatal mistakes which were in fact themselves'.

Like the gear worn by Hido's models, that word 'fatal' is fitting and revealing. For there is something quite creepy and pervy about these beautiful pictures. There is the haunting sense that this is the last photo of X or Y before she disappeared. Now, something like that has always been latent in the very idea of the photograph (Barthes' 'the return of the dead'). If it is felt particularly acutely here that is partly because Hido is using an old-fashioned camera requiring obsolete film (he has a stash) so that there is a discrepancy between when the pictures were taken and – certain technologies being indelibly associated with certain periods – what or, more precisely, *when* they look like. Hence there is another dimension to the way in which the women are stranded: not just between identities (real and constructed) and between places (the whereabouts of the interiors being uncorroborated by exteriors) but *in time*.

All things considered, it is no wonder that these women appear so vulnerable. The camera *poses* the question it is incapable of answering. More exactly, because of the old film stock, it asks the same question in two slightly different tenses: What has become of them? What is to become of them?

Historically, women have been encouraged to become whatever men have wanted them to be. But even those most at pains to devote themselves entirely to the demands of self-effacement retain something of what they are and have been since they were kids – even if (and again it was Arbus who saw this clearly) that thing, that *saving grace*, is a flaw. Contradicting the suspicion that these might be images of the disappeared, this reinforces the inkling – itself consistent with the earlier feeling that a given picture somehow escaped being discarded, lost – that we are looking at the lucky ones, survivors.

On several occasions Hido has expressed his adherence to the idea that 'sources of terror in childhood often become sources of attraction in adulthood'. With reference to these pictures Hido mentions the time he saw his father taking a semi-porno picture of his mother, but remember, it's not a one-way street, photography. It's quite possible that the same things that troubled and inspired him might be at work, just as powerfully, on his models. In at least some of the pictures the tense outcome of the collaboration between photographer and model is the reciprocity of attraction and dread.

2008

Idris Khan

Criticism sometimes achieves the condition of art; certain works of art are also a form of commentary or criticism. Roland Barthes' meditation on photography, *Camera Lucida*, is a classic example of the former. How to respond creatively to a book that has profoundly shaped the way the medium is regarded? A writer might feel compelled to follow George Steiner's grand advice and 'write a book in reply'. And if you're not a writer, but a photographer? If you *do* what Barthes is writing *about*?

Idris Khan's response was to photograph every page of the book and then digitally combine them in a single, composite image. The result of this homage to – and essay on – *Camera Lucida* (English edition) is a beautiful palimpsest: a series of blurred stripes of type in which the occasional word can be deciphered and one of the images reproduced by Barthes – a portrait of Mondrian, by Kertész – glimpsed. Khan did the same thing with *On Photography* by Susan Sontag. The whole of the book can be seen in an instant, but the density of information is such that Sontag's elegant formulations add up – and are reduced – to a humming, unreadable distillation. Already slight, the gap between texts and Khan's images will shrink further if the books are re-issued with his 'readings' of them – surrogate author photos? – on the covers.

It's not just books about photography; Khan also photographs photographs. Bernd and Hilla Becher compiled a comprehensive inventory of architectural building types, such as gas towers, all photographed in a stark, neutral style. Khan's composite, 'Every . . .

Bernd & Hilla Becher Prison Type Gasholder', transforms their rigid geometries into a fuzzy, vibrating mass, more like a smudged charcoal drawing of a shivering iron jelly than a photograph.

These – the Sontag, the Barthes and the Bechers – were the first things by Khan that I came across. It was obvious he was on to something. A better sense of what that something might be can be seen at the Victoria Miro Gallery. Practically everything in this, Khan's first UK solo show, is a composite of some kind but the range and depth of the idea has been extended with – the pun is unavoidable – uncanny success.

Freud, in his famous essay, mentions 'the constant recurrence of the same thing' as a symptom of 'the Uncanny'. In Khan's picture of every page of the recent Penguin edition the black gutter at the centre throbs like a premonition or memory of an Op Art void. It makes you wonder if, as well as psychoanalysis, Freud also invented the Rorschach blot. In the background, two of the paintings discussed by him, Leonardo's *Mona Lisa* and *The Virgin and Child with St Anne*, peer through a shifting sleet of type like emanations of the unconscious or something. It's only a book – only a photo of a book – but it pulses like a living thing.

Khan was born in Birmingham in 1978. His mother, who had trained as a pianist, worked as a nurse. She converted to Islam after meeting his father, a doctor. It was his idea that Idris photograph every page of the Qur'an. Since a significant part of the population believes that the complexities of the world can be resolved by this one book there is a certain logic in taking things a stage further, and reducing the book to a single manifestation of itself. I'm not qualified to speak about the first reduction but the second looks – to boil things down still more – incomprehensible. And lovely. The patterns bordering each page are turned into a solid black frame so that the book becomes – as is often said of photography – a window onto the world. Inside this frame – rigid, unalterable, definitive – all is in flux. Fixed meaning dissolves in a blazing grey drizzle. Words, as one of Don DeLillo's narrators says when confronted by a swirl of Arabic script, are 'design, not meant to be read, as though part of some unbearable revelation'.

Working in a medium wedded to the visible, photographers, perversely and inevitably, have been preoccupied with photographing the invisible. Given his mother's training, music has an obvious allure for Khan in this respect. 'Struggling to Hear . . . After Ludwig van Beethoven Sonatas' is a picture of all of the composer's scores for piano, the impenetrable mass of black serving as a visual corollary of Beethoven's increasing deafness.

Each art form has its own unique advantages and limitations. Words and music unfold successively, through time. Photography is about an instant. By analogy it can ask the impossible: in this case, what if you could hear every note of Beethoven's sonatas in an instant? What would that *look* like? And when we think of a piece of music that we know well, don't we sometimes remember it, not phrase by phrase, but in its amorphous entirety?

It is often said that photographers freeze time, but Khan does the opposite. This can be seen most clearly in his re-mixes of Eadweard Muybridge's motion studies of the 1880s (a well-documented source of inspiration for Francis Bacon). Muybridge used fast shutter speeds to break action into moment-by-moment increments, rendering movement stationary. Khan takes these sequences of isolated moments and *un*freezes time by combining them in a single image. Muybridge's strictly mechanical record of a man getting out of bed becomes a vision of the unconscious lifting clear of the body, a dream of waking. It's like a photographic equivalent of Henri Fuseli's *Nightmare*, an out-of-body experience made flesh – and vice versa.

To learn more about artists' working methods some paintings have been X-rayed so that preliminary versions of masterpieces are brought to the surface. Khan's photographs are a kind of reverse X-ray, laying bare by accretion. Marrying up the eyes of all Rembrandt's self-portraits, reducing them to the same size and layering them digitally together, Khan effectively photographs him with an exposure time lasting the length of the artist's life. 'Rembrandt by Himself' offers an experience akin to the painter looking at the mirror in the moment of his death, when the evidence of a life-time of intense self-scrutiny flashes before his grave-dark eyes in a single instant.

As is always the case with artists of considerable originality there are precedents for these essays in visual condensation. Most recently, there are Fiona Banner's paintings in which a film is verbally transcribed in her own hand so that an entire movie can be seen – but not read – in an instant, on a single canvas. In the 1970s Hiroshi Sugimoto began photographing empty movie palaces and drive-ins. Using an exposure time equal to the duration of the film, Sugimoto reduced the contents of whatever was on screen – car chases, murders, betrayals, romance – to a single moment of radiant whiteness. The most explicit precursors, however, are also the earliest. They also enable us to view Khan's situation and methods in a broader historical and contemporary context.

In the late nineteenth century, photography became an important tool in an alliance between some of the 'scientific' fads of the day – physiognomy, eugenics, racial taxonomy – and attempts by the police and the state to isolate types likely to commit crimes. Writing in 1882, Francis Galton declared that there could 'hardly be a more appropriate method of discovering the central physiognomic type of any race or group than that of composite portraiture'. His composites of convicted criminals duly showed 'not the criminal, but the man who is liable to fall into crime'. Using similar techniques Arthur Batut, in France, made 'type-portraits' to identify the defining traits of particular races, tribes or families (including his own). In a phrase that might have come from Khan's own lips, Batut spoke of these composites as 'images of the invisible', images that shimmer with the same ghostly air that we see in Khan's.

At which point it is worth emphasising that Khan is himself a composite of artist and photographer. For more than a few current practitioners the advantages of identifying themselves as artists rather than photographers can be summed up as a six-word hustle: Print bigger, sell less for more. For my money Khan is as much of an artist – in the simple sense of everything that is left over from just calling him a photographer – as any young photographer currently working. He is a conceptual artist in an equally straightforward sense: thought is implicit in the act of looking at his work. A lot of contemporary British art flogging itself as conceptual has the intellectual depth of a paddling pool and the gravitas of a helium balloon; Khan's work is dense, multi-layered (literally) and profound.

The danger is that this composite thing could just become his shtick. He could do every page of every book, every this of every that. 'Every . . . Photograph Taken Whilst Travelling Around Europe in the Summer of 2002' seems a rather pointless novelty – there's nothing to see. Its relative failure suggests that Khan's method tends to work better when applied to already existing works of art. You can almost hear certain books summoning him to them. It is only a matter of time, surely, before he does every page of Borges' story 'The Aleph', in which the narrator discovers a spot where 'all the places of the world, seen from every angle, coexist'. Needless to say, not everything lends itself equally fruitfully to his attention. Garry Winogrand said that he took photographs 'to find out what something will look like photographed' and Khan, in his mediated way, is motivated by a similarly random curiosity about what might emerge when he opts to give an image the treatment. I'm guessing that a fair amount of stuff gets processed and then discarded once the preliminary findings are in. It's a small price to pay when the successes are as spectacular as the huge 'Caravaggio: His Last Years'. Fifteen late works by the painter who, according to John Berger, depicted a world that 'displays itself in hiding', who found a promise 'in the darkness itself', are turned into a tangled kaleidoscope of disembodied bodies, a swirling knot of light.

In the course of these negative excavations a form of auto-interrogation is at work as Khan's 'discoveries' question the ways in which accumulation can both reveal and obscure essence. 'Every . . . William Turner Postcard from Tate Britain' transforms these great paintings of light and air into a brooding soup with an amoeba-mushroom curdling in the swampy twilight. And yet something glimmers, faintly, through the murk. What could it be?

Walter Benjamin claimed that mechanical reproduction, the process of which Tate postcards are symptoms and which Khan has pushed to an extreme, stripped artworks of their 'aura'. Ironically,

Khan's obsessive reproduction invests works with an aura buried within them. Consistent with Barthes' notion of what makes a photograph special, this is, simultaneously, something that Khan adds to the originals and which, nonetheless, is already there.

2006

Edward Burtynsky

Whether seen on the walls of the Corcoran Gallery in Washington, or in the accompanying book published by Steidl, the photographs in *Oil* bring the viewer face to face with huge and troubling questions. How can we go on producing on this scale? How can we go on consuming like this? Aren't we at the point where we say, OK, enough is enough? Is it sustainable, the level of luxury and lavishness to which we have become accustomed? In short, how many more of these high-concept, high-value Edward Burtynsky productions can we take?

I am being only slightly facetious. Burtynsky (born in Ontario in 1955) hit his stride in the mid-1980s with the large-format, colour views of *Railcuts* and *Mines*, places where raw nature had been scarred and gorged by the agents of economic progress. What resulted, however, was not simply maiming or devastation but a source of potential wonder. By the time of the 2003 retrospective and book *Manufactured Landscapes,* Burtynsky had extended his range to cover quarries, shipbreaking in Bangladesh, oil fields and refineries, compacted mounds of trash . . .

Burtynsky's work has obvious similarities with that of other artist-photographers. Like Richard Misrach (especially in the 'Bravo 20' instalment of his ongoing *Desert Cantos* project), Burtynsky produces images whose beauty is freighted with a political/ecological purpose that is unavoidable and unobtrusive. The pictures can never be reduced to a polemical message, are always compelling – often puzzlingly so – in and of themselves. Some of the quarries, for example, comprise almost abstract blocks of striated marble, floating in a lake of flat, motionless green. Weirdly, the hard, grey-white stones with vertical gouge-scars and veins end up looking like billowing Christo wraps. Even when there are human beings or tools to help us get a fix on things, the scale is hard to comprehend. In some cases, the assault on the landscape is so immense that the idea on which we have long relied to visually orient ourselves – linear perspective – has been abolished. The ecological corollary of this is that we are witnessing something whose consequences are incalculable – if not entirely unprecedented. For it turns out that the template for this outlook was provided by an extraordinary 1932 photograph of a quarry by August Sander (of all people) which hurled the viewer into the vertiginous midst of the picture. Burtynsky's contemporary vision, in other words, is the product of a creative quarrying of the photographic past. Carleton Watkins, William Henry Jackson, Charles Sheeler and others directly inform Burtynsky's work and, in turn, are respectfully interrogated and re-animated by it. Burtynsky, then, is an original artist in exactly the sense described and prescribed by T.S. Eliot: part of a tradition that is actively extended and reconfigured by his contribution to it.

The intellectual background to the wealth of photographs showcased in *Oil* can conveniently be framed by two casual remarks. The first was reported by Raymond Williams, who recalled a miner saying of someone: 'He's the sort of man who gets up in the morning and presses a switch and expects a light to come on.' The other occurred during a conversation I had with the woman who looked after an apartment I was renting in New Orleans during the first Gulf War, in 1991. She was against the war on the grounds that it was really about America's incessant need for oil. I asked if I might have an extra blanket because, at night, it was a little chilly. 'Oh,' she replied. 'You should just turn the heating up a bit.'

To express it as concisely as possible, the photographs in *Oil* seek to make visible the invisible connections between these two opposing views of the world, one predicated on scarcity, the other on limitless abundance. Burtynsky offers a vast portfolio of images, from oil fields to refineries, to highways, cities and industries, to recycling and eventual waste. It's an obviously admirable, important and well-intentioned project by a serious and committed artist.

Why, then, does one baulk at it?

The problem, partly, is that the titular subject – the raw material, as it were – is so pervasive that it ends up being an alternative rubric for a Burtynsky retrospective: the photographic equivalent of an edition of *New and Selected Poems* in which old favourites (arranged in slightly different permutations) are supplemented by some more recent works. OK, there are no quarries or railcuts, but the Bangladeshi shipbreakers are still toiling away, the tyre piles and densified oil drums are still there . . . Well, fair enough, nothing wrong with a bit of recycling, but whereas *Manufactured Landscapes* offered a glimpse of teeming visual possibilities, the totalising vision of *Oil* induces a feeling of satiety. There *are* new things (new to me, at any rate), some of them very good, especially the *Koyaanisqatsi*-style views of the spaghetti tangle of freeways, the cityscapes stretching out to infinity, but once the doubts start to seep in – the suspicion that Burtynsky is photographing the crisis of peak oil and climate change like someone fluently producing company reports – they prove dangerously corrosive.

Burtynsky has long had a fondness for photographing endlessly replicated units of the same thing, whether it's workers at identical benches in a factory, tyres or freight containers – anything, really. Individual examples can be stunning but, in *Oil,* we keep getting replicated instances of pretty much the same thing: multiple versions of multiple cars, multiple versions of locust-like oil derricks . . . We get the point. Then the point is made again with variations so minor that they appear, almost, as an indulgence. Hence the uncomfortable sensation of bloating.

Burtynsky has always avoided wrecking himself on the rocks he has photographed but his enterprise has, nevertheless, contained a lurking potential for self-aggrandisement. In an interview in *Manufactured Landscapes* he admitted to a compulsion to seek out 'the largest example of something – the largest mines, the largest quarry . . .' Attracted to 'massive operations', Burtynsky – more exactly, a Burtynsky photograph – is becoming a bit of a production. One gets the sense, in fact, that this may be as close to stadium rock as a landscape photographer is ever likely to get. There is a similar loss of intimacy, the same dependence on scale and spectacle, on the sheer scale of the spectacle. Now, of course, a crane or helicopter might have been indispensable to the creation of some of Burtynsky's photographs but a crane can so easily become a kind of podium.

Oil invites us to gorge ourselves on Burtynsky's epic catalogue, to gulp down image after image as warnings of impending scarcity and looming resource wars. But it's not just the quantity, not just a case of there being too much of a messianically good thing. No, some of the individual images are stunningly bad. One of Burtynsky's strengths has always been his subtle command of colour, whether muted and rusting or molten and blazing. In images of a 'Truckers' Jamboree' at Walcott, Iowa, or of the parking lot at a Kiss concert in Sturgis, North Dakota, however, the blare of colour seems simply vulgar. Granted, these may not be the most refined or understated gatherings on the planet but, like Hamlet in his rants about his mother's infidelity, Burtynsky wallows in and is tainted by what he observes *without* being able to claim the satirist's exemption of a Martin Parr (he is too high-minded for that). The images of crowds and speedsters at the Bonneville Salt Flats, meanwhile, lack the subtlety and arid grace of rival photographs by Misrach. They also serve as a reminder that Burtynsky has rarely been at his best with people unless . . . Actually, let me pause here to contradict the point I am about to make. One image shows a gang of shipbreakers in Bangladesh, spread out against a near-monochrome, oil-drenched shoreline, a long chain over their shoulders, trudging from one side of the picture to the next. It's as if John Singer Sargent's painting *Gassed* – a procession of blinded soldiers, each with his hand on the shoulder of the man in front – has been relocated to a part of the world in which suffering becomes the stoic norm of an average working day. It's a magnificent photograph – *Oiled*? – but the general point still stands: for the most part, people in Burtynsky serve as indicators of the super-human scale of the work they are engaged in (which becomes, in turn, a testament to the super-human importance of the work in which they appear!); either that or they're a species of the endlessly replicated units to which he is compulsively attracted. In *China* Burtynsky organised a photograph of yellow-jacketed workers arranged in deep perspectival recession along a street lined with yellow factories in Zhangzhou. It was such a striking and successful picture (though not quite as striking as Paola Pivi's controversial piece *100 Chinese* – featuring just that, a hundred Chinese standing in a room – at the Frieze art fair in London, 2005) that Burtynsky decided to try something similar with a bunch of bikers in downtown Sturgis. Earlier I made a comparison with stadium rock; with this image Burtynsky has formed his own tribute band. The result seems to me entirely without merit or purpose except insofar as it is yet another gig on the world tour called *Oil*.

2009

Turner and Memory

I'm not entirely sure that this (see plate 7) is the picture I am writing about.

Three or four years ago . . . And here we have another problem. It *feels* like three or four years ago but time passes at such a rate that, in recent years, there have been quite a few instances when I'd thought something had taken place a couple of years ago only to discover that it actually occurred in the previous century. So it's possible that by 'three or four years' I mean eight or nine.

Anyway, at some point in the last decade I was killing time – however quickly it passes there are always odd pockets that need somehow to be disposed of – at Tate Britain, cruising the Turners. Turner's output was so huge that you are always coming across pictures you've never seen before. On this occasion the painting that took my eye showed – as I remember it – figures in some kind of room or cellar, confronted by a source of intense and radiant light.

Although I can't remember when it happened or exactly what the painting looked like, I remember, very clearly, the jolt of seeing it for the first time. I took some notes that I've been unable to locate and which I never got round to writing up properly. I probably intended using the painting in a piece of fiction, contriving a situation in which someone encountered it in a gallery or in reproduction, or found themselves in a real-life equivalent of the scene depicted.

What kind of scene might this have been? In the late 1990s I spent quite a few nights at underground parties in venues whose settings – the cavernous railway arches near London Bridge, for example –

closely resembled the architecture in the painting. Typically, there'd be a warren of rooms, the exact layout of which could never quite be committed to memory. You wandered from room to room, each promising – courtesy of the light and sound emanating from it – something alluring and magical. Often the lights made the other party-goers seem non-corporeal, spectral. Outside every set of arches you stood on the threshold of beckoning revelation. A revelation akin to the one that Turner's painting simultaneously promises and refuses to reveal.

Since we are talking here about memory I wonder if these words – room, threshold, revelation – immediately suggest to you another cultural artefact . . .

Yes, exactly, Andrei Tarkovsky's *Stalker*! Having guided the Professor and the Writer through the Zone, the Stalker brings them to the threshold of the Room where their deepest wishes will come true. On the brink of being granted this defining illumination they falter and turn back. In place of revelation there is uncertainty, doubt.

It has often been observed that the desolate beauty of Tarkovsky's Zone imaginatively pre-figures the thirty-kilometre Exclusion Zone surrounding Chernobyl, at the heart of which the damaged reactor was sealed in the so-called Sarcophagus. (Many of Robert Polidori's Chernobyl photographs in his 2003 book, *Zones of Exclusion*, could double as stills from the set of Tarkovsky's film.)

The source of recessed light in Turner's painting does not look natural – especially since everything about the interior suggests that it is a cellar, some kind of subterranean dungeon. It is an emanation of pure energy. It is the annihilating light that the artist, according to D.H. Lawrence, 'always sought': a light that would 'transfuse the body, till the body was carried away, a mere bloodstain'. It is the light of definitive or clinching revelation, which, for Lawrence, represents Turner's ultimate vision and ambition: 'a white incandescent surface, the same whiteness when he finished as when he began, proceeding from nullity to nullity, through all the range of colour'.

The picture I remembered seeing was like a representation of Turner moving – or, better, *being drawn* – towards this beckoning but unachievable vision. It gives visual expression to the same longing for transcendence articulated by Shelley (in 1821, in 'Adonais') as 'the white radiance of Eternity.'

This is not the only way in which the painting seems to be an essay on itself and the way it is perceived.

Our memories of works of art have an existence that is independent of but contingent on the works themselves. The ratio of independence to contingency is perhaps determined not just by us – by the vagaries and deficiencies of memory – but by the works themselves. So it is no accident that this painting has failed to imprint itself on my memory with the precision and tenacity of a Canaletto, say, or a Holbein.

The walls – assuming that the picture reproduced here is the one I saw back whenever it was – are insubstantial. The figures are insubstantial. Nothing is as substantial as that core of molten light. Everything else, all that is solid, looks like it could melt into air. The interior depicted has been painted over a view of a landscape so that it resembles a murky X-ray of how it came into being. The painting is a palimpsest, seemingly containing traces or memories of its own earlier existence. And it's obviously unfinished, suspended in the process of becoming what it is. The location and setting are neither given nor ascertainable. The title, *Figures in a Building* (Turner's or cataloguer's shorthand?), could hardly be less specific. The exact date of composition (*c.*1830–35) is unknown. According to the Tate's online catalogue it is 'one of several works where Turner seems to be developing a historical subject without any very clear direction, as if hoping a theme might occur as he moved his paints around on the canvas'. Even the artist, in other words, did not know what the picture might be about, working on it in the hope of a revelation that was never achieved.

Given all of this it is hardly surprising that I couldn't remember the painting clearly – it's *inevitable*. Isn't that exactly what the picture is *about*, the way that some experiences – of art and life – remain inassimilable? (And, while we're at it, unphotographable: almost everything that makes the painting interesting is lost in the version reproduced in this book.) For all its haziness the painting is a precise and lucid depiction of two refusals (both of which have their equivalents in Tarkovsky's film). First, of the world's inexhaustible refusal to succumb to the means of representation (if it did, we would be faced not with the end of history but with the end of art). Second, the refusal of certain artworks to be reduced to memory. That, I think, is what makes the painting unforgettable.

The painting is no longer on display at Tate Britain. It is back in the vaults where, presumably, it blazes away like the light emerging within it.

2009

The Awakening of Stones:
Rodin

I've never been directly interested in Rodin, but so many other interests have drawn me to him that he feels, in some ways, a source to which I have been insistently urged. Can an account of the journey towards it serve as a surrogate description of the source itself?

I first read about Rodin in *Art and Revolution*, John Berger's book about the Soviet sculptor Ernst Neizvestny. Rodin was an important influence on Neizvestny but before discussing the work of either man Berger offers a general consideration of sculpture's relation to space.

'Compare a sculpture with a tree in winter. Because a tree grows, its forms are changeable and this is implicit in their shapes and configuration. As a result its relation to the surrounding space appears to be an adaptive one.' Berger then compares a sculpture with a building and a machine. Having done that, he is ready to specify the way a sculpture 'appears to be totally opposed to the space that surrounds it. Its frontiers with that space are definitive. Its only function is to use space in such a way that it confers meaning upon it. It does not move or become relative. In every way possible it emphasizes its own finiteness. And by so doing it invokes the notion of infinity and challenges it.

'We, perceiving this total opposition between the sculpture and the surrounding space, translate its promise into terms of time. It will stand against time as it stands against space.'

From that point on I was conscious of and curious about sculpture — if only in a vague and passive way.

*   *   *

I next encountered Rodin in connection with Rilke, who had arrived
in Paris in 1902 to write a monograph on the sculptor. 'I am coming
to Paris this autumn to see you and steep myself in your creations,'
he announced to Rodin in June of that year. In spite of the language
barrier – Rilke's French at that time was poor and Rodin had no
German – the young poet was as impressed by the master, when he
met him, as he was enthralled by his creations. Rilke spent a good
deal of time in Rodin's company, wrote his book about him in a month,
and resumed his peripatetic life the following March. Rodin showed
little interest in the book but when he read a French translation, in
1905, he wrote warmly to the man who had 'influenced so many by
his work and his talent'. Expressing affection and admiration, Rodin
invited Rilke to stay at his home in Meudon. The reunion, a few
months later, was everything that Rilke could have hoped for. He
found himself not only integrated into Rodin's busy round of activities
and obligations but helping to organise them. It was a logical next
step – or, perhaps, a temptingly illogical one – for the poet to become
the sculptor's secretary. The arrangement worked well enough for a
while but Rilke soon began to feel over-burdened by his duties. In
May 1906 Rodin discovered that the secretary had become over-familiar
in letters to some of his friends – and sacked him on the spot ('like
a thieving servant', as the grievously wounded Rilke put it).

I read Rilke's book ten years ago, not because of who it was about,
but because of who it was by. Actually, the distinction crumbles even
as it is made since this unique account of genius by a genius, as
Rilke himself told Lou Andreas-Salomé, 'also speaks about me'. If
this became even more evident *after* it was written that is because
Rilke's early exposure to Rodin had such a determining effect on his
subsequent career. From Rodin he became convinced of the absolute
importance of incessant work, of unswerving dedication to a vocation.
It was Rodin, apparently, who advised him to 'just go and look at
something – for example, at an animal in the Jardin des Plantes, and
keep on looking at it till you're able to make a poem of that'. 'The
Panther' may have been the direct result of this suggestion. More
generally, Rilke fought to directly translate what he considered the
sculptor's most distinct quality – his ability to create *things* – into

'thing-poems' (*Dinggedicht*). This entailed more than just looking; as with Rodin, 'one might almost say the appearance of his things does not concern him: so much does he experience their *being*'.

The way that Rodin awakened in Rilke the desire to create poems that were the verbal equivalents of sculptures is quite explicit. 'The Song of the Statue', for example, records a longing to

> be brought back from stone
> into life, into life redeemed.

On his very first visit to Rodin's studio on rue de l'Université Rilke was struck by a bas-relief called *Morning Star*. 'A young girl's head with a wonderfully clear brow, clear, sweet, light, and simple, and deep down in the stone a hand emerges, shielding the eyes of a man, waking, from the brightness. These eyes are almost *in* the stone (so marvellously is the unawakenedness expressed here . . .)' The following day, on his first visit to the pavilion at Meudon, Rilke was exhausted, both by the quantity of things on display and by their snow-bright whiteness – so dazzling that it hurt his eyes. Speculating on the origins of Rodin's own sense of vocation Rilke wondered about the antiquities he must have seen as a youth, in the Louvre and elsewhere: 'There were stones asleep, and one felt that they would awaken at some Judgement Day, stones which had nothing mortal about them, and others embodying a movement, a gesture, which had retained such freshness that it seemed to be preserved here only until some passing child should receive it one day as a gift.' Rodin himself, in *Cathedrals of France*, voiced his belief in sculpture as an 'incantation by which the soul is brought down into the stone'. Looking at the work of Gothic carvers he was amazed 'that one should be able to capture the soul's reality in stone and imprison it for centuries'. Sometimes, Rodin said, a knot of wood or a block of marble made it seem 'that a figure was already enclosed there and my work consisted of breaking off all the rough stone that hid it from me'. On the base of the bronze cast of *Je Suis Belle* he had inscribed lines from another poet, Baudelaire, beginning: 'I am beautiful as a dream of stone.'

As can be seen from this rag-bag of quotations, the relation between these linked ideas is not fixed – not set in stone, as it were. There is a fluid and supple movement between the idea of the stone imprisoning and containing, of its sleeping and dreaming, of its waking and coming back to life. The stone contains the figure and the figure released from the stone imprisons the living being contained within it. The task of Rilke's words – both in his own poetry and in his book on Rodin – was to record this simultaneous sense of deeper and deeper recesses of oneiric inwardness within the stillness of the stone, and of constant awakening, of emerging into being. The process is additionally complicated by the way that Rodin – unlike Michelangelo, who also spoke of freeing figures from stone – did no carving. He was a modeller, forming clay figures with his hands. From the moulds derived from these clay figures plaster versions could be cast; from the plaster figures other moulds could be made, from which a bronze casting might eventually be made. (All the marble versions of Rodin's work were carved by assistants.) There is, in other words, a succession of confinings and freeings, of imprisonment and release, of positives and negatives; a constant inverting of the idea of inside and out, of exterior and interior. As Rilke succinctly phrased it, 'surroundings must be found within'.

Rilke's sense of the importance of what he was experiencing in the course of his immersion in Rodin's work was intense and immediate. So much so that he hinted at how it might appear in retrospect, in the poem 'Memory' (published, like 'The Song of the Statue', in the second, 1906, edition of *The Book of Images*).

> And you wait, you wait for the one thing
> that will infinitely increase your life;
> the mighty, the tremendous thing,
> the awakening of stones,
> depths turned to face you.
>
> On bookshelves, volumes gleam
> in gold and brown;
> and you think of lands travelled through,
> of pictures, of the dresses
> of women lost once more.

And all of a sudden you know: that was it.
You rise, and there before you stand
the fear and form and prayer
of a year gone by.

The idea of the past imagined as a future, of the long-anticipated having already occurred, reflects, in temporal terms, the sense – inherent in Rodin's method of working – of the outside within, of surface being formed within the depths of something else. Rilke came back to this repeatedly: 'the mobility of the gestures . . . takes place within the things, like the circulation of an inner current'. Describing Rodin's technique he wrote, 'Slowly, exploringly he had moved from within outwards to its surface, and now a hand from without stretched forward and measured and limited this surface as exactly from without as from within.' William Tucker, in his book *The Language of Sculpture*, summarises Rilke's observations in terms of 'the identity of external event with internal force: clay is felt as substance, not *over* the surface but *through* every cubic inch of volume'.

These reconciled oppositions – as essential to Rilke's ongoing metaphysical project as they are to Rodin's physical objects – can be seen operating in another way too. Rodin, according to Rilke, saw better than anybody that the beauty of men, animals and things was 'endangered by time and circumstances'. Seeking to preserve this threatened beauty he adapted his things 'to the less imperilled, quieter and more eternal world of space'. As Rodin's career proceeded so the relation of the work to what surrounded it changed; 'whereas formerly his works stood in the midst of space, it now seemed as if space snatched them to itself'. What is going on in the depths of the figures is being sucked to the surface. Hence the intense gestural drama of Rodin's work, the sense of the surface brimming with what is within.

Rilke's discussion of how Rodin adapted the temporally transient to the permanence of space intersects, at this point, with Berger's. Berger, it will be recalled, began by contrasting the relations to space of tree and sculpture but for Rodin the distinction was not as clear-cut. In *Cathedrals of France* he declares that 'between trees and stones [he sees] a kinship', that his sense of sculpture owes much to trees and forests: 'Where did I learn to understand sculpture? In the woods by looking at the trees . . .'

It so happens that a poem of Rilke's about a tree expresses very clearly the dialectic of surface and depth, of inwardness and outwardness, that is so crucial to Rodin's art. To be strictly accurate it is not just the poem itself but the way I encountered it that makes it so pertinent. (Contingency and serendipity play their part in this journey. What is an account of a journey, after all, if not an organised succession of contingencies?) I first read the poem – written, originally, in French – in Gaston Bachelard's *The Poetics of Space*. The lines '*Arbre toujours au milieu / De tout de qui l'entoure*' are here translated as 'Tree always in the centre / Of all that surrounds it'. Curious to see what these French poems of Rilke's were like, I bought *The Complete French Poems*, which presents the original French in tandem with an English translation. In this version the meaning of the passage from 'Le Noyer' ('Walnut Tree') is reversed:

> Tree, ever at the centre
> Of whatever it surrounds . . .

This is clearly wrong – nonsensical, even – but the combination of these two versions accords with Rodin's method of working, the way the figures are always at the centre of whatever surrounds them and are always surrounding whatever is at their centre.

As with sculpture so with photographs . . . The first thing I read about photography was by John Berger. I became interested in reading about photography before I became interested in looking at photographs themselves. Years later, when I became interested in photographs of sculpture, two tributaries joined together, urging me more powerfully in the direction of Rodin (it is appropriate, given the inversion of surface and depth, that the metaphor here tends towards the mouth when I mean the source).

One of the earliest uses of photography was to make visual records of works of art. With the technology not yet responsive to the full range of colours sculpture lent itself more readily to this undertaking than painting. The writer James Hall thinks that 'Louis Daguerre's first relatively permanent photograph was probably a still-life with plaster casts'. In 'Some Account of the Art of Photogenic Drawing' (1839), William Henry Fox Talbot outlined one of the uses to which he intended to put his 'invention', namely 'the copying of statues and bas-reliefs . . . I have not pursued this branch of the subject to any extent; but I expect interesting results from it, and that it may be usefully employed under many circumstances.' Five years later, in *The Pencil of Nature*, his picture of a bust of Patroclus offered abundant proof that 'statues, busts, and other specimens of sculpture, are generally well represented by the Photographic Art'.

So well that David Finn – to leap forward a century and a half – was able to persuade Kenneth Clark and Mario Praz that photographs of sculpture could enable people 'to discover qualities in a work of art that might not be immediately apparent even to a knowledgeable and critical viewer'. Finn also suggests that whereas photographs of complete sculptures often reveal stylistic traits or conventions which date the work and distract the viewer, photos like his (which, typically, isolate parts of a larger whole) reveal what is elemental, timeless. By doing so, by freeing them from the grip of convention and the period in which they were made, the stones are brought to life.

When it comes to photographing the works of Rodin this strategy is both appropriate and, in a sense, superfluous, because the sculptor himself often concentrated on parts of the body. If the fragment is, as Linda Nochlin suggests, 'a metaphor of modernity', then Rodin's eagerness to exhibit dismembered body parts as completed works of art is one of the ways in which the twentieth century can be felt beckoning in the nineteenth. This is not the only congruity between photography and Rodin's working methods.

In her contentious essay 'The Originality of the Avant-Garde', Rosalind Krauss points out that, like Cartier-Bresson, 'who never printed his own photographs, Rodin's relation to the casting of his own sculpture could only be called remote'. The fact that the plasters are themselves casts – i.e. 'potential multiples' – illustrates how deeply

Rodin's method was steeped 'in the ethos of mechanical reproduction'. The same figures recur endlessly, in new contexts, in new permutations, in new arrangements, in new sizes, in new materials. Many of these figures were first glimpsed in the molten swirl of *The Gates of Hell* (which Rodin referred to as his 'Noah's ark'); since the monument was never cast in the sculptor's lifetime – and thus, in a sense, never completed – Krauss views Rodin's as 'an art of reproduction, of multiples without originals'.

Needless to say, any equation of his art with the camera's capacity for copying or passive recording would have enraged Rodin in the same way that allegations that his *Age of Bronze* was cast from life had done in 1877: 'Many cast from nature, that is to say, replace an art work with a photograph. It is quick but it is not art.' Resolutely insisting that 'it is the artist who is truthful and it is photography which lies', Rodin made clear his distaste for photography on many occasions. He was scarcely less obstinate in his aversions as an observer than he was as creator:

> Photographs of monuments are mute for me. They do not move me; they allow me to see nothing. Because they do not properly reproduce the planes, photographs are for me always of an unendurable dryness and hardness. The lens of the camera, like the eye, sees in low relief. Whereas, looking at these stones, I feel them! My gaze touches them everywhere as I move about to see from all sides how they soar in every direction under the heaven and from all sides I search out their secret.

In spite of these specific and generalised objections Rodin, especially from the mid-1890s onwards, took advantage of the full range of opportunities afforded by photography. He used photos as tools to revise and edit his works in progress, indicating in pen changes to be made later to the figures themselves. He included photographs of his sculptures in exhibitions. Alert to their value in making his work available in another, easily disseminated form, he used photographs to publicise, enhance and spread his reputation, to help the idea of his matchless originality to proliferate. After seeing the Rodin exhibition at London's Hayward Gallery in 1986, Anthony Barnett even went so far as to suggest not only that 'the photographic images may often have a stronger presence than the actual works', but that Rodin 'may often have consciously sought for an effect that was aimed at the two-dimensional mass-reproduction of his work, rather than its three-dimensional solitude'.

Rodin did not take photographs himself, preferring to rely on the skills of a small but changing group of skilled and trusted collaborators. The most important of these was Edward Steichen, who achieved in photography the equivalent of what Rilke managed in prose: a supremely individualised account in which the work and the man who made it were perfectly mirrored. Steichen's composite image of Rodin silhouetted in front of *The Thinker* and the *Monument to Victor Hugo* (1902) and the brooding long exposures of the Balzac monument at night (1908) captured the sculptor's imagination in a way that he had not previously believed possible. In person Rodin was, by all accounts, a modest man; at the deepest level, though, the test of photography – its greatest challenge, in fact – was whether it could do justice to his genius. On seeing Steichen's Balzac prints Rodin was immediately convinced, informing him that he would 'make the world understand my Balzac through these pictures. They are like Christ walking in the desert.' Rodin's enthusiasm for Steichen – 'Before him nothing conclusive had been achieved' – was such that it caused him profoundly to re-consider the value of photography, which, he conceded in 1908, 'can create works of art'. The collaboration was mutually beneficial to sculptor and photographer alike. Of the portrait of Rodin and *The Thinker*, Steichen recalled that it was 'undoubtedly the image that launched me in the photographic world'.

I approached Jennifer Gough-Cooper's photographs not with Rodin's magisterial scepticism but with a degree of impatience. There were other things I was supposed to be doing, other things I was meant to be looking at, and I hoped that they would not detain me, that I could look at them quickly. These hopes were accurate and wide of the mark in that it took only a brief look for any desire to move on to be immediately extinguished. Although I didn't realise it at the time the reason for this was, perhaps, that these pictures had brought me so close to the source, to Rodin himself. I couldn't take my eyes off them. Rilke had been dazzled by the snow-bright whiteness of Rodin's work; Gough-Cooper subtly reminds us that white is itself a colour, endlessly susceptible to changes of angle and light. At times it can even seem – how else to put it? – *flesh-coloured*.

As Krauss had seen a connection between the endless reproducibility of the photograph and Rodin's working methods so, here, another, slower relationship was evident: between the images emerging gradually in the tray of chemicals and the figures' emergence into form. 'Stone is so still', sighs the statue in Rilke's song. Still photography is the logical medium for conveying stillness, but one's first reaction on seeing Gough-Cooper's pictures is not of stone's stillness but its *softness*. The figures yield to the oddly tactile gaze of the camera. It is not just flesh but *hair* that plays a part in this response.

Nothing, I suspect, causes sculptors more trouble than hair. How to render it as strands rather than as a finely corrugated lump? Sculpted hair has to be light, but in stone, clay, bronze or marble it tends to weigh the figure down like an anchor. Gough-Cooper makes it possible to believe that if Rodin's figures were tossed into the sea their hair would float above them. Rodin said that 'a woman who combs her hair fills the sky with her gesture'. In Gough-Cooper's photographs the hair of Rodin's women is full of sky; the 'h' becomes silent, their tresses airy.

All this talk of hair, though, is somewhat of an evasion for it was, frankly, the enormous erotic power of the photographs that transfixed me. Undeniable in the originals, the sexual content of Rodin's work is, if anything, more intensely felt in these photographs. Given the volume of sexually explicit visual material currently pouring across the Internet it is initially surprising that photographs of these masterpieces of nineteenth century art can be so charged; but that surprise also provides a clue as to how a medium exclusively concerned with the visible, limited to the surface, can reveal something deeper, something hidden in the depths of the stone.

Generally speaking, Rodin's sculptures of men show them in some kind of torment or anguish. Rodin made much of the idea of himself as the creator – all those versions of *The Hand of God* – but his male creations rarely respond with gratitude. Rather they react like Adam, lamenting his fallen condition in *Paradise Lost* (in lines used by Mary Shelley as the epigraph to *Frankenstein*):

> Did I request thee, Maker, from my clay
> To mould me Man, did I solicit thee
> From darkness to promote me . . . ?

Rodin's male figures show the agony of coming to life, the pain, to put it somewhat clumsily, of becoming alive. This awful jolt into consciousness is felt most clearly in *The Burghers of Calais*.

The immediate inspiration for Rodin's monument was an episode from 1347 when Edward III agreed to spare the rest of the population of the besieged city of Calais if six men turned themselves over to him. Inspired by the example of Eustache de Saint-Pierre, five more of the most prominent citizens of Calais volunteered to join him. The meaning of the finished sculpture goes far beyond the incident in which it originated (and of which many of us today are, in any case, ignorant). Rodin's sculpture shows men weighed down not by fate but by choice, regretting the decision that has emboldened them, pierced and penetrated by the consciousness of what they have done. The gravity of what they have inflicted on themselves causes the sky to bear down on them with atrocious force. Called on to make a gesture – of self-sacrifice – the ennobling ideal of martyrdom is undermined and betrayed by their gestures. Written in damning response to a two-foot-high maquette prepared by the sculptor, an article in the Calais *Patriote* of 2 August 1885 was wildly wrong in its judgement but accurate in its summing up of 'the feelings emanating from the work, in general' as 'sorrow, despair, and endless depression'. The men put themselves forward willingly enough but the force of their decision is not enough to propel them through its consequences. For all its grandeur there is a persistent sense of futility about the whole scene. 'Was it for this the clay grew tall?' Since the question was asked by Wilfred Owen in 1918, in his poem 'Futility', the anguished gestures of the burghers have been repeated and echoed not only in photographs of war and suffering but in sport and on the street. Certain gestures are, as Rodin believed, eternal but it does not follow from this that their meaning is constant, unchanging. What Rodin depicted in the *Burghers* was the birth of a specifically modern *form* of despair: an acceptance that there is no external source of redemption and the knowledge that one's life might not be capable of generating its own capacity for redemption.

What solace is available in the face of this dilemma? One possibility is work ('Adam's Curse', as Yeats called it), the unswerving devotion to a craft that so impressed Rilke. (Perhaps this is why the various versions of the Balzac are so brazenly *un*despairing; the novelist surpassed Rodin in his indefatigable capacity for labour.) The other is the sexual promise offered by women. In his later years Rodin achieved a blissful combination of these possibilities, devoting hours and hours to making thousands of drawings of naked women, often in states of sexual rapture. In Milton – as in the Bible – the Fall comes after Adam has tasted Eve in all her tainted sensuality. This inverts the reality of the situation: that the lure of sex is one of the things that makes the fallen state not simply bearable but desirable. Wittingly or not, Milton provides a glimpse of a paradise that is endlessly regainable:

> Carnal desire inflaming, he on Eve
> Began to cast lascivious eyes, she him
> As wantonly repaid . . .*

Another John – Updike – offers an extended meditation on this towards the end of *Villages*, a novel written in his early seventies:

The Gates of Hell is consistent with Blake's famous insight that Milton was of the devil's party without knowing it. Rodin's hell seethes with voluptuous allure. Every hint of anguish and torment expressed by the males is balanced and compensated by the writhing sensuality of the women. The most intensely sexual elements of the *Gates* are in the box-like tympanum above the lintel on either side of the Thinker. The arrangement has since been adapted by newsagents who stack sexually 'offensive' material out of harm's way – but still within reach – on the top shelf. And if the gates themselves are intended to offer some clue as to *what* the Thinker is thinking then it is hard not to conclude that the figures on either side of him function as the sculptural equivalent of thought-balloons in comics.

Sex is a programmed delirium that rolls back death with death's own substance; it is the black space between the stars given sweet substance in our veins and crevices. The parts of ourselves conventional decency calls shameful are exalted. We are told that we shine, that we are splendid, and the naked bodies we were given in the bloody moment of birth hold all the answers that another, *the* other, desires, now and forever.

Rodin trained himself to draw without taking his eyes off the women who were happy to surrender themselves to him as he abandoned himself to his gaze. (William Rothenstein recalls Rodin 'caressing [his models] with his eyes, and sometimes too with his hands'.) His hand functioned like the needle of an exquisitely calibrated machine, instantly adjusting itself to the models' every move. He wanted nothing – not even himself – to impede the current passing between the model and the paper. Looking and creating art were one and the same. And this late obsession with drawing did not constitute a new beginning or a break with his earlier practice; it was, Rodin insisted, a direct result of his sculpture – or 'drawing in depth' as he called it.

Gough-Cooper's photographs enable us to gaze on Rodin's depth-drawings with the same intensity and absorption that he regarded – in very different ways – the men and women who modelled for him. What she has photographed is nothing less than the awakening of stone, stone awakening to the camera's touch.

2006

The American Sublime

The sublime is no longer what it used to be. In the eighteenth century Edmund Burke used the term to include 'whatever is fitted in any sort to excite the ideas of pain or danger, that is to say, whatever is in any sort terrible'. Kant amended this 'sort of delightful horror' to denote something requiring 'a transcendent scale of reference . . . a greatness comparable to itself alone'. Partly because the landscapes which provoked that original terror have been rendered familiar by the history of art, the older Gothic-tinged patina has worn away and the word has come to connote a source and feeling of grace, of boundlessness. As Wallace Stevens put it in 'The American Sublime':

> One grows used to the weather,
> The landscape and that;
> And the sublime comes down
> To the spirit itself,
> The spirit and space,
> The empty spirit
> In vacant space.

Stevens' poem is not mentioned in the exhibition or the accompanying catalogue, but *American Sublime: Landscape Painting in the United States 1820–1880* at Tate Britain reveals how the transition began to be made. It's a breathtaking show. All the more so because many of the artists in it tended, until recently, to be regarded as second-rate: important in the local history of American painting but minor figures compared with the European masters: Claude, Friedrich, John Martin, Constable, Turner. Artists such as Frederic Edwin Church and Thomas Cole have considerable reputations but the critical consensus was summed up in 1979 by art historian Hugh Honour, who felt that 'few of these American views of mountains and deep and gloomy woods depart very far from formula for depicting sublime prospects established in the eighteenth century and repeated here, as in Europe, until the end of the nineteenth.' *American Sublime* rehabilitates these painters by showing the diverse ways in which individual talents adapted these formulae to the new world. This is the crucial underlying dynamic of the show: the tension between the hold of existing conventions and the raw challenge of a new geography.

For Thomas Cole, writing in 1835, 'the painter of American scenery' could exult in the way that virgin forests and waterfalls 'had been preserved untouched from the time of creation for his heaven-favoured pencil' – but that pencil often made them look distinctly European. Significantly, one of the first paintings in the show, Asher Brown Durand's *The American Wilderness*, looks like the brambly British countryside. It could have been done in Herefordshire. Jasper Francis Cropsey's view of *Starruca Viaduct* inevitably recalls the ruined aqueducts of the Roman Campagna familiar from Claude.

Forward-looking momentum was provided by the project of financial and geographical expansion. Finding new ways of framing the American landscape was part of a larger endeavour of husbanding and exploiting its resources. John Barrell has shown how the stark economic realities of the time are encoded in the depiction of the rural poor in British landscape painting, and something similar could, presumably, be done to illuminate the dark side of the American landscape. Evidence of the fate of Native Americans, however, is almost entirely negative: there aren't any left! Or only a few anyway, and these lone Indians, dwarfed by the all-engulfing landscape, seem like nothing else so much as honorary Americans, symbols of the pioneering spirit that culminated in their near-extermination.

Even when the scenery is unpeopled, the 'pundit of the weather' (Stevens again) has much to say – in Church's *Twilight in the Wilderness* of 1866, for example – about the looming apocalypse of the Civil War. As Tim Barringer points out in one of two excellent catalogue essays, 'only after the war had ended, in "Rainy Season in the Tropics" (1866) was Church able to throw a spectacular double rainbow over the wilderness once more, a symbol of unity'. In *Our Banner in the Sky* (1865) the heavens themselves swore allegiance to the flag: a spangling firmament in one corner combining with bands of crepuscular clouds to form a meteorological alliance that makes up the stars and stripes of Old Glory.

Church was not alone in littering his scenes with historical portents and symbols. Cole went an extravagant step further. In two of the paintings in his five-work series *The Course of Empire* (1834–6), the landscape is transformed into an allegorical movie set on which the artist stages a Hollywood-style Roman epic, one with a limitless budget and a script Gore Vidal could do little to save from ruination (see painting five, the aptly named *Desolation*).

The movies, in this context, are always with us. The extended horizontal vistas of nineteenth-century painting lived on in the CinemaScope Westerns of the twentieth. I was hoping there might be a bit more of this home-on-the-range, *Riders of the Purple Sage*-type stuff but Albert Bierstadt's stirring depiction of an Indian bravely slaying *The Last of the Buffalo* (1889) evidently came too late in the art-historical day. His earlier, stunning *Emigrants Crossing the Plains* (1867) is also sadly absent. Showing a wagon train moving towards a blazing sunset, this film-still in oil alerts us to the loaded and inevitably ambiguous – even contradictory – nature of the sunset in many of the paintings on show.

The setting sun usually indicates decline, the end of things; in nineteenth-century America, though, it is an alluring symbol of the Manifest Destiny of westward expansion. The 'Sunset' Church painted at 'Bar Harbor' in 1854 is meteorologically interchangeable with the 'Sunrise' he did at the same time on the 'Schoodic Peninsula'. One can see the painted sun setting on the long days of European domination (maintained through the resilient conventions of pictorial representation) of American landscape art and, simultaneously, the beginning – the *dawn*, in fact – of an independent American future.

The painters may have started out trying to Europeanise America but, as Stevens concisely argues:

> John Constable they could never quite transplant
> And our streams rejected the dim Academy.

How and where did this take place? Generally speaking, the landscape of the United States gets less and less European as you go west. Yes, Bierstadt's 1872 view of *Cathedral Rocks, Yosemite Valley* looks thoroughly Alpine, just as Napa, today, is a ringer for Tuscany, but bear with me. In Nevada, Arizona or New Mexico the landscape doesn't look like anything in England or anywhere else in Europe. And it was here, in the western deserts, that a vital topographical extension of the sublime took place.

In 1898 John C. Van Dyke, a forty-two-year-old art historian, travelled on a pony into the Colorado Desert and beyond. Three years later he published *The Desert*, a book describing and reflecting on what he had seen. At the time, it should be remembered, the desert was considered to have nothing to offer the civilised eye or mind. Either it was characterised by the lack of everything that made landscapes worth looking at or it was imagined solely in terms of a Saharan expanse of dunes. Impatient with these conventional assumptions ('Where and how did we gain the idea that the desert was merely a sea of sand?'), Van Dyke saw that what had hitherto been considered repellent – the desert's 'grim desolation' – comprised a category of the sublime. 'In sublimity – the superlative degree of beauty – what land can equal the desert?' This was, quite literally, a visionary achievement, so much so that his question – 'who shall paint the splendour of its light . . . the glory of its wondrous coloring!' – went unanswered. Van Dyke – and with him the idea of the sublime – had moved ahead of and beyond what was, at that time, *the frontier of the paintable*.

What lay ahead? In a word, photography.

Painters like Bierstadt and Church were alert to the potential use of the camera to their art. The advantage of the camera – as the painter Thomas Moran's brother somewhat grandly phrased it – was that it did not 'falsify and distort the work of the Creator'. Put more simply, it left little to the imagination. In 1859 Bierstadt travelled with Colonel Frederick Lander on his survey of the south pass of the Rocky Mountains and, despite cumbersome technical obstacles, made a good number of stereoscopic photographs. In this he set a precedent for photographers like Carleton Watkins, who would accompany and document the government- and railroad-sponsored surveys of the next twenty years. This first great era of American landscape photography coincided with the second half of the period of landscape painting covered by *American Sublime*. By the end of the nineteenth century both had fallen into pictorial decline; landscape painting had run its course, could go no further; photography, however, would soon revive and continue the task of mapping the sublime. This can be brought out by a comparison of two responses to the American landscape, its capacity to exceed all imagining.

A witness recalls how, when Bierstadt first saw the Chicago Lakes in the Colorado Rockies in 1863, he 'said nothing but his face was a picture of intense life and excitement'. Anxious to fix the scene in his mind Bierstadt 'began fumbling at the lash-ropes' of the mule that carried 'his paint outfit' and soon fell to making the sketches that were subsequently worked up into the biblical grandeur of *Storm in the Rocky Mountains – Mt. Rosalie* of 1866. Bierstadt's response to this 'glorious scene' is echoed by Edward Weston's reaction when he first travelled to Death Valley in 1937. As his lover Charis Wilson recalled, 'Edward was so shaky with excitement he could hardly set up his camera, and all we could say for some time was, "My God! It can't be."'

It couldn't be – but it was. It was unimaginable – but it was a fact. And the camera, what's more, could prove it. We are, in other words, in the presence of that uniquely photographic and uniquely American phenomenon: the documentary sublime. It is a tradition or trajectory that culminates, logically, in the work of Richard Misrach.

Having honed his technical skills and refined his artistic vision in the deserts of Nevada and Utah, Misrach – who cites Van Dyke as an important intellectual influence on his work – recently published a book of photographs that takes you, metaphorically and literally, as far west as you can get. From his porch in the Berkeley hills Misrach has made hundreds of identically composed photographs of the Golden Gate Bridge. In a way the Golden Gate is a contemporary, man-made equivalent of another tourist-swarmed spot, the Niagara Falls, and just as Church's colossal 'Niagara' (1857) triumphantly surpassed the iconic familiarity of the location, so Misrach's pictures make us see an over-photographed subject in a new light. I mean that quite literally. But the light that shrouds, frames, drenches, curdles around, surfs over and – always – *dwarfs* the bridge is also profoundly historical. It is as if the sky of every one of the paintings on show at Tate Britain has, at some point, ended up in the Bay Area. Church's rainbow even turns up in one of them! All – even the ones that are completely abstract, just air, colour, light – attest to a verifiable truth: at that moment it really looked like this. We have arrived at a vision of the sublime that is literal and absolute. It's impossible to go any further.

2002

D.H. Lawrence:
Sons and Lovers

With the passage of time the great works of the past bunch more closely together. Partly this is because, as the canon is refined, so the quantity of inferior material separating the major works that have remained within it is reduced. More generally, as we look back from the brink of the twenty-first century, the eighteen-year gap between 1895 (when Hardy published his last novel) and 1913 (when Lawrence published his third) seems relatively slight. Joyce and Lawrence were the two writers who most comprehensively and vehemently hauled the English novel into the twentieth century. *Sons and Lovers*, though, now seems to begin directly from where *Jude the Obscure* left off. It starts – literally and metaphorically – in the nineteenth century and grows into the twentieth.

Lawrence began writing the first draft of the novel he was then calling *Paul Morel* in the late summer of 1910. A later version, still called *Paul Morel*, was declined by William Heinemann in July 1912. By then Lawrence had eloped to Germany with Frieda Weekley (whom he had met in March). Incorporating the editorial suggestions of Edward Garnett at Duckworth, and opening himself up to Frieda's considerable influence, Lawrence re-wrote the novel again in Lake Garda, Italy. When he mailed it back to Garnett in November, the manuscript was called *Sons and Lovers* and was, its author believed, 'a great tragedy . . . a great book . . . a great novel'.

To write it Lawrence had delved deep into his own background in a way that he had not attempted in his first two novels, *The White Peacock* and *The Trespasser*. In one way – the evocation of what he would later call 'the country of my heart', the area, that is, of Nottingham and the mining country – this came relatively easy to him. But the composition of *Sons and Lovers* also involved, in Frieda's not over-dramatic phrase, 'facing the dark recesses of his own soul', specifically the intensity of his feelings for his mother ('my first great love'). By the time she died, of cancer, in December 1910, Lawrence realised that this relationship had 'been rather terrible', and had made him, 'in some respects, abnormal'. His love for his mother was inextricably related to an equally passionate feeling against the father whom Lawrence believed he 'was born hating'. When Frieda read *Paul Morel* in September 1912, she thought that 'L. quite missed the point . . . He really loved his mother more than anybody, even with his other women, real love, sort of Oedipus.'

In making this theme more pronounced in the final version of the novel Lawrence was helped by the necessarily vague or *inexplicit* language of sex which was all that he – or any other author – could work with at the time. The vocabulary available for describing Paul's sexual relationships with Miriam and Clara is all but indistinguishable from the language of his passionate, caring, loving, but implicitly incestuous relationship with his mother. If the linguistically unfettered writers of the post-*Chatterley* era have since been unable to avail themselves of these subtleties and inflections of overlapping vocabulary, then that, ironically, is largely the legacy of Lawrence.

The Oedipal theme was perceived by critics soon after the book was published in May 1913; Lawrence, though, was impatient with the way that the Freudians carved 'a half lie' out of the 'fairly complete truth' of the work itself.

As soon as Lawrence received a finished copy of *Sons and Lovers* he declared that he would 'not write quite in that style any more. It's the end of my youthful period.' Quite telling, that 'quite'. Before re-reading it in order to write this introduction I had not looked at *Sons and Lovers* for almost twenty years and, in memory, there was a far sharper split between that novel and *The Rainbow* (1915) and *Women in Love* (1920). Actually, there are many glimpses of the prose – its vocabulary, imagery and rhythms – which I associated with the later works and which I had wrongly remembered as being entirely absent from *Sons and Lovers*. Within a few pages we hear of 'the dusky, golden softness of [Walter Morel's] sensuous flame of life'; later we learn that he has 'denied the God in him'. Throughout, there is much talk of the characters' souls, 'inflamed', 'intensely supplicating' or otherwise. When Paul Morel falls ill he is 'tossed into consciousness in the ghastly, sickly feeling of dissolution'. That word, dissolution (as in 'the river of dissolution'), will become as much a staple of Lawrence's mature style as well-parodied phrases along the lines of *hard gem-like flame* or *loins of darkness*. This aspect of Lawrence's work has not worn well. After *Sons and Lovers*, it seems to me, Lawrence's best writing will be found not in the major novels on which his place in the pantheon is based, but on works which come lower down the traditional hierarchy of genre: in the novellas, stories, travel books, essays and, above all, in his letters. Lawrence never stopped developing as a writer but, as Raymond Williams has pointed out, 'what he lost along the way – what I think he knew he had lost and struggled to recover – may in fact be just as important as what he undoubtedly gained'.

Paul Morel is an artist who works 'a great deal from memory, using everybody he knew'. That this is an accurate reflection of his creator's methods of working suggests the extent to which the novel was earthed in Lawrence's own life. The intensely autobiographical nature of the novel should make us extra careful of reading it *as* autobiography, but Paul's *circumstances* are almost exactly those of Lawrence himself. Lawrence's father, as he expressed it in a later satirical poem, 'was a working man / and a collier was he'; his mother may have been 'a superior soul / . . . cut out to play a superior role / in the goddamn bourgeoisie', but both parents were part of the working class. More exactly (and in discussing the gradations of the English class system one can never be too exact) they were, as biographer John Worthen puts it, part of 'an economically advancing working class' – and Lawrence's mother devoted her own life to trying to ensure that her children would advance beyond it.

Exactly as depicted in the novel, Lawrence's father – who had been working in the pit since he was seven – became ostracised from the rest of the family: 'as soon as the father came in everything stopped.

He was like the scotch in the smooth, happy machinery of the home'. All the children took the side of the mother, none more vehemently than Lawrence. Even with the author's thumb on the scale, however, weighing things firmly against the father, Walter Morel emerges as a figure of considerable sympathy. Not only as the young man and incandescent dancer who woos his bride-to-be (despite her 'high moral sense inherited from generations of Puritans') but also as the old collier whose hands are 'all gnarled with work'. When Paul sells his first picture, Morel remembers his dead son, William; his wife pretends 'not to see him rub the back of his hand across his eyes, nor the smear in the coal-dust on his black face'.

In Ceylon in 1922 Lawrence told his friend Achsah Brewster that 'he had not done justice to his father in *Sons and Lovers* and felt like rewriting it'. Frieda likewise recalls Lawrence saying, 'I would write a different *Sons and Lovers* now; my mother was wrong, and I thought she was absolutely right.' These two hearsay testimonies are corroborated by a third recounting how Lawrence remembered his mother lining up the children to await the return of the drunken father. 'She would turn to the whimpering children and ask them if they were not disgusted with such a father. He would look at the row of frightened children and say, "Never mind, my duckies, you needna be afraid of me. I'll do ye na harm."'

If Norman Mailer was right, if Lawrence in some ways had 'the soul of a beautiful woman', then that can be easily traced to the formative role of his mother. So can the almost religious intensity with which he came to assert his own vision of how life should be lived. If Lawrence is a great writer, however, it is because these feminine qualities were balanced by others derived, in part, from the rejected father. Lawrence's elaborately articulated faith in the wisdom of the blood, the primacy of the instinctual life, is very close to what he came to see as 'the very highly developed' 'physical, instinctive, and intuitional contact' that existed between miners ('to whom so much of me belongs').

Lawrence's sister Emily's lovely memory of their father – 'he knew the names of the birds and the animals and that' – not only echoes what many people remembered of walks with her famous brother;

it also suggests that responsiveness to the natural world – 'his bond with everything in creation,' as Frieda put it, 'just a meeting between him and a creature, a tree, a cloud, anything' – which animates all of his writing.

When Lawrence boasted to Garnett that *Sons and Lovers* was 'the tragedy of thousands of young men in England', he had in mind principally the mother–son strand of the story. My own feeling is that the aspect of the novel still according with the experience of thousands of young men and women deals with Paul's growing up in – and moving away from – the working class. In this regard the book serves as a template for the experience of 'the scholarship boy' of whom Jude was the doomed forerunner. A significant theme in the progress of the twentieth century, this experience has been recorded in different ways by writers like Albert Camus (in *The First Man*, the novel he was working on at the time of his death), John Osborne (whose early, angry vitalism came straight out of Lawrence), Raymond Williams (in the novel *Border Country* obviously, but also in much of his critical and cultural writings) and Tony Harrison, most movingly in *V* and the 'School of Eloquence' sonnets. Written after his mother's death, one of these poems, 'Book Ends', records Harrison and his father ('The "scholar" me, you worn out on poor pay') sitting at opposite ends of the fire ('like book ends, the pair of you' as his mother used to say). As they sit in sullen silence, nothing – not even their shared grief – can hide the fact that 'what's still between's / not the thirty or so years, but books, books, books'. And no book has played a more important role in defining this binding gap than *Sons and Lovers*. As Raymond Williams has pointed out, it ushered in a sub-genre of novel 'pre-formed to end with the person leaving a working class environment, going right away from it'.

Although the scholarship boy's path was well-worn and intricately mapped by the mid-'70s, following it was still a profoundly disorienting experience. When I was fourteen or fifteen a teacher at my grammar school called Bob Beale singled me out for special encouragement and, as a consequence, I fell in love with literature. This led to my studying English at Oxford (Christminster in Hardy's *Jude*) and, later, to my becoming a writer. *Sons and Lovers* was not just a guide to the early part of this journey: it dramatised a process of which reading this novel was an exemplary part. If I had to select a single book to represent what literature meant to me – what difference literature has made to me – that book would be *Sons and Lovers*.

Like Mrs Morel in the novel, my parents hoped that, as a result of my university education, I would become part of the secure and respectable middle class. It didn't happen like that. Because of Lawrence. *Sons and Lovers* ends famously with Paul walking towards 'the humming, glowing town, quickly', poised (like Stephen in Joyce's *Portrait*) to pursue his destiny as an artist, just as Lawrence forged his destiny as a writer. Patti Smith recalls that it wasn't writers' *books* that made her want to become an artist; she 'fell in love with writers' lifestyles'. For Smith, Rimbaud's was the supreme embodiment of the writer's lifestyle. But for working-class boys from England – for *this* working-class boy, at any rate, one who *did* love writers' books – Lawrence was the great role model: because he had come from the same class as me, because his example (leaving England, travelling constantly, living by his pen) made writing a means of – and synonym for – being fully alive: an adventure, in short.

For Williams, 'the tragedy of Lawrence the working-class boy is that he did not live to come home'. In fact, that was a part of his triumph. As Lawrence sought gradually to realise his 'inner destiny' through a series of surges and repudiations, he came to feel that he didn't 'belong to any class'; after years of wandering, of feeling a stranger everywhere, he came to feel 'everywhere . . . at home'. In 1910, when he began writing *Paul Morel*, all of this lay in the future. *Sons and Lovers* pointed the way ahead. It still does.

1999

D.H. Lawrence:
Lady Chatterley's Lover

The immediate inspiration for *Lady Chatterley's Lover* was a trip Lawrence made from Italy to Nottinghamshire, where he was born, in September 1926. He was forty-one at the time and had been travelling or living abroad – in Australia, Italy, Mexico and America – since 1919. This brief return to his native land made a deep and contradictory impression on Lawrence, filling him with 'devouring nostalgia and infinite repulsion'. His sister Ada took him on a driving tour of what he would later call 'the country of my heart', a country in the process of having its heart wrung dry by a bitter coal strike, then in its twentieth week. Reduced to living off 'bread and margarine and potatoes', the miners were returning to work: defeated, defiant, angry, militant. For his part, Lawrence, the miner's son, returned to the Villa Mirenda near Florence in Italy, where, within a few weeks, he began writing the first version of what would become his last novel.

Frieda has left a lovely record of her husband sitting under a pine tree, working on the book. 'There he would sit, almost motionless except for his swift writing. He would be so still that the lizards would run over him and the birds hop close around him. An occasional hunter would start at this silent figure.' Lawrence completed this draft in about six weeks and then, almost immediately, began another version of what he referred to as his 'English novel'. This took longer (about two and half months), partly because he was spending 'much more time painting'. As this period of varied and uninterrupted industry suggests, Lawrence was enjoying one of his rare bouts of good health. He did not fall seriously ill until March 1927 by which time the second version of the novel (now known as *John Thomas and Lady Jane*) was complete and he was researching a series of 'sketches' of Etruscan places. Near the end of July, as he was about to set off on a tour of Etruscan ruins, he suffered a devastating haemorrhage. With the stubbornness that characterised his battle against illness, Lawrence insisted that it was the result of chagrin, rage, trouble in his bronchials – of anything, in fact, but the tuberculosis which, in three years, would kill him. Bedridden for a month, Lawrence then travelled with Frieda to Austria, where he convalesced (i.e. took a break from novel-writing and painting to work on translations, book reviews, essays and so forth).

He began writing the final version of *Lady Chatterley* on about 26 November, soon after his return to the Villa Mirenda. This third version is different in several important ways from the earlier ones but it maintains much of the uninhibited briskness evoked by Frieda's account of his 'swift writing' of the first. This swiftness – evident from the opening pages in which Lawrence quickly and confidently delineates his themes and the circumstances in which they will be enacted by his principal characters – is at the heart of Lawrence's achievement and limitations as a writer. Unimpressed by Joyce's infinite struggle to achieve the perfect sentence, Lawrence was in some ways a rather careless writer. Not surprisingly, the two great novelists held each other's work in mutually low esteem. For Lawrence, *Ulysses* was 'just stewed-up fragments of quotation in the sauce of a would-be dirty mind. Such effort! Such exertion!' For his part, Joyce tired of *Lady Chatterley* after only two pages of 'the usual sloppy English'. As Richard Aldington realised, however, the tendency to 'regrettable splurging' that resulted from an aversion to Joycean exertion and effort – 'was the condition of his genius'. Throughout Lawrence's writing this is manifest in his knack for intensely and instantly evoking a sense of place – and not just of place but of places *in time*, of what, in an essay on Taos Pueblo, he called 'nodality'. Lady Chatterley herself senses a vestige of this in the woods near Wragby Hall:

How still the trees were, with their crinkly, innumerable twigs against the sky, and their grey, obstinate trunks rising from the brown bracken! How safely the birds flitted among them! And once there had been deer, and archers, and monks padding along on asses. The place remembered, still remembered.

A little later Connie walks on into the woods and we get one of those extraordinary passages of which only Lawrence is capable, simultaneously describing the landscape and rendering it sentient:

The air was soft and dead, as if all the world were slowly dying. Grey and clammy and silent, even from the shuffling of the collieries, for the pits were working short time, and today they were stopped altogether. The end of all things!

In the wood all was utterly inert and motionless, only great drops fell from the bare boughs, with a hollow crash. For the rest, among the old trees with depth within depth of grey, hopeless inertia, nothingness.

Connie walked dimly on. From the dim wood came an ancient melancholy, somehow soothing to her, better than the harsh insentience of the outer world. She liked the *inwardness* of the remnant of forest, the unsparing reticence of the old trees. They seemed a very power of silence, and yet a vital presence. They, too, were waiting: obstinately, stoically waiting, and giving off a potency of silence. Perhaps they were only waiting for the end; to be cut down, cleared away, the end of the forest, for them the end of all things. But perhaps their strong and aristocratic silence, the silence of strong trees, meant something else.

Immediately after this Connie finds herself outside the gamekeeper's cottage, conscious both of the gravitational tug that has brought her here and of the social distance still separating her from Mellors. In this respect the book was intended as an extrapolation of something initiated by *The Virgin and the Gypsy*, an exploration of whether people from two such different walks of life could sustain a relationship after the initial, primal attraction and awakening. Some of the changes Lawrence made in his successive re-writings were intended to accommodate difficulties engendered by his own draft answers to the question he had set himself. In his earliest incarnations Parkin (as the lover was known in the first two versions) is unequivocally working class, with none of Mellors' interest in culture, literature, or ideas. In the first version of the novel, moreover, there are no detailed descriptions of Parkin's physical intimacy with Connie, so that the nature of the bond between the lovers is not sufficiently realised at either a bodily or mental level. Parkin also turns out to be a communist who is sternly resistant to the idea of living off Connie's wealth. In the second version, while Parkin remains unambiguously working class, he is not politically driven; also, crucially, his sexual encounters with Connie are described in more detail and have begun to be distinguished from each other.

By the third version Mellors has achieved an ambiguous class status, reflected in the way that he moves, depending on mood and circumstance, between standard English and dialect. The son of a miner, he 'had a scholarship for Sheffield Grammar School, and learned French and things'. Later, in India with the army, he gains promotion to the rank of lieutenant, only to turn his back on the social elevation to which this could have been a prelude to 'come back to England to his own class'. He has continued, however, to nurture the intellectual independence of the autodidact (the range of books in his simple cottage affects Connie as powerfully as the shirts in Gatsby's wardrobe move Daisy) and he has 'a native breeding which was really much nicer than the cut-to-pattern class thing'. In the course of successive re-writes he has, like many of Lawrence's protagonists, moved unmistakably closer to his creator. Like Lawrence 'he had something in common with the local people. But also something very uncommon.' Mellors thereby incarnates Lawrence's own ambivalent feelings about his past, as suggested by the apparent contradiction of two heartfelt letters of 1928. 'Whatever I forget I shall never forget the Haggs,' he wrote to the brother of his first love, Jessie Chambers. 'Whatever else I am I am somewhere still the same Bert who rushed with such joy to the Haggs [the Chambers' family farm].' That was in mid-November, a mere two months after he had written, with equal conviction, 'I am not really "our Bert". Come to that, I never was.' As is often the case – not only in Lawrence but in many creative artists – the contradictions of the life are resolved by the work they animate.

Mellors' combination of physical frailty (the result of pneumonia) and undiminished vitality mirrors Lawrence's. His early sexual history closely resembles Lawrence's relations with Helen Corke and – as imaginatively transcribed in *Sons and Lovers* – Jessie. This is not the only way in which Lawrence's third novel is invoked by his last. Mellors' slurring dialect inevitably recalls that of Walter Morel, the hostile fictionalised portrait of Lawrence's father in *Sons and Lovers*. Mellors, in this light, is an act of creative recompense to the maligned dead father.

In other ways Mellors, like Birkin in *Women in Love* or Somers in *Kangaroo*, is a straightforward mouthpiece for Lawrence's ideas. Many of his diatribes about industrialism and mechanised ugliness are almost indistinguishable from those of Lawrence in essays of the time. Unlike Lawrence, who lived by his pen, however, Mellors has not been able to achieve economic independence from the system he excoriates. Lawrence is unambiguous about the relationship between the wealth of Clifford Chatterley's class and the degradation of man and nature – as exemplified by 'the great colliery which put so many thousand pounds per annum into the pockets of the Duke and the other shareholders' – on which it depends. But, even in the final version of the novel, he comes up against one of the issues that had rendered the first problematic: namely that he cannot afford to investigate where Connie's income – the six hundred pounds a year that will underwrite her and Mellors' future – comes from. Connie might be nicer than Clifford, might even seem 'Bolshevistic' to him, but she is implicated in the same system of economic relations as her husband. This is the unpalatable truth: that to attain his freedom with Connie, Mellors – however free he might claim to be in his soul – must also be a beneficiary of the exploitation he and Lawrence denounce.

It is worth emphasising that this was something of which Lawrence, having lurched to a mature grasp of the political reality on which his (sometimes bonkers) metaphysical beliefs were founded, was painfully aware. Lawrence probably believed and said more stupid things than any other novelist in history. Throughout much of the 1920s he was infatuated by the cult of the leader. Critics like John Carey have seized on Lawrence's not infrequent declarations of enthusiasm in this direction to reduce him to a few 'snarling maxims' (the phrase is Norman Mailer's) and depict him as little more than a raving proto-fascist. This is quite as ludicrous as anything Lawrence himself believed, not least because Lawrence's thought was in a state of constant flux. But by the time of *Lady Chatterley* he had come to believe that nationalising 'the land and industries and means of transport [would] make the whole thing work infinitely better'. (To avoid repeating Carey's habit of misleading by selective quotation it must be conceded that on the same page of this essay, 'Return to Bestwood', Lawrence decrees that 'Hopeless life should be put to sleep, the idiots and the hopeless sick and the true criminal.'). In *The First Lady Chatterley* the broad outline of Lawrence's political journey is nicely summarised by the character Duncan Forbes: 'I've hated democracy since the war,' he declares. 'But now I see I'm wrong calling for an aristocracy. What we want is a flow of life from one to another.' Lawrence himself confessed in 1928 that 'the leader-cum-follower relationship is a bore. And the new relationship will be some sort of tenderness, sensitive, between men and men and men and women, and of the one up one down, lead on I follow, *ich dien* sort of business. So you see I'm becoming a lamb at last.'

Lawrence had long felt that he did 'not belong to any class', but he became increasingly convinced that 'class hatred' was 'the quiet volcano over which the English life is built'. That was borne out by his trip to the Midlands in the autumn of 1926. In the novel the experience is imaginatively transferred to Connie as she makes a journey by motor car, but this extended episode retains the freshness of immediate observation that characterises much of Lawrence's best and most personal responses to things he has seen. On other occasions it is Connie quite as much as Mellors who serves as Lawrence's spokesperson, as when she virtually 'quotes' him to Clifford: 'I believe the life of the body is a greater reality than the life of the mind.' Her reactions to the 'utter negation of natural beauty' and 'the utter negation of the gladness of life' are absolutely Lawrence's own but they are also entirely in keeping with the narrative unfolding of the novel.

They are also part of a recognisable tradition of romantic protest against the dehumanising effects of industrialisation. If Lawrence is the most penetrating voice in this tradition that is because, as Raymond Williams points out, 'his first social responses were those, not of a man observing the processes of industrialism, but of one caught in them, at an exposed point, and destined, in the normal course, to be enlisted in their regiments'. He had escaped, but this served to intensify his horror at the ecological and human cost that he observed on his return.

Some aspects of Lawrence's writing have not worn well. Echoing Lawrence's return to England, the mature reader returns to the site of his or her earlier enthusiasms with a mixture of nostalgia and revulsion. When A. S. Byatt re-read him she found herself irritated 'by his insistent sawing noise' and 'preacherly pulpit-thumping'. But this strain of Lawrence's work – a passionate and *dramatically embodied* advocacy of a more ecologically responsible system of economic production, one that recognises social costs along with economic profits – was prescient and forward-looking. Think of Lawrence's fondness for simple self-sufficiency, his plans for an ideal community to be called Rananim (it came to nothing, predictably) and his final admonition, in *Apocalypse*, that 'we ought to dance with rapture that we should be alive and in the flesh, and part of the living, incarnate cosmos'; add Mellors' suggestion that men wear bright 'red trousers' to this already delirious stew of impulses, and it seems reasonable to conclude that the closest Lawrence's hopes for a transformed and liberated society ever came to realisation was in California, at the dawn of the hippie era!

Closer to home, Lawrence's vision of an England going to the dogs rings true today precisely because neither he nor anyone else was able to do anything to prevent it. Lawrence realised that the colossal ugliness of industrialisation was being succeeded by a different kind of blight: the spread of 'red-bricked semi-detached "villas" in new streets'. This had only just got under way but Lawrence saw it as evidence of the way 'one England blots out another'. 'The blotting out was only not yet complete' and, here and there, Lawrence was still able to detect 'the tattered remnants of the old coaching and cottage England, even the England of Robin Hood'. For Philip Larkin – who, as a young man, was an ardent admirer of the 'weird old beardie' – the blotting-out has, by 1972, become almost terminal. Within a few years, he laments in 'Going, Going', the whole country will be 'bricked in':

> And that will be England gone,
> The shadows, the meadows, the lanes,
> The guildhalls, the carved choirs.
> There'll be books; it will linger on
> In galleries; but all that remains
> For us will be concrete and tyres

Lawrence's and Larkin's worst fears have been miserably realised. Contemporary England may seem far removed from the hideous industrialised Victorian image of Dickens' Coketown, but what might be termed a 'Swindonisation' has taken place whereby every town looks exactly like every other. A journey through 'the vast bulk of England' is now a journey through the almost unrelieved ugliness of post-industrial homogenisation.

This may be the aspect of the novel that has endured best, but it is not the part for which it is infamous. More heavily freighted with its own mythology than any other novel, *Lady Chatterley* comes to us burdened by its long history of sexual notoriety.

From the start Lawrence knew that it was going to be difficult to get his book published. Even publishing it privately in Italy (where the printers knew no English and so were ignorant of the words they were setting) did not prevent trouble: copies were confiscated by the 'censor morons' in the US and Britain. From Lawrence's point of view the corollary of this was still more worrying: the lucrative market for pirated copies created by the legend of the book's impropriety. The power of the book in the early years of its *samizdat* circulation is dramatically conveyed by Ian McEwan's *Atonement*. The first part of McEwan's novel is set at a gathering of the Tallis family's country house in 1935. Like Cecily Tallis, Robbie, the son of the family's housekeeper, has been educated at Cambridge, partly thanks to the financial assistance of Cecily's father. In the course of a sweltering afternoon Robbie writes a letter to Cecily at the bottom of which he scribbles the naked truth: 'In my dreams I kiss your cunt, your sweet wet cunt.' He intends discarding this draft – inspired, partly, by the 'memory of reading the Orioli edition of *Lady Chatterley's Lover*, which he had bought under the counter in Soho' – but mistakenly sends it, with catastrophic consequences. It is as if Mellors has gatecrashed the exquisitely rendered world of Mrs Dalloway.

What would happen if the rest of the public took it upon themselves to do something similar? This was the underlying point of the trial in 1960 when Penguin were prosecuted under the Obscene Publications Act for publishing a cheap, widely available paperback edition of Lawrence's infamous book. The class issue returned with a vengeance during the trial when the prosecutor shot himself in the foot by asking the jurors if this was a book they would be happy for their wives and servants to read. Penguin's acquittal was a watershed verdict that, as Larkin famously claimed in 'Annus Mirabilis', ushered in a new era of sexual freedom. In this sense Lawrence posthumously enjoyed the distinction of profoundly influencing the lives of people who had not even read him. Those who had, like the narrator of John Fowles' *The Magus* (1966), often 'thought [him] the greatest human being of the century'. W.H. Auden nicely conveys the kind of adulation this drew from literary-minded 'women pilgrims' who went up every day to the chapel at Taos, New Mexico, 'to stand reverently there and wonder what it would have been like to sleep with him'. Such reverential curiosity came to an abrupt end in the early 1970s with a new kind of literary-critical trial when Lawrence was convicted of misogyny by Kate Millett in *Sexual Politics*.

Millett's witty attack is all the more devastating for conceding, at the outset, that 'with *Lady Chatterley*, Lawrence seems to be making his peace with the female'. 'Compared with the novels and short stories which precede it, this last work appears almost an act of atonement.' The truth, however, is that Lawrence is the 'most subtle' of sexual politicians, 'for it is through a feminine consciousness that his masculine message is conveyed'. Millett goes on to show how Connie's awakening at the hands – or, more exactly, the phallus – of

Mellors is actually an extended lesson in subordination, a form of imprisonment all the more insidious for being presented in the guise of a liberation. What we are really getting, Millett contends, is 'the transformation of masculine ascendancy into a mystical religion'.

Millett's case is well-made and persuasive, the evidence damning. It is to the credit of Norman Mailer, therefore, that the extent to which the evidence was tampered with became quickly clear. Putting aside his usual tedious bluster, Mailer compares Millett's version of one of Connie's sexual bouts with Mellors with the textual reality. According to Millett, 'Mellors concedes one kiss on the navel and then gets to business' – the business being the need 'to come into her at once'. What has actually passed in the interim is infinitely tender and loving. If one had an objection to the passage it would be that the word 'softly' was over-used:

> Then she felt the soft, groping, helplessly desirous hand touching her body, feeling for her face. The hand stroked her face softly, softly, with infinite soothing and assurance, and at last there was the soft touch of a kiss on her cheek.
>
> She lay quite still, in a sort of sleep, in a sort of dream. Then she quivered as she felt his hand groping softly, yet with queer thwarted clumsiness, among her clothing. Yet the hand knew, too, how to unclothe her where it wanted. He drew down the thin silk sheath, slowly, carefully, right down and over her feet. Then with a quiver of exquisite pleasure he touched the warm soft body, and touched her navel for a moment with a kiss.

All of this, Mailer demonstrates, is censored by Millett in the interests of polemical zeal. It is not surprising that Mailer should go for Millett with all the tenacity that Millett went for Lawrence. What is surprising is that Mailer – often the least subtle of writers – should have articulated the nature of Lawrence's imaginative relations with women with such subtlety and sensitivity. Conceding that 'in all his books there are unmistakable tendencies towards the absolute domination of women by men', Mailer points out that 'he is pathetic in all those places he suggests that men should follow the will of a stronger man'. Until Lawrence, Mailer goes on, there had never been a male novelist 'so comfortable in the tides of [women's] sentiment, and so ready to see them murdered'. If Lawrence 'reminds us of the beauty of desiring to be a man', that is because 'he was not much of a man himself'. For Mailer, Lawrence had been 'a mama's boy' who 'lived with all the sensibility of a female burning with tender love'.

This is well-intentioned and accurate but it does, if anything, understate the extent to which Lawrence dispersed himself among the characters in his novel. In his essay 'A Propos of *Lady Chatterley's Lover*', Lawrence admitted that perhaps he had taken 'unfair advantage of Connie' by paralysing Clifford since that 'made it so much more vulgar of her to leave him'. Unfair to Connie, note, not to Clifford, who, in the novel, is treated with much scorn and remarkably little sympathy – which in itself is remarkable given that Lawrence invests a great deal of himself in the paralysed aristocrat. On only the second page of the book Lawrence concedes that Clifford 'had so very nearly lost his life, that what remained was wonderfully precious to him'. More explicitly, Lawrence's biographer, Brenda Maddox, has pointed out that if Lawrence imaginatively focused 'his longed-for virility on to Mellors', then he 'shifted his sexual frustration on to the impotent Lord Chatterley'. The more circumspect David Ellis concludes that it is 'reasonable to conjecture that at the beginning of 1924 Lawrence and Frieda were no longer having sexual relations in the usual sense of that term'.

From an early stage, however, it seems that Lawrence and Frieda enjoyed sexual relations in the *un*usual sense of that term. For Maddox, the Lawrences' discovery of anal sex in about 1912 was a crucial part in their evolving relationship. 'Anal sex seems to have been the Lawrences' resolution to the conflict between them. Their mutual pleasure in the forbidden zone was part of their strange bond.' Like anything else that Lawrence experienced, the act soon found its way into his fiction – in *Women in Love*, for example – but it is in *Lady Chatterley*, during the night of 'reckless, shameless sensuality', that it becomes a ritual of psycho-sexual apotheosis. Connie 'had to be a passive, consenting thing, like a slave, a physical slave' but by the end of that night 'her sensual self' emerges, 'naked and unashamed'. Ironically, the prosecution at the Penguin trial never picked up on what was happening in this scene (if they had, it is likely that the book would indeed have been adjudged obscene) for the language is coded, rhetorical, inexplicit. This has long been recognised as a major aesthetic flaw in the work. As Lawrence wrote and re-wrote his book he became more determined to free four-letter words from their shameful associations, to use them as part of a frank and healthy expression of physical love. Mellors is glad that Connie 'shits' and 'pisses'; he touches both of her 'secret entrances' but beyond this Lawrence's creative courage apparently failed him. While claiming Connie is free of shame, Lawrence is ashamed – or too timid – to say exactly what passes on that 'night of sensual passion'. A taboo was still in force and this, of course, increased the urge to break down that taboo, which is, in turn, a tacit admission that shame can be an incentive rather than an obstacle to desire.

A related irony attaches to Lawrence's attempt to reclaim the honest language of sex. The battle has been unequivocally won – and Lawrence would, no doubt, have been appalled by some of the consequences of a victory which he, more than anyone else, helped bring about. While writing *Lady Chatterley* Lawrence had warned his English publisher, Martin Secker, that the novel was 'very improper'; by 1968 John Cheever was worried that his new novel, *Bullet Park*, was not improper enough, was, in fact, 'very, very clean. There is not a cock or an arsehole in it and the word fuck does not appear once.' For Lawrence sex was always more than just sex; he had enough of the puritan in him to insist that it had to be the expression of some larger connection of men and women with each other and, ideally, with the living cosmos to boot. As literature has become more and more sexually explicit so this claim has come to seem harder and harder to sustain. The distance from Lawrence to Catherine Millet – or, for that matter, from Millett to Millet – and her blow-job by blow-job account of *The Sexual Life of Catherine M*, for example, could hardly be greater. By comparison, Lawrence's elaborate evocation of love-making has come to seem, if not exactly dated, then almost quaint: a tentative groping for linguistic freedom rather than its consummation.

In this respect one is conscious of how, in matters of sex, literature lags behind the visual arts. This becomes clear if we compare Lawrence's writing about sex with photographic nudes by Edward Weston (who photographed Lawrence in Mexico in 1924) and Alfred Stieglitz (who wrote to Lawrence congratulating him on *Lady Chatterley*). It would be hard to imagine more sexually charged works of art than those made in the 1920s by Weston of his numerous lovers or by Stieglitz of Georgia O'Keeffe. Lawrence sneered at the sight of his philosopher friend in a swimming costume – 'Poor Bertie Russell! He's all Disembodied Mind' – but the work of these photographers is a powerful and timeless expression of precisely the opposite: the embodied mind or mindful body that is perfectly at ease with itself. There is no sense in Stieglitz or Weston of any straining towards a phallic re-awakening of society or some such. On the contrary, there is a frank and untroubled depiction of – and delight in – what, according to Millett, Lawrence could not bring himself to describe: the *female* genitals. Here is Weston on 'a posterior view' of 1929: 'The figure is presented quite symmetrically, great buttocks swell from the black centre, the vulva, which is so clearly defined that I can never exhibit the print publicly.' The problem, Weston concedes, is that 'the lay mind would misunderstand'. That is the crucial difference: Weston and Stieglitz had an aesthetic disdain for the 'lay mind'; Lawrence, nothing if not a fighter, was determined to *make it* understand.

As early as 1915 Lawrence had written to E.M. Forster explaining that if he was 'one of any lot', he was 'one of the common people'. When he returned to England in 1926 there seemed 'a queer, odd sort of potentiality in the people, especially the common people. One feels in them some odd, unaccustomed sort of plasm twinkling and nascent. They are not finished, and they have a funny sort of purity and gentleness, and at the same time, unbreakableness that attracts one.' It was, in other words, the lay mind that Lawrence believed – 'a little droopingly, but with a hopeful heart' – that he had the potential to transform. Clifford, on the other hand, believes that 'the masses are unalterable'. Connie acknowledges that 'there was something devastatingly truthful in what he said. But it was a truth that killed.' Her rejection of Clifford can thus be seen as a dramatised rejection

of Lawrence's earlier contempt for democracy and his absurd infatu-
ation with 'the divine right of natural aristocracy, the right, the sacred
duty to wield undisputed authority'. There is something aesthetically
as well as politically fitting about this, for the alternative to Clifford's
killing truth is, logically, the life-affirming power of *fiction*. Lawrence
himself says as much, jumping naked into the narrative stream to
deliver a Kundera-like *apologia* for the novel:

> It is the way our sympathy flows and recoils that really determines our lives.
> And here lies the vast importance of the novel, properly handled. It can
> inform and lead into new places the flow of our sympathetic consciousness,
> and it can lead our sympathy in recoil from things gone dead. Therefore, the
> novel, properly handled, can reveal the most secret places of life: for it is in
> the *passional* secret places of life, above all, that the tide of sensitive aware-
> ness needs to ebb and flow, cleansing and freshening.

As far as *Lady Chatterley* goes, this is both to over- and understate
his achievement. Parts of the novel are too hastily done, inadequately
conceived or extraneous to its larger design. Parts – like Mellors'
drunken meeting with Connie's father, which descends into 'the old
free-masonry of male sensuality', or Clifford's eventual relationship
with Mrs Boulton (feeling her breasts and kissing them 'in exultation, the exultation of perversity') – affront the reader's expectations
more bizarrely than any scenes involving the lovers. But that is the
way with Lawrence. If he is inexhaustible that is partly because he
was so little interested in restraining the surges of his own creative
intelligence, so gloriously capable of getting things right by letting
them be ostensibly wrong. This is nowhere more apparent than in
that famous apologia for a book whose enduring virtue is that, by
any conventional standards, it is so *im*properly handled.

2003

F. Scott Fitzgerald:
The Beautiful and Damned

Was ever a writer so besotted by failure as F. Scott Fitzgerald? As a young man he craved literary success and achieved it, instantly, with *This Side of Paradise* (1920). In 1918 he had met and fallen for Zelda Sayre, who, a year later, broke off their informal engagement. Fitzgerald won her back and, within two weeks of the book's publication, had married the woman of his dreams. He was twenty-four and had everything he wanted. Even then – or so he later claimed – the pleasure was tainted and enhanced by elegiac projection: 'I remember riding in a taxi one afternoon between very tall buildings under a mauve and rose sky; I began to bawl because I had everything I wanted and knew I would never be so happy again.' That's one way of looking at it; another would be that he was already looking forward to the real business of regret, loss, decline and ruin. Fitzgerald understood that he had to climb to a dizzy height if the fall was going to be spectacular enough to satisfy him. He needed to achieve success in order to be convinced of the colossal scale of his subsequent failure.

By August he was at work on a new novel, which, he informed his publisher, Charles Scribner, 'concerns the life of one Anthony Patch between his 25th and 33rd years (1913–21). He is one of those many with the tastes and weaknesses of an artist but with no actual creative inspiration. How he and his beautiful young wife are wrecked on the shoals of dissipation is told in the story.' The novel was duly completed in the summer of 1921 and published the following March.

For more than a hundred pages *The Beautiful and Damned* does not reveal any kind of advance on *This Side of Paradise*. Isolated moments of insight cannot disguise its stylistic and structural flimsiness. The reader's heart sinks when, after less than twenty pages, Fitzgerald abandons novelistic prose and inserts one of the little playlets that should have been edited out of his *first* novel. In the midst of 'an F. Scott Fitzgerald phase', the writer Richard Yates admired the way that 'every line of dialogue in *The Great Gatsby* serves to reveal more about the speaker than the speaker might care to have revealed'. The characters in *The Beautiful and Damned* say some smart things – 'unloved women have no biographies – they have histories' – but much of the dialogue wilts even as it is spoken. Unleashed as soon as Gloria sets foot in the book, Fitzgerald's tendency to effulgence is, at first, ironically refracted through Anthony's consciousness: 'Surely the freshness of her cheeks was a gossamer projection from a land of delicate and undiscovered shades; her hand gleaming on the stained table-cloth was a shell from some far and wildly virginal sea.' Shortly afterwards it takes on the signature tone of Fitzgerald's own lyrical yearning. A cab 'moved off like a boat on a labyrinthine ocean'; Gloria 'turned up her face to him, pale under the wisps and patches of light that trailed in like moonshine through a foliage'. Fitzgerald never entirely grew out of this kind of thing – he would have been a lesser writer if he had – but he did learn to control it, to ground the lushest imagery in the actual and immediate. That is the problem with the first part of *The Beautiful and Damned*: its themes are declared without being adequately actualised in the specific drama of Gloria and Anthony's relationship.

Significantly, the narrative clicks abruptly into focus on the brink of the first serious breach in their marriage, in circumstances which are like a premonition of the opening of *Tender is the Night*: 'With Eric Mottram, Anthony had been sitting over a decanter of Scotch all the hot summer afternoon, while Gloria and Constance Merriam swam and sunned themselves at the Beach Club, the latter under a striped parasol-awning, Gloria stretched sensuously upon the soft hot sand, tanning her inevitable legs.'

By the time the Patches leave – at Gloria's insistence – Anthony is befuddled with drink. At the railroad station he becomes determined both to pay a pointless visit on some other friends and to assert his power over Gloria and her perceived selfishness. When she continues to insist on going home he grips her arms. The scene that follows is ugly and devastating, all the more so because it is transcribed in such ruthless detail. Its aftermath leaves them changed for ever. To her husband Gloria seems 'a pathetic little thing . . . broken and dispirited', while Anthony has 'killed any love' and 'any respect' his wife ever had for him. Fitzgerald does not leave it there, however. He had a sufficiently subtle understanding of such moments to know that the characteristic of a turning point is that, as often as not, one fails to turn: 'she was aware even then that she would forget in time and that it is the manner of life seldom to strike but always to wear away'.

It is page 168 and we are, quite suddenly and in several senses, on the far side of paradise. Everything Fitzgerald has written up to this point is showy, shallow and – as Jack Kerouac wrote to Neal Cassady – 'sweetly unnecessary'. This is the first glimpse of the mature style and skill that will lead, ultimately, to his crowning masterpiece, *Tender is the Night*. More immediately, his themes are now properly embodied in his characters. From here Fitzgerald's command of his material is, for the most part, considered, assured. (Right at the end he blows it completely, but that is 190 pages away.)

It is difficult to disassociate Fitzgerald's life – especially his relationship with Zelda – from his reputation as a writer. Fact and fiction are constantly informing, illuminating, intruding on and obscuring one another. The temptation to read the novels as a form of vicarious autobiography was, on occasion, sanctioned by Fitzgerald himself. In 1930 he wrote to Zelda – then 'sick as hell' at a clinic in Switzerland – that he wished *The Beautiful and Damned* had been a maturely written book because it was all true. We ruined ourselves – I have never honestly thought that we ruined each other.' Ten years later he told his daughter that 'Gloria was a much more trivial and vulgar person than your mother. I can't really say there was much resemblance except in the beauty and certain terms of expression she used, and also I naturally used many circumstantial events of our early married life. However the emphases were entirely different. We had a much better time than Anthony and Gloria had.' Despite the discrepancy there is not really any contradiction between these two accounts.

It is precisely the intermingling of literal truth and fabrication that gives the novel its imaginative truth.

The 'circumstantial' details include both the renting of a house in the country, the terrifyingly erratic driving that led the couple to it and the binges that became the norm once they had moved in. It is generally assumed that Fitzgerald fell apart due to alcoholism, and while this is, in a sense, obviously true, it is also simplistic – for the simple reason that alcoholism became one of his great subjects. Write about what you know – that is the advice always given to aspiring writers. And what Fitzgerald came to know about was alcoholism. Fitzgerald didn't actually drink that much and took the fact that he got drunk so quickly as proof that he was not nearly as far gone as some of his friends. Hemingway may have known a lot more about drink and drinking but no one has written better about its effects than Fitzgerald. Guy Debord's celebration of his own relationship with booze in *Panegyric* climaxes with an evocation of the state that was close to Fitzgerald's artistic heart. 'First, like everyone, I appreciated the effect of slight drunkenness; then very soon I grew to like what lies beyond violent drunkenness, when one has passed that stage: a magnificent and terrible peace, the true taste of the passage of time.' The passage of time; lost youth: Fitzgerald reiterated his loyalty to these themes so often that Gore Vidal satirically summed up the contents of his *Notebooks* in two lines: 'once upon a time, he was a success and now he's a failure; he was young and now he's middle-aged'.

In *The Thirsty Muse*, his study of 'Alcohol and the American Writer', Thomas Dardis traces the way that booze took its toll on Fitzgerald. This is demonstrably the case – but the irony is that, even before he had succumbed completely to alcoholism, Fitzgerald understood its ruinous consequences so precisely. To paraphrase Blake on Milton, Fitzgerald was of the temperance party without knowing it. In *The Beautiful and Damned* the process by which Gloria and Anthony 'pour into themselves a gay and delicate poison' is painstakingly navigated. An ominous note is struck when, for a wedding present, their friend Maury gives them 'an elaborate "drinking set", which included silver goblets, cocktail shaker, and bottle-openers'. With the accoutrements of booze thereby serving as a symbolic expression of their nuptials, the couple go from getting 'tight' to unconscious dependency and squalor. 'There was the odour of tobacco always – both of them smoked incessantly; it was in their clothes, their blankets, the curtains, and the ash-littered carpets. Added to this was the wretched aura of stale wine, with its inevitable suggestion of beauty gone foul and revelry remembered in disgust.'

Needless to say, Fitzgerald did not discover this subject – indeed, he was consciously under the influence of Theodore Dreiser's *Sister Carrie* while writing *The Beautiful and Damned* – but for no one else was booze so intimately entangled with the romance that it insidiously corrupts. 'There's no beauty without poignancy,' Gloria tells Anthony and, in Fitzgerald, the poignancy is invariably viewed through the bottom of a glass. The mythic status of Fitzgerald in American letters was such that a writer like Richard Yates (born in 1926) was so intoxicated by his example that he spent much of his career – both imaginatively and literally – aspiring to an ideal of ruination exemplified by Fitzgerald.*

Drink is not the only measure of the Patches' decline. Fitzgerald is careful to keep tabs on exactly how much money Anthony has and the rate at which his fortune is dissipated. (The two kinds of dissipation – spending money and drinking – come bathetically together at a scene near the end of the book when Gloria reproaches Anthony for paying 'seventy-five dollars for a case of whiskey' even though they are on the brink of destitution.) As elsewhere in Fitzgerald's writing, this scrupulous accounting has a deep-rooted metaphoric importance; financial ruin is always twinned with what he called, in

---

*Yates' story 'Saying Goodbye to Sally' concerns a writer called Jack Field, who 'had tried for years to prevent anyone from knowing the full extent of his preoccupation with F. Scott Fitzgerald'. Offered a screenwriting job in LA, 'he sat locked alone and stiff with alcohol among strangers in the long, soft, murmurous tube of his very first jet plane . . . It occurred to him then, as he pressed his forehead against a small cold window and felt the fatigue and anxiety of the past few years beginning to fall away, that what lay ahead of him – good or bad – might easily turn out to be a significant adventure: F. Scott Fitzgerald in Hollywood.' A page and a half later, 'in a long-familiar pattern, he began to worry about himself: maybe he was incapable of finding light and space in the world; maybe his nature would always seek darkness and confinement and decay. Maybe – and this was a phrase then popular in national magazines – he was a self-destructive personality.'

the title of a story, 'Emotional Bankruptcy'. As his biographer Matthew Bruccoli puts it, the 'concept of emotional bankruptcy became a key idea for Fitzgerald. He believed that people have a fixed amount of emotional capital; reckless expenditure results in early bankruptcy.' Gloria is willing to live her life on these terms, 'to use every minute of these years' to have the best time [she] possibly can'. After that she won't care and, even if she does, Gloria insists, 'I won't be able to do anything about it. And I'll have had my good time.' Anthony sees through this hedonistic cod-Nietzscheanism: they have *had* their good time and are already 'in the state of paying for it'.

Even this is open to doubt; Fitzgerald was astute about his material when he pointed out that Anthony and Gloria did not have as good a time as he and Zelda. In *The Beautiful and Damned* there is nothing comparable to the enchanted Riviera evenings of *Tender is the Night* or the ecstatic nights in Gatsby's 'blue gardens', where 'men and girls came and went like moths among the whisperings and the champagne and the stars'.* The 'parties' (Fitzgerald himself puts the word in inverted commas at one point!) in *The Beautiful and Damned* are just binges that leave Anthony, in the words of poet Peter Reading, a 'grievously wounded veteran of the / Battle of Bottle'.

That it is not clear what *else* he might have amounted to was part of the novel's purpose. As Fitzgerald explained to Edmund Wilson: 'Gloria and Anthony *are* representative. They are two of the great army of the rootless who float around New York. There must be thousands.' Anthony has vague plans to write but Gloria mocks his inability to settle down to the task. The problem, he retorts, is that she makes 'leisure so subtly attractive'. Anthony is here scratching the surface of what will become one of Fitzgerald's major artistic preoccupations and insights: that if leisure – to which everyone aspires – is akin to ruin then perhaps ruin *itself* is subtly attractive.

---

*Fitzgerald's lyrical evocations of parties continue to cast their spell; in *Brightness Falls*, Jay McInerney seems consciously to invoke those idyllic nights at Gatsby's: 'Fifty yards away, the ocean throbbed against the beach; on the lawn, waiters in tuxedos darted like pilot fish around CEOs in jeans and polo shirts.'

Anthony's attempts at paid employment prove no more successful than his literary and intellectual endeavours. To succeed in the world of finance, he realises, 'the idea of success must grasp and limit his mind'. By comparison the idea of failure seems all-embracing, something that will consume and test his entire being. Perhaps failure will even contain its own kind of majesty. This is the wager at the centre of Fitzgerald's fascination, for failure also necessarily imposes its own limits. From being a person 'of mental adventure, of curiosity' Anthony becomes 'an individual of bias and prejudice'. It is to the credit of Fitzgerald the artist – who, as a man, was prone to shoddy prejudices of his own – that the absolute nadir of Anthony's life, the pitch of degradation, comes when, having been refused a loan, he calls the movie producer Joseph Bloeckman a 'Goddam Jew'.

Even an incident like this demonstrates the capacity of failure to generate some kind of hideous enlightenment. Had everything gone smoothly for Anthony he might never have so nakedly confronted the potential baseness of his own character. In less extreme circumstances failure generates an aura of romance and mystery. Despite his drinking, 'Anthony had rather gained than lost in appearance; his face had taken on a certain tangible air of tragedy, romantically contrasted with his trim and immaculate person.' Fitzgerald was never shy of using the word tragedy but it seems to me that his writing – with the gleaming exception of *The Great Gatsby* – is constantly groping towards an intuition that has historic rather than simply personal resonance: namely that, despite the vaulting claim announced by Dreiser's *An American Tragedy* (1926), in twentieth-century America *failure* had superseded tragedy. Whether this in itself is a failure or a tragedy constitutes the crux of his creative efforts.

The First World War played a major part in Fitzgerald's thinking along these lines. What space was left for individual tragedy in the wake of such a cataclysm? D.H. Lawrence, an English writer living in mainland Europe, began his last novel with the assertion that 'Ours is essentially a tragic age.' For Fitzgerald the fact that he – like Anthony in *The Beautiful and Damned* – missed out on the war only deepened the conviction that Americans were in a post-tragic age. What could be done in such a situation? Could failure and waste be imbued with a tragic grandeur of their own? Zelda came to believe that Fitzgerald succeeded in doing exactly this: 'I do not know that a personality can be divorced from the times which evoke it . . . I feel that Scott's greatest contribution was the dramatization of a heart-broken + despairing era, giving it a new raison-d'être in the sense of tragic courage with which he endowed it.'

As early as *This Side of Paradise* there are moments when Fitzgerald flirts precociously with the prospect of failure. 'I've begun to feel that I was meant to lose this chance,' reflects the youthful hero Amory Blaine at one point. Later, he feels 'an overwhelming desire to let himself go to the devil' but it is not until *The Beautiful and Damned* that Fitzgerald pursues this possibility in earnest. Midway through the novel Fitzgerald sums up Anthony as someone who 'has inherited only the vast tradition of human failure'. While a measure of satisfaction and consolation might be derived from this inheritance Fitzgerald later came to feel dissatisfied with the passivity it implied. The book he was working on in 1932 would therefore 'be a novel of our time showing the break-up of a fine personality. Unlike *The Beautiful and Damned* the break-up will be caused not by flabbiness but really tragic forces such as the inner conflicts of the idealist and the compromises forced upon him by circumstances.' The achieved reality of *Tender is the Night* – as this novel became – would both fall short of this plan and, by failing, exceed it.

By then Fitzgerald was so immersed in his own sense of failure that his capacity to stand by his own judgements was severely compromised. Thus when the novel was not greeted as warmly as he hoped, he revised and rearranged it and, in so doing, made it worse. In 1936 he wrote to his editor Max Perkins: 'This general eclipse of ambition and determination and fortitude, all of the very qualities on which I have prided myself, is ridiculous, and, I must admit, somewhat obscene.' Self-pity of this kind was a justifiable indulgence; having somehow summoned the tenacity and fortitude to write his masterpiece Fitzgerald was no longer relevant to his own achievement. The philosopher E.M. Cioran believed that the autobiographical essays from this period (collected in *The Crack-Up*) in which Fitzgerald 'describes his failure' constitute 'his only great *success*'.* This, however, is radically to underestimate the extent to which Fitzgerald had internalised and pre-empted such a verdict.

Fitzgerald claims that the 'quality which was the best' in Anthony worked 'swiftly and ceaseless toward his ruin'. His fate is altogether less complex than Dick's, and The Beautiful and Damned is a less complex, less profound novel than Tender is the Night. It is both a major step beyond the radiant ease of This Side of Paradise and an indication of the depths Fitzgerald still had to plumb in order to live up to – by breaking – its youthful promise.

2004

---

*Kerouac went further than Cioran; in 1962, having denied that he was himself having a 'Scott Fitzgerald cracup' [sic], he went on to tell Robert Giroux that 'Fitzgerald never wrote better than he did *after* his "crackup".' (My italics.)

F. Scott Fitzgerald:
Tender is the Night *

It was *The Great Gatsby* we were 'doing' for A-level, not *Tender is the Night*, but my English teacher got me to read it anyway. I was seventeen and remembered practically nothing about it – but I never quite forgot it.

This, it turns out, is a not uncommon reaction, or at least a variant of a fairly common one. Putting into practice an idea he'd 'got from Conrad's preface to *The Nigger*', Fitzgerald believed that 'the purpose of a work of fiction is to appeal to the lingering after-effects in the reader's mind'. He was responding to some surly comments about *Tender* from Hemingway, who, as if succumbing to exactly these 'lingering after-effects', later told Max Perkins of a 'strange thing' about Fitzgerald, namely that 'in retrospect his *Tender is the Night* gets better and better'. John Updike bounces this kind of response back into the works themselves. 'So often in Fitzgerald,' he writes, 'we have only the afterglow of a dream to see by.'

I don't remember when I read *Tender* for the second time. Even the note scribbled in the front of my Penguin edition is uncertain: 'Read 2, 3 times (?) before this, Paris, April/May 92.' I had gone to Paris in 1991 to write a novel which, I hoped, was going to be a contemporary version of *Tender is the Night*, so the afterglow of those undated re-readings was, evidently, still strong. Appropriately enough

---

*This piece was commissioned by *The American Scholar* for their Rereading series. They responded to the draft I sent in by asking if I could make it *more* personal, so some of what's here is me being obedient, not self-indulgent! (Note added 2010.)

I made little progress with this novel and, after a visit to the battlefields of northern France, abandoned it in favour of a book about
the Great War. With this in mind it is hardly surprising that, when
I re-read *Tender* in the spring of 1992, it seemed a book saturated
in the aftermath of the First World War or – as Fitzgerald himself
put it – 'the broken universe of the war's ending'.

'This Western front business couldn't be done again, not for a long
time,' Dick explains during a visit to the battlefields of the Western
Front in 1925. 'This took religion and years of plenty and tremendous sureties and the exact relation between the classes.' That's the
passage that always gets quoted, but the book is dominated throughout
by what Dick terms, in a 'half-ironic phrase: Non-combatant's shell-
shock'. The battlefields of northern France, where, as Dick explains,
the dead lay 'like a million bloody rugs', are twinned, through this
image, with the Riviera and 'its bright tan prayer rug of a beach'.

Having got the Great War out of my system, I did eventually write
my Paris novel, but I did not actually read *Tender* again until last
week, when I did so specifically to write this piece. The book I
encountered this time around was radically different to the one I had
read before. Quite literally: up until then I had always read the version
re-organised by Fitzgerald, edited by Malcolm Cowley and first
published in 1951. This time I read the original version, beginning
not with Dick encountering the wounded on his way to Zurich but
with Rosemary's first glimpse of the Divers on the French Riviera.

From Hemingway on, Fitzgerald's fellow-writers have felt free to
be smugly superior about his achievements. In the most wonderfully
snobby aside of all, E.M. Cioran remarks on what seems 'an incomprehensible thing to me: T.S. Eliot wrote to Fitzgerald that he had
read *The Great Gatsby* three times!' After watching the movie of *Tender*
– 'a very good film of a rather poor book' – Evelyn Waugh concluded,
ambivalently, that 'the enormously expensive apparatus of the film
studio can produce nothing as valuable as can one half-tipsy Yank
with a typewriter'. For Gore Vidal 'very little' of what the 'barely
literate' Fitzgerald wrote 'has any great value as literature'.

On this latest re-reading I feared, at first, that he was right. In
places the writing in these early pages is strikingly inept, as when

Rosemary, feeling the 'impactive scrutiny' of strangers on the beach, notices the 'brash navel' and 'facetious whiskers' of a man with a monocle. It all felt like someone *trying* to make his writing interesting – what Nick Carraway calls 'a strained counterfeit of perfect ease' – and succeeding only in drawing attention to its failing. Writing often works best when you are oblivious to it, when you respond to its effects without being conscious of how they are achieved. And so it was here. After that initially uncomfortable period of settling in, I fell under Fitzgerald's tender spell as subtly as Dick's guests fall under their host's. His gift for making people believe in the world he creates while 'leaving little communicable memory of what he had said or done' is of a piece with the effect – more accurately, the lingering after-effect – of *Tender* itself. Other incidental observations hint at this quality of evocative reverberation. Utterly infatuated, Rosemary catches only the gist of Dick's sentences and supplies 'the rest from her unconscious, as one picks up the striking of a clock in the middle with only the rhythm of the first uncounted strokes lingering in the mind'.

It is often thought that Fitzgerald was as besotted by elegance and the wealth on which it is predicated as the teenage Rosemary is by Dick. This is such a distorting simplification of an author who read Marx and conceived of Dick as 'a man like myself', 'a communist-liberal-idealist, a moralist in revolt', that one wonders at its capacity to persist. In a letter of 1938 Fitzgerald wrote, 'I have never been able to forgive the rich for being rich, and it has coloured my entire life and works.' He was the most materialist of romantics, the most romantic of materialists. As representatives of the 'furthermost evolution of a class' the Divers incarnate a way of life which, in its apparent transcendence of all material concerns, is enviably idyllic. But Fitzgerald was one of the first writers to grasp the enervating horror of infinite leisure (in Jane Austen it is simply assumed). Given limitless time and freedom everything, as Dick eventually blurts out at Mary North, comes to seem 'damned dull'. Realising the extent to which Nicole's immense wealth serves 'to belittle his own work', Dick sits 'listening to the buzz of the electric clock, listening to time'. Not the time of striking hours but blank, undifferentiated time. In this eternity of leisure it is inevitable that Dick, though conscious that he has 'lost himself', cannot 'tell the hour when, or the day or the week, or the month or the year'.

About the larger system of global degradation on which this leisure and its attendant virtues of poise and elegance depend, Fitzgerald is, by contrast, explicit and exact: for Nicole's sake, 'girls canned tomatoes in August or worked rudely at the Five-and-Tens on Christmas Eve; half-breed Indians toiled on Brazilian coffee plantations and dreamers were muscled out of patent rights in new tractors – these were some of the people who gave a tithe to Nicole . . .' Poise itself is thereby tainted by the exploitation that finances its cultivation.

If poise and degradation are inescapably entwined then so too – as in the 'Ode to a Nightingale' from which Fitzgerald took his title – are rapture and despondency, celebration and lament. Early on in the novel Nicole observes one of Dick's 'most characteristic moods', 'the excitement that swept everyone up into it and was inevitably followed by his own form of melancholy, which he never displayed but at which she guessed'. From this cocktail of entangled emotions emerges what Philip Larkin – in 'For Sidney Bechet', another, very different elegy for his own idea of the jazz age – calls the 'long-haired grief and scored pity' of the book. Writing it demanded from Fitzgerald a willingness to believe again in every promise of happiness that had been broken by his life.

If the precise trajectory of Dick's failure becomes more difficult to trace with every re-reading, this is a tribute to the book's subtlety rather than an indication of a lack. Dick's disintegration is, of course, a prism refracting Fitzgerald's own. Indeed, the three-way relation between the fictional world Fitzgerald created, the Fitzgeralds as they actually were, and the synthetic myth of the Fitzgeralds that emerged from this inter-relation is as central to the enduring popularity of Fitzgerald's work as it is to the dissenting view that his popularity is based on meagre literary merit. Rather than disentangling these strands consider, for a moment, just *how* intimately they are entwined.

While not portraits of Sara and Gerald Murphy, Nicole and Dick are partly derived from them (Hemingway's initial objections to the book had primarily to do with this). At the same time, as John O'Hara pointed out, 'sooner or later his characters always come back to being Fitzgerald characters in a Fitzgerald world . . . Dick Diver ended up as a tall Fitzgerald.' This protean connection between the lived and the fictive is suggested by Rebecca West's response to a request for her remembered impressions of Zelda.

West had met the Fitzgeralds on her first visit to New York in 1923–4 and again on the Riviera in 1926. Zelda, West wrote in 1963, 'was very plain . . . She was standing with her back to me, and her hair was quite lovely, it glistened like a child's. Her face had a certain craggy homeliness. There was a curious unevenness about it, such as one sees in Géricault's pictures of the insane.' As West continued to mull over the past a 'very unpleasant memory' came to mind of how Zelda 'had flapped her arms and looked very uncouth as she talked about her ballet ambitions. The odd thing to me always was that Scott Fitzgerald . . . should have liked someone who was so inelegant. But she was not at all unlikeable. There was something very appealing about her. But frightening. Not that one was frightened from one's own point of view, only from hers.'

Irrespective of the physical accuracy of West's description of Zelda this seems to me the single most penetrating insight we have – not into Fitzgerald but into his *art* (especially if we bear in mind an earlier occasion when West, in precisely the style advocated by Fitzgerald, commented on 'the *after-image*' of Zelda's face). It reveals the humming circuitry of an artist's imaginative life. In late 1935 Gerald Murphy conceded to Fitzgerald 'that what you said in *Tender is the Night* was true. Only the invented part of our life – the unreal part – has had any scheme, any beauty.' During her first encounters with Dick, Rosemary is aware of 'an act of creation different from any she had known'; 'the intensely calculated perfection' of the Villa Diana becomes evident 'through such minute failures as the chance apparition of a maid in the background or the perversity of a cork'. West's incidental X-ray reveals the fundamental urge – the creative ontology of the writer – behind these variously arranged contrivings. If Fitzgerald's fascination with wealth derived in part from being, as he insisted, 'a poor boy in a rich town; a poor boy in a rich boy's school', then it is not surprising to find that elegance and beauty share a similar proximity to plainness and inelegance. In comparable style, his famous lyrical flourishes work best when earthed in the actual and immediate. To make the same point in terms of the symbolic geography of *The Great Gatsby*, the significance of Gatsby's mansion lies not simply in its 'meretricious beauty' but in its tragic proximity to the ash-heaps of Wilson's garage. By the time of *Tender is the Night* this kind of topographic scheme has been subtly dissolved, psychologically internalised. The lyrical and beautiful are constantly flickering into the abject and desolate.

At this point I need to go back to the novel I went to Paris to write. Taking an aspect of *Tender* and adapting it for my own needs, I wanted to write a book about a failure which also depicted an idyllic period in the life of that failure – but I kept failing to write it. Asked if I am disciplined in my working habits I always respond that I am actively hostile to the idea of writers lashing themselves to their desks for six hours a day, irrespective of how they feel. I write when I feel like it, don't when I don't. My inability to make any progress with my Paris novel, however, did make me suspect that I had become too self-indulgent, too dissolute in my ways. Perhaps I had been seduced by the version of creativity personified by the junkie saxophonist Art Pepper, who claimed he 'never studied, never practiced . . . All I had to do was reach for it.' I kept telling myself that the material I was dealing with was too personal, that I wasn't ready to face it, but I also worried that I simply lacked self-discipline. Failure to write the book gave rise to a less specific sense of failure, so generalised, in fact, that it became part of my life. And then, quite suddenly, without any conscious effort, I began writing the book. It came fairly easily and, I realised quickly, the delay in writing the book – the earlier failure to write it – became an active part in its composition. All sorts of things that had happened in the interim found their place in the book, the most important of which were my experiences with MDMA, or Ecstasy.

Fitzgerald, as we all know, was an alcoholic; booze flows like a river through *Tender.* At that time there was a glamour and promise about drinking that has long since dissipated. In a contemporary context such glamour and promise could only be provided by drugs and so, naturally, the characters in my *Paris Trance* all take E.

On Rosemary's first evening at the Divers' the guests gather for dinner. 'They had been at table half an hour and a perceptible change had set in – person by person had given up something, a preoccupation, an anxiety, a suspicion, and now they were only their best selves and the Divers' guests . . .' This is followed by one of the most famous scenes in the book:

> There were fireflies riding on the dark air and a dog baying on some low and far-away ledge of the cliff. The table seemed to have risen a little toward the sky like a mechanical dancing platform, giving the people around it a sense of being alone with each other in the dark universe, nourished by its only food, warmed by its only lights. And, as if a curious hushed laugh from Mrs. McKisko were a signal that such a detachment from the world had been attained, the two Divers began suddenly to warm and glow and expand . . . Just for a moment they seemed to speak to everyone at the table, singly and together, assuring them of their friendliness, their affection. And for a moment the faces turned up toward them were like the faces of poor children at a Christmas tree.

Of the many descriptions in contemporary literature of people coming up on E, none surpasses this. Certain details in *Tender* – the way Dick is always wearing gloves, or carrying a cane – tie it too closely to the costume drama of the jazz age in which it is set, but scenes like this show its opposite, timeless quality.

Alcohol befuddles and eventually destroys; over time Ecstasy diminishes the user's capacity to enjoy exactly the feelings taking it initially releases. The flood of serotonin induced by Ecstasy leads, ultimately, to a radical depletion of serotonin. It is as if there is a certain, finite quantity of happiness which Ecstasy can lead one to use up quickly. Luke, the central character in my book, blows a lifetime's happiness in a single year-long splurge. By any normal reckoning he is a failure but I wanted also to suggest that, in failing, Luke was somehow being true to his destiny. My faith in this notion was strengthened when I read Peter Matthiessen's *The Snow Leopard*; more exactly when I read the passage from Jung's *The Development of Personality* that is quoted in the book: 'The fact that many a man who goes his own way ends in ruin means nothing . . . He *must* obey his own law, as if it were a daemon whispering to him of new and wonderful paths . . . The only meaningful life . . . is . . . a life that strives for the individual realization – absolute and unconditional – of its own peculiar law . . . To the extent that a man is untrue to the law of his own being . . . he has failed to realize his life's meaning.'

This passage of Jung's was in turn obviously derived from Nietzsche, specifically from the essay 'Schopenhauer as Educator', one of the *Untimely Meditations*. Sometimes the very pervasiveness of an influence makes it difficult to trace. It is quite possible that my own inkling that an individual's failure might not derive solely from an inability to realise his potential but, on the contrary, from an ability to access a deeper level of that potential, was nurtured by prolonged exposure to Nietzsche's thought. By the same token, the germ of the idea might also have come from those early, dimly remembered readings of *Tender is the Night*. On the other hand again perhaps it was because the germ of this idea was latent in me that I was so susceptible to *Tender* in the first place and so prone, subsequently, to regard Dick in this somewhat peculiar light.

Certainly now, in the wake of having written a book which was both a version of *Tender* and an attempt to dramatise this theory of failure/destiny, I see what happens to Dick almost as the opposite of a collapse: a standing firm, an assertion rather than a weakening of will. This is why Dick's failure is accompanied by the affirming sense that he is not falling short of but living up to his destiny, fulfilling it. E.M. Cioran got as close as anyone to the mysterious heart of *Tender* when he said of the Fitzgeralds' time in Europe – 'seven years of waste and tragedy', as Fitzgerald himself termed it – that in this time 'they indulged every extravagance, as though haunted by a secret desire to exhaust themselves'. Elsewhere, without even referring to Fitzgerald, Cioran writes that 'the man who has tendencies toward an inner quest . . . will set failure above any success, he will even seek it out. This is because failure, always essential, reveals us to ourselves, permits us to see ourselves as God sees us, whereas success distances us from what is most inward in ourselves and indeed in everything.'

On a more mundane level Dick is like millions of people who end up settling for a lot less than they had once promised. But he is also, far more unusually, someone who seeks out his 'intricate destiny' despite the huge detour of his early success. This is especially arduous since, unlike Nicole, who contains 'in herself her own doom', Dick, according to Fitzgerald's notes, is 'a superman in possibilities'. He has an array of talents and opportunities at his disposal, talents that must, to re-phrase things only slightly, be disposed of. First he has to allow his early ambitions to be a good psychiatrist – 'maybe to be the greatest one that ever lived' – to dissipate amid the affluence of the world to which Nicole's wealth grants him access. But here too his 'fine personality' and 'great personal charm' (Fitzgerald's notes again) ensure that he becomes a virtual Prospero of the Riviera. To go from here to the small town where he ends up will require not a dissipation but a massive assertion of will. Ostensibly it might be a lack of strength that leads him to squander his talents but the further movement into charmless drunkenness and bigotry, brawling and self-ostracism, is as much a rising to the surface of Jung's 'daemon' as it is a descent. The belated consummation of his affair with Rosemary is less an act of faithlessness to Nicole than of fidelity to a long-buried urge to shatter his life:

'We can't go on like this,' Nicole suggested. 'Or can we? – what do you think?' Startled that for the moment Dick did not deny it, she continued, 'Some of the time I think it's my fault – I've ruined you.'

'So I'm ruined, am I?' he inquired pleasantly.

'I didn't mean that. But you used to want to create things – now you seem to want to smash them up.'

She trembled at criticizing him in these broad terms – but his enlarging silence frightened her even more. She guessed that something was developing behind the silence, behind the hard, blue eyes . . . It was as though an incalculable story was telling itself inside him, about which she could only guess at in the moments when it broke through the surface.

A few pages later, Dick's voice has become 'serene' and his face shows 'none of the lines of annoyance she had expected. It was even detached.' And then, as if to hint, delicately, at the extent of Dick's achievement, Fitzgerald grants him a kind of lyrical – almost a signature – blessing. 'He turned away from her, toward the veil of starlight over Africa.'

In this light, the episode of supreme humiliation – when he fails to perform a gymnastic feat which he would have 'done with ease only two years ago' – is actually a definitive triumph. Word has already got around that 'Dick is no longer a serious man' and, as if to validate such rumors, he inflicts a kind of tragic slapstick on himself. Three times he tries – even though on the third attempt he 'couldn't have lifted a paper doll' – and three times he fails to get up, his impotence made embarrassingly public. From this point on – Nicole regards him with 'contempt', 'everything he did annoyed her now' – there is nothing to endear him to anyone. No one stands in his way. He is free, free at last, to realise his true and wretched destiny.

2001

James Salter:
The Hunters and *Light Years*

James Salter is the great enigma of post-war American letters. Hailed as a 'writer's writer' (at once the highest accolade and a tacit admission that he has never enjoyed commercial success), he is both underrated and occasionally over-praised. The author information in the UK edition of *Cassada* (first published in the US in 2000) explains that 'with the publication of his second novel in 1961, his reputation as an author was established'. According to Salter himself, in his 1997 memoir *Burning the Days*, this second novel 'disappeared without trace'. (Things are additionally complicated by the way that *Cassada* is actually a revised and re-worked version of that second novel, originally published under a different title, *The Arm of Flesh*.) *Burning the Days* was adorned with admiring sound bites from some of America's most prominent writers, among them Richard Ford, who believes that 'sentence for sentence Salter is the master'. So it's odd, on first encountering these sentences, that a number of them seem ungainly, as if Salter's stylistic distinction renders part of what he intends to convey at variance with the syntactical demands of the language: 'There was an elevator within the steel framework and we had once gone up in it, perhaps in my imagination, even the Olympian view.' This is not a definitive judgement; it takes a while to adjust, to feel at home with the unsettled rhythms of his prose. The uncertainty surrounding Salter's reputation and craft is exacerbated by *A Sport and a Pastime* (1967). An account of a passionate sexual affair in France, Salter's best-known novel is also the one that has fared least well with the passage of time.

All of which makes the re-issue of *The Hunters* and *Light Years*, as Penguin Modern Classics, doubly welcome: a cause for celebration and appraisal. *The Hunters* (1957) was Salter's first novel and remains the most concise expression of his talents. It is based closely on his own experience as a pilot flying combat missions in Korea. The war in the air proceeds in tandem with a near civil war on the ground as the pilots vie with each other to achieve the coveted five kills which will make them aces. The conflicting demands between ensuring the safety of comrades (the 'sacred' duty of the wingman) and the individual daring – recklessness, even – needed to shoot down MiGs threaten to destroy the central character, Cleve Connell.

In *Burning the Days* Salter recalls a friend advising him that 'The original form of storytelling is someone saying, I was there and this is what I beheld.' As soon as he began writing, Salter knew that his time as a fighter pilot would give his storytelling this elemental immediacy and power. (The magnificent climactic scene of the novel involves an incident mentioned briefly in the memoir, when two planes, out of fuel, are forced to glide back to base.) Earlier still, when he was learning to fly, Salter had fallen under the spell of the most famous writer-pilot of them all, Antoine de Saint-Exupéry: 'it was his knowledge I admired, his wholeness of mind, more than his exploits . . . In [his] footsteps I would follow.' (This tradition – or perhaps trajectory is a better word – has recently been extended by Jed Mercurio. Part of his novel, *Ascent* (2007), about Soviet pilots flying MiGs in Korea can be read as a commentary on – or duel with? – Salter, whose novel, presumably, served as template and inspiration.) *Cassada* has at its core an event which is in some ways a re-working of the kind of crisis imaginatively depicted by Saint-Exupéry in *Night Flight* as two lost planes drift past their landing strip, cut off from the earth by darkness and rain clouds. *The Hunters* contains a direct allusion to the master, a translation of the lyricism of *Wind, Sand and Stars* ('Below the sea of clouds lies eternity') into the argot of the jet age, the dawn of the right stuff: 'There was a mission when they conned across seas of eternity, never catching sight of the ground except at the beginning and end.' Not that Salter is lacking in his own lyric gifts. The experience of flight, the mysteries of the sky, remain as intoxicating and magical as they were for the pilots of propeller-driven biplanes:

> Suddenly Pell called out something at three o'clock. Cleve looked. He could not tell what it was at first. Far out, a strange, dreamy rain was falling, silver and wavering. It was a group of drop tanks, tumbling down from above, the fuel and vapour streaming from them. Cleve counted them at a glance. There were a dozen or more, going down like thin cries fading in silence. That many tanks meant MiGs. He searched the sky above, but saw nothing.

The movement of this passage is entirely characteristic: an inventory of the procedural dialogue of the cockpit dissolves into lyrical evocation, which is then identified and absorbed as data – to be computed, worked with, responded to. At the start of the novel, when Cleve is a passenger en route to Korea, gazing out the cabin window, Salter stresses that 'His eye was the flyer's. He saw the hostile mountains, the absence of good landmarks, and the few places flat enough to land in an emergency.' But in Cleve's later straining to make out exactly what he is seeing in the 'dreamy rain' and his failure to see the MiGs that he knows *must* be there Salter hints at a potential flaw in his protagonist's make-up. For pilots the eyes are everything: 'It came down to that, time after time, who could see the farthest.' Cleve's wingman and rival, Pell, has vision so good – 'he can see a bird's nest from forty thousand' – it amounts almost to a kind of second sight.

Everything in the novel is rendered from within the world-view and idiom of the fighter pilots (the planes are almost always referred to as ships!). It is, without question, one of the greatest flying novels ever written. However meticulously and faithfully rendered, though, flying is important not simply as an end in itself but as a test of character, of how one reacts in the face of destiny (again there are echoes of Saint-Exupéry here). You do everything you can to control what happens but at some point – to return to *Burning the Days* – you are left 'facing the unalterable'. Cocooned in his cockpit, as alone 'and isolated as a deep-sea diver', the pilot achieves – or fails to – a state of grace in and through his isolation.

This is at the heart of Salter's ethic of solitary splendour. It is part of the sheer definition of self attained by Rand, the climber-hero of his later novel *Solo Faces* (1979): 'There is something greater than the life of the cities, greater than money and possessions; there is a manhood that can never be taken away. For this, one gives everything.'

Even here there is ambiguity, however. For Rand also basks in recognition. 'A kind of distinction surrounded him, of being marked for a different life. That distinction meant everything.' It is the same with Cleve and the other pilots; their kills have to be recorded on film or vouched for by others to be verified. Cleve craves the bestowal of public acclaim that five kills will grant him. Only when that has been achieved can it be rejected; until then failure stalks him like a curse. On leave in Tokyo Cleve explains to a girl he has met that 'truth doesn't always come from truthful men'. In a defining twist he ultimately achieves his moment of truth through a kind of falsehood; having 'searched the whole heavens for his destiny and godliness' he ends up finding them 'on earth'. His triumph lies in attaining what he has most sought and then voluntarily renouncing it – and all the acclaim that should have gone with it.

In this light it is difficult not to see the fictionalised version of Salter's flying experience in *The Hunters* as a prophetic allegory of his subsequent career as a writer. Cleve longs to succeed, both in the hermetic isolation of the cockpit and through the admiration of his peers. When Salter finished *Light Years* he 'wanted glory' and craved praise, 'widespread praise'. To an extent this was achieved in America. In Britain the novel was published thanks to the intervention of Graham Greene, whose 'opinion of it was higher than the English critics''. This is not just gossipy irrelevance, for in *Light Years* one of Salter's characters addresses the issue nakedly: '"The thing I would really like to know is," Nedra said, "must fame be a part of greatness?"' It is the question that haunted Cleve – and it is a question that brings Nedra's husband Viri to an appalling realisation of his own insufficiency: 'fame was not only part of greatness, it was more. It was the evidence, the only proof. All the rest was nothing, in vain. He who is famous cannot fail; he has already succeeded.' On a general level this explains why Fitzgerald, with all his early success, could wallow in his later, ostensible failure. In Salter's case it offers a dramatic and unusual instance of a writer's work and his reputation coming into mutually illuminating adjacency.

If *The Hunters* is Salter's most perfectly achieved novel, *Light Years* is his strangest, the most complex and ambitious. It depicts the idyllic life of a young couple, Nedra and Viri (possibly the most irritatingly named characters in literature), living in upstate New York. Their lives are bathed in a domestic, earthly version of the crisp radiance that illuminated the pilots in their planes (or, for that matter, Rand on his mountains). 'Autumn morning. The earliest light. The sky is pale above the trees, pure, more mysterious than ever, a sky to dizzy the *fedayeen*, to end the astronomer's night. In it, dim as coins on a beach, fading, shine two last stars.' At first an atmosphere of abundance – economic, familial – pervades the novel. It opens in 1958 and – *pace A Sport and a Pastime* – the passing years have favoured it in one very simple way. Viri is always driving into and out of Manhattan, to work or for dinners. The prospect of having to do that now is enough to fill anyone with dread; back in the late '50s and early '60s the commuter's lot is enviably uncongested.

The novel is so saturated with its own intensity that it is surprising to see the seasons roll quickly by, to witness the narrative extend itself so extravagantly. As Viri and Nedra's marriage grows strained it becomes evident that the stress had been there from the start, was inseparable, in fact, from its apparent or backlit perfection. They both have lovers; their children grow up; friends die or simply drop out of sight; the couple divorce – and the novel follows them after they move, separately, abroad. In a weird way Salter's account of his characters' lives seems both definitive and haphazard, inconclusive. If we take Ian McEwan as the master of a certain kind of novelistic execution whereby every thread and hint is neatly tucked in and subsequently tied up then *Light Years* is chaotic, a draft, full of holes waiting – in vain – to be filled. Incidents that are crucial are not worked through or resolved; affairs are begun but we sometimes learn nothing of how they end (or even develop) . . . And yet there is an assurance about these apparent inadequacies, a purposefulness about the hesitancies.

Salter offers an important guide to the nature of his unusual and oblique form of authorial command in *Burning the Days*. In 1972 he completed a sixty-five-page outline:

> I was nervous and elated. I knew what I wanted: to summarize certain atti-
> tudes towards life, among them that marriage lasted too long. I was perhaps
> thinking of my own. I had in mind a casting back, a final rich confession,
> as it were. There was a line of Jean Renoir's that struck me: The only things
> that are important in life are those you remember. That was the key. It was
> to be a book of pure recall. Everything in the voice of the writer, in his way
> of telling.

With this in mind the book's weirdnesses begin to melt away, its lacunae become part of an essential, overarching design. It becomes an extraordinary, light-inflected narrative made up of defining moments, an unfolding reminder that certain instants can be so charged that their consequences do not merit recounting.

Salter thought, with justification, that he was on to something, but he had trouble persuading a publisher of his intentions. When it was eventually finished and accepted, Salter explains in *Burning the Days*, his editor sent a note that offers a brisk summing-up of his ambiguous status as an American master: 'An absolutely marvellous book in every way, probably.'

Remember Nedra's line about fame and greatness? By the terms of that question, and Viri's reaction to it, it is not just Salter's *reputation* which is changed by *Light Years* being installed as a Modern Classic; the text itself, the very words on the page, are also subtly altered. His editor's qualifying 'probably' can be edited out.

2007

Tobias Wolff: *Old School*

Youth, J.M. Coetzee's first book after the Booker-winning *Disgrace,* was published in the UK as 'a novel' even though it was self-evidently the sequel to *Boyhood,* his memoir of a provincial childhood in South Africa. You could be forgiven for thinking that something similar is going on here. Billed as a novel – a *very* eagerly awaited one, what's more – Tobias Wolff's *Old School* exudes memoirness from every pore. Then, about halfway through, you realise that it's turning, subtly and gradually, into the great novel it was always intended to be.

As with *In Pharaoh's Army,* Wolff's memoir of his time in Vietnam, each section of the new book is built around an incident or episode that is arranged into an aesthetically satisfying and self-contained shape. Chronologically it bridges some of the gap between that phase of Wolff's early adult life and the boyhood recorded in *This Boy's Life.* This is the period in the late 1950s when he has won a scholarship to a prestigious prep school on the east coast. Wolff immerses us in this world with the unfailing fidelity of observation, gesture and phrase that one would expect. Such, such are the joys!

The school has a proud literary tradition, maintained, each year, by a competition in which the boys submit a piece of writing to be judged by an eminent writer who then visits the school. All the pupils benefit from this but only the winner is granted a personal audience. The dramatic portraits of these visiting legends are considerable feats of anecdotal recreation in their own right. One year it's Robert Frost (snowy-haired, red-cheeked, homely as a favourite uncle and imposing as Mount Rushmore), the next it's Ayn Rand (a sub-Nietzschean apostle of her own personality cult, instilling awe – swiftly followed by intense disillusion – in all who meet her). All this is as nothing, however, compared with the tremor that goes through the school when it's announced that the next visitor will be none other than Ernest Hemingway.

The narrator – who, like the school, is unnamed – is so besotted with Hemingway that he has taken to typing out stories like 'The Killers' word for word as a form of literary apprenticeship. It's as if Borges' 'Pierre Menard, Author of the *Quixote*' has been relocated and re-imagined in strictly realist mode. Such is the narrator's desperation to win an audience with Papa that he's unable even to *start* writing a story of his own. The desire to become a writer effectively stops him being one. As Fitzgerald put it in *This Side of Paradise*, 'It was always the becoming he dreamed of, never the being.' At his wit's end, crushed by the weight of his own literary yearning, he embarks on a simple and ultimately devastating subterfuge.

It is difficult to summarise much of the story of *Old School* without sabotaging the experience of reading it. Suffice it to say that around this point one starts to realise that an apparently simple book, which has been engrossing and enjoyable from the first page, is assuming the shape of a complex masterpiece. It also begins to look like the culmination of everything that Wolff has written. In these circumstances the urge to cross-refer to the earlier books becomes irresistible.

Wolff first established a reputation as a writer of stories. One of these, 'Smokers', from his first collection, *In the Garden of the North American Martyrs*, is set in a school that closely resembles the one in the novel. The ban on smoking in both places is absolute (immediate expulsion, no exceptions) and, in both novel and story, the narrator narrowly escapes detection. In the story, moreover, the narrator helps out a class-mate by inventing 'a fictionally interesting person' as a way of fulfilling an assignment his friend is struggling with. In real life the young Wolff had by then already invented 'a fictionally interesting person', namely himself. *This Boy's Life* explains how he only obtained his scholarship by systematic deceit: 'I felt full of things that had to be said, full of stifled truth. That was what I thought I was writing – the truth. It was truth known only to me, but I believed in it more than I believed in the facts arraigned against it.' (While he is frank about the way he entered the school under false pretences he is elliptical about how he made his exit. 'In my last year I was asked to leave,' he writes. 'But that's another story.' Is *Old School* a version of that story?)

Actually, Tobias was not the first to fess up to his early transgression. In *The Duke of Deception* (1979), his brother's memoir of their father, Geoffrey Wolff tells how Toby gained admittance to the Hill School in Pottstown, Pennsylvania, 'by forging letters of recommendation' and 'a letter-perfect transcript on a stolen form'. According to Geoffrey, 'Toby had my father's facial gestures and facial tics, and certain maneuvers with his hands and voice that made him resemble our old man more than I did, as he still does.' Their father – who, Geoffrey informs us, despised *This Side of Paradise* but loved the line from it quoted earlier – was a serial fraudster who ended up in jail. The influence of the errant father and his gift for multifarious deceptions – or fictions – is felt in much of Tobias' writing. 'He appalled me and frightened me,' he confesses in *Pharaoh's Army*, 'because I saw in myself the same tendencies that had brought him to grief.' 'I didn't want to be like him,' he continues. 'I wanted to be a man of honor.' Honour: the fates of several characters in *Old School* – including the narrator's – come to hang on that single word.

At odd points readers familiar with these various records of Tobias' life will notice a number of inconsistencies appearing between the world of the novel and that of the memoirs. We learn, to take a tiny example, that the narrator stopped going to confession after his mother died; in *This Boy's Life* she meets him off the train when he eventually leaves school. It is difficult to separate the narrator of the novel from the Toby of record but, as the former realises when he is reading Hemingway, 'a certain confusion of author and character [is] intended'. This 'deliberate blurring' is apparent again when, after leaving school and doing an assortment of odd jobs, the narrator 'enlisted in the army and ended up in Vietnam'. Simultaneously emphasising the similarity and generalising beyond this particular instance, he adds, 'If this looks like a certain kind of author's bio, that's no accident.'

The narrator of *Old School* goes on to become a successful writer who, on the evidence presented, is all but indistinguishable from its author. As the novel proceeds the layers of fabrication and truth become more and more entwined and mutually dependent. That was exactly how Wolff senior, the prodigal father, lived his life; in this fictive rendering of the past, the father never once allows 'that his son had anything to be pardoned for'. This line once again draws one back to the 'official' record of the memoirs, specifically the letter quoted by Geoffrey in which he asks their father to 'suppose for a moment, thinking back to your fictions, that you could will them to be true. Would this make you happy?'

Having come this far the reader trusts Wolff as unreservedly as the fictive father does his son. One has faith in his command of the novel form even when, in the final section, he swerves sharply from his own path to tell the story of one of the teachers at the school (who, until this late stage, has barely featured except at the level of hearsay). Like everything else in the book this bold disruption of narrative expectations turns out to be assured, measured and, ultimately, extremely moving. There is just one line – and it is, needless to say, at the centre of the fictive carpet – that one *has* to take issue with: 'The life that produces writing can't be written about.' Every line in the book – including this one! – proves it to be untrue: mere fiction, in fact.

2003

Richard Ford:
The Lay of the Land

Richard Ford's writing is the product of such powerful convergences that, viewed in context, there is a certain inevitability about it. Saul Bellow's first novel, *Dangling Man* (1944), began with the narrator, Joseph, explicitly booting aside the Hemingway model of fiction as an imaginative transcription of action – fighting bulls, shooting big game – in favour of a record of 'inward transactions'. Instead, Joseph talks about himself and his troubles.

Appropriately enough, Ford's first book, the hard-boiled *A Piece of My Heart*, was runner-up for the 1976 Hemingway Award. His second, *The Ultimate Good Luck*, was so tough that the opening paragraph was boiled down to a single sentence: 'Quinn knew he needed to get lucky.' Then, in *The Sportswriter* (1986), Ford combined the clarity of Hemingway's declarative sharpness with Bellow's legacy of loquacious inwardness in the voice and consciousness of Frank Bascombe. Thirty-eight, living 'the normal applauseless life of us all', in Haddam, New Jersey, Frank's 'no-frills voice' uncovered 'simple truth by a straightforward application of the facts'. There were no Joycean epiphanies (denounced as falsehoods), just a steady drip of incident and insight that posited resignation as a mode of enlightenment.

By the time of *Independence Day* (1995), Frank, who had quit serious writing to become a sportswriter, had quit sports writing to sell real estate. He was still in Haddam, still contemplating life with that deadpan tone of 'low-wattage wonder'. The Bellovian gift of the extended gab was more pronounced, there was a fair bit of slack, but, at a moment's notice – *pow!* – we could be snapped back into the midst of scenes as tangible as the houses Frank was flogging.

The Lay of the Land takes place in 2000. Frank is fifty-five, still working as a realtor, but has moved out to a place overlooking the ocean. He's doing well, or would be except: a) he has prostate cancer, b) his second wife has left him to go back to a previous husband who for years was missing, presumed dead and, c) things are about to get worse. As in the previous books the action (such as it is) is organised around a holiday, this time Thanksgiving. Frank's daughter, Clarissa, back in the heterosexual fold after a happy stint as a lesbian, is coming home to visit; so is Paul, the son with whom Frank undertook the nearly calamitous trip recorded in *Independence Day*. Various other characters from the earlier books crop up, most in worse shape than they were last time around. As before, these and others appear in sharp focus the moment they shuffle onto the page: 'It's as if Lloyd became an undertaker because one day he gazed in a mirror and noticed he looked like one.' Frank goes about his business, showing properties to potential buyers, preparing for the holiday and coping with whatever life throws or fails to throw at him.

A lot of *Independence Day* was spent following Frank as he drove up 80, headed west to Hackensack and so forth. Here the reader is perched on his shoulder like a slo-mo speed camera, monitoring his every move as he stops at a red light on Franklin, turns left here and – because of the prostate – gets out for a piss there. Hand in hand with an ongoing inventory of the area's real estate, the narrative tailgating is exhaustive and a little exhausting. And then, in the midst of this cataloguing of the quotidian, epiphanies (of sorts)! During one of his piss-stops Frank comes across 'a chartreuse cell phone, a little Nokia that's been tossed in the urinal as a gesture, I suppose, of dissatisfaction with its service'. Discoveries like these prompt Frank to drift off into 'quasi-philosophical' wonderings about the world as he finds it. 'This civilization, future thinkers will conclude, liked beer. They favoured wood-paper products as receptacles for semen and other bodily excretions. They suffered haemorrhoids, occasional incontinence and erectile dysfunctions not known to subsequent generations.'

That's on page 45. It's a terrific passage but already, by then, you're wondering if the Bellovian bequest – yak on and on about anything – could do with cauterising. (Tom Wolfe, remember, defined hell as a bus ride across America with only *Mr. Sammler's Planet* for company.) *The Lay of the Land* is full of good things. Like its predecessors it is an unerring thesaurus of gestural tells, a trove of briskly rendered asides ('We shook hands limply, in the manner of a cold prisoner exchange on the Potsdam bridge'); but it is also full of unheeded warnings about the lay of the narrative land.

Good, bad or great, *all* writers are like inept criminals: they leave their prints on everything they touch. In this case readers need no training in literary forensics to see the text offering clues about why it feels bloated. Or, to put it another way, Bascombe has become a mole, subtly working against his creator's best interests by giving voice to the reader's doubts about the distension of which he is the agent. 'I was vamping,' Frank confesses at one point; at another he dismisses the background to his present crisis as 'a chronicle I wasn't that riveted by' – this only pages after 'Cutting (blessedly) to the chase.' More simply, we have, variously: 'On and on, and *on* and on'; 'Wrong, wrongety, wrong, wrong, wrong'; 'No, no, no, no, and no again'; and, more simply still, 'Yakkedy, yakkedy, yakkedy'.

As the words accumulate so the temptation mounts to read the book in accordance with Frank's own 'telescoped version of the whole cancer rigmarole: blah, blah, blah, blah, in earnest hope of gaining blah, blah, blah, blah, and better blah, blah, blah, blah . . .' Over the years Frank has learnt that 'you rarely miss anything by cutting most people off after a couple of sentences'. There are, likewise, few novels that would not benefit from having some sentences cut from them. The ontological problem with *his* style of indefinitely extended narration, though, is that once you start cutting it's nigh-on impossible to know when to stop. The irony, of course, is that there is something perfectly Bascombian about this predicament.

2006

Denis Johnson: *Tree of Smoke*

Who'd have thought that Denis Johnson had this kind of whopping, mega-ton novel in him? His last, *The Name of the World*, ran to a mere 120 pages but still managed to sneak onto the shortlist for the bi-annual *Irish Times* International Fiction Prize. Consider that for a moment. A slender, almost plotless piece of ostensibly slipshod prose was judged – alongside substantial competition from Michael Ondaatje and Philip Roth – to be one of the best novels published in the English language over the two-year period 2000–01. What made it so intriguing was that it seemed to be the work of a writer who, at some level, did not know how to write at all – and yet knew exactly what he was doing. *Jesus' Son*, his best-known book, is even skimpier: a collection of stories about strung-out losers unfolding in meticulously addled prose overspilling with transcendence, lyricism or just addledness. 'Where are my women now, with their sweet wet words and ways, and the miraculous balls of hail popping in a green translucence in the yards?' A writer, then, of distinctly American graininess: a metaphysical illiterate, a junkyard angel.

Needless to say, he is not everybody's cup of tea. After I'd recommended *The Name of the World* a highly literary friend responded with an email – Subject: 'The Correction of Taste' – contrasting Johnson's self-described 'zoo of wild utterances' with Bellow's infinite loquacity. For me, the effect of the comparison was counter-productive: Bellow instantly seemed as old and venerable as George Eliot.

And now we have what is in some ways a Victorian novel: 600 pages, zillions of characters and a plot that offers a key to the variously contested mythologies of American involvement in South East Asia (Vietnam, principally, but with substantial sections in the Philippines as well). What makes it a distinctly modern key is that, with every turn, the promised revelation is more securely concealed. We are talking CIA here; we are talking, more generally, about a literary mission that invites comparison with DeLillo, Robert Stone, Conrad (especially towards the end) and, of course, Graham Greene (one of the characters is undecided whether he is a Quiet American or just an ugly one).

However extensively the novel's story is summarised, it is going to be sold short. It starts in 1963, a year in which nobody gives a damn about Larkin, Chesil Beach or Lady Chatterley. 'Tree of Smoke' is some kind of CIA project. Skip, an operative of uncertain status but intense dedication, is working for the Colonel (who also happens to be his uncle). Skip has an affair with Kathy, a Seventh-Day Adventist whose aid-worker husband has been kidnapped, possibly killed. Years pass. History – as they used to say of shit – happens. Kurtz-like, the Colonel's methods become increasingly unsound. (Martin Sheen's famous line from *Apocalypse Now* also holds good for Johnson: 'I don't see any method at all.') At the sharp end are the seriously messed-up Houston brothers (who previously saw service in Johnson's very first novel, *Angels*). Trung, a North Vietnamese – who once tried to assassinate the Colonel – is being recruited as a double agent, but, at the same time, Trung's assassination is being plotted by the same guy – a German – who killed a priest with a blow pipe in the Philippines, back in 1963. Twenty years later, in Arizona, the Houston brothers . . . Ah, forget it. There may be no smoke without fire but in this case you can't see the wood for the tree of smoke or something.

People and events loom out of the dense narrative foliage and then disappear. The writing can appear humdrum. Stuck in a quagmire of incantatory banality, the dialogue seems to be contributing nothing except its own capacity to keep on coming. But . . .

Whatever else might be said about my talents as a reader, my ability to quit is undisputed. I can give up on any book – and I never for a moment considered abandoning this one, even when it seemed

1. 'Palm Beach' by Jacob Holdt.
See 'Jacob Holdt's America', page 33.

2. 'Acropolis, Athens, Greece' by Martin Parr.
See 'Martin Parr's *Small World*', page 43.

3. 'Ruins of Drop City, Trinidad, Colorado, August 1995.'
Photography and text by Joel Sternfeld. See 'Joel Sternfeld's Utopian Visions', page 49.

Ruins of Drop City, Trinidad, Colorado, August 1995.

Three of the original founders of Drop City met as art students in Lawrence, Kansas, in 1961. They referred to their practice of painting rocks and dropping them from a loft window onto the busy street below as 'Drop Art.'

By 1965 the founders' desire to live rent free and create art without the distraction of employment led them to a six-acre goat pasture outside Trinidad, Colorado, which they purchased for $450. Naming their community after their gravity-driven art was the easy part; building it a little harder. But having recently attended a lecture by Buckminster Fuller and now joined by a would-be dome builder from Albuquerque, they began with scrap materials and visionary optimism. Sheet metal was stripped off car roofs (for which they paid a nickel or a dime) and attached to the grid of a dome. These building materials not only provided shelter, but they also emblemized the group's refusal to participate in consumerist society. Money, clothing and cars were shared, and they lived as quasi-dumpster divers.

Initially the community flourished. With a core group of twelve, it functioned as the founders had intended, a hotbed of art-making. But a steady flow of publicity in underground and mainstream media, encouraged by resident Peter Rabbit, led to a torrent of guests. It has been reported that Bob Dylan, Timothy Leary and Jim Morrison visited, but the historian's chestnut, the primary account, may be less than reliable when it comes to the 1960s. By the time the community decided to abandon its open-door policy, it was too late: the founding members had left, and conditions had taken hold that would bring about a final dissolution in 1973. In 1978 the site was sold; proceeds helped rent space in New York City for exhibitions of the group's work and to publish it in *Crisscross* magazine.

The domes sat on the land of A. Blasi and Sons Trucking Company until recently, when they succumbed to gravity.

4. 'Peter's Houseboat, Winona, Minnesota', from *Sleeping by the Mississippi* by Alec Soth. See 'Alec Soth: Riverrun', page 53.

5. Photograph by Todd Hido.
See 'Saving Grace: Todd Hido', page 81.

6. 'Oil Fields #19a' (Belridge, California) by Edward Burtynsky.
See 'Edward Burtynsky', page 93.

7. 'Figures in a Building' by J.M.W. Turner, circa 1830–35.
See 'Turner and Memory', page 99.

8. 'Danaid' from *Apropos Rodin* by Jennifer Gough-Cooper.
See 'The Awakening of Stones: Rodin', page 103.

to be going nowhere. Even though the story had disappeared like a path overrun by vegetation the novel retained its uniquely slippery kind of traction.

Why? Because, at any moment it was capable of stumbling into the sharpest focus. Some kind of slanted truth seemed always close to hand. Let me give a tiny example and comparison. In Alan Hollinghurst's *The Spell* we learn that the characters all felt a bit 'hectic' from drinking wine at lunch. So much is fixed so exactly with that single, perfectly chosen word. Here is Johnson's swilled-out version of the same observation as applied to a sailor on shore leave in Honolulu: 'He strolled the waterfront with the beer thudding inside his head.' Ditto. Now imagine that sloshy accuracy about beer 'thudding' around your head cropping up throughout the massively distended narrative that is *Tree of Smoke*. There are hundreds of things like this – 'He stood right in the crashing-down light of the tropical morning'; 'The dark was thick enough to drink'; 'The smoke from the burn piles of deadfall and trash had the odour of legend, the chicken droppings, even' – and you never see them coming. I skipped (the central character's name dares the reader to do just that) but always had to go back and read properly from exactly the point where I began skimming.

Central to Johnson's dramatised world-view is the belief that it is the mangled and damaged, the downtrodden, who are best placed to achieve – 'withstand' is probably a better verb – enlightenment. It's like an inversion of the idea of the law of the jungle where trees vie with each other to reach for the sky, the light. For Johnson the real revelations are at ground level, amid the degradation of mush and swamp. As such there are moments of extreme ugliness and horror. A snake – 'a brindle python longer than any of them, longer than all of them together' – tries to make a getaway from the man pursuing it. 'He ran after and brought the rake down hard, hoping to trap the reptile's head, but sank the splines rather farther down its spine, and like that, with frightening energy, the snake wrenched the handle free of his hands and swivelled off wildly, still skewered, dragging the rake into the bush.' In 1968 a GI spoons out the eye of a VC prisoner and James Houston – the moral equivalent, one might have hoped, of the slave who tries to prevent the blinding of Gloucester in *King Lear* – yells: 'Give it to the motherfucker. Make him holler.' Thus encouraged the soldier 'grabbed the man's eyeballs hanging by the purple optic nerves and turned the red veiny side so the pupils looked back at the empty sockets and the pulp in the cranium. "Take a good look at yourself, you piece of shit."' A little while earlier James had emerged from a firefight in the aftermath of which 'every blurred young face he looked at gave him back a message of brotherly love'. But then his buddy got wounded and ended up in hospital 'like the Frankenstein monster laid out in pieces, wired up for the jolt that would wake him to a monster's confused and tortured finish'. The book is a monster in that sense, jolted constantly into life by its own damaged circuitry, a mass of spare parts (which are essential and which superfluous is difficult to say) all held together with a relentlessly deranged sense of purpose and – for good measure – suture-quotations from Artaud and Cioran.

Johnson is all over the place and he is an artist of strange diligence. It is as if his skewed relationship to the sentence – not really knowing what one is and yet knowing exactly what to do with it – operates, here, at the level of structure. *Tree of Smoke* is as excessive and messy as *Moby Dick*. Anything further removed from the tucked-up, hospital-corners school of British fiction is hard to imagine. It's a big, dirty, unmade bed of a book, and once you settle in you're in no hurry to get out.

2007

Ian McEwan: *Atonement*

The twists and turns of Ian McEwan's fiction are built on a knack for simply sustained illusion: when he writes 'glass of beer' we do not just see it; we are willing to drink from it vicariously. The ballooning accident (imaginatively transcribed from footage of an actual incident) which immediately immersed us in *Enduring Love* is a spectacular example, but the ability to actualise the invented animates every nuance of his work. The novels' psychological acuity derives, always, from their fidelity to a precisely delineated reality. Needless to say, the more disturbing or skewed that reality (in the early stories and novels, most obviously) the more finely McEwan tunes his readers to it. Moral ambiguity and doubt are thereby enhanced – rather than resolved – by clarity of presentation. This is why the themes of the novels (with the exception of the enjoyably forgettable *Amsterdam*) linger and resonate beyond the impeccable neatness of their arrangement. He is, in other words, a thoroughly traditional original.

Atonement does not feel at first like a book by McEwan. The opening is almost perversely ungripping. Instead of the expected sharpness of focus the first seventy or so pages comprise a lengthy summary of shifting impressions. One longs for a cinematic clarity and concentration of dialogue and action but such interludes dissolve before our – and the participants' – eyes.

Unlike Martin Amis, say, or Salman Rushdie, McEwan is an invisible rather than flamboyant stylist. Even so, the pallid qualifiers and disposable adverbs (a 'gently rocking' sheet of water, the 'coyly drooping' head of a nettle) come as a surprise. The language used to distil the scene – a gathering of the Tallis family at their country house on a sweltering day in 1935 – serves also as a wash that partially obscures it.

Various characters come and go but the novel, at this point, seems populated mainly by its literary influences. Chief among these is Virginia Woolf. The technique is not stream of consciousness so much as 'a slow drift of association', 'the hovering stillness of nothing much seeming to happen'. The book later contains a critique of its own early pages – or at least of the draft from which they derive – in the guise of a letter from Cyril Connolly, editor of *Horizon*, who advises that 'such writing can become precious when there is no sense of forward movement'. The requisite propulsion is provided by the un-expected intrusion, as it were, of two other novelists from the inter-war years.

Cecilia, the eldest daughter of the family in whose house we are imaginatively lodged, was at Cambridge with Robbie, the son of the Tallises' housekeeper, whose education was funded by Cecilia's father. They become aware, on this sultry day, of some kind of current – animosity? irreconcilable attraction? – passing between them. Robbie tries to articulate this in a letter, at the bottom of which he scribbles the naked truth: 'In my dreams I kiss your cunt.' He discards that draft and intends to send another, blander one but, in keeping with Freud's analysis of such slips, accidentally sends the shocking letter to Cecilia via her adolescent sister, Briony, who opens and reads it. The consequences of the go-between coming between them like this are liberating and incriminating in unequal measure. What Lawrence called the 'dirty little secret' of sex besmirches the Tallises' world or – as Lawrence would have insisted – reveals how besmirched that world really is. It is as if quotations from the obscene bits of McEwan's early stories had been daubed on the walls of Brideshead.

Another crisis soon follows, this one imported from E.M. Forster's India. Cecilia's young cousin, Lola, is sexually assaulted in the grounds of the house. Lola does not know by whom but Briony – an aspiring writer – compounds her earlier transgression by convincing her and everyone else (except Cecilia) that Robbie is the culprit. Unlike the incident in the Marabar Caves, this one does not end in a retraction and Robbie, the proletarian interloper, is convicted.

In the second section of the novel the pastel haze of the first part gives way to an acrid, graphic account of Robbie's later experiences in the British rout at Dunkirk. McEwan is here playing more obviously to his strengths. The highly decorated novelist deploys his research in an effective if familiar pattern of narrative manoeuvres. Refracted through Robbie's exhausted, wounded view of history in the making, the retreat unfolds in a series of vividly realised details and encounters. In the atrocious context of battle, Briony's apparently motiveless crime is rendered almost insignificant. 'But what was guilt these days? It was cheap. Everyone was guilty, and no one was.' In similar fashion, the partial democratisation of Britain that results from the social upheaval of war is prefigured by Cecilia's turning her back on her family and allying herself with Robbie, the working-class graduate (whose smouldering sense of grievance and displacement will be vehemently embodied on the post-war stage by Jimmy Porter).

Part three shifts back to London where Briony is training as a nurse, struggling to cope with the influx of casualties from Dunkirk. McEwan's command of visceral shock is here anchored in a historical setting thoroughly authenticated by his archival imagination. The elliptical style of the opening part has no place in these pages as the graphic horrors of injury, mutilation and death pile up before Briony's eyes. She loosens the bandage around a patient's head and his brain threatens to slop out into her hands. Does this devotion to the victims of war wash her hands of her earlier guilt? Does her atonement depend on Robbie's survival? Or can it – can at-one-ment – be achieved through the eventual realisation of her literary ambitions, through a novel such as the one we are reading? Who can grant atonement to the novelist whose God-like capacity to create and re-work the world means that there is no higher authority to whom appeal can be made?

It is a tribute to the scope, ambition and complexity of *Atonement* that it is difficult to give an adequate sense of what is going on in the novel without pre-empting – and thereby diminishing – the reader's experience of it. Suffice to say our initial hesitancy about style, our fear that, for once, McEwan is not in control of his material, all play their part in his larger purpose.

On the one hand McEwan – to go back to something hinted at earlier – seems to be retrospectively inserting his name in the pantheon of British novelists of the '30s and '40s. But he is also, of course, doing more than this, demonstrating and exploring what the mature Briony comes to see as a larger 'transformation . . . being worked in human nature itself'. The novels of Woolf and Lawrence did not just record this transformation; they were instrumental in bringing it about. McEwan uses his novel to show how this subjective or interior transformation can *now* be seen to have interacted with the larger march of twentieth-century history.

While he was working on *The French Lieutenant's Woman* John Fowles reminded himself that this was 'not something one of the Victorian novelists forgot to write' but it was 'perhaps something one of them failed to write'. A similar impulse underwrites *Atonement*. It is less about a novelist harking nostalgically back to the consoling certainties of the past than it is about creatively extending and hauling a defining part of the British literary tradition up to and into the twenty-first century.

2001

Alan Hollinghurst:
The Line of Beauty

Alan Hollinghurst's first novel, *The Swimming Pool Library*, was set in the pre-AIDS summer of 1983, 'the last summer of its kind there was ever to be'. This historical moment is the starting-point for Hollinghurst's fourth and most ambitious novel. After coming down from Oxford to begin a doctorate on Henry James, the aptly named Nicholas Guest becomes a lodger in the family home of his friend Toby Fedden, whose father, Gerald, is a Tory MP. Like the mirror in the hallway of the Fedden's vast Notting Hill house, Nick 'monitor[s] all comings and goings', while keeping his own discreetly under wraps. After his first date – in the sense of first *ever* – with Leo, a young black man, Nick takes advantage of his keyholder's privileges to use the private garden in the square at the back of the house where they have deliriously unprotected sex. This episode could be said to stand for the whole first part of the novel: Nick's excited entrance to the twilight of the *belle époque* of gay life and, courtesy of the Feddens, his sudden access to the *haut monde* of the English ruling class. The balmy west London nights are imbued in these pages with the lyric promise that captivated another Nick – Carraway – as he observed guests coming and going on the lawn of his fabulous neighbour, Gatsby.

Hollinghurst is as infatuated by wealth and elegance as Fitzgerald; a first frisson of unease – what in *The Swimming Pool Library* is called 'a faint flicker of calamity' – comes when Leo turns up at the house. Gerald answers the door, calls Nick and stands back 'to see if there was going to be any kind of trouble'. Gerald then retires to the kitchen where he is overheard explaining that the visitor is 'some pal of Nick's . . .' and a few moments later, 'No, black chappie.' Nick and Leo are still at the door when a cab pulls up.

> It stopped just in front of them, and the driver clawed round through his open window to release the rear door. When the passenger (who Nick knew was Lady Partridge) didn't emerge, a very rare thing happened and the cabbie got out of the cab and yanked the door open himself, standing aside with a flourish which she acknowledged dryly as she stepped out.

Nick politely introduces Lady Partridge to Leo:

> She smiled and said, '*How* do you do?' in an extraordinarily cordial tone, in which none the less something final was conveyed – the certainty that they would never speak again.

I quote at length – though not at the length I would like; the temptation is to go on quoting paragraph after wonderful paragraph – because this little incident reveals many of the qualities that make this novel such a magnificent achievement. Plenty of English writers can come up with smart turns of phrase and lines of occasional beauty, but Hollinghurst's are the product, always, of precision and patience of observation. Unerringly receptive to the tell of gesture, his astuteness probes the psychological make-up of even a minor character like Toby's girlfriend Sophie, who makes a mock-complaint 'with the crossness that hides a sweetness that hides a toughness'. All of this, needless to say, is interwoven and substantiated by a deft attentiveness to what, even within a narrow sampling of society, are the endless subtleties of class distinction – to say nothing of the 'shock of class difference' when Nick visits Leo's family.

A familiar type in Hollinghurst's fiction, Nick is shy, bookish. Initially he peers into 'the world of actual existing gayness' with 'recurrent vague snobbery'. Snobbery and the way that it can be the product both of a capacity for fine discrimination and its opposite is as central to the book as its gayness. Gayness democratises Nick, stretches his social horizons – even if only through the search for sex – beyond those of his straight friend Toby.

This proves crucial even when we jump ahead four years to find Nick perched pleasantly in the world of gayness *and* extreme wealth. By now he is involved in a clandestine affair with Wani – Lebanese, gorgeous, loaded and exquisitely depraved – who introduces Nick to a new line of beauty: cocaine (which, back in 1987, cost a whopping 'one-twenty a gram').

Wani's limitless carnality echoes the unbridled hedonism of bad-boy Danny in Hollinghurst's last novel, *The Spell*. For some readers the exclusively male homosexual milieu of that book was indicative of an imaginative shortcoming so overt that it amounted to a tacit misogyny. Consciously or not, *The Line of Beauty* is a rebuttal of such claims. Toby's sister, the vividly realised Catherine, is in some ways the most important character in the book, its wayward, economically implicated conscience. A more daring feat of imagination, though, is to have Margaret Thatcher turn up at a party at Gerald's house. By this stage Nick, like many other characters in the book, is courting calamity. In a surge of coke-induced confidence he asks the Prime Minister to dance. Perhaps it is to flag the dual audacity of character and author that Hollinghurst has Nick observe of The Lady that 'she noticed nothing, and yet she remembered everything'. Which, as Hollinghurst is certainly aware, is pretty much how Maxime Du Camp remembered Flaubert!

Not that Flaubert is the book's presiding literary spirit. After the Thatcher party Nick and Wani end up snorting charlie off an edition of Henry James. A similar point has been made earlier when a dinner guest asks Nick 'what would Henry James have made of us?' Nick replies, 'He'd have been very kind to us, he'd have said how wonderful we were and how beautiful we were, he'd have given us incredibly subtle things to say, and we wouldn't have realised until just before the end that he'd seen right through us.'

In describing the arc of his own novel in this way is Hollinghurst succumbing to the hubris he dissects? Most definitely not. There are moments where he falls short of his own standards of subtlety and settles for something approaching satire. When Nick is reading John Berryman we know that an authorial trap is being baited for Lady Partridge (who obligingly launches into a discussion of John *Betjeman*).

Such lapses are rare indeed. More characteristic is the moment when Gerald smiles at the person beside him with 'the fine glaze of pre-occupation of someone about to make a speech'. Or the glimpse of a woman at the party, 'sedately jiving' with 'a look of exhausted good manners'. There are literally thousands of impeccably nuanced touches like this in the novel. Hollinghurst, in James' own words, is one on whom nothing is lost.

In the course of a spat with James, H.G. Wells grumpily concluded 'I had rather be called a journalist than an artist, that is the essence of it.' *The Line of Beauty* makes one aware of how many contemporary novelists might better be described as feature writers with a twist of plot. Hollinghurst reminds us that the vaulting claims made by James on behalf of the novel – 'the force and beauty of its process' – still hold good today.

2004

Lorrie Moore:
A Gate at the Stairs

Did it matter – did it gnaw away at her – that in spite of the high critical standing enjoyed by her stories Lorrie Moore had not come up with the big novel by which writers, American ones especially, tend to be judged? Yes, there was *Anagrams* (1986), but the fact that a third of it also ended up in last year's *Collected Stories* slightly undermined its claims to unity. And then there was *Who Will Run the Frog Hospital?* (1994) – nice enough but suggesting that, like a boxer moving up a weight division, litheness was having to compensate for lack of bulk. The stories, meanwhile, got better, deeper, darker and – yes – *heavier*, but maybe a voice and talent so exquisitely adapted to the shaped imperatives of brevity would come to be defined and measured by what it *couldn't* do. 'I can't do this,' says the distraught Mother-Writer in the famous story 'People Like That Are the Only People Here'. 'I can do quasi-amusing phone dialogue. I do the *careful ironies of daydreams*. I do *the marshy ideas upon which intimate life is built* . . .' Hence the mix of excitement and trepidation which even adoring readers will bring to her third novel. Would it be great? Would Moore prove that she was not synonymous with less?

Hell, yes, it is and she does. You can sit back and have the time of your life reading *A Gate at the Stairs*, if you're prepared to make a bunny hop of critical faith: what might be called – I'm showing my age here – the Jimmy Clitheroe Concession.

Moore was born in 1957; her narrator, Tassie, is looking back to the time, shortly after 9/11, when she was a student in the Midwest town of Troy. At the alleged time of writing she is in her mid-twenties but the voice and, to a lesser extent, the *eyes* are those of someone old enough to be her mother.

Lorrie M's characters and books have always been light-footed. *Self-Help*, her first collection of stories, was all wit and sad dazzle. *Anagrams* was so loaded with gags that the reader suffered occasional quip fatigue. No surprise, then, that Tassie has a GSOH, but for someone claiming to be 'fresh from childhood' she seems to be lugging around an extra quarter-century of adult life. A couple of times she remarks on the quirks of 'our generation' – the way, for example, that 'everything either "sucked" or was "awesome"' – but they're exactly the things that strike people of Moore's and my generation.

It's tricky. The main symptom of over-ageing in this coming-of-age novel is also intrinsic to its effect. Precocity enables you to play the piano at six but wisdom – like the 'half-life of regret' that also haunts these pages – only comes later. You find it, as Blake knew, in the desolate market – where few come to buy.

This is not to minimise the purchases made there – the grief visited upon and witnessed – by Tassie in the brief period covered by the novel. Short of cash, she gets a part-time, all-consuming job baby-sitting for a middle-aged couple who are adopting a mixed-race baby. Much of the book details Tassie's time with the foster mother, Sarah, and her adopted child, Emmie. Smuggled – the word turns out to be more apt than one might imagine – into an overwhelmingly white town, Emmie's arrival prompts Sarah to organise a series of evenings in which other mixed families serve as a scathing mock-chorus on the state of race relations in idyllic-seeming Troy.

The neurotically energetic Sarah runs a ludicrously upmarket restaurant whose potatoes are grown by Tassie's dad. At Christmas Tassie goes home to the family farm where her brother, Robert, is poised to join the army. She will return there during the intensely moving – and, in places, brilliantly weird – final phase of the book. So the immediate focus of the novel – life in a college town – is framed by the immensity of the surrounding prairie whose seasons and endlessly changing monotony are captured in a series of virtuoso passages. (Moore, in this book, is very consciously the heir of Willa Cather.)

Tassie learns that despair means 'mistaking a small world for a large one and a large one for a small' but how to avoid such an error when small and large – college and prairie – are prey to the same implacable meteorological and historical forces?

But let's stick, for a moment, with the small stuff, with Moore's eye for absurdist, hi-def detail: the mouth of the meth addict with its 'crooked teeth, bits of shell awash on a reef of gum'; the fortune cookie that looks like 'a short paper nerve baked in an ear'; the wonderful, late-night glimpse of married life when Tassie overhears Sarah saying to her husband: 'You emptied the top rack of the dishwasher but not the bottom, so the clean dishes have gotten all mixed up with the dirty ones – and now you want to have sex?' There's tons of this kind of thing, cute and psychologically acute, but there's also the sense of something sky-vast and doom-laden, 'full of sorrow and truth', bearing down from the past or about to loom up from the future.

The past trauma turns out to be Sarah's, though it will taint the present and be passed on to Emmie, one of whose first attempts at speech is 'Uh-oh!': 'She already knew both the sound and the language of things going wrong.' The future history, so to speak, is latent in Robert's posting to Afghanistan and by the way that the Brazilian boy Tassie is dating turns out – a tad implausibly – to be . . .

Ah, but that would be telling, wouldn't it? Critics are not supposed to give the game away even though certain works – the best ones, arguably – are not harmed by spoilers. On first reading *A Gate at the Stairs* one can become not frustrated exactly but a bit impatient with Moore's determinedly lackadaisical way of proceeding. Second time around, when you know what's going to happen, when you give yourself up to the book's unusual and distinctive rhythm, it quivers on the brink of being a masterpiece. That quivering, that slight feeling of uncertainty (like 'candlelight vibrating the room'), is entirely appropriate given Moore's hesitant engagement with the demands of a big novel and the protracted gestation of this, her eventual response and solution. Uninterested in narrative locomotion Moore advances her story while appearing to let it drift sideways, roll backwards or even, at times, to stall. In the middle of Tassie's first conversation with

Sarah – at a point in the novel when convention decrees that *this* scene and *these* characters are fixed in the reader's mind – Tassie remembers instead how her father 'took to driving his combine down country roads to deliberately slow up traffic. "I had them backed up seventeen deep," he once boasted to my mom.' And after a while, he might have added, none of them wanted to be any place else. They were glad to be along for the ride.

2009

Don DeLillo: *Point Omega*

Don DeLillo's spectacular career seemed to have reached some kind of Omega Zone almost twenty years ago. After the red-hot streak of *The Names*, *White Noise* and *Libra*, his tenth novel, *Mao II*, was so self-derivative that one wondered how much he had left in the tank. The answer came in the form of *Underworld*, an epic rejoinder that left the reader doubly pummelled: by the scale of the undertaking and the sustained intensity with which it was achieved. *The Body Artist* felt like a warm-down after such titanic exertions, but it was followed, disastrously, by the high-concept self-karaoke of *Cosmopolis*. *Falling Man* was a partial return to form – if the 9/11 subject-matter had not demanded a good deal more.

His new novel, *Point Omega*, begins and ends with Douglas Gordon's *24-Hour Psycho* (installed at the Museum of Modern Art in 2006), in which the ninety-minute Hitchcock original is slowed so that it would take a full day and night to twitch by. The uncanny beauty of 'the actor's eyes in slow transit across his bony sockets' or 'Janet Leigh in the detailed process of not knowing what is about to happen to her' are conveyed with haunted lucidity. Being DeLillo, of course, it's the deeper implications of the piece, what it reveals about the nature of film, perception and time, that detain him. He – an unidentified spectator – is mesmerised by the 'radically altered plane of time': 'the less there was to see, the harder he looked, the more he saw'. This prologue and epilogue comprise a phenomenological essay on one of the rare artworks of recent times to merit the prefix 'conceptual'. As soon as one puts it like that, however, questions beg to be asked. How does this persuasive interrogation of the visible benefit from *not* being an essay, from being novelised? What is gained by the choreography of post-*noir*ish suspense – 'He watched two men enter, the older man using a cane and wearing a suit that looked travelled in' – and the slow whir of third-person thought ('He understood for the first time . . .')?

The answer is adjacency to the stuff in the book's middle, the meat in a slender fictive sandwich. Turns out the old guy with the cane was a scholar who worked with the Pentagon on 'risk assessments' (the classic DeLillo occupation) and provided theoretical guidance in readiness for the invasion of Iraq. The young guy, Jim Finley, another familiar DeLillo type, was trying to persuade Elster to take part in a film he wants to make. That's how they end up in the Sonoran Desert, in a house together, sitting on the deck mainly, drinking, shooting the DeLillo breeze (which also sounds rather Mametian at times!). They're joined by Elster's daughter, Jessie, and it's almost idyllic – 'vast night, moon in transit' – in a zero-humidity sort of way. There's even a hint – 'a random agitation in the air' – of erotic possibility. Then something happens or doesn't happen to Jessie. The men search for her; the desert presses in on them, a desolate end-zone of ancient time.

At which point it's worth mentioning that Gordon did another of these time-expanding pieces which Elster and Jim could almost have driven to see. Installed for just one weekend in the desert near Twenty-nine Palms, *5 Year Drive-By* re-projected part of *The Searchers* in real time – i.e. the five years John Wayne spent searching for his abducted niece. Unwinding at the glacial rate of about one frame every twenty minutes, it makes *24-Hour Psycho* look like the Keystone Kops and might have sated even Elster's need for slow time.

He came to the southwest to get away from the sped-up, *Koyaanisqatsi*-style time of the city, the 'endless counting down'. In the desert he can feel 'Time becoming slowly older. Enormously old. Not day by day. This is deep time, epochal time.' He'd had a premonition of this when Jim took him to see *24-Hour Psycho*, an experience he likened to 'watching the universe die over a period of about seven billion years'.

Elster's and Finley's movements are painstakingly inventoried, enhanced and isolated from the flow of action: 'He paused and drank and paused again.' The intention seems to be to slow the prose down so that it works like Gordon's artwork, halting along frame by frame, sentence by sentence. The result, whether in the emptiness of the desert or the confines of MoMA, is a contradictory mix of the stripped down – 'This is what he thought. Then he thought about combing his hair.' – *and* the padded-out – 'He wasn't carrying a comb. He would have to smooth down his hair with his hands once he got in front of a mirror . . .'

Same with the dialogue, the call and response of incantatory demotic where the response takes up the call and pitches it back.

> 'Okay. We'll take a drive.'
> 'We'll take a drive,' he said.

Not that these liturgical duets are devoid of purpose and effect:

> 'Heat.'
> 'That's right,' Jessie said.
> 'Say the word.'
> 'Heat.'
> 'Feel it beating in.'
> 'Heat,' she said.

Hypnotically compelling, isn't it? Um, yes, as long as you've forgotten the tour-de-force verbal seduction in *The Names*:

> Do you feel it? Tell me if you do. I want to hear you say it. Say heat. Say wet between my legs. Say legs. Seriously, I want you to. *Stockings*. Whisper it. The word is meant to be whispered.

'Too many goddam echoes,' exclaims Elster at one point, himself a character who seems – a voice that sounds – like a ghost-refugee from the earlier novels. The good bits in *Point Omega* keep reminding you of older good bits which turn out also to be better bits. Jessie says she likes 'old movies on television where a man lights a woman's cigarette. That's all they seemed to do in those old movies, the men and women.' Pretty good, but not as smart and funny as the contingent precision of this (from *Americana*): 'It was one of those old English films in which people are always promising to meet at Victoria Station the moment the war is over.'

The film Finley has in mind involves Elster talking straight to the camera. 'Just a man and a wall,' Jim explains. 'The man stands there and relates the complete experience, everything that comes to mind,' all filmed in 'one continuous take'. It's a re-make of the kind of thing David Bell talked about almost forty years ago, in *Americana*: 'The monologue. The anti-movie. The single camera position. The expressionless actor. The shot extended to its ultimate limit in time.' David sees this as 'part dream, part fiction, part movies', which also sounds like a prophetic summing up of the novel, *Point Omega*.

The title is derived from the philosopher Pierre Teilhard de Chardin; Elster mentions him a couple of times, sketches his idea about the way 'consciousness accumulates . . . begins to reflect upon itself' until, eventually, it reaches the Omega Point.

We've had hints of a not dissimilar place before. 'Film is more than the twentieth-century art,' explained the director Volterra, in *The Names*. 'It's another part of the twentieth-century mind. It's the world seen from inside. We've come to a certain point in the history of film. If a thing can be filmed, film is implied in the thing itself.' Within the more circumscribed realm of literature this is where DeLillo has staked his mighty claim. He has reconfigured things, or our perception of them, to such an extent that DeLillo is now implied in the things themselves. While photographers and film-makers routinely re-make the world in their images of it, this is something only a few novelists – Hemingway was one – ever manage. Like Hemingway, DeLillo has imprinted his syntax on reality and – such is the blowback-reward of the Omega Points Scheme for Stylistic Distinction – become a hostage to the habit of 'gyrate exaggerations' (the phrase is in *The Body Artist*) and the signature patterns of 'demolished logic'. *Point Omega* starts out by contemplating a re-projection of a classic film. It's barely had time to get going before it ends up reflecting on the oeuvre of which it's the latest increment and echo: a 'last flare' that – we've been here before too! – may not be the last after all.

2010

The Goncourt Journals

Before setting off to interview Nicholson Baker – who, in *U and I*, had devoted a whole book to the subject – Martin Amis reminds us that writers' lives 'are all anxiety and ambition'. Among many other things the Goncourt journals are a vast archive of anxiety and thwarted ambition. The brothers, Jules and Edmond, began keeping them on what was, for them, a momentous occasion: the publication, on 2 December 1851, of their first novel. Unfortunately, it was also a momentous day for France: Napoleon III seized power in a coup d'état. With the city under martial law, their eagerly anticipated debut made almost no impact. So the journals became a repository of all the woes and disappointed hopes suffered in their 'hard and horrible struggle against anonymity': critical indignities, lack of sales, the perfidy of reviewers, the unmerited success of friends (some of whom, like Zola, were celebrated for techniques the Goncourts claimed to have pioneered). As happens, lack of success only increased the brothers' sense of neglected worth. 'It is impossible to read a page by them,' André Gide confided in *his* journal, 'where that good opinion they have of themselves does not burst out from between the lines.' He was referring to their novels (now almost entirely forgotten) but this sense of wounded self-esteem greatly increases the pleasure of the journals for which they are remembered. 'Oh, if one of Dostoevsky's novels, whose black melancholy is regarded with such indulgent admiration, were signed with the name of Goncourt, what a slating it would get all along the line.' That's in 1888; by 1890 the tone is of comic resignation (there is much comedy in these pages) as Edmond realises that he has devoted the whole of his life 'to a special sort of literature: the sort that brings one trouble'.

It's not just the brothers themselves; their friends are constantly sniping about each other's success or bemoaning the lack of their own. Zola, 'whose name echoes round the world', is particularly 'hard to please'. Permanently 'dissatisfied with the enormity of his good fortune', he is 'unhappier than the most abject of failures'. (This also finds an echo in Amis: specifically his shocked realisation that Norman Mailer, the 'much-televised headline-grabber, suffers from a piercing sense of *neglect*'.)

Forgive the name-dropping – in this context it is inevitable and appropriate; an abundance of famous names renders the most banal entries compelling. 'A ring at the door. It was Flaubert.' 'Baudelaire was at the table next to ours.' Even people who make only a cameo appearance are fixed with a precision to match that of the recently invented camera. The glimpse of Baudelaire continues: 'He was without a cravat, his shirt open at the neck and his head shaved, just as if he were going to be guillotined.' Unlike photographs, these verbal pictures develop and change over time, according to fluctuations in the fortunes and health of the people concerned and their shifting relationships with the authors of the journals. Part of the ambition behind the project was to show the Goncourts' acquaintances – many of whom happened to be the great writers of the age – 'as they really are, in a dressing-gown and slippers'. At one point a fellow guest is shocked by Flaubert's 'gross, intemperate unbuttoning of his nature' but the reader is grateful that the Goncourts were on hand to witness such things, even when – especially when – the conversation among these men of letters becomes – as it often did – 'filthy and depraved'. Among all the talk of fornication, hookers, venereal disease and drunkenness there is some literary discussion too – and not just about 'the special aptitude of writers suffering from constipation and diarrhoea'. The journals are shot through with observations which cut to the critical quick. On first hearing Flaubert read from *Salammbô* the brothers are disappointed to discover that he 'sees the Orient, and what is more the Orient of antiquity, in the guise of an Algerian bazaar. Some of his effects are childish, others ridiculous . . . [T]here is nothing more wearisome than the everlasting descriptions, the button-by-button portrayal of the characters, the miniature-like representation of every costume.' The brothers are often vehement participants in debate – blasphemously insisting that 'Hugo has more talent than Homer' – but much of the time they are eager flies on a wall, conscious of the privilege of witnessing a master like Flaubert as he illuminates what, to him, is truly shocking about the author of *Justine*: 'there isn't a single tree in Sade, or a single animal'.

By the time they meet the author of *Madame Bovary* he is already a celebrated writer, already 'Flaubert'. Others, like the 'strange painter Degas', enter inconspicuously with none of the aura subsequently bestowed upon them by fame. When they first encounter their 'admirer and pupil Zola' he strikes them as a 'worn-out *Normalien*, at once sturdy and puny' but with 'a vibrant note of pungent deter- mination and furious energy'. (Another, more recent echo: Christopher Isherwood records how, in April 1948, a 'young man' called Gore Vidal introduces himself; he reminds Isherwood 'sometimes of a Teddy bear, sometimes of a duck', but is obviously 'a shrewd operator' with a good deal of courage and 'a desire for self-advertisement'.)

Many people come strolling through the journals but one young man who went on to distinguish himself in the world of letters does not merit so much as a mention (in this selection at least). When Henry James met Edmond ('and his dirty little companions') in 1885 he was struck by 'something perverse & disagreeable' about him. Expanding on this in an interminable review of the journals, James is baffled by the way that the 'weakness' of these 'furious *névrosés*' 'appears to them a source of glory or even of dolorous general interest'. The fact that they do not appear anything like so sickly or neurotic to us is proof of a sort that the Goncourts were right: their malaise was indeed proof of their modernity. The self-styled 'John-the-Baptists of modern neurosis' prided themselves on being 'the first to write about the nerves'. The 'shameless vanity' of this claim irks Roberto Calasso – who, in *The Ruin of Kasch*, insists that 'Nerves and the modern find definitive voice' in Baudelaire – but the Goncourts certainly played their part in articulating an emergent feeling of unease and anxiety that will become a staple of twentieth-century literature.

('We are the future!' Jules yells at Saint-Beuve.) The sickliness that so repelled James was what, according to Susan Sontag, gave later writers such as Nietzsche, Kierkegaard and Kafka their authority: 'Their unhealthiness is their soundness, and is what carries conviction.' To a table that would soon be groaning beneath the weight of accumulated anguish the Goncourts brought their signature note of affected disaffection: 'There are moments when, faced with our lack of success, I wonder whether we are failures, proud but impotent. One thing reassures me as to our value: the boredom that afflicts us. It is the hallmark of quality in modern men.' Again, this is a note sounded repeatedly by such quintessentially modern masters as Fernando Pessoa (in *The Book of Disquiet*), E.M. Cioran and Roland Barthes (who brings together the twin themes of sickness and ennui by wondering if boredom might be his form of hysteria).

The atmosphere of metaphysical sickness is clearly related to the dark shadow cast by actual physical illness. In 1861 the death of their friend Henri Murger had prompted an agonised reflection on mortality:

the orgies of work at night, the periods of poverty followed by periods of junketing, the neglected cases of pox, the ups and downs of an existence without a home, the suppers instead of dinners, and the glasses of absinthe bringing consolation after a visit to the pawnshop; everything which wears a man out, burns him up, and finally kills him; a life opposed to all the principles of physical and spiritual hygiene, which results in a man dying in shreds at the age of forty-two, without enough strength in him to suffer, and complaining of only one thing, the smell of rotten meat in his bedroom – the smell of his own body.

Once again, this is a passage whose resonance extends well beyond the date and circumstances of its composition. Alter the odd detail and the Goncourts' elegy for 'the death of Bohemia' in mid-nineteenth-century Paris can be read as a catalogue essay for Nan Goldin's photographs of the Lower East Side in the 1970s and '80s.

The unnamed illness that kills Murger was mysterious and rare; syphilis was so pervasive that in 1877 Maupassant, initially, was 'proud' to have caught 'the magnificent pox. At last!' By then Edmond had had seven years to mourn the utterly unmagnificent death, also from syphilis, of his beloved brother. Jules' passing made Edmond 'curse and abominate literature' to such an extent that, after describing with clinical precision and agonising detail the gradual collapse of his brother's physical and mental capacities, he decided to abandon the journals.

The habit of daily transcription was not so easy to break, however, and Edmond soon returned to the task. With the Franco-Prussian War, the Siege of Paris, and the Commune, history comes crashing in on the daily accounts of visits, incidental observations and reflections. The entries from the post-Jules period are as varied, fascinating, compelling and odd as anything that has gone before. (I am particularly fond of the passage describing 'the mania for fighting' which so takes hold of Drumont that 'Nature is nothing for him now but a setting for affairs of honour. When he took the lease on his house at Soisy, he exclaimed: "Ah, now there's a real garden for a pistol duel."') But these later sections are interesting in two additional and complicating ways.

As early as 1867 the brothers had reflected on the transience of all pleasures:

> Everything is unique, nothing happens more than once in a lifetime. The physical pleasure which a certain woman gave you at a certain moment, the exquisite dish which you ate on a certain day – you will never meet either again. Nothing is repeated, and everything is unparalleled.

Naturally, this affirmation of the unrepeatable uniqueness of all experience – especially once his brother is no longer there to share, record and analyse it with Edmond – encourages recollection and reverie. As Edmond ages so he becomes more and more absorbed by memory. While in no way dimmed, his responsiveness to what is going on around him is all the time having to compete for attention with events from the past. At one point he recalls seducing a sixteen-year-old virgin: 'She was a strange creature, that girl, with the ecstatic pallor of her face when we made love together, the inert passivity of

her body, in which nothing was alive but the pounding of her heart,
and the expression in her big blue eyes.' Later she becomes the
mistress of one of Edmond's friends; later still, as part of a 'wish to
degrade her', he arranges for her to sleep with Jules: 'My brother,
after making frenzied love to her for several weeks, decided that she
was too melancholy, and even rather frightening, with the sort of
lethargy into which love-making plunged her, and with the far-away
look which came into her great blue eyes; and he dropped her.' The
journals are full of notes on atmosphere, details of psychology and
gesture – the kind of raw material which, once processed, finds its
way into fiction; they are also full of off-the-cuff misogyny. Here, it
is as if the ghost of a novel, a darkly erotic *Bildungsroman*, at once
repressed and in the process of formation, begins to emerge, unbidden,
from the pages of the journals.

The second factor in the distinctive quality of the latter parts of
the journals derives from the fact that in 1886–7, after much reluctance, Edmond begins publishing them. As a consequence the
journals from that date onwards have to come to terms with how
the earlier ones have been received – both by the critics and by the
people mentioned, described or quoted in them. The journals, in
other words, start being about themselves. (At the risk of making the
journals seem modish in an old-fashioned way, it's worth recalling
that in a 1967 essay – 'French Letters: Theories of the New Novel'
– Gore Vidal was struck by the way that 'the writers whom Robbe-
Grillet and Nathalie Sarraute most resemble' are 'the presently
unfashionable brothers Edmond and Jules de Goncourt'.)

Plenty of people felt embarrassed, upset, outraged or betrayed by
the Goncourts' record of things they had said or had said about them.
As indicated earlier, this is part of the journals' charm and value.
Christopher Isherwood, when he finished reading them, on 5 July
1940, was in no doubt as to their importance in this regard: 'Here,
gossip achieves the epigrammatic significance of poetry. To keep such
a diary is to render a real service to the future.' This realisation may
well have been an incentive to persist with *his* diaries, which have
since acquired a similar value of their own. Or, to put it another way,
it is as if the journals, which caused people to discuss – and thereby

add to – their content, continue to prompt the same reaction and so, in a sense, are still being incrementally extended by a constantly expanding cast of characters, readers and contributors, from the nineteenth century to Gide, Isherwood, Vidal and beyond.

Obviously the Goncourt journals have been a wonderful resource for historians and biographers alike but not everyone has concurred with the verdict of Proust's narrator in *Time Regained*: 'Goncourt knew how to listen, just as he knew how to see.' Coming as it does from a work in which fiction and fact are famously and intimately entwined, this character reference is itself unreliable and inadmissible. Certainly it is contested by a conversation recorded by Gide in a journal entry from January 1902: '"According to what I have been able to verify," says Jacques Blanche, "nothing is less true than their journals."' Claiming to remember perfectly certain conversations which the Goncourts had falsified, Blanche flatly contradicts Proust: 'I assure you, Gide, that they didn't know how to listen.'

Blanche rants on, furnishing more and more examples, only to have the rug pulled from beneath his feet by the author of *The Counterfeiters*. '"But", I say, "the words that he puts into the mouths of various people, however false they may be according to you, are almost never uninteresting. Watch out, for the more you reduce his stature as a stenographer, the greater you make him as a writer, as a creator."'

We only have Gide's word that he had the last word in this exchange, but it reminds us that what we are dealing with here is not simply a resource but a compendious work of literature. 'A book is never a masterpiece,' the brothers declare in 1864. 'It becomes one.' The process of becoming is inevitably more awkward for a journal – which did not even set out to be a book; its imperfections and indiscretions, its lack of artistic and thematic organisation – all the things, in fact, that make it a pleasure to read – militate against its ever becoming one. But while Sainte-Beuve – a major player in these pages – believed his notebooks to be 'the lowest drawer of the writing desk', the Goncourt journals have come to deserve a place in the highest.

2007

Rebecca West:
Black Lamb and Grey Falcon

The author of a guide book should have no artistic personality. Entirely at the mercy of the place being written about, he or she is ideally an anonymous conduit of reliable information about bus times, places to stay and museum opening hours. At the other end of the spectrum, in his book *Fiction*, the photographer Michael Ackerman claims that 'places do not exist. A place is just my idea of it.'

Travel literature thrives between the extremes represented by the guide and the solipsistic Ackerman. The best travel writers may be of only limited reliability when it comes to bus times but they express timeless truths about the buses of a given country – or at least about their relationship with those buses. Take D.H. Lawrence, whose responsiveness to places was both instantaneous and profound. Editors and publishers were keenly aware of this gift and Lawrence was eager to turn it to financial advantage.

When Rebecca West visited Norman Douglas in Florence in 1921 he joked that although Lawrence had been in town only a few hours he was probably already hammering out an article, 'vehemently and exhaustively describing the temperament of the people'. To West this seemed 'obviously a silly thing to do', but Douglas was right: they turned up at Lawrence's hotel to find him doing just that. At the time West thought that Lawrence did not know enough about Florence 'to make his views of real value'. It was only after his death that she appreciated that Lawrence 'was writing about the state of his own soul at that moment' and could only do so in symbolic terms. For this purpose 'the city of Florence was as good a symbol as any other'

West wrote this in 1931. She had not yet made the first of the trips to Yugoslavia which would form the basis of *Black Lamb and Grey Falcon* but the importance of this realisation for her own *magnum opus* is considerable. Indeed, relative to the size of the finished book, her experience of Yugoslavia was pretty skimpy. As Edith Durham, a noted authority on the Balkans, bitchily put it at the time, 'The novelist Miss West has written an immense book on the strength of one pleasure trip to Yugoslavia, but with no previous knowledge of land or people.' For the record, Miss West had made three trips to Yugoslavia: the first, at the invitation of the British Council, to give lectures in the spring of 1936; a second with her husband, Henry Andrews, in the spring of 1937; the third in early summer of the following year. Initially she had hoped quickly to write 'a snap book'; four months after the second trip this potentially profitable venture had grown into a 'wretched, complicated book that won't interest anybody'.

In the course of researching its 'long and complicated history' West clarified her ideas about Yugoslavia – and about much else besides. To adapt Italo Calvino's comment on *The Ruin of Kasch* by Roberto Calasso, *Black Lamb and Grey Falcon* takes up two subjects: the first is Yugoslavia, and the second is everything else. By the time it was published – in two volumes totalling half a million words – West was somewhat at a loss to discover why she had been moved 'in 1936 to devote five years of my life, at great financial sacrifice and to the utter exhaustion of my mind and body, to take an inventory of a country down to its last vest-button, in a form insane from any ordinary artistic or commercial point of view'. As the 'mass of my material' swelled and changed so this 'inventory' became an immense and immensely complicated picture not simply of her own soul but that of Europe on the brink of the Second World War. The result, which she feared 'hardly anyone will read by reason of its length', is one of the supreme masterpieces of the twentieth century.

Like the book itself its reputation is rather odd. West is considered a major British writer. If she is not regarded as a writer quite of the first rank that is largely because so much of the work on which her reputation should rest is tacitly considered secondary to the forms in which greatness is expected to manifest itself, namely the novel. As a novelist West is clearly less important than Lawrence, James Joyce (whose genius, in *Ulysses*, was to have 'invented a form and exhausted its possibilities at the same time') or E.M. Forster ('a self-indulgent old liberal with hardly a brain in his head'). Her best work is scattered among reportage, journalism and travel – the kind of things traditionally regarded as sidelines or distractions. The success of *Black Lamb and Grey Falcon* is due in no small part to the ingenuity with which she contains this tendency to dispersal by *giving it free rein*. The book is manifestly a work of literature but since literature in English (at least as far as prose is concerned) is synonymous with the novel – with an agreed upon *form* of writing rather than a certain *quality* of writing – it is tacitly removed from the company in which it belongs. Palpably inferior works – novels – sit far more securely on the literary syllabus than an awkward tome whose identifying quality is a refusal to fit. In danger of dislodging other volumes from the top canonical shelf – or, more radically, of bringing the whole shelf crashing down – *Black Lamb and Grey Falcon* topples from its rightful place and is tacitly stocked in a lower, less prominent but safer place.

Even some commentators who claim the book as a masterpiece have little to say about *why* it is one. In *Abroad*, Paul Fussell's highly regarded survey of 'British literary travelling between the wars', West (unlike Waugh, Lawrence or Greene) does not get a chapter-compartment to herself and her book receives a mention more or less in passing. Victoria Glendinning, in her biography of West, has no doubt that *Black Lamb and Grey Falcon* is 'the central book of her life, the work in which Rebecca West formulated her views on reli-gion, ethics, art, myth and gender'. Beyond that, she has almost nothing to say about it. Is the book doomed to repel attempts to articulate the awe that it inspires?

To try to make good this lack let's begin, uncontentiously, by observing that it is a key book about Yugoslavia. I read it in 1993 after visiting Serbia (for the British Council, as it happens) to learn about Yugoslavia – or ex-Yugoslavia, as it had by then become. The book had been re-issued in response to the outbreak of a conflict

West had, in some ways, foreseen. In the Prologue West remembers herself 'peering' at old film footage of the king of Yugoslavia, 'like an old woman reading the tea-leaves in her cup'. The book's prophetic quality is hinted at as early as page 10 when West writes that 'it is the habit of the people, whenever an old man mismanages his business so that it falls to pieces as soon as he dies, to say, "Ah, So-and-so was a marvel! He kept things together so long as he was alive, and look what happens now he has gone!"' I can still remember how weirdly disorienting it was to read this in 1993 when the blaze of contemporary events was fierce enough to make one wonder if she was writing not about Franz Josef, but Tito. Much later in the book, in Kosovo, West's chauffeur, Dragutin, grabs a Croat boy by the ear and says with a mixture of irony and threat, 'We'll kill you all some day.' Even in my own minuscule experience of Serbia and Montenegro there have been many times when the scene unfolding before my eyes seemed to have been faithfully enacted from the pages of *Black Lamb and Grey Falcon*. As a book about Yugoslavia, then, it is of 'extraordinary usefulness' as a kind of metaphysical *Lonely Planet* that never requires updating. (As West herself observed, 'sometimes it is necessary for us to know where we are in eternity as well as in time'). The book's practical worth is nicely suggested by the journalist Robert Kaplan, who remembers taking the book with him everywhere in Yugoslavia. 'I would rather have lost my passport and money than my heavily thumbed and annotated copy of *Black Lamb and Grey Falcon*.'

If you are not in – or interested in – the Balkan peninsula the number of pages devoted to the history of the region can seem offputting. Except this is history as it might have been written by Ryszard Kapuściński or Gabriel García Márquez. Take the extraordinary scene from Sarajevo in 1914 when, shortly before his assassination, Archduke Franz Ferdinand finds the reception hall he is standing in crammed with the half-million beasts he has, 'according to his own calculation', killed in his career as a hunter:

One can conceive the space of this room stuffed all the way up to the crimson and gold vaults and stalactites with the furred and feathered ghosts, set close, because there were so many of them: stags with the air between their antlers stuffed with woodcock, quail, pheasant, partridge, capercailzie, and the like; boars standing bristling flank to flank, the breadth under their broad bellies packed with layer upon layer of hares and rabbits. Their animal eyes, clear and dark as water, would brightly watch the approach of their slayer to an end that exactly resembled their own.

When Susan Sontag directed Beckett's *Waiting for Godot* in Sarajevo during the siege it was widely felt that what was happening on stage offered some kind of absurdist commentary on events beyond the theatre. In a café in Mostar – a place which became stitched into international consciousness in the same way as Sarajevo – a comparable fable had unfolded before West's eyes in the 1930s:

Young officers moved rhythmically through the beams of white light that poured down upon the acid green of the billiard-tables, and the billiard balls gave out their sound of stoical shock. There was immanent the Balkan feeling of a shiftless yet just doom. It seemed possible that someone might come into the room, perhaps a man who would hang up his fez, and explain, in terms just comprehensible enough to make it certain they were not nonsensical, that all the people at the tables must stay there until the two officers who were playing billiards at the moment had played a million games, and that by the result their eternal fates would be decided; and that this would be accepted, and people would sit there quietly waiting and reading the newspapers.

West's intention was 'to show the past side by side with the present it created' and part of her achievement is to reveal how even an apparently ahistorical sensation – the scent of a plucked flower, say – is saturated with the smell of the past. Geography and history, to make the same point rather more sweepingly, cannot always be distinguished from one another – hence the way that certain places 'imprint the same stamp on whatever inhabitants history brings them, even if conquest spills out one population and pours in another wholly different in race and philosophy'. Impatient readers tempted to skip the historical bits are taking a big risk because the past – the narrative history – can melt into the immediate present with zero notice.

The most spectacular instance comes after a lengthy disquisition – a bit too long, I was thinking – on events in Prishtina during the reign of Stephen Dushan in the fourteenth century. After twenty pages or so we learn of his death:

> In the forty-ninth year of his life, at a village so obscure that it is not now to be identified, he died, in great pain, as if he had been poisoned. Because of his death many disagreeable things happened. For example, we sat in Prishtina, our elbows on a tablecloth stained brown and puce, with chicken drumsticks on our plates meagre as sparrow-bones, and there came towards us a man and a woman; and the woman was carrying on her back the better part of a plough.

Isn't that the boldest jump-cut – the most daring time-shift, the most outrageous deduction – ever? And West does not stop there. The sight of this man and woman prompts her to return to one of the major themes of the book, the vexed relations between men and women:

> Any area of unrestricted masculinism, where the women are made to do all the work and are refused the right to use their wills, is in fact disgusting, not so much because of the effect on the women, who are always taught something by the work they do, but because of the nullification of the men.

And West does not stop there either – she loops this vision back to the death of Stephen Dushan before leaving the table to go to 'a lavatory of the Turkish kind':

> The dark hole in the floor, and something hieratic in the proportions of the place made it seem as if dung, having been expelled by man, had set itself up as a new and hostile and magically powerful element that could cover the whole earth with dark ooze and sickly humidity. I felt as if the place were soiling me with filth which I would never be able to wash off because it was stronger in its essence than mere mild soap and water.

And West does not stop there either… Let's loop back for a moment. The book's inexhaustible capacity for self-fuelling discussion, for examining the implications of everything that it touches upon, is central to West's structural and stylistic method. Any conclusions she draws are tied to the process (a key word in the book) by which they are being teased out. Something catches West's attention; the incident – a Mozart symphony coming on the radio in a restaurant on page 507, say – is conveyed with vivid immediacy. As West articulates and processes this experience, she takes us on a vast discursive journey before returning us to the exact spot or occasion from which we started. Franz Ferdinand's assassin, Princip, is in this way the active representative of the author's own purpose: 'He offered himself wholly to each event in order that he might learn in full what revelation it had to make about the nature of the universe.'

How, with this in mind, could *Black Lamb and Grey Falcon* have been anything other than a vast book? Even enthusiastic readers of Robert Fisk's *The Great War for Civilisation* are likely to feel that its impressive bulk is due solely to accumulation, to the mass of material contained in it. *Black Lamb and Grey Falcon* earns its size *as a work of art*. Like W.H. Auden in his 'Letter to Lord Byron' (1936), West needed 'a form that's large enough to swim in'. The scale of its conception is imprinted internally in its syntax and composition. Ostensibly convenient and alluring, the edited selection offered in *The Essential Rebecca West* feels like an aesthetic violation. There is, in fact, something inappropriate about reducing such a book to its essentials. I suspect that some of the passages that most delight me are, by the kind of limiting definition West repeatedly decries, the bits that might be considered in*essential. I don't want to diminish the importance of *Black Lamb and Grey Falcon* as a book about Yugoslavia; it is predicated on 'a coincidence between the natural forms and colours of the western and southern parts of Yugoslavia and the innate forms and colours of [West's] imagination', but while many of the parts I value have their origin *in* they are not unique *to* that part of the world. A few examples from hundreds: the 'erotic panic' of a horse which 'rolls the eyes not only in fear but in enjoyment, that seeks to be soothed with an appetite revealing that it plainly knows soothing to be possible, and pursues what it declares it dreads'; the woman who had 'the beauty of a Burne-Jones, the same air of having rubbed holes in her lovely cheeks with her clenched knuckles'; the Muslims for whom 'the reward for total abstinence from alcohol seems, illogically enough, to be the capacity for becoming intoxicated without it'.

Black Lamb and Grey Falcon is digressive and meandering – you never know what's going to happen next – but this is not to say that it is shapeless. It may sprawl – it *is* sprawling – but remember, for a start, how what is offered as an account of a single journey has in fact been stitched seamlessly together from three separate trips. Over time we have grown familiar with the complex organisation of works like *Bleak House* or *Ulysses*; in contemporary fiction we admire the intricate interweaving of plot, character and themes in the novels of Ian McEwan. Making different demands on the reader's expectations of order, *Black Lamb and Grey Falcon* has the unity and fluidity of a sustained improvisation in prose. As with a saxophonist or trumpeter the controlling factor, the thing that allows West to range so widely without ever losing her way, is *tone*. The book's bold demonstration of the way that tone can take over some of the load-bearing work of structure is crucial to its innovatory importance. Within an overall constancy of tone West moves easily between registers. She can be witty: 'The visit had been extraordinarily pleasant, though it had been nothing at all, and least of all a visit'. She can be playful:

'Then why did we not bring the book?' asked my husband. 'Well, it weighs just over a stone,' I said. 'I weighed it once on the bathroom scales.' 'Why did you do that?' asked my husband. 'Because it occurred to me one day that I knew the weight of nothing except myself and joints of meat,' I said, 'and I just picked that up to give me an idea of something else.'

She can be lyrical ('As we drew nearer the shore the water under the keel was pale emerald where the diving sunlight had found sand') and fantastical at the same time:

Beyond the bridge the river widened out into a curd of yellow water-lilies, edged with a streak of mirror at each bank, in which willow trees, standing above their exact reflections, amazed us by their shrill green and cat-o'-thousand-tails forms; they were like static fireworks.

As happens when she dismisses a woman she meets in a hotel in Bosnia, West can be abusive and intemperate: 'she was cruelty; she was filth'. Most surprising of all in a book of such length West has the gift of brevity: 'We fell again through Swissish country'; 'A naked range as black as night, its high ridge starred with snow'; 'the first heavy pennies of rain'.

The progress of this essay is in danger of being impeded by the quantity of superlatives it has already had to take onboard but room must be made, ultimately, for a brief consideration of West's thought. A few years after *Black Lamb and Grey Falcon* was published West sat down to consider a proposal from her American editor, Ben Huebsch, that she write a book on the British Empire. It was something she would have liked to have done, but 'except for the fancy bits on religion and metaphysics that I would throw in in my demented way', she decided, there was nothing new she could contribute to such a study. It is, of course, these 'demented' bits that make *Black Lamb and Grey Falcon* a great book of ideas. In the Epilogue West comments on the way that, in her teens, Ibsen 'corrected the chief flaw in English literature, which is a failure to recognise the dynamism of ideas'. With characteristic vehemence she later decided that 'Ibsen cried out for ideas for the same reason that men call out for water, because he had not got any'. To say that West has them by the gallon is an understatement. *Black Lamb and Grey Falcon* is, along with everything else, a vast flood of ideas. As with Lawrence it is impossible to say where sensation stops and cogitation begins. Observation and metaphysics, thought and responsiveness to 'the visibility of life', are all the time flowing into each other.

The book's biggest idea is also its simplest, so simple that it should be no more than a preference 'for the agreeable over the disagreeable'. The problem is that only part of us is sane:

only part of us loves pleasure and the longer day of happiness, wants to live to our nineties and die in peace, in a house that we built, that shall shelter those who come after us. The other half of us is nearly mad. It prefers the disagreeable to the agreeable, loves pain and its darker night despair, and wants to die in a catastrophe that will set back life to its beginnings and leave nothing of our house save its blackened foundations.

As West wrote this Europe was hurtling towards just such a catastrophe; in 1993, when I first read *Black Lamb and Grey Falcon*, TV screens were full of images of the blackened foundations of houses in the very places she had described. West had enough of the disagreeable in her nature to realise that an affirmation of the agreeable is part of an ongoing personal and political struggle. Her faith in this idea is echoed by Auden in the commentary appended to his sonnet sequence *In Time of War* (published in 1938 while West was immersed in writing her book):

> It's better to be sane than mad, or liked than dreaded;
> It's better to sit down to nice meals than to nasty;
> It's better to sleep two than single; it's better to be happy.

In both cases the modesty of the conclusion is proof of its wisdom – and vice versa. *Black Lamb and Grey Falcon* is a vast, ambitious and complex book which repeatedly stresses the kinship between homely and universal truths. By making a cake for friends, West insists, 'one is striking a low note on a scale that is struck higher up by Beethoven and Mozart'. In Montenegro West encounters a woman who is trying to understand the many hard things that have befallen her. The meeting persuades West that if 'during the next million generations there is but one human being born in every generation who will not cease to inquire into the nature of his fate, even while it strips and bludgeons him, some day we shall read the riddle of our universe'. And if, once or twice a century, a book like this appears the wait will be only a fraction as long.

2006

John Cheever: *The Journals*

Chances are most readers will come to John Cheever's *Journals* via his fiction. That is natural and proper. Whatever value his journals might have in their own right, their viability as a publishing proposition was conditional on the interest of the large readership of his novels and stories. Depending on your point of view, that audience's loyalty had already been tested or its curiosity whetted by his daughter Susan's memoir, *Home Before Dark*, and the selection of letters edited by his son, Ben. This 'rapid posthumous invasion of [Cheever's] privacy', as John Updike deemed it, seemed modest and discreet in the face of the relentless, remorse-filled exposure of *The Journals*.* For more than forty years, it turned out, Cheever had subjected his liver-damaged soul to a daily regimen of self-excoriation.

All of this – memoir, letters, journals and, to bring things right up to date, Blake Bailey's massive biography – would normally be regarded as retrospective trellising around which the great works could be shown to have blossomed. A degree of shock, in such circumstances, is not unusual. In Cheever's case, the gulf between the received image of the revered author and the revealed truth, as a well-known editor put it, of 'a writer who had just masturbated (he kept a record of that), doodling in the margins of his despair or boredom or occasional euphoria while waiting to hit the bottle' was, in some quarters, a cause for profound dismay.

---

*Throughout, 'journal' or 'journals' refer to the unedited mass of material as written by Cheever; *The Journal* or *Journals* to the published selection that follows.

But *The Journals* disturbs readers' assumptions in another, more subversive and complex way. For Cheever was in that very weird minority of writers – Christopher Isherwood and the Goncourt brothers spring immediately to mind – whose private, unpublished, writings contained much that was as good as, possibly even better than, the stuff which made their posthumous publication feasible. I would go further and suggest that this selection from his journals represents Cheever's greatest achievement, his principal claim to literary survival.

Cheever constantly voiced doubts about his writing. Already, by 1959, he found his early stories 'too breezy', and was soon trying to resign himself to being an 'inconsequential writer'. Reading *The Naked and the Dead* made him despair of his own 'confined talents'. He worshipped Bellow, admired and bitched about Updike, fretted that while Roth and others were 'playing stinkfinger and grabarse I admire the beauty of the evening star'. Not surprisingly, these admissions of literary inadequacy were always tempered by a wounded defensiveness. Firmly rooted in 'the genteel tradition', his 'old-fashioned fiction' about 'the country-club set' served as a tacit rebuke to the unfettered excesses of 'the California poets'.

Actually, some of the fiction – the 1962 story 'A Vision of the World', for example – is a lot stranger than one imagines it to be, or remembers it being. And while many stories are set in the suburbs they often have the quality of 'violet-flavored nightmare' that Cheever admired in Nabokov's *Pale Fire*.

Inevitably, *The Journals* reveals the germs of much that will eventually be transformed in the fiction. In 1972 we can observe the first faint, drunken glimpse of *Falconer*, so faint that when Cheever sobers up 'it doesn't seem to amount to much'. The reflection in 'The Death of Justina' (1960) about how the soul might not leave the body but 'lingers with it through every degrading stage of decomposition and neglect' is there, almost word for word, in a journal entry from the previous year. After you have read this passage in the starker context of *The Journals* – Cheever has run out of booze, is thinking of his dead mother while drying dishes – its force in the story is reduced by the knowledge that it has been craftily insinuated into the narrative.

This happens time and again. Things we admire in the fiction – the eye for 'travelling acres of sunlight', the telling psychological detail, exuberant lyricism tinged with a residue of the last (or anticipation of the next) hangover – are spilled straight onto the pages of his journal.

The Journals also contains numerous hints of a kind of writer we do not expect Cheever to be. It's not such a surprise to find that he can do proto-Carver – 'On Sunday afternoon my only brother comes to call. He is told that if he drinks again he will die, and he is drunk' – but we don't expect him, reflecting on the Shea Stadium, in 1963, to anticipate the famous opening of DeLillo's *Underworld*:

> I think that the task of the American writer is not to describe the misgivings
> of a woman taken in adultery as she looks out of a window at the rain but
> to describe four hundred people under the lights reaching for a foul ball.
> This is ceremony. The umpires in clericals, sifting the souls of the players;
> the faint thunder as ten thousand people, at the bottom of the eighth, head
> for the exits. The sense of moral judgements embodied in a migratory
> vastness.

Cheever is here describing a specifically American trajectory; fragments like the one about 'law-abiding murderers' or the encounter with an old class-mate and his wife are the kind of abbreviated fables Kafka might have written had he been born thirty years later, in Shady Hill or Bullet Park.

The neurasthenic strain in modern European literature – a strain which reaches breaking-point in Kafka's *Diaries* – could be conveniently arranged under a quotation from Kierkegaard's *Journal* entry of 1836: 'I have just returned from a party of which I was the life and soul; wit poured from my lips, everyone laughed and admired me – but I went away – and the dash should be as long as the earth's orbit ————————————————————————— and wanted to shoot myself.'

Cheever was all too familiar with the gin-sodden, mid-twentieth-century residue of this sentiment: 'you drink too much at cocktails you talk too much you make a pass at somebody's wife and you end with doing something foolish and obscene and wish in the morning you were dead'. On the very first page of *The Journals* Cheever records a trip to church on the second Sunday of Lent. It is presented as part of the normal round of Westchester life but the threat of damnation, the fear that he is a sinner standing 'outside the realm of God's mercy', is measureless. His milieu may seem circumscribed – Martinis, swimming pools, lawns – but it has the infinite brevity of that Kierkegaardian dash. The comfortable specificity and familiarity of the setting – the way rows are routinely and silently choreographed around the morning's toast and eggs – is part of a larger torment. Cheever's flickering back and forth between a yearning for light and the lure (alcoholic, carnal) of darkness, his urge to destroy himself – more subtly, his sense that 'the most wonderful thing about life is that we hardly tap our potential for self-destruction' – is rendered on a scale that is at once 'ingrown' and vast.

Any reader of *The Journals* will quickly notice that Cheever's incessant inventories of light and landscape have their own peculiar resonance. Once it becomes evident that he is talking about 'the moral quality of light' or 'an emotional darkness' then the adoring evocations 'of light and water and trees', of corner drugstores in summer twilight – all the signature elements of Cheever's topography – begin to hum with a dangerous current. A 'hint of aberrant carnality' is never far away. Entire landscapes, however idyllic-seeming, become coded expressions of longings and dread: 'The morning light is gold as money and pours in the eastern windows. But it is the shadow that is exciting, the light that cannot be defined.' As the years pass the message becomes steadily more explicit, unavoidable. On Easter Sunday 1968, sixteen years after that first church service, thoughts of 'the empty tomb' and 'life everlasting' are interrupted by intimations of obscenity: 'All those cocks and balls drawn on toilet walls are not the product of perverse frustrations. Some of them are high-hearted signs of good cheer.'

Cheever, then, was wrong to talk about his talent being 'confined', but it is entirely appropriate that, like a tongue probing an aching tooth, this was a word to which he insistently returned. As he explained in 1976, *Falconer* did not come from his experience of prison but from the myriad different kinds of confinement he had experienced 'as a man'. What he does not say – how could he? – is that the forms in which he gave dramatic expression to this sense could be enlarged manifestations of confinement. Richard Yates griped about the way that 'John fucking Cheever' was always getting published in *The New Yorker* – an honour that was constantly denied Yates – but, for Cheever, the shaping demands of the short story, his acquired habits of fictive resolution, all the aspects of hard-won craftsmanship that stood him in good stead at *The New Yorker*, worked against his being able to plumb the complex depths of his being. Only in the shapeless privacy of his journal could he do that. If he was 'writing narrative prose' Cheever believed that 'every line cannot be a cry from the heart.' So he stopped crying. In the journals, meanwhile, he went the other way, wept 'gin tears, whiskey tears, tears of plain salt' and stopped worrying about narrative. The irony is that while he was instinctively hostile to the splurging of Kerouac and 'the California poets', his own best writing would derive ultimately from a sustained forty-year word-binge with no thought of form, or – at least not until very near the end – of publication. A further irony follows: that the consummate craftsman should end up being reliant on the posthumous inter-vention of an editor to turn this repetitive mass of belly-aching, 'booze-fighting' and self-lament into a book with immense narrative power. This power derives from three, closely intertwined, sources.

One is the story of a marriage with its epic sulks, sexual lock-outs ('Looking for a good-night kiss, I find the only exposed area to be an elbow.') and – though this is easily overlooked – interludes of long-shadowed harmony. The second is the author's descent – already under way by the time *The Journals* begins – into (and eventual recovery from) alcoholism. Unless you are a recovering alcoholic – in which case you have had more than enough experience of this – it's worth reading a couple of pages of *The Journals* when you get home at night, after you've got drunk at a dinner or in a pub. Let's say it's eleven at night. In an hour you'll be asleep. But before you nod off imagine what it must be like, being as drunk as this – no, a lot more drunk than this – not just every night but pretty much all day every day for decades. (A not untypical entry from 1968:

'Dear Lord – who else? – keep me away from the bottles in the pantry. Guide me past the gin and the bourbon. Nine in the morning. I suppose I will succumb at ten; I hope to hold off until eleven.') It must have been a form of insanity – albeit a madness Cheever shared with an extraordinary number of American writers. The unanswerable questions remain: even though drinking did him no good at all, even if by 1972 he seemed, in Bailey's words, 'permanently impaired by alcohol', was it integral to what he ultimately achieved? Did he need its blurry delirium? Was it essential fuel for the journey?

The third strain is Cheever's struggle to overcome, satisfy and understand his sexual urges. He resolved, in 1959, not to become 'the kind of writer through whose work one sees the leakage of some noisome semi-secret', thereby announcing what, precisely, was in store. Effectively, Cheever's slow discovery and eventual acceptance of his sexual identity conforms to the larger story of homosexuality in the twentieth century. In rough chronological order – and with many overlaps, contradictions and relapses – we have: memories of adolescent horsing around with his friends ('cobbling', as he terms it); sustained attempts to bury the allure by aping the censoriousness he fears would be visited on him if people only knew; periodic failures to resist the promptings of the body followed, predictably, by crippling remorse and renewed determination to suppress those urges (and corresponding increase in loathing for those who don't even try); gradual acceptance ('I am queer, and happy to say so'), celebration, and realisation that real harm was caused not by one's sexual nature but by 'the force that was brought to crush these instincts and that exacerbated them beyond their natural importance'.

Cheever's eventual accommodation with his sexuality is not merely the story of personal rehabilitation; consciously or not, he is the beneficiary of a larger political struggle waged by and on behalf of men and women like him. In 1967 Cheever wonders if he will ever be 'caught up helplessly in the storms of history and love?' The irony is that the journals of this self-absorbed, solipsistic, allegedly 'friendless man' are freighted with history. And not only in the area of sexual orientation.

In 1962 there is a description of a scene in which, at the end of the day, people leave a beach: 'It is always, for me, a moving sight, to see people pick up their sandwich baskets, their towels and folding furniture, and hurry back to the hotel, the cottage, the bar. Their haste, their intentness, is like the thoughtlessness of life itself . . .' Lovely, exact, poignant, it displays the observational grace and sweep typical of Cheever. But it is preceded by these two sentences: 'I spend the day, as do many others, in watching Glenn orbit on TV, and I torment myself for not working. Once the man is in orbit, the crowds leave the beach . . .' So that timeless description of beach-life and its aftermath was Cheever's take on a specific and major historic event. Most entries lack that introductory, establishing context but, thus alerted, we wonder how many more of these free-floating fragments are imbued with undated history. Combine that with the way in which the landscape and houses are an encoded – perhaps the better word is 'scrambled' – inventory of psycho-sexual currents and you have a sense of why so many entries in *The Journals* are possessed of 'something much more mysterious than [the] bare facts' that occasioned them.

In seeking to define the narrative drive of any writer's journals there is a danger of marginalising what is essential to their appeal, namely the way that the incidental and irrelevant do not get pushed aside as must happen in the course of more streamlined narratives. So it should be added that, in the course of trips to Rome and Russia, Cheever reveals himself to be a brilliant, if intermittent, travel writer; that he was an insistent and penetrating reader of a wider variety of literature than we might have expected ('I read George Eliot and find myself to be so physical a person, so tactile, so crude, that when anything is touched – when Deronda at last puts his hand around an oar – I am thrilled'); that, finally, he succeeded according to his own stated terms:

> To disguise nothing, to conceal nothing, to write about those things that are closest to our pain, our happiness; to write about my sexual clumsiness, the agonies of Tantalus, the depths of my discouragement – I seem to glimpse it in my dreams – my despair. To write about the foolish agonies of anxiety,

the refreshment of our strength when these are ended; to write about our painful search for self, jeopardized by a stranger in the post office, a half-seen face in a train window; to write about the continents and populations of our dreams, about love and death, good and evil, the end of the world.

2009

Ryszard Kapuściński's African Life

Suppose we were to launch a spacecraft with the intention of establishing literary contact with the residents of some remote part of the galaxy. If we had room for only one contemporary writer, who would we send? Bellow? Márquez? Atwood? Rushdie? I'd vote for Ryszard Kapuściński because he has given the truest, least partial, most comprehensive and vivid account of what life is like on our planet.

For almost thirty years he was a roving foreign correspondent for the Polish press agency. During that time he witnessed twenty-seven revolutions and coups. Though dutifully fulfilling his brief, he was also a kind of narcotic-free gonzo journalist, suddenly breaking contact with Warsaw and disappearing without trace to throw himself 'into the jungle, float down the Niger in a dugout, wander through the Sahara with nomads'. In *The Soccer War* we learn that in Nigeria in 1966 he was 'driving along a road where they say no white man can come back alive. I was driving to see if a white man could because I had to experience everything for myself.' At the first roadblock he was beaten and allowed to drive on after he had paid a toll. At the second roadblock he was beaten again, doused in benzene but, after handing over the rest of his money, allowed to drive on rather than being set alight. Which meant that by the time he came to the third roadblock he was penniless and highly inflammable . . . Kapuściński survived, sent in a hair-raising account of what happened, and received a telegram from his boss ordering him 'to put an end to these exploits that could end in tragedy'.

Fat chance. The early pages of *The Shadow of the Sun*, a compendium of further adventures in Africa, find him in Dar es Salaam, in 1962, where he hears that Uganda is about to gain independence. He and a friend, Leo, promptly set off for Kampala via the Serengeti with its teeming wildlife. 'It's all improbable, incredible. As if one were witnessing the birth of the world, that precise moment when the earth and sky already exist, as do water, plants, and wild animals, but not yet Adam and Eve.' They have no maps, they're lost and they're confronted with an enormous herd – 'stretching almost to the horizon' – of buffalo. They press on regardless. It gets hotter and hotter. 'The burning air started to quiver and undulate.' Kapuściński begins to hallucinate. By the time they come to a hut in the middle of nowhere Kapuściński is 'half dead'. He slumps down on a bunk only to discover that his hand is dangling inches from an Egyptian cobra. He freezes. Leo approaches gingerly and slams down an enormous metal canister on the snake. Kapuściński hurls himself on the canister as well, whereupon 'the interior of the hut exploded. I never suspected there could be so much power within a single creature. Such terrifying monstrous, cosmic power.' Eventually the cobra dies and they make it to Kampala. Kapuściński is still delirious, not just from heat-stroke but – it turns out – malaria. Cerebral malaria. He's just about recovered from malaria when he goes down with TB . . . All in about twenty pages!

Kapuściński, it has to be said, trowels it on. On every other page he is 'drenched in sweat'. Having risked life and limb to get *into* Zanzibar – another coup, naturally – he tries to sneak *out* in a boat, only to get caught in an imperfect storm that tips him from the precipice of a wave 'into a roaring abyss, a rumbling darkness'. Then the engine floods and cuts out. In the Sahara the sun beats down 'with the force of a knife'. Step out of the shade and 'you will go up in flames'. In Monrovia there are roaches 'as big as small turtles'. Is there a touch of exaggeration in all of this? Kapuściński himself alerts us to the possibility by observing that he 'could embellish' the stuff with the roaches but decides against it because it 'would not be true'.

The possibility, though, is always there. Experience is only the beginning – and some writers can get by on very little of it. I think it was Camus who pointed out that it is possible to lead a life of great adventure without leaving your desk. At the other extreme Joe Simpson can function as a writer only on condition that he remain roped to the cliff-face of personal experience. But what about someone who has the experience *and* is possessed of consummate intelligence and literary gifts? Then you have what Nietzsche considered 'something very rare but a thing to take delight in: a man with a finely constituted intellect who has the character, the inclinations and *also the experiences* appropriate to such an intellect'. Then you have Kapuściński.

It is often unclear whether he is recycling dispatches sent forty years ago or is only now writing up this hoard of experience. Chronology is deliberately uncertain, the sequence fragmented. Rival tenses jostle for dominance within the same page. Like this, his prose has the unsteady immediacy of the moment and a measure of historical reflection. What was happening in one part of the continent in the '60s affords a glimpse of what will happen elsewhere years later, in Liberia or Rwanda.

Robert Stone was over-generous when he likened Philip Gourevitch to Kapuściński. Gourevitch's *We Wish to Inform You* . . . is an outstanding book of reportage, but Kapuściński's work is of a different order of achievement. A great *imaginative* writer, he not only processes his material but goes beyond it. They may be rooted in his own experience but his books are full of amazing digressions, little essays – in *Imperium* – on how to make cognac, on the history of the Armenian book, on anything and everything. And yet these digressions are always integral to the conception of the work. In his nomadic life he has described real places – like the city of crates in Angola in the famous opening of *Another Day of Life* – that are as fantastical as Calvino's invisible cities. In Ethiopia he meets 'a man who was walking south. That is really the most important thing one can say about him. That he was walking north to south.' It's as if Coetzee's Michael K has just wandered into *The Shadow of the Sun*. Dozens of mini-novels and their characters stray briefly into view and then move on: 'All of Africa is in motion, on the road to somewhere, wandering.'

He is lyrically succinct – in the stupor of noon a village was 'like a submarine at the bottom of the ocean: it was there, but it emitted no signals, soundless, motionless' – and often hysterically funny. Terror gives way to absurd slapstick, and vice versa. Either way, an endless capacity for astonishment holds sway. He is an unflinching witness *and* an exuberant stylist.

And yet many fiction writers I've spoken with seem not even to have heard of him. In this respect he is the victim of a received cultural prejudice that assumes fiction to be the loftiest preserve of literary and imaginative distinction. It is instructive in this (rather dim) light to compare him with a highly regarded novel that touches on events to which Kapuściński has returned repeatedly. Ronan Bennett's *The Catastrophist* is set amid the historical upheaval surrounding the independence of Zaire and its aftermath (Kapuściński, needless to say, was there), including the death of Patrice Lumumba. Despite its distant location Bennett's well-crafted novel never strays from a familiar template of conventions. Kapuściński's radically unconventional approach, on the other hand, is entirely novel in the literal sense that no one else attempts anything like it. His material generates an apparently ad hoc aesthetic that draws on the chaos threatening to engulf him. The outcome – the *formal* outcome – is perpetually uncertain, in the balance. Hence the suspense.

There is perhaps a superficial resemblance to *The Songlines* but *The Shadow of the Sun* shows Chatwin for what he was: the rich man's Kapuściński! Kapuściński is steeped in the politics of everything he sees. His daring – actual and literary – is underwritten by an awareness of how politics complicates empathy, and of how sympathy implicates politics. There he is, a white man in Africa at the moment when countries are liberating themselves from the shackles of colonialism. But Kapuściński is from a country that has been repeatedly ravaged by the imperial ambitions of its neighbours. He knows what it means 'to have nothing, to wander into the unknown and wait for history to utter a kind word'. This is one of the reasons he feels at home in Africa, among the wretched of the earth. In other respects, he is utterly alien, making the attempt 'to find a common language' more exacting. To Kapuściński it is not Manhattan or La Défense in Paris 'that represent the highest achievement of human imagination' but a 'monstrous' African shanty town – an 'entire city erected without a single brick, metal rod, or square metre of glass!' The torpor of the wretched is matched by a quite phenomenal resourcefulness. Likewise, he never plays down the corruption or violence he has witnessed – on the contrary, its prevalence makes the survival of kindness all the more remarkable.

'There is more in men to admire than despise': this was the great truth dramatised by Camus in *The Plague*. Having narrowly escaped death in *The Soccer War*, Kapuściński is more direct: 'There is so much crap in this world, and then suddenly, there is honesty and humanity.' In the new book he puts it more simply and subtly. Summing up his dealings with a man serving as his driver, Kapuściński eventually achieves the human – rather than strictly economic – relation he craves, one rich in 'tenderness, warmth and goodwill'. He is not being naive or sentimental: the goodwill was genuine, heartfelt – but it could only be bought. Does this inhibit him from seeing the spirit of Africa? The answer is revealed, magnificently, on the very last page of the book.

By virtue of the fact that it's translated non-fiction, *The Shadow of the Sun* is ineligible for a number of literary prizes. The best thing to do would be to vault the problem by giving him a couple of Nobels – for literature and for peace.

2001

W. G. Sebald, Bombing
and Thomas Bernhard

The first thing to be said about W. G. Sebald's books is that they *always* had a posthumous quality to them. He wrote – as was often remarked – like a ghost. He was one of the most innovative writers of the late twentieth century, and yet part of this originality derived from the way his prose felt as if it had been exhumed from the nine-teenth.

The second is to concede that what Arthur Penn said of film – that it trembles constantly on the brink of being boring – also holds true for Sebald. It is the trembling, the perpetual uncertainty, the hovering on the edge of infinitely tedious regress (a yawning chasm, so to speak), that generate the peculiar suspense – the sense, more exactly, of suspended narration – that makes Sebald's writing so compelling. This was most pronounced, paradoxically, in *The Rings of Saturn* (the second of his books to be published in English), where the flatness of the landscape, the profound inaction described, accen-tuated the dizzy psychological depths plumbed. Like *The Emigrants* (his first), it held one's interest constantly because any clues as to what was going to make the book work always seemed likely to be hidden in the least interesting passages, the passages one was most tempted to skim. The reader was thereby forced to attend (in every sense) with a patience-straining diligence that proceeded in tandem with the narrator's weary tramping through the Suffolk lowlands.

Sebald's hypnotic prose lulls the reader into a stupor of height-ened attention. After a while (long after you might normally be prepared to wait) you sense that the studied avoidance of anything resembling momentum *has* generated a purpose and direction of its own: not a story as such but the process and chance encounters from which a more conventional novel could have been coaxed.

By the time of *Austerlitz* we had become sufficiently acclimatised to this weird literary terrain to feel that we knew exactly what was going on. 'Exactly' in the sense of, well, vaguely. In the course of his trips to Europe and London the narrator (indistinguishable from the 'I' of Sebald's other books) from time to time runs into his acquaintance, Austerlitz, who delivers perambulatory, Sebaldian lectures on architecture, the science and construction of fortifications. Austerlitz also gives a fragmented account of how, in 1939, at the age of five, he arrived in Wales and was brought up by Calvinist foster parents. Of his life prior to that he had, for a long time, no memory, but the obliterated past keeps coming to the surface through troubling coincidences. Sites of physical dereliction have such a powerful hold on him as to suggest a clue to his own sense of acute psychic abandonment. Tormented by the feeling that he has no idea who he is, his head ringing with echoes whose origin he cannot fathom, Austerlitz gradually accumulates details of how he was placed on one of the Kindertransports from Prague by his Jewish mother, Agata, whose fate slowly and painfully becomes known to him.

As in all of Sebald's books photographs are pasted into the text. These pictures anchor the author's history-drenched investigations in a documentary reality but – since they are always uncaptioned, impossible to vouch for – the surrounding prose is all the time dissolving the very reality they appear to support. In similar style, an exhaustive fidelity to empirical accuracy leads to interludes of deliriously plausible speculation. Actual journeys dissolve into discursive ones; the narrator's story melts into Austerlitz's, the former's familiar 'dull despair' giving way to the latter's 'soul-destroying' mental paralysis. In turn, Austerlitz's story is a prism refracting those of the people *he* meets. Apparently insignificant details become, quite literally, *telling* as the tangible landscape yields involuntarily to the buried claims of memory. In this light it is difficult not to regard Austerlitz – to quote David Thomson on Peter Lorre – as the 'wild-eyed spirit of ruined Europe'. Sebald, by extension, was the medium through whom that spirit spoke.

On the Natural History of Destruction goes to the epicentre of ruination, examining the Allied bombardment of German cities in the Second World War. Given the scale of the calamity, Sebald asks, why have German writers been so silent about it? How had it come about that 'the sense of unparalleled national humiliation felt by millions in the last years of the war had never really found verbal expression, and that those directly affected by the experience neither shared it with each other nor passed it on to the next generation'?

Given that much has been written in English about the bombing campaign, a good deal of it fiercely critical of Bomber Command, this comes as a shock to British readers. From the outset there was heated debate here as to whether terror bombing – or area bombing as it was euphemistically known – was morally justified and strategically worthwhile. The commander-in-chief, Arthur 'Bomber' Harris, had no doubts on this score, least of all ethical ones. In *Bomber Command*, Max Hastings reports how, when Harris was stopped by a police constable for driving so fast that he 'might have killed someone', he snapped back, 'Young man, I kill thousands of people every night!' According to Sebald there is much to support Solly Zuckerman's suggestion that Harris was a man who 'liked destruction for its own sake'. Understandably, the decision a few years ago to erect a statue of Harris in London generated intense controversy within Britain.

The bombing was initiated by a desire to do *something* to the enemy at a time when no other options were available. Once that decision had been made a massive amount of resources – far in excess, it was argued, of any industrial damage caused – was directed to this end. In the closing months of the war a deranged logic of industrial surplus demanded that bombing went ahead – because there were so many bombs and bombers – even though it served no purpose.

This aspect of *On the Natural History of Destruction* brings into focus part of the larger story of aerial aggression examined – in a book as original and aesthetically inventive as any of Sebald's – by Sven Lindqvist in *A History of Bombing*. Where Lindqvist is outraged and fiercely polemical, Sebald is characteristically curious and vexed as he looks at the ways in which the calamity is glimpsed in the work

of Heinrich Böll and others. The relative paucity of material is proof
to Sebald of 'people's ability to forget what they do not want to know,
to overlook what is before their eyes'.

The book is derived from lectures given by Sebald in Zurich in
1997. In those lectures Sebald sought to show how, even though he
was born in a village in the Allgäu Alps in 1944 and was 'almost
untouched by the catastrophe then unfolding in the German Reich',
it had 'nonetheless left its mark on my mind'. Sebald apparently illustrated this claim with lengthy references to his own work which he
chose not to reproduce in the book – a decision that makes the text
more recognisably Sebaldian. With characteristic vagueness Sebald
mentions that in one of his 'narratives' he described how, as a boy,
he had assumed that *all* cities were made of ruins. In the course of
trying to track down this reference it quickly became obvious that
several other passages in *Vertigo* (translated into English after *The
Emigrants* and *The Rings of Saturn*, but written before both) could be
seen to have their origin in the aftermath of the bombing. Near the
end of the book the narrator is in London, where, 'before the blazing
strip of sky on the western horizon, rain fell like a great funeral pall
from the dark-blue cloud that hung over the entire city'. The novel
closes with the narrator's description of a dream which merges with
an account from Samuel Pepys' diary of the Great Fire of London
that imaginatively anticipates – or should that be *recalls*? – the firestorm
that swept through Hamburg: 'we saw the fire grow. It was not bright,
it was a gruesome, evil, bloody flame, sweeping, before the wind,
through all the City.' (How far into critical meteorology – weather as
metaphor – should we go with this? To what extent does a down-
pour in Sebald recall what Edith Sitwell, in 'The Shadow of Cain',
called 'the terrible Rain' of bombing?)

Sebald wryly concedes that the 'unsystematic notes' of *The Natural
History of Destruction* do not do justice to the complex ways 'in which
memory (individual, collective and cultural) deals with experiences
exceeding what is tolerable'. That, of course, is the theme under-
pinning the complex architecture of *Austerlitz*. The extreme lethargy,
the 'lack [of] any real will to live', that Sebald observes in Böll's characters is shared by Austerlitz, who falls prey to a 'dreadful torpor

that heralds disintegration of the personality'. *The Natural History* derived its title from a planned report on the ravaged city of Köln by Zuckerman. The project came to nothing because what he had seen 'cried out for a more eloquent' piece of writing than he could manage. Austerlitz takes this to an extreme, succumbing to a breakdown so total that sentences come to consist of meaningless clumps and fragments of words.

If *The Natural History* sends us back to the earlier books in this way, it also looks ahead to narrative journeys that will not now be undertaken. Alert 'to the few points at which my own life touches the history of the air war', Sebald tells us that he lives near one of the many air fields in Norfolk from which the raids were launched.

'Grass has grown over the runways, and the dilapidated control towers, bunkers, and corrugated iron huts stand in an often eerie landscape where you sense the dead souls of the men who never came back from their missions, and of those who perished in the vast fires.' In turn this passage haunts us like the daybreak of a book that Sebald never came back to write.

After Sebald had delivered his lectures he received a number of letters confirming his belief 'that if those born after the war were to rely solely on the testimony of writers, they would scarcely be able to form any idea of the extent, nature, and consequences of the catastrophe inflicted on Germany by the air raids'. This came as a surprise since he had thought that his thesis 'would be refuted by instances which had escaped [his] notice'.

Now, at this point the book becomes extremely curious, for if we cross the border into Austria and use 'German' to refer not to a people but a language then we have, in Thomas Bernhard, an instance that refutes Sebald so thoroughly as to constitute a mirror-image of the lacuna he describes. That Sebald doesn't acknowledge this is all the more extraordinary given that Bernhard would seem to have been a significant influence on him. It is possible that the similarities between the two appear more striking in the English translations than the German originals but it was, surely, from Bernhard that Sebald derived the inverse telescoping whereby the reliability of the narrative recedes and diminishes the more incessantly it is vouched for.

'You concealed your shock very well, I said to the Englishman, Reger said to me,' writes Atzbacher, the narrator of Bernhard's *Old Masters*. 'I was particularly anxious, Vera told me, said Austerlitz,' writes the narrator of Sebald's *Austerlitz*. (If the aim of history is to go back to the primary sources then the indefinitely extended hearsay of these vicarious monologues is its wilful stylistic opposite.) The comic obsessiveness and neurosis common to many of Sebald's characters – their unnatural capacity for distraction – is like a sedated version of the relentless, raging frenzy into which Bernhard's narrators habitually drive themselves. 'For all the apparent quietness of Sebald's prose, exaggeration is its principle, an exaggeration he has undoubtedly learned in part from Thomas Bernhard,' writes James Wood. 'I've cultivated the art of exaggeration to such a pitch that I can call myself the greatest exponent of the art that I know of,' declares the narrator of Bernhard's last novel, *Extinction*. 'No one has carried the art of exaggeration to such extremes, I told Gambetti.'

Bernhard's influence was most explicit in *Austerlitz* – the pages of unparagraphed meandering even *look* Bernhardian. In the grip of a breakdown, Austerlitz discovers that, however much or little he has written, on subsequent reading it always seems 'so fundamentally flawed' that he has 'to destroy it immediately and begin again'. The passage itemising this collapse goes on for several pages; Bernhard's crazed narrators are imprisoned in unchanging variations of this infinite feedback loop for book after book after book.

Most significantly for the present discussion, the first instalment of Bernhard's five-volume autobiography, *An Indication of the Cause* (originally published in German in 1975, included as part of *Gathering Evidence* in 1985), dwells at length on his experience of the bombing campaign.

Bernhard was born in 1931; in 1944 he is at school in Salzburg, watching the 'hundreds and thousands of droning, menacing aircraft which daily darkened the cloudless sky'. Sebald notes that at some level perhaps the German people felt they deserved this retribution and, in a childish version of this impulse, Bernhard and his pals, 'while afraid of an *actual* bombing raid', 'secretly longed for the *actual* experience of an air attack'. It happens soon enough and Bernhard emerges from the shelter to be confronted by 'huge piles of smoking rubble, under which many people were said to be buried'. When Sebald asked Zuckerman about Köln the only details he could recall were the blackened cathedral and a severed finger he found nearby. In the course of one of his strolls through the ruined city the young Bernhard 'stepped on something soft lying on the pavement in front of the Bürgerspital Church. At first sight I took it to be a doll's hand . . . but in fact it was the severed hand of a child.' As this section of Bernhard's autobiography proceeds the reader realises that it is *exactly* the kind of thing that Sebald says does not exist. Every detail that he claims is buried beneath a blanket of silence is exhumed by Bernhard. Sebald discusses the Germans' delight in their ability to stage concerts soon after the bombing and, as if to dramatise this in miniature, the young Bernhard doggedly continues his violin lessons – until his violin is destroyed. One could go on quoting passages interminably (Bernhard is nothing if not interminable) to show how Bernhard, in an extraordinary pre-echo of Sebald's own phrase, evokes what was 'developing into the greatest catastrophe the world had known'. But the important thing to emphasise here is that at one point Bernhard looks back and – stressing the psychic fallout posited by Sebald – realises that 'whenever I walk through the city today, imagining that it has nothing to do with me because I wish to have nothing to do with it, the fact remains that everything about me, everything within me, *derives from this city.* I am bound to it by a terrible, indissoluble bond.'

Bernhard is the most perversely contradictory of writers. How *perfect*, then, that this book which refutes Sebald's thesis absolutely should simultaneously confirm it:

whenever I speak to people about what happened, nobody knows what I am talking about. In fact everybody seems to have lost all recollection of the many houses that were destroyed and the many people who were killed, or else they no longer want to know when someone tries to remind them. When I visit the city today, I always ask people what they recall of that terrible period, but they react by shaking their heads. To me these shocking experiences are as vivid now as if they had happened only yesterday. Whenever I visit the city, I suddenly remember sounds and smells which they, it seems, have blotted out of their memories. When I speak to people who are old inhabitants of the city who must have been through what I went through, I meet only with extreme annoyance, ignorance, and forgetfulness. It is like being confronted with a concerted determination not to know, and I find this offensive – offensive to the spirit.

Again, this is Austria not Germany (Bernhard insisted that the rhythms of his prose were Austrian, not German). If someone adopted a similar critical ploy, using an American writer to correct a perceived traumatised silence in British writing, this would be discredited by the simple fact of geographical distance and historical difference. But Austria is right next to Germany and, more importantly, the experience Bernhard describes ('So-called total war was getting closer and closer and had now made itself felt even in Salzburg') is practically indistinguishable from the one Sebald is concerned with. If we accept the comparison as valid, two intriguing possibilities result. One is that by failing to take account of Bernhard it is as if Sebald has in some way fallen victim to his own thesis, succumbing to the amnesia he describes. The other is that because of their intense stylistic similarities we already have a premonition of how Sebald himself might have made good the lack he laments.

2003

Regarding the Achievement
of Others: Susan Sontag

To what extent is it possible to be a great prose writer without being a great writer of fiction? Or, to put a similar question in a different way, can one's achievements as cultural commentator and critic be enough to make one a writer in the specially valued sense of those one has written about? Don Paterson, in *The Book of Shadows*, is Manichaean on this score. 'Well, critic: fair criticism. But at the end of the day, she did; you didn't.'

The thing about Susan Sontag is that she both did and didn't. As essayist and thinker her stature is assured. The authority, rigour, clarity, discernment and range of her expository prose helped configure the cultural landscape of the last forty years. For almost the whole of that time Sontag had also been writing fiction, from the modish avant-gardism of *Death Kit* and *I, Etcetera*, to the later, substantial novels, *The Volcano Lover* and *In America*. As her son David Rieff points out in a moving foreword to *At the Same Time*, a characteristically varied collection of essays and speeches, 'she valued her work as a fiction writer more than anything else she did'. And it is here that a major discrepancy opens up, between how Sontag regarded herself and the way she is regarded – and will be remembered – by others.

Speaking personally, my love of her writing would be undiminished if she had never published a novel. (I remember thinking, when *In America* won the National Book Award, that the prize was thoroughly deserved – as long as one assumed that it was given for everything *except* the book in question.) 'Literature', she contends, 'is knowledge', but dozens of writers, some with only a fraction of her intelligence and knowledge, have produced novels that are many times more impressive – to say nothing of enjoyable – than hers. This makes her case especially interesting. It is, I am tempted to say, what *At the Same Time* is predominantly, if tacitly, *about*. A quick diversion will enable us to see why and how.

J.M. Coetzee has just published *Inner Workings*, his latest instalment of critical writings. As one would expect from a novelist of his abilities, these essays – the result of careful ladling between two closely related activities – are of a consistently high standard but they are not the work on which Coetzee would stake his claim to greatness. As far as I am aware, no such collection is forthcoming from Lorrie Moore. Moore is one of those writers whose intelligence and perception find perfect expression in fiction. Little of her talent has spilled over into the realm of commentary. She feels perfectly *at home* with fiction. So there was a certain irony when Sontag cattily dismissed Moore's work – especially the 'famous story' about 'the infant having cancer' – on the grounds that it was so trivial 'you don't respect yourself for finishing it'. As a writer of fiction Sontag strikes one as having to proceed like Jackson Pollock in reverse, finding ways of coaxing spillage back into the confines of the pot. Thus the most extraordinary moment in a collection marked by unflinching intellectual honesty is also the most deluded. It comes during the Friedenspreis acceptance speech, when Sontag describes herself as 'a storyteller'. To put the matter crassly, she couldn't tell a story to save her life. (Her reaction to learning about her first diagnosis of cancer was not to fictionalise the experience but to examine it analytically, in the benchmark essay, *Illness as Metaphor*.) What she did manage, with *The Volcano Lover*, was to find a way – just – of turning her distinctive discursive habits into a mode of historicised fictional narration. As for *In America*, I respected myself so much for finishing it that I felt I deserved a prize myself.

The irony is that whereas for Sontag the essays were a compelling distraction from what she felt she should be doing, the commitment to fiction was, to many of her admirers, an interruption from her ongoing critical project. Her best writing recorded, with a trademark combination of precision and breadth, the experience of being a reader of – and looker at – other people's works. Except it was not quite as simple as that.

Critics are always working the room. The way they do so changes over the course of a career. Young critics like to disparage and tear down. Later, when they write about the real heavyweights, it is not so much the subjects – Tolstoy, Proust etc. – as their own ability to go toe-to-toe with greatness that comes under examination. Once this test has been passed a reversal takes place when an unknown, under-rated or neglected figure is deemed worthy of the attention of a particularly respected critic. The mere fact that, in the current volume, Sontag considers the case of Victor Serge – at length, brilliantly – is a vicarious affirmation of his status.

But this kind of employment was not enough for Sontag, either as reader or as writer. For someone who valued literature so highly and, more importantly, who understood so well what it took to produce literature of lasting value, Paterson's 'She did, you didn't' would have gnawed away like a constant reproach. So she had to believe that fiction was her real home – and had to have her right of residence recognised.

As *At the Same Time* repeatedly demonstrates, Sontag was both moralist and aesthete, democrat and elitist. Her political commitments were matched by her unyielding adherence to standards of excellence, to the belief – as she famously quipped – that 'literature is not an equal opportunity employer'. She wanted to meet people on equal terms. It's just that the people she most wanted to meet were right at the top of the cultural totem pole. And she couldn't meet them on equal terms simply as a critic so the fiction, the fiction that (to her) was more important than – and, *at the same time*, palpably inferior to – everything else she wrote, had to be hauled (or, if you prefer, smuggled) up there too. How? By claiming that the magisterial pronouncements *about* literature were a side-effect of having produced it. This had the additional side-effect of giving her political and critical interventions even more weight because of the sacrifice or opportunity cost (foregoing the real business of writing fiction) of doing so. But it is of course these distractions (five years later her off-the-cuff 9/11 piece seems a profoundly considered reaction, not only to what happened but to what lay ahead) that constitute her real and enduring achievement.

2007

The Moral Art of War

The question of whether writers should engage with the big events of the day can never be permanently settled. Sartre conceded that a writer was under no obligation to deal with the threat of nuclear war – but you couldn't be wholly sincere in writing poems about birds if you were scared of 'dying like a rat'. Sometimes – as Orwell argued on behalf of Henry Miller – important work will come out of an extreme aversion to the claims of history. Certainly, there is no correlation between a willingness to grapple with big themes and the quality of the work that results. But it happens that, at this moment, the defining story of our time – the Al Qaeda attacks on New York and the Pentagon, and the subsequent wars in Iraq and Afghanistan – is being told in some of the greatest books of our time. It's just that these books are not coming in the shape and form commonly expected: the novel.

In very roughly chronological order of ground covered – there is, inevitably, a degree of overlap – the shelf of masterpieces already includes: Steve Coll's *Ghost Wars: The Secret History of the CIA, Afghanistan and Bin Laden, from the Soviet Invasion to September 10, 2001*; Lawrence Wright's *The Looming Tower: Al Qaeda's Road to 9/11*; George Packer's *The Assassin's Gate: America in Iraq*; Rajiv Chandrasekaran's *Imperial Life in the Emerald City: Inside Baghdad's Green Zone* and Dexter Filkins' *The Forever War*. Lower the bar only slightly and room would have to be made for Evan Wright's *Generation Kill*, Thomas E. Ricks' *Fiasco: The American Military Adventure in Iraq* and its follow-up, *The Gamble*. Broaden the catchment area somewhat and Jane Mayer's *The Dark Side: The Inside Story of How the War on Terror Turned into a War on America's Ideals*, and Ahmed Rashid's *Descent into Chaos: The World's Most Unstable Region and the Threat to Global Security* would also make the cut.

There is no sign that this surge of war books will stop any time soon. David Finkel's *The Good Soldiers* is the result of eight months spent with the US 2-16 Infantry Battalion in Baghdad, part of 'the surge' confidently announced by President Bush in January 2007. Sebastian Junger's *War* is an account of his time embedded with a platoon of American soldiers at 'the tip of the spear' in the lethal Korengal Valley in Afghanistan. Jim Frederick's *Black Hearts* is a devastating investigation of the disintegration, under intolerable pressure, of a platoon of American soldiers of the 502nd Infantry Regiment in Iraq's 'triangle of death', in 2005–6, culminating in the rape and murder of a fourteen-year-old Iraqi girl and the execution of her family by four members of the platoon.

As Packer put it in his recent collection of essays, *Interesting Times*, 'The press redeemed in Baghdad what it had botched in Washington.' Reportage, long-form reporting, contemporary history – call it what you will – has left the novel looking somewhat superfluous.

The novelist's lobby might respond in the style of Zhou Enlai when asked about the consequences of the French Revolution: it's too soon to tell. A decade of literary silence followed the Armistice of 1918. It wasn't until 1929 that a novel appeared which made imaginative sense of the First World War. Erich Maria Remarque's *All Quiet on the Western Front* answered an unspoken need and helped create the conditions in which other war novels might, in the words of the hopeful Richard Aldington, 'go big'. Since then, however, the lag between a given war and the appearance of books about it has shrunk. Norman Mailer's *The Naked and the Dead* appeared in 1948. In terms of its timing, Joseph Heller's *Catch-22* (1961) was a strange and fortuitous case: a novel about the Second World War that seemed to anticipate the absurdity of Vietnam. The defining prose work to come out of *that* conflict was a book of reportage, Michael Herr's *Dispatches* (1977). This is not to ignore *Dog Soldiers*, *The Things They Carried* or *Machine Dreams*, but, like teams competing for lower places in a league whose winner has already been confirmed, Robert Stone, Tim O'Brien and Jayne Anne Phillips concede the top spot to Herr – or to journalist Neil Sheehan for his epic history, *A Bright Shining Lie*. The potential exception to this judgement, *The Sorrow of War* by the Vietnamese author Bao Ninh, raises the interesting possibility that, if a great novel does emerge from the current conflict, it might be by a writer from Iraq.

No major novel came out of the first Gulf War; it received its most memorable prose expression in Anthony Swofford's account of his time in the Marines. *Jarhead* (2003) may not have been a first-rate literary achievement, but the power and skewed originality of the narrative was such that even a director as ham-fisted as Sam Mendes was able to turn it into a decent film.

The precedent set by Herr and followed, in off-kilter fashion, by Swofford, seems unlikely to be reversed. If there was a time when the human stories contained within historical events – what Packer calls 'the human heart of the matter' – could only be assimilated and comprehended when they had been processed by a novel (*War and Peace* is the supreme example), that time has passed. Given the high quality of reportage about the current conflicts, it is difficult to see what the novelist might bring to the table except stylistic panache (we will return to this) and the burden of unnecessary conventions. As David Shields put it in his recent manifesto, *Reality Hunger*, 'A while ago the imaginative thing – the supposedly great thing – would have been to write a "novel about Vietnam", but I just feel in my bones how little I could read that.' You don't have to sign up for Shield's anti-novel *jihad* to feel that what he says about Vietnam holds good for Iraq – *only more so*.

But aren't I forgetting those novelistic trumps, character and story? The characters are there in the non-fiction accounts, fully realised in flesh and (often awash in) blood, in exactly the way that we expect fictional characters to be. Lawrence Wright has spoken of how, in the process of researching the 9/11 attacks, he came to realise that certain people could serve as 'donkeys', to bear the weight of larger historical drives or circumstances. Part of the success of *The Looming Tower* derives from the way that these donkeys are presented as complex and developing individuals, never simply as beasts of narrative burden. And while their destinies fatefully converge on the Twin Towers in a way that is almost novelistic, the book's suspense and momentum do not reduce the idea of narrative to page-turning compulsion. At their best – as Wright and his colleagues remind us – narrative and story are forms of cognition and understanding.

Finkel has seen most of what he records, but removes himself absolutely from his own narrative. In this respect *The Good Soldiers* is like a traditional third-person novel, with a near-omniscient narrator – or an Isherwood-style camera, recording but not judging. What this camera records – what the soldiers endure – almost defies belief. The combat is dreadful, the immediate aftermath worse. 'Someone, maybe a medic, was pushing up and down on his chest so violently it seemed every one of his ribs must be breaking. "You need to go harder and faster," the doctor in charge told him. The medic began pushing so hard that pieces of Reeves' shredded leg began dropping on the floor.' The long-term aftermath is worse still, as the central character, Lieutenant Colonel Ralph Kauzlarich, visits the ruined soldiers and their families – recovering and not recovering – back in the States. 'There was so much of Duncan Crookston missing that he didn't seem real. He was half of a body propped up in a full-size bed, seemingly bolted into place.'

In the course of the book you see Kauzlarich – 'Lost Kauz', as he becomes known – and other good men 'disintegrate before your eyes'. Their efforts are heroic and futile. Wright's idea of the donkey has been enlarged so that the experiences of one group of soldiers encapsulate the larger quagmire of the US in Iraq – a quagmire that is tactical, strategic, moral and political. (Frederick does something similar in *Black Hearts*.)

The starkness and magnitude of Finkel's material demands an unerring control of tone. Even at its most matter-of-fact, his prose finds a hypnotic calm in the interminable repetition of exposure to extreme danger: 'Eyes sweeping, jammers jamming, the convoy moved along route Pluto . . .' At times there is an eerie, damaged lyricism: 'Hours later, as the sun set, the sky took on its nightly ominous feel. The moon, not quite full, rose dented and misshapen, and the aerostat, a grey shadow now rather than the bright white balloon it had been in daylight, loomed over a landscape of empty streets and buildings surrounded by sandbags and tall concrete blast walls.' One of these details acquires hideous poignancy later, when a soldier is shot in the head; he survives but his head assumes the 'dented and misshapen' aspect of the moon. With touches like this Finkel demonstrates how the chaos of events can be given narrative shape by scrupulous observation and phrasing.

A lesser but still thrilling book, *War* plunges the reader into the adrenalin-mist of combat. Like the soldiers around him, Junger is less interested in 'the moral basis of the war' than the immediate experience of combat and its 'twisted existential' ramifications whereby 'each moment was the only proof you'd ever have that you hadn't been blown up the moment before'. Often his senses were so overwhelmed by the experience that it was only by consulting video footage he had shot during firefights that he was able to understand and write up what had been going on. This feeds into another of Junger's interests: the complex mixture of military training and biochemical processes – the body's emergency surges and shutdowns – that enable a person to function in extreme danger while the instinct for self-preservation programmes him to curl up in a ball or flee. Actually, it turns out not to be so complicated after all. Courage, Junger learns, is love: a willingness to lay down your life for others who, you know, would do the same for you, because in certain situations there is no such thing as 'personal safety' ('what happened to you happened to everyone'). There is also the fact that combat is so 'insanely exciting' that 'one of the most traumatic things about [it] is having to give it up.'

War is written in the first person; unlike Finkel, Junger is present in the events he records, but discreetly, unobtrusively. The most extreme contrast to Finkel's narrative self-effacement, however, is represented by the author who sits right next to him on alphabetically arranged shelves – and operates at a comparable level of literary excellence: Dexter Filkins, author of the jagged collection of dispatches, *The Forever War.* Junger and Evan Wright are actors in their respective books, but neither has the authorial swagger of Filkins.

He might be employed by the stylistically conservative *New York Times*, but Filkins is obviously an heir of Herr.

This can be a little grating at first. He is so bad boy, so gonzo. Apart from a few details of transport and costume this early glimpse of the Taliban could have been lifted straight from Hunter Thompson's *Hell's Angels*: 'Man, they were scary. You'd see them rolling up in one of the Hi-Luxes, all jacked up, white turbans gleaming; they were the baddest asses in town and they knew it, too.'

A man who has 'lived through everything, shootings and bomb blasts and death', Filkins is the latest incarnation of the reporter as renegade, 'untethered, floating free, figuring out the truth by a different set of standards'. Like Junger he is willing to get to the place of maximum danger, but tends, when he gets there, to drift into a digression that winds us more tightly into the scene. At which point, a still more illustrious antecedent comes to mind: Ryzard Kapuściński. (Once you begin looking for precedents it's difficult to know where to stop: perhaps we can also glimpse the ghost of Alan Moorehead, the great Australian reporter of the Second World War.)

This willingness to digress, to operate in territory that shares a border with fiction, does not meet with universal approval. I once went to a talk given by Jon Lee Anderson, who had just published *The Fall of Baghdad*. During the Q and A afterwards I asked if he felt any tension between the *New Yorker's* famous emphasis on factual accuracy, and the urge to embellish – even if that tugged one away from an objective reporting of the facts – that made Rebecca West and Kapuściński great writers, if potentially unreliable reporters. Quite a clever question, I thought, but Anderson dismissed it with magisterial contempt. With the bullets flying, any thoughts of literary embellishment were luxuries he couldn't afford; his only concern was to report things accurately. Filkins, I'm guessing, would have been more sympathetic, as even an atrocious incident – coming across the head of a suicide bomber who has detonated himself in a crowded market, for example – can become a source of horror–comedy: 'They'd placed it on a platter like John the Baptist's, and set it on the ground next to an interior doorway. It was in good shape, considering what it had been through . . . . The most curious aspect of the face was the man's eyebrows: they were raised, as if in surprise. Which struck me as odd, given that he would have been the only person who knew ahead of time what was going to happen.'

It's not just a question of tone. As with Kapuściński's *The Soccer War*, the pieces in *The Forever War* often have the narrative shape and moral resolution of fiction. 'Pearland' recounts an episode from the assault on Fallujah in which Filkins and a photographer are responsible for the death of twenty-two-year-old Lance Corporal William Miller. The story ends with multiple layers of dreadful, poignant and unresolved irony.

Taking our cue from Junger's observation that the platoon, the group, counts for so much more than the individual, what – leaving aside particular merits or otherwise – do books of this kind reveal about larger questions of documentary versus fiction, about the ways in which the wars in Iraq and Afghanistan are recorded and represented?

They make one feel thoroughly duped, for a start, by Kathryn Bigelow's Oscar-winning film *The Hurt Locker*. As with the HBO adaptation of Evan Wright's *Generation Kill* (written by David Simon and Ed Burns) the viewer is totally immersed in the experience of the American military in Iraq. Both are relentlessly gripping, especially *The Hurt Locker*, where every bit of trash – and there's a lot of trash – is potentially life-threatening. Indeed, *The Hurt Locker* is so nerve-shreddingly tense that it's only when you re-emerge into the safety of daylight that you see quite how ludicrously you have been manipulated, how shallow the experience has been. There is a thematic continuity here within Bigelow's work: *The Hurt Locker* serves up a military equivalent of the thrill-trips that Lenny Nero was hustling in her earlier *Strange Days*. Lenny sells virtual reality experiences of everything from a girl showering to armed robbery. And that – right down to the same camera techniques – is exactly what we get here. The new twist is in the nature of the simulated environment: all the thrills and spills of combat and bomb disposal in the privacy and safety of your own home-entertainment environment! So impressive is the technical accomplishment that one forgets that the action, while ostensibly unfolding in the context of a real and recognisable war, is operating safely within the absurd liberties of Hollywood convention. As if his life as a bomb-disposal expert were not exciting enough, as if it weren't stretching belief that a top bomb-disposal outfit could suddenly morph into a crack sniper team, we are treated to a Bourne-style interlude in which William James implausibly and absurdly pulls on a hooded sweatshirt, takes a pistol and goes on a one-man search for vengeance–justice (in Hollywood the two are dangerously synony-mous) *at night,* in Baghdad – and makes it back in one piece! Throughout, the inflexible rigour of military discipline appears merely optional. While we're at it, the whole character of James is patently absurd: a short-haired and uniformed reincarnation of Patrick Swayze, still seeking the ultimate ride, not in the surf and skies of *Point Break,* but in the heat and dust of Baghdad.

The TV adaptation of *Generation Kill* is, along with everything else, a sustained critique of the structural and conventional fictions of *The Hurt Locker.* Taking no liberties with the facts of Wright's account, the series follows a convoy of US marines as they make their way from Kuwait to Baghdad. Certain characters have more screen-time than others, but there are no heroes. As in a platoon everything comes down to team-work and ensemble playing. The action is never contrived to assume the shape imposed by the demands of a good story. This is one of the reasons why, ultimately, the immersion in the experience of war is more complete than in *The Hurt Locker.* Despite their expertise and marksmanship the extent to which the marines control their own destinies is minimal; it pretty much ended, in fact, before the series began, when they signed up. From the start we are sealed within the acronym-intensive argot and world-view of the USMC. Our p.o.v. is absolutely that of the marines. The lessons dished out by their experiences are never moralistic, but, as the situation deteriorates around them, the larger ethical and strategic impossibility of their position and purpose becomes unavoidable.

We are back to the quandary observed by Finkel in *The Good Soldiers.* We are also back, more generally, to the relative strengths of non-fiction over fiction. Of course, one could easily imagine a novelist taking none of the liberties enjoyed by Bigelow. But we would be left, then, with a novel that was almost a carbon copy of the best of the non-fiction books discussed here. For the assumed skills of the novelist – an eye for telling detail, stylistic flair and so on – are deployed in abundance by many of these reporters, at least the ones who are – there's no dodging this bullet so we might as well bite it – *American*.

Within every comparable category or type of book on Iraq and Afghanistan the Americans do it better than their British counterparts. On either side of the Atlantic the books by journalists are, naturally, better than those by the people they are writing about. It is clear from *Generation Kill* that Nathaniel Fick is a remarkable officer and human being. In his own book, *One Bullet Away*, however, Fick is not able to impose his authorial personality on his version of the story from which he emerges with so much credit in Wright's account. Similarly, *Desperate Glory* – British journalist Sam Kiley's Junger-esque account of his time in Helmand with Britain's 16 Air Assault Brigade – is a better piece of writing than *The Junior Officers' Reading Club*, former soldier Patrick Hennessey's memoir of his tours of duty in Iraq and Afghanistan. This is inevitable; we don't expect Wright and Kiley to be able to shoot more accurately or march further in full equipment than Fick or Hennessey. But once we start comparing like with like – soldier with soldier, journo with journo – the Americans come out unambiguously ahead. Fick's book is more accomplished than Hennessey's. Wright and Junger make Kiley seem at best a competent reporter.

Americans, in other words, possess an overall advantage – and the reasons for this are not hard to fathom. Print journalists lucky enough to be working for *Rolling Stone* (Wright), *Vanity Fair* (Junger) or *The New Yorker* (Packer) are like the soldiers with whom they are embedded: both benefit from the economic might of America while their cash-strapped British equivalents make do with scantier resources.

More generally, American journalists writing about the US military are the beneficiaries of the all-round flexibility and versatility of American English as deployed by the soldiers on whose lives they depend. Officers and non-coms alike share a common idiom which is varied and animated by the racial and cultural make-up of the army. In the

British military, by contrast, the lack of this shared linguistic medium reflects the basic class division of the army, between officers and enlisted men, toffs and proles. Instead of variety there is a straight choice. And this applies not just to reported speech, but to the register adopted by writers when operating outside the class perimeter of inverted commas. As can easily happen when choice is demanded, the worst possible result is a compromise that rinses out everything that might make either idiom compelling. This is exactly what we get in Hennessey and Kiley: a lumpen version of educated English which lacks both the clipped polish of Sandhurst and the vitality of unschooled demotic. (Conveying the latter in print requires the highest literary ambition and skill.) The experiences might be bloody, violent and extreme, but the idiom ends up being anodyne. 'Just as the Liverpool vs. Chelsea game kicks off, and some angelic signaller appears out of nowhere with hot dogs, and it seems life is as good as it gets, the message comes through about more casualties, which leaves the football forgotten, and even the bad luck Liverpool apparently suffer doesn't matter a shit against the good luck that it's not any of our boys . . .' That's Hennessey: not terrible writing; just bland and more than a little clumsy.

Kiley is 'mad keen' to get the job done, but even when the experiences he records are terrifying, the writing is always comfortably unthreatened, except by clichés which are often, as they say in the military, danger-close. Hence the undermining sense that any moderately talented writer could have come up with the following *without* leaving his desk. 'The air fizzes and crackles with bullets. There seems to be no space between them as if they are being poured from a hose. Rounds are smacking into the ground; the dust is leaping around their feet. Des can hear the fizzing sound made by bullets which are within a foot of his ear. He can feel the hot whip of them on his face . . .' Writing is not a bravery contest; it's a writing contest. Junger is as experience-dependent as Kiley, but his prose ('he saw a line of bullets stitching towards him in the dirt . . .') works like one of Lenny Nero's virtual trips, sealing us within the experience described.

It's not just a question of individual talent, though. Hennessey and Kiley are both victims of Britishness, hostages to the fact that as soon

as you open your mouth you are class-identified. Among the marines
engaged in the fight for Fallujah, Filkins is 'self-conscious of my age
and my profession and my education' but not, it is worth noting, his
accent. When Evan Wright arrives at the marine base in Kuwait, ready
to roll with them into Iraq, they resent him as an outsider, but he
never has to resort to the American equivalent of 'mockney'; linguistically, he is equally at home with officers and enlisted men. The
traffic between reported speech and narrative voice is unchecked and
constant. There may be a certain amount of shared linguistic ground
between British officers and men – 'Fuck fuck fuck', Hennessey repeats
to himself at a moment of danger. 'It's the most versatile word in the
language' – but Americans would seem to have the edge in politically incorrect invention and invective. From the moment Evan Wright
arrives and overhears a marine discussing an Asian girl whose 'eyes
were so small and tight you could have blindfolded her with dental
floss' he knows that a good part of his job will just be keeping his
ears open and getting it all down.

This is not to say that, by turning their attention to Afghanistan
or Iraq, American reporters and journalists are on to a sure-fire winner.
When Jon Krakauer became interested in the story of Pat Tillman,
he must have thought that he had found (in Wright's terms) the
perfect donkey: All-American boy wins lucrative pro-football deal,
but, after 9/11, chucks it in to join the army and goes to Afghanistan
where he is killed in an ambush. Even more of a hero. Then word
begins to creep out that he was killed by friendly fire, and the military try everything in their power to conceal the truth.

It's a potentially great story and even though *Where Men Win Glory*
reveals Krakauer's limitations as a writer – for the historical background, he gulps down hunks of Coll and Lawrence Wright without
ever adequately digesting them – it remains an interesting failure in
several unexpected ways. Krakauer sees that the military want Tillman
to fit into their own heroic narrative, both specifically (the ambush)
and generally (football star sacrifices career to join army and then
sacrifices himself). But the buck does not stop there, for it is clear
that Krakauer has seized on Tillman as the latest incarnation of the
ideal of rugged and tragic individualism that made his earlier books

Into Thin Air (about a doomed Everest expedition) and *Into the Wild* (the story of Chris McCandless' death in the Alaskan wilderness) so compelling. Viewed in this light the book compounds the kind of exemplary appropriation that it investigates.

There is another reason why an obviously flawed book repays serious attention – a reason which, paradoxically, reinforces the case for non-fiction generally that this particular instance would seem to undermine. One of the Tillman family's grievances was that the army – specifically a lieutenant colonel who was also an evangelical Christian – over-rode Pat's explicit wish for a secular funeral. Later, after the family had refused to accept the findings of several investigations into Pat's death, that same lieutenant colonel gave an interview in which he suggested that the Tillman family's continuing dissatisfaction was due to their lack of religious faith.

In the larger scheme of Krakauer's book it's a fairly minor point, but the Christian lieutenant colonel turns out to be none other than Ralph Kauzlarich, the enormously sympathetic central character – the donkey carrying the heaviest load – in Finkel's *The Good Soldiers*. Just as characters interconnect with each other within a novel so these non-fiction books and real-life characters interconnect with and segue into each other to form an epic, ongoing, multi-volume work-in-progress. The name of this constantly revised, unfinishable book, I guess, will eventually be *History*.

The biggest question mark about this proto-book concerns the way in which it is illustrated. Years ago, in *The Missing of the Somme*, I suggested that a caveat needed to be added to Adorno's famous claim that there could be no poetry after Auschwitz: there would, instead, be photography. I wonder now if that amendment is itself in need of amendment. As Packer wrote in the essay quoted earlier, the press may have excelled itself in Baghad, but 'Iraq has not been a photographer's war'. Really? When there are so many strong pictures coming out of the current wars by Sean Smith, Michael Kamber, Tim Hetherington (who was with Junger in Afghanistan and co-directed their documentary *Restrepo*) and others? Perhaps these are the exceptions that prove the rule, for Packer, it's important to note, is talking about photograph*ers*, not photography. In Iraq and Afghanistan we are perhaps glimpsing the end of the era of the combat photographer as a special category of occupation, the twilight of the photographer *as novelist* in the way that Capa (whose famous photo from the Spanish Civil War is now believed to be a fiction) and Eugene Smith were visual novelists. Current photography from the frontline is defined absolutely by what it is *of* rather than who it is *by*. No photographer has been able to stamp a visual identity on what he depicted in the way that Capa or Tim Page managed, respectively, on D-Day or in Vietnam. Perhaps photographs are now simply too ubiquitous for that. So ubiquitous that, in a devastating passage in Finkel's book, 'photographs' refers not to actual physical records of the kind collected by Wilfred Owen (who carried photos of the dead and injured in his wallet), but a way of seeing, a state of damaged mind. Suffering from post-traumatic breakdown, one of the most heroic soldiers in the battalion explains that he keeps seeing 'photographs . . . Like a picture of Harrelson burning, in flames. I can't get that out of my head right now . . . It's just a slideshow in my head.'

Even when it comes to marketable images photography no longer needs someone with special skill and sensibility or even a special set of equipment: *anyone* with a free hand and some kind of image-gadget will do. Capa thought a bit of blur lent a dangerous immediacy to his images; photographs now seem most 'real' when they look as though they were taken not with a camera but through a cell phone or (it can't be long before this becomes possible) the scope of a sniper's rifle.

Consistent with this, the debate about current combat photographs is less about their quality than whether it is appropriate or in good taste to publish them. Last year AP caused a fire-storm of controversy by distributing a photograph from Afghanistan taken by Julie Jacobson. Lacking any of the formal elegance of Burrows, just about in focus, it was unremarkable in every way – except that it showed twenty-one-year-old Lance Corporal Joshua Bernard in the gory process of dying from wounds after getting hit in the legs by an RPG. Bernard's family were adamant that they did not want the picture published and were outraged when AP went ahead anyway on the grounds that it showed the human reality of war. Now, Filkins and Finkel witness events just as harrowing, and describe them in far

more explicit detail. Their verbal records of these events became tributes for which they receive the gratitude of the bereaved and wounded.
Anyone who was there with a camera and an auto-wind could have
taken a picture of the quality of Jacobson's. Only a few supremely
gifted – and courageous – individuals could have recorded the deaths
of Miller or Reeves with the skill and power of Filkins or Finkel.
They are, to adapt a phrase of Martin Amis', 'moral artists'.

The phrase is from an essay in *The Moronic Inferno* in which Amis
claims that the non-fiction novel, as practised by Mailer and Capote,
lacks 'moral imagination. Moral artistry. The facts cannot be arranged
to give them moral point. There can be no art without moral point.
When the reading experience is over, you are left, simply, with murder
– and with the human messiness and futility that attends all death.'
The essay is an old one, and the point can now be seen to contain
its own limitation and, by extension, refutation. We are moving
beyond the non-fiction *novel* to different kinds of narrative art, different
forms of cognition. Loaded with moral *and* political point, narrative
has been recalibrated to record, honour and protest the latest, historically specific instance of futility and mess.

2010

Is Jazz Dead?

Duke Ellington died on 24 May 1974. Within days Miles Davis had recorded a tribute, 'He Loved Him Madly' (alluding, of course, to Ellington's 'Love You Madly'). Across the Atlantic, Philip Larkin was also moved by Ellington's death: 'Let us bury the great Duke', he wrote (alluding to Tennyson's poem on the death of Wellington). 'I've been playing some of his records: now he and Armstrong have gone jazz is finally finished.'

Miles Davis died on 28 September 1991. On 12 October Keith Jarrett and his trio recorded 'For Miles' and 'Blackbird, Bye Bye' as their tribute to him.

In the fall of 1996 Jarrett became ill with Chronic Fatigue Syndrome. If that is a more accurate name for what is popularly known as ME, for Jarrett, it was a 'stupid' understatement. 'It should', he said, 'be called Forever Dead Syndrome.' He couldn't do anything, couldn't play the piano. For someone who claimed that 'playing the piano' had been his 'entire life', it was like not existing.

Recorded at his home studio in rural New Jersey, *The Melody At Night, With You* (1999) was the album of Jarrett's convalescence. In a way it was a very modest offering: an hour of old love songs and standards played solo, on the piano, with little sign of the surging improvisational gusto that marked Jarrett's epochal Köln Concert of 1975. When he took a break from playing improvised music to begin recording Bach in 1987 Jarrett remarked, 'This music doesn't need my help.' This time around it was the pianist who needed the help

of loyal old tunes like 'Someone to Watch Over Me' and 'I Got It Bad
and That Ain't Good'. Finding themselves *needed* and profoundly
appreciated, the songs flickered back to life.

If this seems a sentimental reading consider Jarrett in the wider
context of jazz at the tail-end of the century through which it streaked.
Was it not appropriate – inevitable, almost – that one of the greatest
living jazz musicians should have succumbed to exhaustion when
the medium in which he was working had utterly exhausted itself?

From the early '40s to the late '60s, jazz strode confidently into
the future, constantly revolutionising itself. Such was the speed of
development during this period that, in its aftermath, musicians could
build careers stocktaking the immense hoard of cultural riches laid
in by the likes of Charlie Parker, John Coltrane and Miles Davis (with
whom Jarrett played in the early '70s). As a consequence, the forward
momentum of the music diminished to the point where it became
choked by the enormous weight of the past. Like the Mississippi, the
jazz delta began to silt up. Two directions were possible: backwards,
into the past, or sideways – east more often than not – to the edges
of the form, into world music.

Recorded in May 1961, 'Olé' is one of the first tracks on which John
Coltrane can be heard moving east. On this occasion he looked only
as far as Spain, but later stages of the journey can be traced by the
simple geography of titles like 'Africa/Brass' and 'India'. Not everyone
viewed this odyssey sympathetically. Larkin held Coltrane largely
responsible for the 'racket of Middle East bazaars' that came in his
wake. Larkin was a musical bigot but anyone listening to the screeching
'chaos' and 'absurdity' – Larkin again – of *Om* (1965) would concede
that he had a point.

On the title track of *Olé*, however, Trane's soprano solo begins with
extraordinary discretion and delicacy. It comes after a blazing flamenco
bass duet between Reggie Workman and Art Davis. At first you do
not even realise that the soprano sax has taken over: it sounds, instead,
like a stringed instrument, as if one of the bassists is straining into
the higher register of the violin. Or, to alter the angle of approach
slightly, as if the interplay between the basses is so tight that the

soprano can insinuate itself into the mix only by passing itself off as a kindred instrument.

On *Yara* (1999) by the Lebanese oud player Rabih Abou-Khalil one experiences exactly the opposite sensation. For this, his tenth album, Abou-Khalil was joined by two Frenchmen, Dominique Pifarély (violin) and Vincent Courtois (cello). At one point on the opening track, 'Requiem', the violin sounds like a soprano sax before gradually assuming its usual musical identity.

What happened in the thirty-eight-year interim, between *Olé* and *Yara*?

To put it as concisely as possible, jazz *as jazz* died. Perhaps, ironically, that is why we had to wait until 2000 for a comprehensive documentary series like *Jazz* by Ken Burns: jazz is history. That may also be why, having ridden the crest of a stylish jazz revival when first released, movies like *'Round Midnight* and *Bird* have rapidly acquired the patina of period pieces or costume dramas. The same point can be made the opposite way: some of the best new jazz releases are actually old releases re-mastered and re-packaged. Specialist publications aside, the only place where jazz commands extensive media attention is on the obituary pages, when living legends die. Not surprisingly, concerts by jazz giants often have the reverential stuffiness of improvised mausoleums.

I hear a clamour of objections. Isn't this simply another of the 'premature autopsies' denounced by Stanley Crouch? Aren't these concerts almost always sold out? Isn't the audience invariably ecstatic with gratitude? Since old rock bands keep coming back from the dead, re-forming, touring, why shouldn't old jazzers keep playing for as long as their fingers are nimble? Why shouldn't talented young musicians have the chance to explore the legacy of Charlie Parker? They can, they should. But jazz is like Woody Allen's shark: it has to keep moving, going forward, otherwise it dies. That's inherent in the idea of its animating characteristic: improvisation. The Who can play 'Won't Get Fooled Again' again and again, forever and a day, without undermining the song's credibility. Every rock song aspires to the status of an anthem. But as soon as a jazz tune becomes anthemic it is no longer jazz – it's elevator music. (Yes, 'A Love

Supreme' is played in *elevators*.) Change is immanent to jazz. Wynton
Marsalis has done much to raise awareness of the jazz tradition but
his conservative approach drew an inevitable rebuke from the late
Lester Bowie, who energetically espoused an alternative tradition of
change, innovation and revolution. The problem – as anyone who
has heard Archie ('gonna be a Re-re-revolution') Shepp perform in
recent years will testify – is that the modes of change have themselves become dated, fixed (gonna be a Re-re-repetition). The allure
of the avant-garde turns out to be primarily nostalgic. (There is something pleasingly apposite about the section labelled 'Secondhand
Avant-Garde' in Ray's Jazz store in London.) Borges said that the
problem with Apollinaire's experimental poetry is that 'not a single
line allows us to forget the date on which it was written'. One's enjoyment of contemporary jazz quartets and quintets playing bop of a
very high standard may not be diminished but it must be *informed*
by the fact that music like this was first heard more than half a
century ago. It's not as thoroughly quiff-bound and retro as rock 'n'
roll but jazz, now, is not just part of the American academy, it's part
of the American heritage industry.

Another objection: could something similar not be said of classical
– or, to use the jazzer's term – straight music? If Mozart is timeless
why isn't Coltrane? Well, he is, clearly. The status of the masters is
assured. The issue, again, has to do with the peculiar dynamic of
jazz, the thing that makes it jazz. Dizzy Gillespie once said that
the only way this music – jazz – was going was forward. If it's not
going forward then it's not jazz – it is instead a species of classical
music, an archive. Compared with the *Giant Steps* made by Coltrane,
or the *Change of the Century* announced by Ornette Coleman, or
the 'Directions in Music' taken by Miles, jazz in the last twenty
years has been relatively staid. Meanwhile, other forms of music
– world and dance music most obviously – developed so fast that
jazz, relatively speaking, seemed either to be standing still or moving
backwards.

Standards are constantly being re-interpreted. More recent compositions – Wayne Shorter's 'Footprints', say, or Ornette Coleman's 'Lonely
Woman' – become part of the inherited repertoire of material that is

improvised on and around. Plenty of jazz musicians experiment with
new instrumental permutations . . . These are some of the ways in
which jazz keeps faith with Ezra Pound's rallying cry, 'Make it new.'
Which is a good thing, isn't it? Yes, yes it is. But then you realise the
devastating truth of Joseph Brodsky's suggestion 'that the true reason
for making it new [is] that "it" [is] fairly old'.

The standard formats of jazz – quartets or quintets comprising
various permutations of saxophone or trumpet together with rhythm
section of bass, drums and piano – are musically active only in the
most passive sense (they still exist); judged by their potential to
generate the molten eruptions of Coltrane or Pharoah Sanders,
however, they are practically extinct. Technically, there are phenom-
enally advanced players around but even the most fertile soil – found
on the slopes of Mount Coltrane – has become exhausted by over-
use. In this respect, a moment of prophetic intensity can be heard
on a live recording of another version of 'Olé', by Pharoah, from
January 1982. Having taken his solo to a shrieking pitch of extremity,
Pharoah simply abandons the horn and *screams*: a recognition – at
once celebratory and frustrated – that the instrument has come to
an unsurpassable frontier of expressivity. This is why the frenzy generated by more recent efforts in this direction often sounds like an
academic exercise in excess.

The case of Norwegian saxophonist Jan Garbarek is more complex.
Not only is Garbarek one of the world's greatest saxophonists, he has
also been one of the musicians most willing to move beyond the
boundaries defining jazz as jazz. Garbarek's collaborations with
Pakistani singer Ustad Fateh Ali Khan (*Ragas and Sagas*, 1992) and
Tunisian oud player Anouar Brahem (*Madar*, 1994) have helped tilt
the geographical balance of jazz further eastwards. Four years after
Madar, Brahem released an album that would probably not have come
about without his having played with Garbarek. On *Thimar* Brahem
was accompanied by Dave Holland (bass) and John Surman (soprano
saxophone and bass clarinet). On the title track, Surman, who is
masterful throughout, sounds so like Coltrane – in high eastern mode
– as to suggest that it is here, in a distant outpost of the crumbling
jazz empire, that the saxophone finds most rewarding employment.

(The saxophone in John Ashbery's wry lines would doubtless have 'something to say / about all this, but only to itself'!)

In the same way that many people were turned on to Brahem by Garbarek, so I heard of Abou-Khalil because of another musically nomadic saxophonist, Charlie Mariano, who was part of the magnificent Arabic-jazz ensemble put together by Abou-Khalil for his album *Blue Camel* (1992). Effectively, then, the most adventurous spirits in jazz have led us away from its centre, to the edges of jazz – and beyond.

Jarrett's extraordinary productivity has been due in no small measure to his refusal to restrict himself to jazz. At the same time, however, his trio has spent much of the last fifteen years in an extensive curatorial reappraisal of the jazz backlist. His biographer, Ian Carr, considers these recordings of standards to be among the best Jarrett has made.* I disagree. The format of most of these albums has been similar: fifty minutes of standards and ten minutes of amazing Jarrett originals. Typically this original track develops seamlessly out of a standard, as 'The Fire Within' comes blazing out of the smouldering familiarity of 'I Fall in Love Too Easily' on *At The Blue Note* (or, more modestly, when 'Blame It on My Youth' gives way to a darker 'Meditation' on *The Melody at Night, With You*). They are like exotic birds, these original compositions, gliding clear of still water in a blur of colour and motion. Exceptions to this formatting rule are *Changes*, a series of free improvisations from the first *Standards* sessions of 1983, and *Changeless* (1989), an album compiled from the improvised segments of four 'standard' concerts (one of the best trio recordings in the history of improvised music). But it is the other, as it were, 'unspliced' albums that offer the more telling ratio of progress to tradition – of new to old – currently available even to a supreme

---

*The question posed by the title of this piece was somewhat rhetorical but, since it was first published, Ian Carr, Lester Bowie and – tragically – Esbjörn Svensson have all passed away. When my first novel came out I published an article about jazz in *The Guardian*. Ian got in touch to say how much he had enjoyed both the article and the novel. It turned out he lived just round the corner, in Brixton, and we met up from time to time. The kindness and encouragement of a highly respected musician and writer on jazz meant a great deal to me. (Note added 2009.)

genius like Jarrett. By the time of *Tokyo '96* we got only five minutes out of eighty (though what a blissful five minutes it is, as 'Caribbean Sky' bounces clear of 'Last Night When We Were Young'). Recorded in Paris in 1999, *Whisper Not* was made up entirely of standards. *The Melody at Night* was, in this light – this twilight, rather – a kind of destiny, for Jarrett and for jazz.

This can be heard in another way too. A crucial part of the jazz tradition has been the way that debility – think of Django Reinhardt's fire-scarred fingers – can enhance. One could go further and suggest that, in jazz, a diminution of power can produce a dramatic heightening of effect. It is no surprise, then, that Jarrett's last solo album was haunted by the ghost – the touch – of the damaged god of the keyboard, Bud Powell. The history of jazz has been the history of people picking themselves up off the floor. This is the rough truth articulated so delicately by *The Melody at Night* – and that's why there is nothing depressing about it. On the contrary, what we hear after Jarrett's 'long privation and powerlessness' is what Nietzsche called 'the gratitude of a convalescent': 'the rejoicing of strength that is returning, of a reawakened faith in tomorrow and the day after tomorrow, of a sudden sense and anticipation of a future, of impending adventures, of seas that are open again, of goals that are permitted again, believed again'.

On 26 July 2000 Jarrett's trio played in London. I had read in interviews that the need to conserve his energy meant that Jarrett would be playing be-bop. I went along in the same spirit that, years before, I had gone to see Miles Davis in exactly the same place: not for what I would hear but because of who I would see. My expectations could hardly have been lower. Jarrett, DeJohnette and Peacock took to the stage, started to play an original Jarrett composition. In minutes we were in the incomparable Jarrett zone. When that first piece ended I thought, 'That's it, now we're going to have forty minutes of standards.' But no, they kept playing category-defying music. In the interval I bumped into Ian Carr and other friends. We were all blown away – exhausted and exhilarated by what we had heard.

It was an incredible concert (parts of which can be heard on *Inside*

Out [2001]) but it also begged the questions it appeared to answer. Was this a break with the 'standards' format or a further extension, a demonstration of the way that free playing had itself become standardised? Had the archival investigation of jazz history reached the point that free jazz could now be incorporated into the repertoire? And, relatedly: to what extent does the recovery of one individual genius enable us to extrapolate, to make a more general prognosis about the fate of jazz to come? Will anyone be around – to put things slightly differently – to offer the kind of tribute to Jarrett that Jarrett did to Miles, that Miles did to Ellington?

To answer that we have, characteristically, to begin elegiacally. I have never been as moved by the death of a public figure as I was by the death of Don Cherry in October 1995. Unlike Larkin, however, I was not prompted to reflect that jazz was 'finally finished', for although obituaries referred to him as 'a jazz musician' or 'trumpeter' Cherry – the embodiment of all that is best in the term 'world music' – had moved beyond all limiting descriptions. Since his death, the invocation of Cherry's name or spirit is an invariable sign of musical broadmindedness – and it is to Cherry that Nils Petter Molvaer's trumpet alludes, unmistakably, on the title track of his groundbreaking 1997 debut, *Khmer*. The other influence on Molvaer's trumpet sound is John Hassell but, in terms of his larger musical conception, Miles is the dominant presence, especially in his electric phase, from *In a Silent Way* to *Agharta*. 'He Loved Him Madly' – the Stockhausen-inflected Ellington tribute – is absolutely central to this stage of Miles' career: a brooding, proto-ambient piece, finishing, as Ian Carr puts it, 'with a long, grooving pulse that transforms all the grieving into something positive and even optimistic'. To Larkin, of course, it would have sounded a singularly inappropriate tribute: a cause for deepening pessimism, more like.

When I first got into jazz I would have been tempted to agree. I regarded this phase of Miles' career as a disastrous step in the direction of jazz-funk and jazz-rock (Return to Forever – ugh!) from which the music only recovered with the re-emergence of acoustic post-bop in the '90s. Under the influence of Cherry and others I drifted away from 'jazzy' jazz towards world music and, at an embarrassingly late age, embraced dance and electronic music. The trajectory may not have been typical but the destination was, in many ways, inevitable.

The pre-coma part of Douglas Coupland's *Girlfriend in a Coma* takes place at the end of 1979. Karen, the girlfriend in question, recalls a premonition she's had of the future. 'People seemed to be more . . . *electronic*,' she says. Consistent with this, Carl Craig, co-director of the first Detroit Electronic Music Festival in 2000, was exaggerating only slightly when he said that 'every music is electronic music right now'. (Who knows, maybe the quality of silence has been subtly changed – the air itself altered – by all the electronic information passing through it?) As a consequence, Miles Davis' pioneering electric music from the '70s now sounds more contemporary – less tied to the moment it was created – than 'My Funny Valentine' or 'So What'. As well as having a new electric sound, *Bitches Brew* was one of the first 'jazz' albums created as much in the editing as it was during the recording sessions. Like 'He Loved Him Madly' it anticipates not just the sound and textures but the methods of contemporary music-making.

Within the field of electronic music-making the soloist's art has, to a degree, been taken over by that of sampling and re-mixing. Both *assume* an accumulated body of material to be re-combined and re-processed. When 'In a Silent Way' and 'He Loved Him Madly' were re-mixed by Bill Laswell (for the 1998 album *Panthalassa*) the technical proximity of source and subsequent processing meant something even more remarkable occurred: the proto-contemporary became super-contemporary. (It may have been a defect on my part, but it was not until hearing *Panthalassa* that I realised the extent to which pieces like 'Shhh/Peaceful' anticipated the ambient wash of chill-out.)

Which brings us back to Nils Petter Molvaer. In a sense he is continuing Miles' practice of looking outside jazz to what is going on in other kinds of contemporary music. But whereas Miles, like his accomplices in fusion Wayne Shorter and Joe Zawinul, defaulted to funk, Molvaer has not simply immersed himself in, but, to a considerable extent, been *formed by*, the most advanced electronic music around: drum 'n' bass, jungle, techno, ambient, triphop. In the late 1990s all sorts of compilations were vying with each other to showcase the Future Sound of this, that or the other but the future was *already* being heard in Oslo. But was it jazz? If we have to use the word at all I would prefer to call it post-jazz since so much of its distinctive character depends on elements that are alien to the prerogatives of the form. To call it jazz, also, is to give insufficient emphasis to the staple elements (programming, sampling, scratching) of dance and electronic music on which Molvaer depends. Jazz is a crucial but not *defining* element. If Molvaer was extending the jazz tradition he was doing so by drawing a line under it. To revert to Brodsky's formulation, the 'it', here, is not being made new, the 'it' is itself new. Crucially, Molvaer's trumpet sound – even when it has not been fed through a vocoder or processed in some other way – sounds somehow electronically inflected. Consciously or not he has realised that, for the moment at least, the trumpet had to shed its earlier brassy, vaulting confidence in favour of – Miles' influence again – a more muted role. It is not just that the computer technology of electronic or dance music-making complements the soloist's art: the two are indivisible. If Molvaer is a great jazz musician that is largely because he is not just a jazz musician.

Khmer was followed, over-eagerly, by *Solid Ether* (2000). The Cherry-Davis-Hassell-inflected trumpet sound was as exquisitely brooding as before but often the arrangements dissolved into a hectic clatter of drum 'n' bass. This seemed, actually, to illustrate a larger conundrum whereby if drum 'n' bass were to advance it was doomed to quickly exhaust all possible permutations of which it was capable unless it changed into something else – whereupon it would cease to exist! The dance-electronic inspiration on which Molvaer had relied to extend and illuminate the long twilight of jazz was itself plunging into creative darkness. Nothing demonstrated this more bleakly than *Recoloured*, an album of poor-quality re-mixes that comprehensively failed to enhance any of the original tunes. Inevitably, that was not on ECM and nor was Molvaer's next 'proper' release, *NP3* (2003). The album didn't hail any great advance and succumbed in places to a vulgarity of arrangement that has characterised the 'new concept of jazz' proclaimed by Molvaer's fellow Norwegian Bugge Wesseltoft. But there were enough lyrical interludes to suggest that Molvaer was taking stock of the immense technical and artistic resources already at his disposal rather than lunging recklessly ahead. The fact that so much of the momentum had drained from dance music gave him pause – a pause incorporated into the melodic hiatus of the exquisite post-ballad 'Little Indian'. That track was re-worked on Molvaer's most recent album, *Streamer* (2004), recorded live in London. It provided ample evidence that he remains one of the most exciting and contemporary-sounding makers of music in the world.

If Molvaer's music is termed post-jazz, then the Necks' might with some justification be regarded as post-*everything*. They are sometimes categorised as a jazz trio – which is fine as long as this is immediately qualified by adding that they've completely re-conceived the idea of the jazz trio.

The rapturous response to the Esbjörn Svensson Trio at the Royal Festival Hall in 2003 at the London Jazz Festival was claimed by some to be a sign of how the torch of innovation had passed from America to Europe – specifically to Scandinavia. Imagine how far EST are removed from the kind of stuff that was routinely dished up by the likes of the Tommy Flanagan Trio and you have an idea of how far the Necks have gone beyond EST. Which means, if we are locating advancement geographically, that the new frontier of jazz is being forged in Australia.

I say 'new' but Chris Abrahams (keyboards), Tony Buck (drums) and Lloyd Swanton (bass) have actually been playing together for more than fifteen years. They're all from Sydney and maybe this distance from the traditional centres of jazzing excellence accounts, in part, for their groundbreaking originality. It might also explain why their following, though devoted, is still relatively small.

Whether on stage or record a typical performance by the Necks consists of a single, hour-long piece that builds slowly in intensity and complexity. Emphasising this steady continuity, their second album, *Next* (1990), started with ten seconds of their first, *Sex* (1989). The sublimely minimalist *Aether* (2001) took this approach – or rather, *reduced* it – to an entirely new dimension: a whole piece based around a single, shimmering chord. I love the uncompromising inconvenience of this, the way that, in a culture largely predicated on a deficiency of attention, listening to the Necks requires the kind of single-minded immersion demanded by Indian ragas.

When playing live they usually perform acoustically; the studio albums supplement piano, bass and drums with some swirling Rhodes and electric organ that lend a hint of early 1970s Miles Davis to their sound (particularly evident on *Hanging Gardens* [1999]). Miles borrowed from and incorporated what he judged – sometimes mistakenly – to be the best in other fields of contemporary popular music, and the Necks – like Molvaer – have taken on board the hypnotic repetition of the best electronic music. As a concession to 'live' performance, makers of programmed music sort of improvise but it usually amounts to little more than a bit of cosmetic knob-twiddling. Here the infinite loops, bass figures and drum patterns of electronica are back in the hands of freely improvising musicians who set up an endless groove. There are echoes of the free-flowing Jarrett trio whom the Necks sometimes resemble (particularly on 'Pele' – from *Next* – which clocks in at what, by the band's normal standards, is a modest half-hour). At other times they seem on the brink of shifting into full-on dance music. It never quite happens but the brooding expectation generates incredible suspense. This accounts for the sense of the music being driven – again there are similarities with Indian classical music – by what is latent within it.

As the title suggests, their 2004 album *Drive By* is great driving music – and not just in the way that it motors towards a constantly receding horizon. (I wonder if, in the early '70s, one or more of the Necks were besotted by the 'Motorik' or 'Apache' beat of NEU!)* This is music that contains the space through which it passes. The Necks might be inspired by Miles' ability to imbue his music with space but it seems likely that the open-ness of their style has deeper

---

*I feel sure someone was: 'Abillera', the last piece on *Chemist* (2006) – a highly unusual album in that it consists of three tracks, each a mere twenty minutes long, and features Tony Buck on electric guitar – sounds like a homage to the Krautrock pioneers. (Note added 2009.)

roots in the immensity of the Australian outback. In keeping with this you could be lulled, at times, into finding them monotonous – then you realise that the music has changed, totally, but you can't tell *when* it changed. It's changeless and constantly changing. Themes and motifs approach from the horizon and recede into the distance as if one impulse behind the album was to map the musical possibilities of the Doppler Effect. There's no telling where this tranced-out journey might take us, where we might end up. As D.H. Lawrence wrote when he was in Australia in 1922, there is 'a sort of lure in the bush. One could pass quite out of the world, over the edge of the beyond.'

Drive By glides through an ambient dream-time of 'found' sounds: a children's playground, crickets, a beehive. Where the previous albums are reliable, slightly embellished records of sustained improvisations in 'real time', this one was built out of segments that were then overdubbed and re-structured in the edit, like a soundtrack for a road movie waiting to be made. I don't know if it's jazz but it's a great record and I love it; you'd be mad not to.*

2004

Drive By had the potential to be the album which saw the Necks break through to a mass audience. Lest this was perceived as any kind of softening of purpose it was followed, in 2005, by a two-CD set, *Mosquito/See Through*, which was abstract, minimalist and as demanding as anything they had ever recorded. Since then we've been treated to three masterpieces in a row: *Chemist* (2005); a recording of a churning, oceanic live set, *Townsville* (2007); and, most recently, the epic *Silverwater* (2009), which sees the band pushing ahead again into uncharted territory. (Note added 2009.)

Editions of Contemporary Me

People with initiative and imagination use the valuable interlude between leaving school and starting college to enlarge their experience. They travel to exotic places, work abroad at unusual jobs. Faced with this opportunity in 1977, I filled the nine months at my disposal by working in an office in the provincial town where I had grown up. I lived with my parents. In the evenings I played badminton or squash and read Dickens and George Eliot. My job was as a clerk in the actuarial department of Mercantile & General Reinsurance (a company that insured insurance companies). One of the trainee actuaries, Rob, was a guy in his early twenties who had moved to Cheltenham from London with his wife soon after they'd graduated. Rob was a hi-fi nut and invited me round to their semi-detached house to hear his system in action. Jazz-rock was his thing. I was mainly interested in the rock bit of this alliance. My tastes had been formed by prog (Van der Graaf Generator) and heavy (Mountain) rock but I had recently bought my first Bob Dylan album: *Desire*. I was ready for a change – in music if not in circumstances.

Rob had the best stereo I had ever heard or, for that matter, seen: each speaker loomed like the monolith in *2001*. The first track we listened to that evening was by Return to Forever. It was followed by a very heavy piece by Miles Davis from *Live-Evil*, and parts of a record with a really nice cover (pieces of fruit or something on a sky-reflecting puddle?) by someone called Keith Jarrett. The last track we listened to was by Tangerine Dream. I'd been a big Hawkwind fan so I had an idea where this stuff was coming from: outer space, presumably.

Speaking of which, I also had another couple of graduate friends whom I'd met at the Cheltenham Science Fiction Group. I didn't like sci-fi but I did collect superhero comics and there was a tacit overlap between the two things. In any case, I'd only joined to try to make some friends. Paul and Jan were more alternative than Rob and his wife (it was at their house that I ate my first ever vegetable curry). Musically they were mainly into Little Feat and Robert Palmer (whose first album, lest we forget, was very cool) but, like Rob, they were heavily into Tangerine Dream; they were also keen on an album by Weather Report called *Mysterious Traveller* (which had a sort of sci-fi cover).

The connections between some of these sounds – back then one always referred to music as 'sounds' – to which I had been exposed will be evident to everyone reading this. Jarrett, Wayne Shorter, Joe Zawinul and Chick Corea had all played with Miles Davis during his groundbreaking electric phase. (Jarrett actually plays on 'What I Say', that stomping track from *Live-Evil*.) This didn't registered with me at the time; nor did the bigger point – that for squandering nine months in a tedious office job in Cheltenham I had been compensated by accidentally stumbling on some of the most advanced music being made anywhere in the world. I emphasise the circumstances because there was nothing exotic about my discovery of what I would later come to recognise as the ECM sound: it came sandwiched between Return to Forever and Tangerine Dream. The importance of the shift in taste that came in its wake, however, was enormous. This became obvious in the summer when I drove around France and Germany for a month with two friends in a Mini Cooper. We had each made compilation tapes of our favourite tracks and my main memory of this, my first trip outside Britain, is of driving for hours on end, arguing about what music to play. I wanted to hear selections from *Belonging*, *Dansere*, *Arbour Zena*, *Agharta* and *Black Market*. My friends lobbied for Supertramp and Be-Bop Deluxe.

I rest my case.

A special significance attaches to the first piece of music you play on moving into a new place – especially if it's the first place you've ever moved into. After setting up my stereo in my room at college I played Jarrett's 'Long As You Know You're Living Yours'. This was how I announced my arrival musically to my neighbours. These neighbours might have guessed a jazz nut had taken up residence but my small stash of ECM LPs had not lured me more deeply into jazz. I recognised some of the names (Jan Garbarek, Terje Rypdal) that cropped up on various albums but I didn't hear or see what this distinctive ECM sound – and look – was an offshoot of. And because I didn't know what had gone before I didn't fully appreciate the novelty of what I was hearing. It was years before I found out because my interest in this kind of music tailed off as I was drawn towards more mainstream student fare. The remainder of my time at Oxford was dominated by Bob Dylan (who played Earls Court and Blackbushe in 1978) and, belatedly, in my third year, punk. In the early '80s, when I moved to London, I was completely caught up in the new wave or post-punk scene.

I didn't return to ECM until the mid-'80s, when I moved into a shared house in Brixton. Chris, one of the people in this house, had a big jazz collection and many ECM records I'd never seen or heard before. None of us had jobs, which meant we were free to spend the days reading theory (which I'd not done at university, oddly), smoking pot (which, even more oddly, I'd also neglected to do at university) and listening to music. This was when I got properly into the history of jazz – and the starting-point, as often as not, was ECM. What had once been the vanguard was now part of the heritage that ECM – a new vanguard – drew upon and reinvigorated. By making a tradition accessible ECM offered a way back into jazz; but it also pointed ahead to the kinds of music I would listen to for the next twenty years. This is worth stressing, not simply with regard to the reception of the material (listening) but with its creation in the first place. To have provided excellent recording opportunities for American jazz musicians would have been a worthy but limited enterprise; the ECM agenda was more far-reaching: to establish conditions and ways of working most conducive to the emergence of new musical possibilities.

Chris had a bunch of records by the Art Ensemble of Chicago. I loved the pretentious name, and the picture on one of the albums of these nice guys sitting outside a French café, but much of their music was just a din. Then Chris played a track called 'Charlie M', which turned me on to both the Art Ensemble *and* Mingus. Chris also played the various Old and New Dreams albums a lot and it was through them that I got into Ornette Coleman. In some ways the original version of 'Lonely Woman' on *The Shape of Jazz to Come* still seems to me to be a re-working of the one I first heard, by Charlie Haden, Don Cherry, Ed Blackwell and Dewey Redman.

I was starting to see how the web of collaboration, influence and innovation extended the jazz tradition into the present – and, as the Art Ensemble insisted, into the future. ECM was expanding my musical horizons not just through time and history but geographically, across space. No one played a bigger part in this than Cherry. I first heard of the great Egyptian singer Om Kalsoum in the dedication to 'Arabian Nightingale' on *El Corazon*. It was years before I heard her voice but that was the first mention of her name. I started listening to Augustus Pablo after hearing Cherry play Pablo-style dub melodica on 'Roland Alphonso', also on *El Corazon*. That's another point about ECM: although there is widespread agreement that Jarrett's *Köln Concert* is crucial to any account of the label's development there is, I suspect, a huge diversity of opinion as to which albums have had the biggest impact on individual listeners. Objectively, *El Corazon* – a series of duets between Cherry and Blackwell – is not a major album but it's at the heart of my collection. There is, in other words, something profoundly democratic about the ECM approach; great moments crop up anywhere, in any format and combination of musicians. Greatness is always a possibility, partly because the distinction between leader and supporting musicians in these circumstances is often hard to fix.

Grazing Dreams is another obviously canonical record. Officially it's a Collin Walcott-led production but I came to it because Cherry was part of it. This was one of the first albums on which I consciously heard a tabla being played; the second was Zakir Hussain's *Making Music*. These two albums led the way to Indian classical music – and for me *that* began with ECM too: Shankar's *Who's To Know* and *Pancha Nadai Pallavi*. I am not saying, of course, that ECM was the only possible starting point (how had I missed out on Shakti?) but in my case it almost always was. The corollary of this is that even when it wasn't, it could have been.

I have never loved the voice of a female singer the way I love R.A. Ramamani's. I first heard her singing on an album with Charlie Mariano and the Karnataka College of Percussion (what a blow it was to learn that she was married to the head of the college). This wasn't an ECM record but it was, essentially, a live version of an album recorded years earlier on ECM. My friend Chris had first played this for me, and years later he told me of a new album that Mariano had recorded with a Lebanese oud player. The tail, it turned out, was wagging the dog. Mariano was one of a number of musicians guesting on *Blue Camel* (on the Enja label) by Rabih Abou-Khalil – whose first album, *Nafas*, had been released by ECM.

ECM, in other words, was the pattern at the centre of the carpet of almost all the music I was listening to. And the figure at the centre of this pattern was Jarrett. There were ECM albums I didn't care for, there were Jarrett albums that I didn't like so much – but there were no ECM albums that I was more entranced by than Jarrett's. I mean that literally.

What changed when I went round to my friend Rob's house back in 1977 was not just the kind of music I could listen to but what I listened to music for, how I listened to it. By the 1980s this had become a matter almost of habit: what I wanted more than anything else from music was to trance out to it. No album of Jarrett's was more trance-like than *Eyes of the Heart* and I was surprised to discover that people who knew more about music than me did not share my sense that this was a masterpiece. (What a bore it must be to have impeccable taste!) It's a recording of a live performance from 1976, the opening phase of which features Jarrett on soprano sax – mind-boggling in itself. He then moves over to the piano, setting up rhythmic ripples with Haden and Paul Motian. Although it's a quartet recording, Redman is nowhere to be heard (he'd gone to the bar to get a glass of wine, apparently) and after a while Haden also drops out. In his biography of Jarrett Ian Carr explains that the pianist spent much of the gig vamping, just waiting for the others to come in. In this vacancy, Carr claims, can be heard the imminent disintegration of the group. Well, I was happy to wait indefinitely, the longer the better in fact, because the infinitely prolonged suspense makes the climactic *re*integration of the group – with just five minutes of the second side left to run – all the more intense. And the waiting, in any case, never felt like waiting; it felt like being where you wanted to be, never wanting to leave, but still curious to know who else might turn up, what else might happen. I never have this feeling when the Jarrett–Peacock–DeJohnette trio play standards but I get it every moment when they play those surging originals: 'Sun Prayer', 'Dancing', 'Endless', 'Lifeline', 'Desert Sun', 'The Cure'. Except that's not quite true, because the greatest moments of all occur when standards give way to Jarrett originals, when 'Autumn Leaves' reveals that the trio really are 'Up For It' on the eponymous live album recorded in 2002. These transitions express in miniature the larger contribution of ECM to musical history as the accumulated riches of a tradition give way to something that lies beyond it, new, but waiting to be discovered. At the risk of projecting a listener's response onto the music's creators it seems to me that an unspoken assumption under-writes many of the most successful ECM recordings: namely, that by the late twentieth century you could only make jazz if you were simultaneously trying to find a way out of it. These days I spend an inordinate amount of time listening to the Australian trio, the Necks. This wouldn't have happened – it's possible, in fact, that the Necks wouldn't have got into their hypnotic, hour-long grooves – had Jarrett's trio not led the way.

Throughout the 1980s one of the main ways in which I heard new music was to get together with my friends Chris and Charlie and listen to whatever one or the other of us had recently come across. It was incredibly nerdy but it was frequently momentous too. Music-ally we went through many of the same phases together and then, in the early '90s, Charlie began to immature with age. We couldn't believe it but our friend, the person with whom we had listened to Coltrane, to Hariprasad Chaurasia (first heard on *Making Music*), to Nusrat Fateh Ali Khan (not to be confused with the Khans singing with Garbarek on *Ragas and Sagas*), began listening to . . . house music. Then techno. It was one thing to trance out to Jarrett or Trane but the idea that you could escape Samsara by freaking out to psyche-delic trance! Chris and I were both – I was going to say sceptical but incredulous would be a better word. Inevitably, my incredulity turned to evangelical zeal once I too had succumbed. For the next several years, in fact, I listened only to dance music. Circumstances meant that Chris – married with two kids, unable to go out all night – never followed suit. He was stuck at home, listening to his boring old ECM records. Besides, he was never quite convinced that the stuff we were listening to was anything other than drug- or party-music. Until, that is, Nils Petter Molvaer released his first album. *Khmer* (1997) was not strictly speaking dance music but neither, strictly speaking, was it jazz. Molvaer's sound obviously owed as least as much to various kinds of dance and electronic music as it did to jazz (specifically, to take us right back to where we started, to Miles' electric period of the early '70s). And, amazingly, it was on ECM – who even came up with re-mixes of some of the tracks.

I've forgotten much of the music I heard during this ecstatic inter-lude and I'm embarrassed by some of the little I can remember – but I've never stopped listening to Nils. Recent ECM releases are of a very high standard but in many ways *Khmer* is a highpoint in the ECM project precisely because it seems so conspicuously at odds – sampling! re-mixes! – with the ethos of the company. (Having the courage of one's convictions is, as Nietzsche pointed out, a pretty modest virtue; 'having the courage for an attack on one's convictions' is another matter altogether.) The ECM sound is as recognisable as Blue Note's from the 1960s. It's a style of music as much as a label; unlike Blue Note it has never become a reductive or formulaic one. Which is why, of course, we are still listening to the old records (a CD of *Arbour Zena* is winging its way to me in the post; what will that be like, twenty-five years after first hearing it?) and listening out for what's coming next (a new double live CD of Jarrett playing solo piano is due out soon; what will that be like?).

The music playing on my stereo as I write this is the first ECM track that I ever listened to, the piece I heard round at my friend Rob's house, back in Cheltenham in 1977 after a day's clerical drudgery at the Mercantile & General Reinsurance Company: Jarrett's 'Long As You Know You're Living Yours'. I couldn't have lived mine without these editions of contemporary music to keep me company, to show me how.

2006

Fabulous Clothes

'*The world's made fabulous*
by fabulous clothes.'
Mark Doty, 'Couture'

Our Eurostar was still creeping through the Kent countryside when my minder from *Vogue* HQ expressed her first doubts about my mission.

'Do you actually know what couture is?'

'Yes, I do,' I replied. 'Yes, in the sense of . . . no, not really.' Detecting an *I-thought-as-much* look flicker across her face, I reassured her that this was no cause for concern. Since the readers of *Vogue* obviously knew what couture was it made no difference that the reporter didn't. I banged on about this for some time, rounding off my defence with a well-chosen pun. 'I think we're about to enter the Chanel tunnel,' I said. It was my way of letting her know that I knew more than I let on.

The first show – Christian Dior – was at the Hippodrome on the outskirts of Paris. We drove there in an unmarked car. Security was tight but I had not lost my invitation so it was OK. I have a vague memory of entering a tent or marquee or something but the interior had been transformed so totally that, by the time I had taken my seat, all sense of the world outside – *le monde sans couture* – evaporated. The entrance to the runway was marked by a vast wall of light boxes, illuminated, for the moment, by two signs with the letters CD in blazing red. Such is the familiarity of those initials that it seemed possible that we had actually travelled back in time and were about to witness the launch of a technological breakthrough that would render the LP obsolete. Certainly there was a major sense of expectation. The lights dimmed. The wall of lights came alive in pulsing rectangles. Music roared and pumped. Show-time . . .

Thin as legend claims, the models streamed into view. The Spanish element was unmistakable. A friend once told me that the thing about flamenco was that you had to do it with a serious expression on your face and the Dior models brought to their task a sternness of expression befitting the judges at Nuremberg. Whether 'face' is an adequate term to describe the site of this seriousness is a different matter entirely. 'Face' is powerfully suggestive of something human but make-up and paint had here been applied to make this seem a quaint, possibly unfounded assumption. It quickly became apparent that flamenco was just one bee in the designer's swarming bonnet. There was a bit of everything going on. The models appeared, variously, as flappers, can-can dancers, sprites, zombies – you name it. A seasoned fashion writer said to me later that this show had actually been comparatively tame: 'There were things in it that you might even *wear*,' he said. Nothing brought home to me my ignorance of couture more clearly than this crestfallen lament. To my untutored eye what was on offer here had nothing to do with clothing as traditionally understood. Looking at the coats – which seemed capable of almost anything *except* keeping you warm or dry – I was reminded of Frank Lloyd Wright's response to clients who grumbled about the roof leaking: that's how you can tell it's a roof. And so it was here: it was primarily by their extravagant refusal of the function for which they had been nominally intended that they could be defined as clothes. No, this was a form of pure and vibrant display that took the job of covering the human body only as a necessary jumping-off point. An ecstatic poetry was, as Mark Doty puts it in 'Couture',

> raveled around the body's
> plain prose

And how lovely it was, this celebration of our capacity to produce *excess*. What progress we have made from the cave-dwelling days when arguments would break out over whose turn it was to wear the hide.

The music surged and changed. It was like a firework display in that you wish it would never end – though even as you wish this you know that you would be bored rigid if it lasted a moment longer than it does. At the end of it all Galliano came stomping up the runway, looking like a cross between a toreador and Conan the cross-cultural Barbarian. I say 'Galliano' but I only learned that it was him after I turned to my chaperone and asked if he was Christian Dior. No, it is not, she replied. The reason for this, apparently, is that Dior has been dead for about a hundred years. Well, as Larkin said, 'useful to get that learnt'. It was obvious that only a response of the utmost gravity would redeem me in the eyes of my chaperone. 'Ah, yes,' I said. 'But his spirit lives on in Galliano.'

This impression was confirmed – or, for all I knew, refuted – when Galliano appeared on TV later that evening. I was right about one thing: there really was a bit of everything going on. He talked about the way his collection had been inspired by Spain, his travels in India, African ceremonies, and he ended by saying that it had all been done for his father. Just as couture has floated free from any anchoring in function so no one feels under any compulsion to anchor what is said *about* it in something as humdrum as sense. No one would have batted an eyelid if Galliano had said that he'd intended the whole show as an offering to the gods of the Incas. I shall return to this point.

After the Dior show I went to have a look round the Ungaro atelier where this kind of high-end clobber is actually made. It was, to say the least, a far cry from the sweatshops of Bangkok. Everyone wore white medical jackets, creating the impression that they were engaged in work that was vital to the health of the human race. And who is to say that they were not? For it would be a dreary old planet if there weren't the chance to create stuff so far in excess of what anyone could ever need. 'Nothing *needs* to be this lavish,' Doty exclaims in rhetorical astonishment. To which the only riposte – as the poet himself was surely aware – is Lear's: 'Oh, reason not the need!' I was reminded, watching *les petites mains* at work, of the painstaking labour and inventiveness that goes into the preparation of exquisite food, that same devotion to transcending the body's base requirements.

Many of the people here had worked for Ungaro for years and years. They seemed a contented and fulfilled workforce, proud of their skills and of the chance to deploy them to such extravagant ends. I thought of my mum, who, for years, mended my clothes when they were torn and took them in if they were too large or long. Having completed one of these tasks she always said that she would love to have been a seamstress. Not a seamstress for a designer; just someone whose skills would be sufficient to earn a modest living. Maybe this is the greatest excess and waste in the world: the huge reservoir of abilities that never get a chance to be used.

My visit culminated with admission to a room where *le maître* himself was putting the final touches to one of his creations. The model wearing it was long, blonde and lovely but her face conveyed the suggestion – in Don DeLillo's words – of lifelong bereavement over the death of a pet rabbit. She turned from Ungaro and gazed at herself in the mirror. I say gazed at 'herself' but this form of words fails to do justice to whatever it was she beheld in the glass. She had glimpsed what she would become during the show: the incarnation of something more than herself. Already, after just a few hours, I was starting to realise that there was more to couture than meets the eye.

Versace wasn't doing a show: just a presentation in a tent (with chandelier) at the Ritz. It was like being at a museum in the process of formation, the exhibits consisting of a bag, a shoe, a brocaded jacket . . . There was one model, though, in an airy dress and a mink coat with ostrich feathers. Her hair was not hair so much as a kind of super-deluxe candy floss. People regarded her in the same way tourists do the soldiers on Horse Guards Parade, *peering* at her while she was being photographed. One of these peerers was me. I wondered what it must be like to exist in this *I-am-seen-therefore-I-am* trance. Her eyes were no longer the instruments of vision, merely its object.

Although the compulsion to stare at her was overwhelming it was difficult to detect her nationality, her race, even, frankly, her *species*. She was laboratory-bred to look amazing on magazine covers. If anything she reminded me of drag queens I'd seen a few weeks earlier at the Gay Pride march in New York. It wasn't that she looked like a man dressed up in women's clothes, but there was the same obsession with expressing an idea of femininity by its accoutrements. It was *Priscilla, Queen of the Desert* meets *Mad Max*, a combination that might one day result in a co-production called *Back-combed to the Future*. Surrounded by clothes displayed like museum exhibits it was as if she had been cryogenically preserved, the sole survivor of a catastrophe so devastating that the means to bring her fully back to life were no longer quite functioning and so she was unable to explicate the creation myth of *haute couture* of which she was the embodiment and apostle.

Nor could she have explained how, twenty minutes later, we were in the Gursky-space of Palais Omnisports, doing the Mexican wave, waiting for the Rolling Stones. It was a huge venue but, in the context of stadium hugeness, quite small. There was no sense of scale, none of the perspectival recession that enables one to make sense of distance. Cheers went up for no reason, just to give vent to the terrible burden of expectation. I had heard a rumour that the Stones' wives might become clients of Ungaro but it seemed that the Stones husbands were themselves in more urgent need of vestimentary assistance. People speak of Mick Jagger's extraordinary longevity and wealth but that is only half the story. The other, more interesting, half is how, despite this wealth, he has managed to dress so badly for so long. Like the other Stones he favours tight trousers which make him look like a Cruikshank drawing of a character in a Dickens novel, one of the interminable ones that has been adapted for TV so many times you know it off by heart without ever having read it. And so it was with this truly dismal concert. The enthusiastic consensus was that the Stones could 'still do it' – though what this 'it' was, and whether 'it' was worth doing, remained a source of mystery.

*   *   *

This was all the more striking given that the music at the shows is so cool: the Chanel show at the Cloître de l'Abbaye in Port Royal featured under-seat audio that turned the cloisters into a night club. Or *day* club, rather, for it was only ten in the morning. Photographers descended on a blonde woman in the front row who turned out to be Kylie Minogue. Jack Nicholson had been at the Dior show but I had not caught a glimpse of him. After the Stones gig, at Chez Paul, I pointed out to my chaperone that there was a Keanu Reeves look-alike at a nearby table. He looked so like Keanu Reeves that it did not occur to us that he really was Keanu Reeves until he left, posing for photographs and signing autographs for our fellow diners. So it felt good to start the day with a confirmed celebrity sighting.

That afternoon, a screaming comes across the sky . . . A fly-past by high-end military aircraft, slipping the surly bonds of earth or whatever. It's not only the linguistic coincidence of the runway that links *haute couture* and *haute aviation*. The procedure is essentially the same: the full range of state-of-the-art aircraft – fighters, bombers, helicopters – cruise by in a straight line, strutting their edge-of-the-envelope stuff for all to see, unhindered by anything as tedious as budgetary restriction. It lasted ten minutes, after which I expected to see either the planes' designers or the Air Vice Marshal take a victory roll.

Next up was Lacroix at the École Supérieure des Beaux-Arts. The models emerged from a seaweed tangle of glowing bulbs, luxuriant as the growth of an electrically powered forest, the entrance to a grotto of unimaginable fabulousness. The runway was curved and blue and the models came floating down this river of pure glamour. Faint applause pattered down from one of the rows behind me. My neighbour explained that when you heard applause from the back like this it almost certainly emanated from one of the women who did the sewing. I felt so happy for the woman in question: how lovely to see your skills paraded before the world like this and to applaud what they had resulted in, anonymously, from the back. By contrast, I had heard that a well-known fashion writer had got all bent out of shape because she had not been given a seat in the front row. I felt so sorry for her: how sad to invest even a fraction of your self-esteem in something so trivial, especially since the view from the second row was perfect.

There seemed to be elements of some kind of national costume in Lacroix's collection – but which nation could it be? One with a GNP larger than that of the whole continent of Africa and an amazing array of tropical birds. One October day in 1981 John Cheever found himself thinking about the beautiful autumns they must have in those countries that make brilliantly coloured carpets. 'How else could the Persians have hit on the idea of gold and crimson underfoot?' In the same way, I was becoming more and more convinced of an essential connection – no less essential for being lost over time – between the extravagant contrivances of couture and the forces of the natural world: a magical connection, what's more.

There seemed to be a House of Usher thing going on at Givenchy. There were a lot of colours but, at the outset, they were all black, grey or charcoal. The look was that of a nineteenth-century business woman – and the business was undertaking. The show was in le Grand Hôtel, in a ballroom that could, just as easily, have been a church. The moment it ended people began scrambling for the exits. Sokurov's film *Russian Ark* ends with the aristocracy trooping out of a ball at the Hermitage, stepping down the staircase, patiently descending in to the maw of history. There was no semblance of grace or patience here. It was like someone had issued the order to abandon ship and word had got round that not all the lifeboats had an adequate stash of champagne. It was over – and we were *outta* there, scuttling for our driver who, in turn, jockeyed for position, battling with the other drivers who were caught up in the micro-jam of traffic generated by the show.

We were only going to be at the Théatre de l'Empire – for the Ungaro show – for an hour but people were so desperate for upgrades, for seats nearer the front, you'd have thought we were crammed in for a flight to Sydney. But some people *were* – in it for the long-haul, I mean, and their faces revealed the same tiredness as those ageing flight attendants who have been around the global equivalent of the block (i.e. the world) so many times that there is no longer any difference – especially when you factor in jetlag – between coming and going. Fashion writers live seasons not years so if you want to calculate the age of a fashion writer in normal human terms you probably have to multiply it by at least two. The vocabulary alone is enough to do for you. No one should have to use a word like *toile* more than three or four times in a lifetime but fashion writers routinely expose themselves to several times the recommended lifetime dose in a single year.

The models entered through geometric pearl arches suggestive of jet-age elegance. Movie-score strings evoked a Hollywood epic whose entire budget had been blown on costumes. By comparison with some of the stuff we'd seen earlier in the week this collection seemed almost understated. Minimalism can come in many guises. There was even, I realised now, a minimalism in the realm of excess. Perhaps I had a soft spot for Ungaro because I'd caught a glimpse of a fraction of the effort that went on behind the scenes. But this, surely, is not enough to account for the surge of happiness when I recognised, flaming and flickering down the runway, the model wearing the outfit I'd watched her try out the day before.

Of course it's not. There was more to it than that.

Later that day we went to shows by Valentino (climaxing with an appearance by the dark goddess, Naomi Campbell) and Gaultier (who introduced an innovation of ankle-spraining originality: shoes that were quite unwearable) but by now it was the similarities of these events rather than their quirky differences that absorbed me.

'The ceremony is about to begin . . .' Jim Morrison's line was always in my head as we waited for a show to start. Whatever the setting, the form taken by this ceremony varied only in detail: the march of the individual models, including, as often as not, a wedding dress, followed by the appearance of the designer (greeted ecstatically by the audience), who would walk off either arm-in-arm with the bride (of Frankenstein, so to speak) or surrounded by his magnificent creations. Obviously this form had not come about by accident, even if the people who arranged a given manifestation of it were not conscious of the origins of the template to which they conformed.

The number of couture customers is falling off. There are practical reasons for this (the rise of ready-to-wear) but this dwindling of initiates is appropriate in other ways. Saint-Laurent once said that *haute couture* consisted 'of secrets whispered down from generation to generation', emphasising that it is not just a set of skills but a form of esoteric knowledge. Much is made of the astronomical expense of couture but perhaps some other kind of transfer – of which the garment is no more than the outward or symbolic expression – is at work here. Nietzsche pointed out that beneath the grace of Greek tragedy lay a primitive force that had earlier found uninhibited expression in singing and dancing rituals. In the same way this fabulous extravaganza had about it something instinctual, primeval. Could it be that the couture show is an immensely sophisticated and commercialised residue of an arcane rite or fertility ceremony?

In this light the models and their outfits really might be an offering to some kind of god. Not, as I had joked earlier, the old god of the Incas but the great modern god of the camera, waiting at the end of the runway like the rising or setting sun – except this sun is not just the source of life but its meaning and content too.

Still not convinced? Try looking at it another way. Imagine you came across an event like this – the costumes with their amazing surfeit of plumage and jewels, the models with their unnatural, clippy-cloppy, equine walk – in the Amazon. Wouldn't you think that you were witnessing some attempt at harnessing the characteristic powers of certain revered birds or animals and incarnating their spirit in human form? Wouldn't you assume that the designers were endowed with some alchemical or shamanic power? If the couture show is itself a residue of older rites then a residue of what this show originally appealed to is still there, in equally etiolated form, in some recess of our own psyche. How could people invest couture with so much importance were it not also the contemporary manifestation of something primal: not an extravagance, in other words, but the practice of a belief? How else to account for that weird sensation that something as transitory as a *fashion show* has about it a quality of timelessness?

2003

The 2004 Olympics

After the unbearable tedium of the European Championship (the fact that the final was an exact repeat – Greece 1, Portugal 0 – of the opening game put the redundancy of most of the intervening ones beyond doubt) this enthusiast approached the Athens Olympics with a sense of weary duty. I wondered if I still had the hunger, the discipline, to sit through the gruelling schedule of late-night medal ceremonies and re-runs of races that I'd already watched a dozen times. To be honest there were moments, before it all started, when I considered hanging up the remote.

Such doubts proved short-lived as the Games got off to the best possible start with an unscheduled, possibly even mythic event: the mixed doubles motorcycle sprint time trial and road race. Only one team took part but the rumour, eventually confirmed, that 'the Greek pair' – as Kederis and Thanou became contemptuously known – had ended up in hospital provided the first twist in a series of engrossing stories within the all-consuming narrative of the Games. We expected this one to conform to an established template for reactions to positive drug tests: outright denial followed by qualified admission ('it was the cough mixture!') leading to eventual confession ('I was so full of pills that I rattled'). As it turned out, though, our craving for justice was simultaneously satisfied and thwarted by the story's non-denouement. By handing in their accreditation the Greek athletes denied us definitive closure. This was all the more palpable since, in every other way, the modern Games have sought to eliminate uncertainty. The technology of the photo finish is so finely calibrated as to make the idea of a dead heat seem an archaic residue of the failings of the human eye. Even if the three Kenyan steeplechasers had tried to cross the line together they would have been shown to have done so successively.

In every event (the gymnastics, most controversially) sportsmen and -women are constantly outstripping our ability to assess what they are doing without the adjudicating support of technology. This did not, at first, appear to be the case with Team GB, who left us contemplating the not unfamiliar prospect of serial humiliation in event after event. In those early days the Acropolis loomed above the traffic, as Don DeLillo puts it in *The Names*, 'like some monument to doomed expectations'. Things ended up rather nicely – climaxing with the alchemical surge of the final Saturday – but one of the defining moments of the Games was, of course, the catastrophic meltdown suffered by Paula Radcliffe in the marathon.

Victory and triumph over adversity (as supremely achieved – twice! – by Kelly Holmes) are uplifting, but defeat and failure can be utterly transfixing too. The nature of the race and the unique demands made on participants by the marathon meant that what happened to Radcliffe lay beyond the usual explanation that 'on the day' Mizuki Noguchi was the better runner. This was not just long-distance Henmanism; it was an encounter with destiny in the form of a series of intensely compressed, incremental realisations.

When Elfenesh Alemu went past her Radcliffe realised that not only would she not win gold but that she was out of the medals. As soon as she realised this it became clear that there was no point even finishing – which meant that she was finished. Athletes often talk of hitting the wall. Radcliffe had been through that wall so often she didn't know it was there. And then, weirdly, the road itself had become a wall and it was all around her and there was no end to it in sight. It was like watching someone having a complete crack-up before your eyes. As such it made superb television. (The grassy verge on which she ended up even lent a Zapruderish touch to the footage.) Athletes deny nine-tenths of themselves – to adapt what John Berger said of Mondrian – so that they can pack the remaining tenth with incredible intensity and purpose. While plenty of people succumb to the urge to give up (going to the gym, trying to be an artist) it goes pretty much unnoticed. But for Radcliffe this was both a public and complete *ontological* collapse. And it happened, let's not forget, on the very day that that icon of modern despair, Edvard Munch's *The Scream*, was stolen. Who needs art when you've got sport?

Tears of one kind or another were everywhere in evidence at these Games. Enough were shed on my sofa to leave me repeatedly and blurrily amazed by sport's capacity to reach depths of emotion that used to be regarded as the preserve of high art. The American novelist Andrew Holleran is right: most of the time 'tears on TV are like the come shot in a porn film'. At a time when our responses to everything – especially so-called tragedy – are consistently being cheapened, coarsened and pre-programmed, sport accesses some zone of shared feeling which remains mysterious in spite of the familiarity of the clichés by which it is routinely articulated. Wordsworth claimed to have thoughts that lay 'too deep for tears', but the tears that left Matthew Pinsent a quaking hulk on the podium came from so far within they were practically chthonic.

Moving though that was, what really got to me were the comments from Barney Williams of the Canadian crew, who said that being 'part of one of the most exciting races of all time [was] as stimulating as winning a gold medal by three or four seconds'. The majority of the occasions that left me blubbing involved some display of sportsmanship like this: when the decathletes, shattered by their exertions of the last thirty-six hours embraced each other; when the beaten Bernard Lagat shared El Guerrouj's joy at winning the 1500 metres that had eluded him for so long.

By contrast, the idea that winning is the *only* thing has become so entrenched in football as to render the sport abhorrent as often as it is thrilling (it was also one of the reasons why the Euros ended up being such a bore). Two days after the Games began Jimmy Floyd Hasselbaink scored a goal against Newcastle with his hand, thereby making a nonsense of the whole game (it's called *foot*ball for a reason). Again and again in the course of the Games we were reminded not simply of the rightness of the Olympic ideal, that taking part is glorious in itself, but that this quaint idea might actually *enhance* the greater glory of winning. (Perhaps, to put it more cynically, the great virtue of the Games is that the cheating takes place offstage, invisibly, chemically.)

The joy of taking part holds good irrespective of the perceived worth or silliness of the sport in question. There is always a great deal of debate about whether minor sports deserve to be included. On the evidence of these Games the debate should be whether the big ones need to be excluded. The results suggest that, for leading tennis players and football teams alike, an Olympic gold medal, far from being the ultimate prize, is an international equivalent of the League Cup (or whatever it is now called). The sports that work best are those for which the Olympics are the unquestioned summit of exposure, recognition and achievement. Take badminton, for example. The badminton rocked! A million miles away from the dreamy country-house idyll of David Inshaw's lovely painting in Tate Britain, the semi-finals of the mixed doubles had an intensity to rival that seen in any sport. It was the intensity of concentration that was especially marked and this, I suspect, is another reason why I and so many other people found some of the less visually rewarding events so engrossing. Attention Deficit seems less like a Disorder, more a glimpse of the next stage of human evolution. There will come a time when the ability to concentrate on *anything* for more than a few minutes will appear as mysterious as a Chardin. In the meantime we have those photographs of table tennis players, fixing their attention on a white ball floating in the middle of their foreheads like a bubble of pure thought.

Sorry, where was I? Oh, right, the so-called minor sports . . . That's another thing that always amazes about the Olympics: how interesting it is to watch sports in which one has no interest and which one has never even considered playing. I draw the line at basketball (an 'armpit sport' as DeLillo calls it) but I *really* like watching sports I would hate to have to play. Hockey, for instance: a game that involves so much stooping that getting a puck in the teeth actually comes as a relief from the chronic pain in your lower back. For back pain, though, the gold medal has to go to the weightlifters. I loved watching the weightlifters (though while doing so I was often and unfortunately reminded of Craig Raine's line about dogs who 'shit like weightlifters'), especially the super-heavyweights, lifting really super-heavy weights. Can you imagine trying to do that? The breakfasts alone – twenty eggs, a dozen steaks – would have been enough to kill me but, as a spectacle, it was utterly addictive, watching the bar bend under the weight, wondering if someone might actually *burst* before your eyes. I also found it strangely soothing to turn on the TV and find the lone sailor Ben Ainslie – an Ahab in the era of downsizing and cost-efficiency – duking it out in some endless and, as far as one could determine, fiercely one-sided battle against the cruel sea. It was good to know that he was out there and, for me at least, he still is. We will come back to this.

Some of these minor sports would undoubtedly benefit from a change of costume. It is extraordinary that the judo jacket has remained unchanged for so long since the participants have to spend so much of their energy wrestling it back into some kind of order. The showjumping would be more fun if the participants dressed like cowboys and jumped over bits of abandoned wagon trains. In other sports a more radical overhaul is needed. Archery would be improved if the archers were shooting at moving targets: antelope maybe, possibly human beings, ideally (and this would really make a sport of it) each other. Come to that, why not combine three-day-eventing, trap-shooting and archery and just call it Cowboys and Indians?

The most compelling events, though, need no dressing up because they have such a naked connection to their biological origins: the ability to run away from or catch up with something or someone; to jump over a yawning chasm or river; to swim across a lake. (The corollary of this is that it's difficult to imagine a scenario in which the triple jump might be of use. Stepping stones in a wide stream, perhaps?) One might go further and say that an event's pulling power is directly linked to the stage at which it emerged as a human activity. After running, jumping and swimming came throwing, fighting, gymnastics (or tumbling, anyway) and all the equine stuff pioneered by the Mongol hordes or some such. Eventually you got the invention of the ball (as significant in its way as the invention of the wheel) and, as we became adept at using and making tools, so we saw the development of racket sports, the pressurised tennis ball, Air Jordans and so forth. But the primal origin of the basic athletic events means that, give or take a few details, they are pretty well unaltered by technological refinement. Plutarch might have been writing for the *Observer Sports Monthly* when he wrote of 'men who, for deftness of hand, speed of legs, and strength of muscle, transcended human nature and were tireless'.

And what could be more basic – what could be more grounded in the make-up of the species – than our love–hate relationship with what we now know to be *gravity*? There's no point making light of it: the Olympics would be nothing without gravity, especially those events in which, as Bob Dylan put it, they're all doing their best to deny it. A certain number of falls – sacrifices, I suppose you could call them – is essential to the spell of gymnastics: they remind us that, in the course of almost every manoeuvre, the bar or beam is regained against all odds (and how lovely it is to see the coaches of the gymnasts on the bars, standing by, ready to catch them should they fall). What in the Bible was termed a miracle is now known as a Ginga.

The extreme degree of difficulty that characterises the performances pervades every aspect of gymnastics. Photography, which does so well by other sports (the intense temporal concentration of the sprints, for example, is matched by the visual compression of the telephoto lens), has great difficulty *isolating* the split-second of weightlessness which is, quite literally, the highpoint of many gymnastic moves. (The problem, paradoxically, is the ease with which fast shutter speeds render *any* instant weightless.) We, in turn, have great difficulty judging what we are seeing – and so, it seems, did the judges. The reason for this is tangled up in the idea of perfection. In *The Marriage of Cadmus and Harmony* Roberto Calasso writes that 'Perfection doesn't explain its own history but offers its completion.' This is not true of gymnastics. Gymnastics gives us a glimpse of perfection – but every time it does so it instantly raises the bar of the possible (how about throwing in another half-twist?), thereby postponing the idea of completion. It is also constantly commenting on its own history, quoting from the previous masters and the moves – the Katchev, the

Korbut – named after them. (This form of worship has reached its most extreme, monotheistic tendency elsewhere, in the high jump, or the Fosbury as it has now, effectively, become.)

We will, as they say in sports broadcasting, return to the gymnastics shortly, but let us first concede what has become increasingly obvious over the past decade: that the Olympics are, along with everything else, a great festival of Eros. Whatever your preferred body type or sexual orientation, there is someone here to fixate on. Personally, the Bulgarian female hammer-throwers don't do anything for me but there is, as they say, a bun for every burger. For fans of women's weightlifting the highlight of the Games in this respect was probably the opportunity to see Nataliya Skakun's amazing snatch. There seemed almost no consensus among my female friends as to which events worked best for them. Several felt that no one on the track could rival the laidback sexual magnetism of the man in the commentary box. No, not Jonathan Edwards – Michael Johnson! Some liked the sprinters; others found them too muscle-bound, an opinion widely denounced by male gay friends who expressed widespread disappointment that, in the pool, amphibious, dolphin-grey speed-suits had taken over from what Alan Hollinghurst, in *The Line of Beauty*, terms 'knob-flaunting Speedos'. Their interests were better served by the synchronised divers and, of course, by the male gymnasts.

In *The Farewell Symphony* Edmund White recalls how, in the '70s, intensive work-outs left him with forearms the girth of a horse's withers, a 'waist as slender as a napkin' and a 'butt as imposing as a diva's bosom'. The problem was that he became so muscle-bound that he could no longer scratch his back or peel off a t-shirt. The bodybuilder's goal is appearance not action. It was only when watching the gymnasts do something mortal – applying chalk or tying on wrist supports – that the quotidian superfluousness of their arms really became apparent. On the apparatus those boulders of muscle on arms and shoulders represented the *minimum* size necessary to perform the superheroics demanded by the sport.

As for my old-fashioned hetero self, it's the leggy jumpers that have always done it for me. (Oh lucky sand, to have had Heike Drechsler landing in it all those years!) This time around it was the women's beach volleyball that was the unquestioned erotic epicentre of the Games. The sexual element is latent in the word 'beach' but even here it was both intended and incidental. That's the great thing about it! The athletes are not using their perfect bodies just to model all that lycra – and that makes it even sexier. If this kind of thing becomes more overt it will be diminished. Yes, part of me longs to see the outfits get even skimpier. Another part of me realises that would be a bit cheesy – and then another part of me thinks, well, it's only every four years.

And that's the killer. We'll have to wait another four years to live through all this again because it's over. It's over – and the thought of that is too much to bear. For those few weeks in August our lives were packed with meaning and purpose (get home and watch the Olympics – or, in my case, since I was at home already, just *watch the Olympics*). It was great watching the old faces (Svetlana Khorkina, the tragic diva of the asymmetric bars; Frankie Fredericks looking like he had been running since the dawn of time); and it was great watching the new faces (Jeremy Wariner springing to the front of the 200 metres like sprinting's answer to Eminem), but it was actually great just watching. We spent half the day watching and a lot of the next morning reading about what we had watched and, as a result, we felt . . . fulfilled. One day led perfectly to the next. We were never bored and even if we were bored at least there was something on telly. How did we get by without it? What are we going to do without it? How are we going to survive until 'the youth of the world' – a swelling bit of oratory from the closing ceremony that always brings a tear to the eye – gather again in Beijing? For the moment all I can do is think of Ben Ainslie. I like to think he's still out there somewhere, doing battle against the waves, like some Japanese soldier of the Second World War, refusing to admit defeat, refusing to admit that it's over.

2004

Sex and Hotels

Hotels are synonymous with sex. Sex in a hotel is romantic, daring, unbridled, wild. Sex in a hotel is *sexy*. Even if you've been having a sexy time at home you'll have an even sexier time in a hotel. And it's even more fun if there are two of you.

Yes, so far we've only been talking about masturbation, an activity which, at home, often has a hurried, lavatorial quality to it. In a hotel – and I should add that 'hotel' throughout this piece is short for 'expensive hotel' – it's something to luxuriate in. At home you want to watch news, sport or documentaries about human rights abuses. If you are watching TV in a hotel, on the other hand, you want to see things going in and out of other things in extreme close-up. Ideally, to square the circle, the porno you watch in your hotel room will be *set* in a hotel room.

And what will you be wearing as you watch hotel porn in your hotel room? Why, a fluffy white bathrobe, of course. Even though they are frequently stolen these fluffy white bathrobes are theft-proof in the sense that almost as soon as you get them home they lose that fluffy quality. How do hotels maintain robes in that state of perpetual fluffiness? Keeping them white is easy; keeping them fluffy is one of life's enduring mysteries. Is it a question of using gallons of fabric conditioner? Apparently not (I've tried it). The answer can only be: because they are not just fluffy white bathrobes – they are fluffy white *hotel* bathrobes.

Not only are they fluffy and soft and white – they are also *clean*. And the chances are that you too are clean beneath your fluffy white robe because everything about a hotel is clean. Cleanliness might not be next to godliness but it is certainly adjacent to horniness. A hotel room is horny because it is clean: the sheets are clean, the toilets are clean, *everything* is clean, and this cleanliness is a flagrant inducement to – what else? – *filthiness*. Ideally, the room is so clean as to suggest that it has never been used. It cries out to be defiled. If the room is, in a sense, virginal, then the act of breaking the seal on bars of soap and other stealable accessories has something of the quality of breaking its hymen. Slightly archaic it may be, but to speak of '*taking* a room' is, in this context, pleasingly suggestive.

In an effort to keep the rooms unsullied by that dirty stuff *air*, urban hotel rooms are almost always sealed off from the outside world, cocooning you totally in the ambient hum of overnight luxury. It doesn't matter where you are on the planet, you could be anywhere. More exactly you could be *nowhere*. The luxury hotel is a quintessential example of what the French theorist Marc Augé calls the 'non-place' of super-modernity. In *The Right Stuff* Tom Wolfe pointed out that the defining architectural feature of the motel – namely that you don't 'have to go through a public lobby to get to your room' – played a major part in the 'rather primly named "sexual revolution"'. In international hotels, however, the passage through the lobby – a process of which checking in is the ritualistic expression – is also a passage from place to non-place. By checking in and handing over your credit card or passport you effectively surrender your identity. By becoming a temporary resident of this non-place you become a non-person and are granted an ethical equivalent of diplomatic immunity. You become morally weightless. In the confines of the hotel you are no longer Mr or Ms Whoever, you are simply the occupant of a room. You have no history. The act of the porter carrying your stuff up to your room means that you are, as they say, not carrying any baggage. As a result (I am basing this claim on zero medical evidence!) men are less liable to be impotent in a hotel than in any other environment. If a man goes to a motel with his mistress he cheats on his wife. In a luxury hotel, on the other hand, there is no moral liability, only financial.

As befits this utterly amoral environment everything is available –

for a price. If hotels are, as I claimed at the outset, synonymous with sex, then the two are coeval with money. Basically, the more expensive the hotel the more arousing it is. There is, in other words, almost no distinction between the building itself and the prostitutes who ply their trade in it. In the bar of a very expensive hotel the feel of potential sex in the air is almost palpable. If you are in the bar alone, a casual encounter seems more likely with every over-priced drink you sign for. This impression is so strong that a hint of the one-night stand is imparted to a late-evening drink with a partner of twenty years. Almost certainly the most commonly enacted fantasy in a hotel bar involves a couple pretending that they are strangers who have just picked one another up, that one of them is a hooker.

The reality, too, is a kind of historical fantasy. Luxury hotels offer the chance to live – for a while – like an eighteenth-century libertine for whom life consists entirely of pleasure because there is a retinue of servants to clear up the mess. Every whim is catered for. A hotel is a chore-free zone, leaving you free – DO NOT DISTURB – to engage in limitless carnality. Every hint of the mundane – even turning down the covers of your bed – is taken care of by other people, by the staff. As a consequence your actions have no consequences. What the British writer Adam Mars-Jones calls 'treating the facilities to mild abuse' is certainly the privilege of every hotel guest, but major abuse is also tolerated (as long as it's paid for). The rock star's famed tendency – obligation, almost – to trash hotel rooms simply takes this to its extreme. Every day is a new beginning. Everything broken can be replaced. Every day the room and its contents are wiped clean of staining evidence and incriminating finger-prints (a fact which, in turn, feeds into the sense of rampant amorality that is at the heart of the hotel experience). This has its dangers, of course; it takes an effort of will not to succumb to the delusion that the mere fact of being in a hotel room is both prophylactic and contraceptive.

At this point a slight qualification is needed, namely that in some ways a room is more erotic than a suite. A suite subtly revives the division of labour and leisure on which the architecture of the house is predicated. In a suite the bed is kept separate as an adjunct or option. In a room the bed is all-dominating and unavoidable. However big the room, the bed expands proportionately to fill it up. Since the outside world scarcely exists the bed becomes the world ('This bed thy centre is, these walls thy sphere', as the great hotelier John Donne put it). You do everything in or from this bed: you read, write, watch porno, have sex, sleep, make calls . . . Basically, the only time you're not stretched out on the bed is when you're stretched out in the king-size bath, which is, effectively, a liquid bed.

The St Martins Lane hotel, smack in the heart of London's Covent Garden, is exemplary in every regard. It is extremely, ludicrously, expensive. The rooms are white, the sheets are white (though the lights over the bed can be adjusted to impart a discreet purple, yellow or greenish glow to the whiteness), the walls are white, the towels are white. Everything is so white it's like it has been designed as a camouflage for cocaine, that other component of sex-hotel-money nodality. If certain styles of architecture – courts and police stations, most obviously – are inherently judgemental, this is a style of interior design that acknowledges no moral currency other than American Express. It goes without saying that the rooms are completely soul-less (one might as well expect a credit card to have a soul). The fact that they are also small manifests itself mainly by its implicate opposite: the all-engulfing hugeness of the bed. In addition, there is the spatially amplifying illusion of a life-size mirror. Ah, the mirror! This, of course, is another indispensable part of hotel erotics. The mirror is a virtual porn channel in which fantasies of hotel sex are simultaneously enacted and broadcast, to the delight of participants and viewers alike.

'The point of rooms is that they're inside,' writes Don DeLillo in a famous passage in *White Noise*. 'People behave one way in rooms, another way in streets, parks and airports. To enter a room is to agree to a certain kind of behaviour. It follows that this would be the kind of behaviour that takes place in rooms.' Some rooms, though, are more inside than others. Hotel rooms, for example. As such, they generate a special sub-set of room behaviour that one might term *hotel room behaviour* – otherwise known as sex.

So there you are, behaving appropriately in an extremely expensive, hermetically sealed, totally safe, utterly artificial environment. You look out through the smear-free windows at the soundless city which could be any city. No one can see you, and even if they do it's not *you* they see: all they can make out – as in a memorable sequence from Ryu Murakami's *Tokyo Decadence* – is a figure silhouetted in the window: a figurehead and totem of the depraved, atrocious, inhuman sexiness of hotels.

1999

What Will Survive of Us . . .

The first one I saw was on the corner of West 36th Street and Sixth Avenue: a racing bicycle, painted completely white (tyres, saddle, spokes – everything) and chained to a street sign ('Left Lane Must Turn Left'). Plastic flowers had been threaded through the wheels and around the crossbar. New York, that week, was hosting a clutch of art events so I assumed that the white bike was a spin-off from the Pulse or Armory art fairs; either that or a harmless bit of street art. Or maybe it was a prop belonging to one of those irritating mimes, like the ones you get in Covent Garden, presumably painted in matching white and performing nearby. But no, there was no human accompaniment, just this white bike with – I could see as I drew close – cards attached to the sign and to the crossbar:

DAVID SMITH
63 Years Old
Killed by Car
December 5, 2007

A memorial, then, but unlike any I had ever seen before.

The habit of placing flowers or other tributes at the scene of a murder or fatal accident is well established in Britain and America. Two recent novels offer vivid essays in contrast between the default style of commemoration in London and New York respectively. For the East End-based narrator of Emily Perkins' *Novel About My Wife*, these 'tawdry plastic sheathes of flowers in memory of a loving colour-photocopied mum or restless young chav who's got in the way of somebody else's crack-fuelled Stanley knife' are 'a new form of urban decoration, mawkish post-Diana grief'. The Lower East Side equivalent, as seen in Richard Price's *Lush Life*, is altogether more extravagant:

> There were dozens of lit botanica candles, a scattering of coins on a velvet cloth, a reed cross laid flat on a large round stone, a CD player running Jeff Buckley's 'Hallelujah' on an endless loop, a videocassette of Mel Gibson's *The Passion* still sealed in its box, a paperback of *Black Elk Speaks*, some kind of unidentifiable white pelt, a few petrified-looking joints, bags of assorted herbs, coils of still-smouldering incense that gave off competing scents, and a jar of olive oil.

Just four nights later this wild, neo-Kienholzian shrine is on its way to becoming visual compost. Already it seems 'all wrong, sodden and charred, sardonic and vaguely threatening; as if to say, this is what time does, what becomes of us mere hours after the tears and flowers'.

This bike, though, had advanced the practice to a far higher level of commemoration and artistic expression. With its poignantly flat tyres the white bike was unmissable and yet, even in the crowded streets of midtown Manhattan, it didn't get in anyone's way. Robert Musil writes somewhere that nothing is as invisible as a monument; this un-monumental memorial was distinctly visible and yet so discreet as to be *almost not there*. As they waited to cross the street several people touched the bike: a casual version of the gesture made by Catholics, of crossing themselves when they pass over a threshold. By virtue of the white bike a completely innocuous corner of Manhattan – one of thousands – had been imbued with a uniquely gentle aura. Perhaps I am being sentimental but it felt as if this was the safest intersection in the whole of the city.

I had no idea how the white bike came to be there or how it was regarded by the authorities. After a few more months would the chain be cut and the bicycle discreetly removed? Or would it be allowed to remain perpetually in the sun and rain, like the cars and bikes that have been left to fade, rust and rot at Oradour-sur-Glane in

France since the massacre that took place there on 10 June 1944? I assumed it was a one-off guerrilla action but, in the course of a week in the city, I noticed two more of these white bikes: at Houston and Lafayette, and on the Hudson bike path (in memory of Eric Ng, aged twenty-two), right by the Pulse art fair:

Eric Ng
22 Years Old
Killed By
Drunk Driver
December 1, 2006
Love & Rage

So these bikes *were* part of an organised, if unofficial, campaign of remembrance. As far as I can work out the first so-called ghost bike appeared in St Louis, Missouri, in 2003. The ongoing initiative is now part of a loose alliance of websites and organisations such as Visual Resistance and the NYC Street Memorial Project (another strand of which commemorates pedestrian fatalities). According to ghostbike.org there are now similar memorials in more than thirty cities across the world. I've never seen one in London but there are, apparently, ghost bikes in Manchester, Oxford and Brighton. On the ghostbike website, Ryan, a volunteer, had written about the creation of the bike I had seen outside the Pulse art fair:

I started making ghost bikes for strangers in June 2005. A year and a half later, my friend Eric Ng was killed by a drunk driver while riding on the West Side bike path. Eric was 22 and had just started teaching math in a Brooklyn high school. He was the kind of person that made you want to live a little more. A year later I still expect to see him when I show up some-where. His death ripped a hole in my heart.

When we make ghost bikes we tap into the hurt of the world. Each person is part of the soul of their city. These stories can make headlines one day and are forgotten the next – we try to make the city remember. We choose to honor that stranger we know could just as easily be our friend, our sister, our own self. That choice makes us whole.

As well as being part of a web of activist organisations, the ghost bikes can be seen in the context of the ad hoc accumulation of street art generally, from loutish graffiti litter to Banksy's ironic – now ironically iconic and commodified – stencils, to community-based murals. In civic ambition the ghost bikes are like a quiet and respectful aspect of the old Reclaim the Streets initiatives – except they proceed from the premise that the streets do not need to be reclaimed by confrontation, that they are *already* ours. But the bikes also throw into relief something about the inadequacy of public art generally and 'official' memorial art in particular.

At its worst public art in Britain typically defaults to the level of the Norman Wisdom sculpture outside Edgware Road tube station or the justly derided couple kissing goodbye at St Pancras. The fact that the latest round of proposals for the fourth plinth at Trafalgar Square included Tracey Emin's idea for a little group of sculpted meerkats as 'a symbol of unity and safety' re-confirms what everyone already knows: that it is possible to gain a reputation as a serious and important artist on the basis of work devoid of seriousness or importance. With the odd honourable exception – Antony Gormley's *Angel of the North*, for example – most contemporary public sculpture prompts the viewer to echo the question posed fifty years ago by Randall Jarrell in *Pictures from an Institution*: 'It's ugly, but is it Art?'

Rituals of remembrance now come freighted with worries about whether they will be properly observed. As the singing stops and the players find their spot 'around the ten-yard circle that until / tonight seemed redundant' (Paul Farley, 'A Minute's Silence') the possibility that homage will turn to insult hangs over football stadiums like a threat of terror. State-sponsored memorials like the Diana Fountain in the Serpentine are distinguished by their failure to give voice to the sum of individual feelings they are designed to articulate. In Britain one has to go back to the numbed aftermath of the First World War, to Charles Sargeant Jagger's statue of a soldier reading a letter at Paddington Station (by Platform 1) or to the Cenotaph (designed by Sir Edwin Lutyens) on Whitehall to find memorials of high aesthetic quality that are also in step with the needs of a grieving populace.

Most deaths, of course, cannot be expected to be recorded and memorialised on the official monuments of a large city. Nor should artists be required to devote themselves to creating anything other than exactly what they feel like making at any given time. But the hope that the larger needs of society might coincide with the deepest, uncoerced urges of the best artists can never be entirely extinguished. Perhaps it is a sign not only of the solipsism of the contemporary art world but of a wider social failing, that it is on the margins – and beyond – of the competitive, hedge-fund-powered art market that one finds evidence that art, rather than being an amusing diversion or a profitable investment, might be integrated with a broader goal of social progress. The flipside of the art boom of recent years has been that one notion of value – cash – has become so engorged as to have caused other, ultimately more valuable, ones to wilt. This is not to hark back to the earnest early 1960s when John Berger, then art critic of the *New Statesman*, was content to ask a single simple question of any piece of art: 'Does this work help or encourage men to know and claim their social rights?' Nor does it date back to the heady days of the Bolshevik Revolution when artists eagerly put their shoulder to the Soviet wheel which would eventually break them. No, this takes us much further back, to the prehistoric dawn of art and of human consciousness, to the realisation that, as Lewis Mumford famously expressed it in *The City in History*, 'the performance of art itself added something just as essential to primitive man's life as the carnal rewards of the hunt'.

The Temple of Tears and the Temple of Joy were created by David Best at Burning Man, Nevada, in 2001 and 2002 respectively. Made out of the wooden off-cuts from a toy factory these huge, Balinese-style structures were constructed by changing teams of volunteers in the course of the week-long festival. As the temples were being built people left photographs and keepsakes, or wrote prayers and messages on the wood to loved ones who had died. On the understanding that suicide places the greatest burden on the ones who are left behind to mourn, the altar of the Temple of Tears was dedicated to those who had died by their own hand.

Needless to say, there were no notices or guards stipulating appropriate behaviour. (Solemnity, it is worth remembering, is usually a form of decorum, a way of behaving that is entirely compatible with a *lack* of feeling.) The boom of sound systems could be heard in the distance; people wandered through in their wild, sex-crazed costumes, but the atmosphere of compassion and kindness was palpable – overwhelming, in fact. In scale and intensity of effect these Temples were comparable to Lutyens' memorial to The Missing of the Somme at Thiepval. The difference, of course, is that whereas Lutyens' monument was built to last, the Temples were built in order to be ceremoniously burned within days of their completion. In a post-religious culture that lacks appropriate rituals of grieving and mourning – and the solace provided by such rites – there was something perfectly appropriate about this: a memorial predicated on transience, a work of art that was absolutely inseparable from the temporary city and the community it was designed to help and to please.

In their less spectacular, more modest – and, already, more lasting – way the ghost bikes do the same thing: honouring the dead, delighting the living, making the world a safer, nicer place. If that is too humble a definition of art then one wonders why it is so rarely achieved elsewhere.

Postscript: a few days after this essay was published in the *Guardian* a reader who had been in New York about a month after me sent a picture of the first ghost bike I'd seen, the one on 36th and Sixth. It had been completely vandalised: wheels buckled, signs and tyres torn off. This was sad but, in a way, the mangled bike looked even more poignant than in its original pristine condition.

2008

On Being an Only Child

'Autobiography begins with a sense of being alone.'
John Berger

My mother often quoted with approval the maxim 'Spare the rod and
spoil the child.' Unfortunately she thought this was intended as exhor-
tation rather than warning. The mother's instinct to indulge her only
child was thereby reinforced by a higher authority. I was so spoiled
that on the day my parents unexpectedly came to pick me up at
primary school in the middle of the morning – I was about eight at
the time – I told the teacher that it was probably because they wanted
to buy me a toy. In fact it was to go to Shropshire where my grand-
mother was dying. I was also spoiled because I was such a sickly
thing. I spent so much time away from infant's school that the truant
officer visited our house to see what was going on. What was going
on was that I was always ill. When I went into hospital to have my
tonsils and adenoids out – a panacea in those bountiful days of the
NHS – my parents brought me a Beatrix Potter book each day. I
missed having brothers and sisters but I liked the way that I didn't
have to share my toys with anyone else. It also meant I got more
presents at Christmas and on my birthday.

This kind of pampering was balanced by the way that my parents
had grown up in the Depression of the 1930s. They have spent their
lives saving. My mother worked as a dinner lady – serving school
dinners (i.e. lunches) in the canteen of the school I went to until I
was eleven. Later, after I had left home, she became a cleaner at a

hospital. My father worked as a sheet-metal worker. They have always been able to make more money by saving than by earning. It has never been worth their while to employ anyone to do anything for them. On the one hand, then, I was spoiled constantly – because I was an only child, because I was a skinny, sickly little boy; on the other, life consisted entirely of small economies, of endless scrimping and saving that became second nature. If I grew up having everything I wanted that is partly because my desires soon became shaped by the assumption that we could not afford things, that *everything* was too expensive, that we could do without almost anything. Many times, when I asked my dad if I could have something that had taken my eye in a shop, he responded by saying, 'You don't want that.' To which I wanted to reply, 'But I *do*.' And then, after a while I stopped wanting things. (I now wonder if my father was unconsciously using 'want' in an earlier, archaic sense of 'lack', a distinction capitalism has since pledged all its energies to rendering obsolete.)

If I wanted replica shorts worn by my favourite football team, Chelsea, my mother bought cheap blue ones and then stitched the authenticating white stripes down each side. Clothes for my Action Man? My mum would make them. A Subbuteo soccer pitch? She bought a piece of green baize and painted-on the lines. We never used a trolley in the supermarket, only a basket. We always bought the cheapest versions of everything. When I was a bit older – about fourteen, I think – and wanted a Ben Sherman shirt my mother explained that it was just 'paying for the name'. We hardly ever went on holiday, mainly because it involved the activity that my dad hated more than any other: spending money. When we did go to Bournemouth or Weston-super-Mare for a few days – never abroad; I did not fly on a plane until I was twenty-two – it was no fun. On the cloudy beach one day I buried my mum's feet in the sand. Half an hour later, having forgotten all about this, I plunged my spade into the sand and into her feet. Often it rained and so we went to the cinema – something we never did at home – to see big-screen versions of the TV shows we watched at home: *Morecambe and Wise*, *Steptoe and Son*. My dad was happier using his time off work to work on the house (concreting the drive, building a garage).

Whatever form it takes, your childhood always seems perfectly normal. It took years for me to understand that I had grown up in relative poverty. If we had enough money for everything we needed that was only because of the extent to which economising – a voluntary extension of the rationing introduced during the Second World War – had been thoroughly internalised. As with most things connected with parental influence this later manifested itself in my behaviour in two contradictory ways. As soon as I left home I became a splurger: if I bought a bar of chocolate then instead of rationing myself to one or two squares I would gobble down the whole thing. I became a gulper not a sipper. But I have also been able to live on very little money without any sense of sacrifice (a valuable skill, almost a privilege, for anyone wishing to become a writer). Going without things that most of my contemporaries took for granted never felt like hardship. I spent years living on the dole, more than happy with the trade-off: little money, lots of time. Even now, aged fifty, it is agony, for me, to have to take a taxi in London.

We lived in a terraced house in a neighbourhood full of families. There were always plenty of kids to play with in the lane that ran behind our row of houses. Next to my school – less than ten minutes' walk away – there was the Rec where you could play football or just run around. There was no shortage of companions but always, at some point, I would have to go back home, back to being on my own, back to my parents. And some days there was just no one to play with. Bear in mind how huge afternoons were back then. For a child the hours stretch out interminably. After my father was made redundant from his job at Gloster Aircraft, he worked nights for a while, at a factory where nylon was made. On afternoons when I had no one to play with I had to be quiet because my dad was sleeping. When I think back to my childhood now, these are the afternoons that I remember. It almost seems like a single afternoon of loneliness and boredom. I've never shaken off this propensity for being bored, in fact I've gotten so used to it that I don't even mind it that much. As a kid I was so bored I assumed it was the basic condition of existence.

When we drove to my grandparents' damp house – another example of the working holiday: there was always something to be mended or built once we got there – we never went on the newly constructed motorways which, back then, had a glamour that seems almost inconceivable now that they are synonymous with the *opposite* of speed, with delays and mile-long tailbacks. It was as if there were a tacit toll on using the motorway; somehow it was cheaper to take the regular roads – cheaper because slower. (One of my dad's most pointless economies was never to fill up our car with petrol; he always put in just half a tank at a time so that we seemed constantly to be stopping for petrol.) Doing things slowly was a way, somehow, of saving money. We were always overtaken by everyone. 'He's in a hurry,' my mum would say as someone whizzed past our sky-blue Vauxhall Victor. I remember wishing that *we* could be in a hurry, just once. Being in a hurry looked like *fun*. It wasn't just driving; everything we did was done slowly. I was always waiting. My parents kept telling me that patience was a virtue. I have, as a consequence, turned into a raging inferno of impatience. If I have matured at all it has been in the style of D.H. Lawrence, who said that when he was young he had very little patience; now that he was older he had *none at all*. I love hurrying. It still seems like fun. I remember how relaxing it felt when I first went to New York, to be in a place where everyone was in a hurry all the time. And yet, at the same time, the life I have ended up leading has effectively re-created those afternoons when I had no one to play with and nothing to do and so had to come up with something to amuse myself. As a kid this meant drawing or making something; as an adult it means writing things like this. I'm not only used to having, I *need* hours and hours of uninterrupted free time if I'm ever to get anything done. And yet, at the same time, I never love the life of the writer more than when I *have* someone to play with, when I'm down at the park, playing tennis on a Monday – or Tuesday, Wednesday or Thursday – afternoon. If you fancy a game I'm always free.

Our life was completely devoid of culture, both in the selective sense of music, art and literature, and in the larger sense. There was no community life, none of the remembered richness of working-class life that served as ballast for Raymond Williams and Tony

Harrison when they left home and went to university. There was just my mum and dad and me and the television. We bought a record player but after about a month my dad gave up on buying records ('The Green, Green Grass of Home' by Tom Jones was the last). Sometimes we visited relatives like my uncle Harry and auntie Lean in Shurdington. Harry kept whippets. Their house smelled of dogs and I always ended up sneezing because, as well as being ill the whole time, I was allergic to cats and the fine hair of the whippets. My auntie Joan lived a few doors down, in the gloomy council house, full of stuffed birds, where she and my dad and my other aunts had grown up. Joan kept poodles and her house smelled even worse than uncle Harry's. I think these visits were the first things I ever *endured*. I only had one cousin – herself an only child – who was close to my age. The rest, most of whom lived in another part of the country, were all a lot older. My parents were never very social: my mum had been brought up as a Methodist and so did not drink. Occasionally, in the summer, we would drive out to a pub with a garden for chicken-in-a-basket but my dad never went out on his own to meet friends in a pub. We never went to restaurants. Basically, except for visits, we stayed home and saved money. I loved it in the winter when it got dark early and we locked the doors and drew the curtains and *stayed in*.

So: no brothers, no sisters, just one cousin – and no pets except for the occasional goldfish which expired soon after it was brought home from the fairground in a polythene bag full of water. My dad was dead against pets. He hated dogs because they yapped. He hated cats because they were cats. The lack of pets and siblings had a bad effect on me. Love was coming at me in vast quantities from my parents but because I was never allowed to have pets I had no experience – apart from the instinctive love of child for parent – of learning to love or to take care of someone or something more vulnerable and needy than me. (Several girlfriends have said that I am a terrible hugger. Basically I just stand there, draped like a coat around the person I am supposed to be hugging. At some level I assume that I am the one who needs to be hugged, comforted.) Perhaps the lack of pets and siblings is part of the reason why I have never wanted to have children. Actually, that puts it too mildly. It's not just that I have never wanted to have children; I have always actively hated the idea. Frankly, I can't understand why *anyone* wants to have them. As I get older, in fact, I find it more and more astounding that anyone can feel or think differently to me about anything. I am amazed – and often furious – that the world does not resemble more closely my own preferred idea of how it should be. Perhaps that has something to do with being an only child too.

It was natural, since I didn't have to share my toys with any siblings, that I became a collector. I collected all sorts of cards, Airfix soldiers and comics. I loved *arranging* my things – whatever they were – and putting them into some kind of order. I still love doing this. I spent much of my time making model aeroplanes and doing jigsaws: things that you can do on your own. (My mother had a particular way of doing jigsaws: we sorted out the side pieces and made a hollow, unstable frame, then filled in the middle. Our approach to jigsaws was, in other words, methodical, rigorous. Work had entered into every facet of my parents' lives; even leisure activities had about them some of the qualities of labour.) I would like to say that I displayed the single child's customary ability to develop a rich imaginative life but I don't think I did – unless finding ways to play games intended for two or more players on your own counts as imaginative. In my late thirties I bought a flat in Brighton on the south coast of England. It was a big place, big enough to accommodate something I'd long wanted: a ping-pong table. The problem was that I knew almost no one in Brighton and except on weekends when friends from London visited I had no one to play with. It took me right back to my childhood, that table. In its immense, folded uselessness it symbolised all the afternoons I spent playing games on my own. I played Subbuteo on my own – almost impossible since you have to flick both the attacking players and control the opposing goalkeeper simultaneously. I played Monopoly on my own. I played Cluedo on my own. When I eventually got round to it, masturbation seemed the natural outcome of my childhood.

A few years after hitting upon this solitary activity I discovered another: reading. I had passed the 11-plus and gone to Cheltenham

Grammar School, where, for the first four years, I was an indifferent student. Then, at the age of about fifteen, under the influence of my English teacher, I started to do well at school and began to spend more and more time reading. I passed all my O-levels and stayed on for A-levels. During my first year at grammar school we had moved from a terraced house to a semi-detached with three bedrooms. I wonder if I would have had the peace and space to study if I had had brothers and sisters. It's impossible to say, but reading and study filled the vacuum of boredom that had been there for as long as I could remember. But reading created a gap as well as filling one.

When I was trying to decide which A-levels to do my father said not to bother with History because it was all in the past. He also gave me another piece of advice that I have come particularly to cherish: 'Never put anything in writing.' From the age of about sixteen on, most of the advice my parents gave me was best ignored. Still, I ended up doing Economics instead of History.

It became obvious, early in the lower sixth form, that I would go to university. I would be the first person in my family to do so – I was already the first to be doing A-levels or their equivalent. And then, as the time for the exams approached and it became evident that, unless I messed up, I would get very high grades, my English teacher advised me to try for Oxford. My parents only knew of Oxford through *University Challenge*. Of course they liked the idea of my going to Oxford but they made a big fuss about how other parents wouldn't have let their children stay on at school; other children would have had to start bringing money into the house. I hated this because it was stupid and because it was so obviously untrue. Even if they didn't know what Oxford was, they were as excited by the prospect of my going there as I was. We had many arguments, in the course of which I often became furious. During one such argument – I forget what it was about – my father and I became involved in a scuffle. My mum tried to intercede and, in the process, my father accidentally elbowed her in the nose. 'That's me nose gone!' she said, a remark so idiotic that I became incandescent with rage. It is strange and unfair but, even now, that rage has never entirely gone away. I am angry at the way that my parents were oppressed but at some level I am angry with them for having internalised their oppression.

In Raymond Williams' *Border Country* the autobiographical protagonist tells a friend that every value he has comes only from his father.
'Comes only from him.' Many of my values come from my parents:
honesty, reliability, resilience: the bedrock values. But there are other
qualities I have been attracted to – vivacity, charm, light-heartedness,
grace, urbanity, doing things quickly – which had no place in my
parents' world: they were privileges. Also, because my parents had
always worked hard – for practically nothing – I never set any store
by hard work. My father was very proud of never having been on
the dole in his life. During the summer between A-levels and the
start of the Oxbridge term I had a part-time job in a shop, which
meant that the pay I received counted against my entitlement to
benefit. Effectively I was working for nothing. My father thought it
better for me to give up my time to work at this crap job than it was
for me to get the same money from the state. It is no exaggeration
to say that I hated him for this. My parents' view of the world was
just too simple: it was suited to the Depression but not to the 1970s.
I, on the other hand, had the contemporary idea that the world owed
me a living.

This became more acute after I passed the Oxbridge exam and got
a so-called Exhibition (a form of scholarship) to Corpus Christi,
Oxford. From then on the gap between my parents and me widened
as I realised that, as well as an intangible intellectual world different
to the one I had grown up in, there was an actual social world too.
This, the classic quandary of the scholarship boy, has been thoroughly
documented in many novels. Here I will mention just two representative episodes. In my second year at university I came back home
for my twenty-first birthday. My mother had made a cake and my
father had paid to have it decoratively iced in the shape of an open
book with a bookmark down the middle. Printed across the cake,
like print on the open pages, was the name of my college: Corpus
Christi. It had the look of a shrine or totem, which in some sense it
was, an expression of the mysterious and vast symbolic power of
books. This mystery, needless to say, was enhanced by the way that
my father had never actually read one. My uncle Peter took a photo-

graph of that cake and it seems the proudest thing in the world – and the saddest.

In my final year at Oxford I came home unexpectedly and turned up at my old primary school where my mother still worked in the canteen. She opened the door in her dinner lady's blue uniform. We both started crying and embraced each other. We held each other because we both had an inkling that part of my education was to understand that it was more than just education. I was my parents' only child but the life I would go on to lead would be so different to theirs, and the most important part of this difference was the way that it could never be explained and articulated to them by me.

What does this have to do with being an only child? Everything. Let's suppose I'd had a younger sister. Perhaps she would have been influenced by my example and gone on to university and would have begun to have a different life to the one we had grown up to expect. Then, as a family, we could all have moved along together. Alternatively, if my brother had left school early and led the life that someone from my background might have been predicted to lead it would have bound me more closely to the world I had come from. There would have been more ballast. Either way, there would have been an intermediary. I wouldn't have been the oddity, a weird exception that no sense can be made of or conclusions drawn from. I had a friend who went to Cambridge while his brother left school after A-levels. For a while they drifted apart but then, in their different scenes, they independently discovered a common interest: drugs. I like to think that if I'd had a relationship like this with a brother who had, say, left school early and then worked as a bricklayer or an electrician we would have been more of a family. It wouldn't have just been my parents and their son who had gone to Oxford and led this strange life of doing nothing. As it was, my parents remained cocooned in a late-twentieth-century version of the 1930s. For a time, while I was at university and in the years immediately afterwards, I tried to get my mum to read proper books (*Jude the Obscure*, *Sons and Lovers*: novels that initiated and articulated the process we were living through) and to get my dad to read the *Guardian*. I played them some of the music I was listening to (Keith Jarrett), tried to get them to try different teas, real coffee, to eat nicer food. They didn't like any of it. (From time to time we still have conversations about diet. 'You know, you really shouldn't be eating eggs and chips the whole time,' I say. 'Well, we've been eating them for our whole lives and it's never done us any harm,' says my dad. 'You don't think that the fact you had cancer of the rectum and have had a colostomy counts as harm?' 'Get away with you,' says my dad. 'That was nothing to do with that.')

If there is a special loneliness that is intrinsic to the single child there is a particular isolation that attaches to the scholarship boy or girl. Most people come from families with brothers and sisters. And most people in the world I have been part of for the last twenty years are from middle-class families: they speak the same way as their parents, they go to the same things, have similar interests. The terrible truth is that, ostensibly, I have more in common with my wife's parents – her dad is an academic, her mum a piano teacher – than I do with my own. Almost everything that counts for anything in the world I have been part of has been learned, acquired. Most of the things I grew up knowing about are irrelevant.

Except – and the importance of this can hardly be overstated – my parents have a sense of humour! They're funny. What greater gift can parents pass on to their children? In my impatient maturity anyone without a sense of humour bores the crap out of me. This is not the only way in which something I picked up from my parents manifests itself. My parents, as I have said, laid great stress on being reliable, punctual, dependable. We are encouraged to think of reliable people as boring, dull, and perhaps for a brief while, after leaving university, I briefly flirted with this in that I was drawn to carefree, careless people. Then I realised that unreliable, dishonest people are the most boring people in the world. One of the advantages of the way that new social opportunities open up to you – and for me this began happening after university – is that you can have it both ways: there are plenty of people out there who are fun, pleasure-loving, clever and reliable. It's got to the stage now, in my late forties, where I try to minimise contact with unreliable, unpunctual people. For different reasons – for my parents it was a moral judgement, for me it's just impatience – we have ended up sharing an aversion to particular forms of behaviour. Especially lying. I am told that if you have brothers and sisters you learn to lie – about each other, or in collusion with each other to your parents. I don't know if this is true but I do know that I have grown up with almost no capacity for lying (I like scams and dodges but that is different; that is part of a battle of wits). My parents made me believe that as long as I was honest everything would be OK. I am still almost incapable of lying in real life. And it took me a long time to learn how to do so on the page.

It wasn't until 1987 that I really understood how liberating the task of writing fiction could be. I was twenty-nine and writing a book based very closely on the life my friends and I were leading in Brixton, south London. At that time I was going through a phase of wishing very badly that I had a sister. I'd had these longings before, but never as intensely. It came to me in a flash – and it should be obvious by now that this is not the first time that I have belatedly realised something that everyone else has either known for ages or taken for granted – that if I wanted a sister I could just invent one! It was as easy as that. And not only could I invent a sister, I could invent the *perfect* sister – one you were sexually attracted to. Friends who have sisters say that only someone who didn't have one would think in these terms but I think that hint of incest added a useful quality of unease to the novel. Anyway, it worked. I never again had a craving for a sister.

2008

Sacked

I intended giving a full, frank and unadorned account of how I came to be fired from my first proper job after leaving university but that has proved more difficult than I imagined. It's not just that I can't remember things clearly enough; what really happened has been overlain by the re-created version of events in my novel, *The Colour of Memory* (1989). The fiction has coloured my memory to such an extent that it is nearly impossible for me to get at the literal truth of what occurred.

The facts, or what remains of them, are as follows: I came down from Oxford in 1980 with no real idea of what I intended to do. Having applied, without success, for various jobs in advertising and television I moved to London, where I got a job teaching part-time at a tutorial college in Chelsea and at Lucie Clayton Secretarial College. Both of these jobs were for just one term. After that I worked in Harrods during the busy period of their January sale. I was not sacked from that job but a friend who worked in Personnel and had access to my employee assessment form told me that I had been classified as someone never to be re-employed. For most of 1981 I lived on the dole before starting teaching again at another tutorial college in September. I also applied again for more jobs in journalism, TV and advertising. One of these jobs was at the Periodical Publishers Association (PPA). The company was run by a Tory MP whose name – Tom Something? – I have forgotten. My first interview took place at the House of Commons while my prospective employer was taking a quick break from a masochistic-sounding part of the democratic process called a Running Three Line Whip. My second interview was at the offices on Kingsway. To my amazement I got the job.

I began work in September while living in Islington, renting a friend's room while he was on holiday for a month. I know this because I can distinctly remember cycling to work down Rosebery Avenue, past Sadler's Wells Theatre. I also remember being astonished at the amount of time a job soaked up. If you went for a drink after work – I mean 'went for a drink' in the English sense of 'got totally plastered' – the whole day was shot to hell.

London was exciting to me back then. There were many things I wanted to do – like going to Kensington market to buy clothes – and having a job seriously interfered with my ability to do these things. I can't remember what my job involved but I assume it was boring and completely pointless.

One day the second-in-command took me out for lunch. It was the first free lunch I'd ever had, even though it wasn't really a lunch, just some disgusting sandwiches on white bread smeared with too much butter. I thought I was going to be sick, partly because of all this rancid butter and pink ham, but mainly because this pink-faced deputy-boss was a rancid old bore. He told some stories he had reheated hundreds of times before. I was a vehement young leftie at the time and spent quite a bit of the afternoons debating politics with my colleagues. Gallingly, the other graduate who had been hired at the same time as me was a member of the Tory party and, even more gallingly, had actually published some short stories in glossy magazines. He shared a house with Ian Hislop, who would go on to become editor of *Private Eye* and a TV celebrity. This other new employee and I had many arguments about politics and I greatly preferred arguing with him to doing the work for which I was being paid. Some days I didn't do any work at all, I just larked around. It could be said that I had a bad attitude, in fact it probably *has* to be said that I had a bad attitude. All I've ever wanted from a job is to skive. Skiving is a whole way of approaching – in the sense of avoiding – work. It's not the same as slacking, because skiving can involve a far greater investment of energy and initiative than doing the work could have ever have necessitated. Get in late, knock off early and do fuck-all in the interval except steal stationery: that's my attitude to work. Get paid for something you haven't done. Why? Because this stupid job required that I give up my valuable time, time which I would rather have used in some other way even if I did nothing with it.

I think the reason I have this bad attitude to work is because of my background. My parents worked hard and I didn't like the look of it at all. University made me realise that you didn't have to flog your guts out working at some piss-bin job. It also gave me a taste for leisure which has, if anything, increased over the years.

After about a month I was called into the deputy-boss' office and sacked. I can't remember exactly what happened, only that he gave me a month's pay to sort myself out. For a more precise and extended – though not necessarily accurate – account of what took place, the curious reader is directed to the first chapter of *The Colour of Memory*.

After leaving the office I met my friends Robert and James at a cocktail bar, where we got totally plastered. I felt pretty bad – not because the sacking was unjustified but because, effectively, I'd been caught, found out. I deserved to get sacked. (I am all for firing people. More people should be sacked from all sorts of jobs. The number of people doing jobs and doing them badly – thereby creating extra work for other people – is incredible. The world is an inefficient place and sacking people can only make it more efficient.) Although I felt pretty bad about being sacked I realised that it was not for me, this world of work, that I was too selfish to do a job, that I actually valued my time – my life – so highly that I would rather waste it than work at a job.

My memories are a little vague from this point on. I know I moved into a house in Balham. Fortunately, I only stayed there for a short while. After six weeks I moved into a house in Brixton with a whole bunch of people who, like me, were on the dole. From there, to cut a longish story as short as possible, I ended up becoming a writer.

That's all I can manage in terms of recalling the period of getting sacked from my job. The more I think about it the more confused events become. The chronology is uncertain. I just can't untangle the sequence of events. I've had to give up. Perhaps there's a connection here with getting sacked from that job. Getting fired turned out to be a good thing – even though it felt like a very bad thing – and I have tended to carry the lessons I learned from it into the rest of my life. That is to say, I've adopted a policy of quitting, of getting by without persevering. As soon as I get fed up, bored, tired or weary of anything I abandon it. Books, films, writing assignments, relationships – I just give up on them. (Is it possible to live entirely without perseverance? I think it is, as long as one perseveres with the idea of doing so.) So I should, by my own principles, have given up, without a second thought, on this attempt to write about being sacked. But something about this period of my life continues to gnaw at me. I'm curious about it, would like to learn more about it – and, fortunately, I've just had a breakthrough.

I'm writing this in New York, where I landed what I thought was going to be a cushy teaching gig for a semester but which actually involves a certain amount of work. My wife is in London and a few days ago I asked her to have a rummage around in my filing cabinet to see if she could find my old diaries for the early 1980s.

"81 or '82,' I said. 'Hopefully in September or August there'll be an entry saying "Started work at PPA" or something.' This turned out not to be the case but in my little 1982 diary she did find the following entry, dated 24 September, 'Sacked from PPA'. Significantly, I had noted the date I was fired but not the date I'd started work. My wife is coming to visit this weekend and she's bringing the diary. All will be revealed.

I have the diary in front of me now. How funny, to end up being one's own biographer, to have to resort to the kind of research required by writing someone else's life. On the evidence of this diary, though, it's not surprising, either that I have so little memory of what was going on or that I got sacked. If ever there was a case of un-unfair dismissal this was it. The diary is two and a half inches by four, not all the entries are legible; many are blurred as if by damp or by time itself. That's what amazes me most about this diary – the simple passage of time between my writing it then and reading it now. To think that I am looking back at things that happened *more than a quarter of a century ago* . . .

At the beginning of the year I was living in Brixton, sharing a flat with my friend Robert, who was working as a solicitor at one of London's most prominent left-wing legal firms. (I no longer know any lawyers but there was a time, I see now, when I was surrounded by them.) Robert had gone to the same school – Cheltenham Grammar – as me and had been a year ahead of me at Oxford but I only got to know him afterwards. I was teaching at a tutorial college over in west London. I see I was always going to gigs (a quick selection: Bow Wow Wow, the Au Pairs, Pig Bag, 23 Skidoo, Kid Creole and the Coconuts), night clubs (the straight nights at Heaven, the Language Lab, the Kareba, the Beat Bop) and films (*Circle of Deceit*, *Reds*, *The Passenger*, *Badlands*, *The Battle for Chile*, *State of Siege*, *Barry Lyndon*, *Prince of the City*, *The Loveless*, to mention a few). It seems that most weeks I went to the cinema and clubs twice and probably to one or two gigs as well. I was also reading a great deal, far more than I do now. (I used to keep lists but the one for 1982 has gone missing.)

When my wife first looked through the diary she was surprised to discover that as well as going to the cinema a lot (which I still enjoy now) I had also gone to hear the London Symphony Orchestra a great deal (something I never do now). This, I see now, was a code. On Friday 12 February Robert and I went to meet a client of his in the branch of McDonald's near Warren Street tube. She was waiting with a copy of the *Evening Standard* newspaper folded up in front of her. We were there to buy LSD (some code, huh, changing the D to an O?) but when we walked back to her squat in King's Cross she unfolded the newspaper to reveal a considerable quantity of heroin. Did we want some? I definitely didn't. Just the acid was fine, thank you very much. But my friend Robert was adamant. This was something we had to do, an experience we had to have. So I did have some of this experience and most agreeable it was too. We spent a couple of hours there, snorting this brown powder with Robert's client and her moronic boyfriend. Robert was violently sick, both in his client's flat and on the Tube on the way home. I felt fine and went to meet friends (principally Caroline, Robert's cousin, who he was always trying to sleep with) at a party at the Royal College of Art. Robert felt better the next day so we took the acid that we had bought. We walked around Brockwell Park and sat in the blue room of our place in Brixton. It was winter in the park and the walls in the blue room rippled and breathed. The floorboards were painted a glistening blue and sitting on the sofa, watching the walls ripple and breathe, was like being on a raft in the middle of a calm blue lake. The sun sank into the gas fire on the horizon.

There's another coded entry for 18 March: 'A!!' This meant that I had anal sex, for the first time ever, with Jane. 'I would love to fuck you in your arse,' I said. I used the porno words, but this was before I had ever seen any porno. Back then we were anti-porno. Porn was woman hatred. I said it in this relaxed way but in reality I was as tense as Jeremy Irons in one of his uptight Englishman roles. Certainly I was a lot less relaxed than Jane, who coolly responded, 'Then why don't you?' I had never done this before, but Jane had (she had also slept with women). She was the first woman I had been out with who was really *interested* in sex.

The next day Robert and I took heroin again with his client and the day after that we did two micro dots of acid each. Jane cooked a huge vegetarian meal for us. She didn't take acid but she smoked a lot of pot (which I didn't do back then because I hated the idea of smoking).

5 April: 'Pink Flamingo club.' It's all coming back to me now. It's a reference to the Soft Cell song ('standing in the doorway of the Pink Flamingo, crying in the rain . . .') and it meant I had split up with Jane. Immediately after this I fell ill with gastro-enteritis. (Looking through my diary I see that I got ill an awful lot more then than I do now.) My second interview at the PPA was at 10 a.m.

7 May: 'Camden Palace – French girl.' Another New Romantic-type evening. The French girl was a hotel chamber maid. We came back to Brixton on the night bus and we had nothing-special sex. This was on the same day (I remember this, though I've not noted it) that I sprained my ankle playing five-a-side football: the first of a number of occasions when I have torn the ligaments in my ankle.

What resilience, though: going to a night club after spraining an ankle!

I had become quite friendly with one of my students, James, a rich, charming guy who'd been expelled from Eton and who was now re-taking his A-levels (though his only real ambition in life was to become a heroin addict). Another of my students was a promising tennis player. He was a member of the club – conveniently located round the back of my tutorial college – where, every June, there is a grass-court tournament which serves as a dress-rehearsal for Wimbledon. When my tennis-playing pupil did not need his card (either because he had classes or some other obligation) he lent it to me so that I could go and watch the matches. Members were allowed to take a guest and so, one afternoon, after we had completed our tutorial, James and I dropped some acid and went to watch McEnroe and Connors in their respective quarter-finals. James was wearing fluffy blue slippers. I remember Connors or McEnroe complaining about these slippers because we were in the front row (it was a very intimate tournament back then, like watching top players in furious competition at the vicarage) and James had his feet resting on the net post. Well, that's how it seems in retrospect. Certainly they were resting on the canvas barrier separating the small crowd from the court. According to my diary I went to the club again on Friday the 11th, took acid again on the 12th and went to see Connors beat McEnroe in the final on Sunday the 13th.

30 June: I went round to Jane's and we spent the day having sex. She was living in Sydenham Hill, a short bus ride from Brixton. I don't recall the exact nature of our arrangement but over the course of several years after we had split up, if circumstances were propitious, we would have blissful sex together.

The next day I took a train to Italy en route to Corfu, where I was due to meet James. I stopped off in Venice, where I spent two nights sleeping outside the station so that I would not have to pay for a hotel. I also went to Florence. One night, in fact, I took trains back and forth between Venice and Florence just so I could sleep comfort-ably. It was a shitty way to see both cities because I was so tired all the time I could barely keep my eyes open but I was obsessed with not spending any money.

Things got much better when I arrived in Corfu, via Brindisi. This, of course, was in the days before email and although I knew the name of the village I didn't know exactly the *pensione* where James was staying. Miraculously, the first place I tried turned out to be his place. He was there with his girlfriend, Julia, who was gorgeous. I booked into a cheaper boarding house and then the three of us took acid and went down to the beach and got sun-burned. It was the start of an amazing week. A football match was arranged between tourists and the local Greeks. We were one-nil down, I scored the equaliser but then the game had to be abandoned because there was so much animosity between the two sides. We got to know all the other tourists in the village and went carousing every night. It was like Ibiza before raving and E and house music, which means we got plastered every night at the disco. Julia was becoming increasingly upset by James because he was so bent on seducing a woman from Norway. It was probably to get back at him that Julia ended up having drunken sex with me in my squalid room. James came in while we were still lying there. I remember him going out and saying to someone next door, 'I need a cigarette quite badly.'

A few days later Julia suddenly took off. The note she left read: 'James, I can endure your company no longer. Last time I left you my soul, this time I leave you money.' James was depressed by this because, contrary to what Julia had said in her note, there was no money to be found. Shortly after this he and I went on to Alexandria and Cairo. There are photos of us riding stallions in the Sahara, near the pyramids, on the edge of Cairo. James had said that one of the great things about Egypt was that you could go into a pharmacy and buy drugs over the counter but this turned out not to be true. We kept going into pharmacies and asking for amphetamines but they shook their heads and looked at us like we were junkies. Alexandria had nothing going for it. It wasn't attractive and there was none of that Lawrence Durrell feel about it as far as I could tell (though I hadn't read the *Alexandria Quartet* at that point and still haven't).

*   *   *

Back in England for the late summer I drove with Robert from Cheltenham to Hay-on-Wye, doing hits of amyl nitrate on the way. Why did we do that? Not only is amyl a horrible drug, but it is a totally inappropriate drug for a trip to a place like Hay. In late August I must have started my job. I had only been there a few weeks when I went on holiday to Dublin with Robert and James. The reason for going to Dublin was to visit my old girlfriend Claire, who was now at art college there. She lived in a house with three other women and they all slept in the same room, on a row of adjacent mattresses. One morning, when everyone else had got up, Claire and I had sex quickly for no particular reason and without much pleasure.

Back in London I got sacked on Friday the 24th. The entry for Sunday the 26th is more representative of this period. '*The Conversation* at NFT. LSO with R[obert]. Fucked C[laire], in love with C.' Claire was only in London for a few days and I can't remember why she had come. After she went back to Dublin I moved into a room in a new flat in Notting Hill. I was now being paid by James' parents to give him tutorials for the Oxbridge entrance exam, which meant that our relationship reverted to its semi-formal, semi-recreational basis. James had gone from wearing slippers to going barefoot. This behaviour was sufficiently unusual to give a police constable cause to stop, question and search him, whereupon he was busted for possession of grass.

The room I'd moved to in Notting Hill was only available for a month and I had to begin looking at a new place almost immediately. At a rental agency I got chatting to one of the women working there. Her name was Lucy and we went out, first to see *Blade Runner*, then to a club called the Bat Cave.

Some of the codes for this period don't make sense, or at least I no longer understand them. 28 October: 'C + S!!! at Alison's', for example. I can't remember who Alison was. Maybe she was a tall woman with back-combed blonde hair who I met when the Clash played at the Lyceum. One imagines the C stands for coke and the S for speed but I don't think I ever came across coke at that stage. Being October, though, I certainly came across a lot of magic mushrooms, partly because James and I spent so many of our tutorials looking for them. The weather must have been mild and wet because there was a bumper crop that year. On the evidence of my diary it seems I did mushrooms twice a week for about six weeks. I even put together a little collection of writings about some of these escapades and made five photocopied booklets on blue paper. I called it *Memories of Hallucinogenics* and gave copies to Robert, Claire and James. Lest we get too transcendental about the whole thing, though, a not untypical entry – for 10 November – shows how casually tripping had been integrated into the normal rhythm of the day's social life. 'Some mushrooms – evening in pub with James.' That was at the tail-end of a season which had come to a climax on Saturday, 30 October when Lucy and I had gone to Brighton for the day. She had a bag full of an unspecified number of dried mushrooms. We took half each and within ten minutes the world went completely berserk. The beach was as tidal as the sea. We were delirious. The walls of a bouncy red castle swayed over us. We spent the whole day clinging to each other, shrieking hysterically, trying to stay out of trouble. We both agreed that we had never been so out of it in our lives. When we got back to London – punch-drunk, bedraggled, relieved to not be permanently deranged – I assumed we would go home together but Lucy didn't want to. We met again on Monday and went to a club called Sound and Vision and she asked to come home with me because it had been a mistake not to on Saturday.

The next day I moved into a room in the house in Balham and, in the evening, went to see the Thompson Twins. James had started going out with a woman called Sammy who lived in Flood Street in Chelsea. There was a tremendous glut of mushrooms and everyone who passed through that apartment seemed to be off their heads on something. There didn't seem anything unusual or untoward about this but an unremarkable entry from 3 November suggests, I think, how routinely unacceptable our behaviour had become: 'Met James and Rob at Master's [a bar, presumably] – got thrown out, then went to Lucy's.'

On Sunday the 14th I saw Bob Dylan's four-hour-long film *Renaldo and Clara – for the second time.* The stamina I had back then! Lucy phoned to say she didn't want to see me any more. I said I had the right to some kind of explanation or appeal. She told me to stop hassling her. It was around this time that I finally got the hang of smoking grass. I'd never smoked cigarettes and on the few occasions people had passed me joints – when, for example, we went to see *Ciao! Manhattan* at the Scala – I was violently sick. It was James who insisted that if grass was smoked without tobacco it would be fine – and he was right . . .

From this point on, I think it's fair to say, things got really crazy. I started sleeping with Sammy – who I fell in love with (and who I was still in love with when she started fucking Robert) and James started sleeping with this very druggy, privileged girl called Bella (the kind of person, I used to think, Dylan might have had in mind when he wrote 'Like A Rolling Stone'). At some point I must have torn out part of the page itemising what took place on 9 December but later, in an attempt to at least partially restore the historical record, I added, on the opposite page, 'The Flood St massacre!!!' God knows what happened.

Everything got messier and messier – and things didn't get any less messy when, in January, I moved into the shared house on Brixton Water Lane with five other people (all of whom – like me – were living on the dole). I'm not sure how it happened but after a while these five were joined by a sixth, James' friend Bella, who I hated. I tried, unsuccessfully, to have her evicted from the house on some kind of ideological grounds but the others decided she should stay on the same grounds – because it would be good for her political education. Having been infatuated by James' poise, wealth and decadence I now found myself starting to loathe him for his poise, wealth and decadence. In the course of an argument about something I punched him in the face.

'I won't take this lying down,' he said, from a prone position. One day a brick was thrown through the window of our front door; no one knew why. We were always having parties at our house, and we were always in the local pub, the George Canning. I fell in love with Bella. We went out together for about three or four months, during which time we took a trip to Venice. Then, when I was out of London, visiting my parents, she called to say she had started sleeping with Karen, a woman who lived near by. Shortly after this Bella moved out of the house on Brixton Water Lane and deeper into the local anarcho-lesbian-squatting scene. She worked for many years at Brixton Cycles and was the first woman I knew to completely shave her head. A couple of other people moved out of our house and new people moved in. A new phase began which was, in many ways, a continuation of the previous phase. I gradually moved out of this very druggy phase into more of a stoner phase with occasional mushrooms thrown in. Later that year I published my first book review – of a new translation of Milan Kundera's *The Farewell Party* – in the listings magazine *City Limits*.

I hope the foregoing provides some context to my getting sacked from the PPA. It had taken two years to find a proper job and less than a month to lose it. It is tempting to say that I decided to become a writer at that moment but this is not the way things work. Certainly, getting sacked was one of the things that contributed to my becoming a writer but, more immediately, this job was another possibility – another possible direction – that came to nothing, led nowhere. This is part of the process of becoming a writer. As often as not one *ends up* being a writer as attempts at doing other things fail to pan out. Writing is what you are left with. It remains a possibility, even when – especially when – nothing else is available. Having said that, my novel *The Colour of Memory* starts with me getting sacked from my job so in this invented version of things (which is, in many ways, the most truthful version) my life as a published writer did literally begin on that day.

I am no longer in touch with any of the people in this account. James achieved his ambition and became a heroin addict. I think he lived in Thailand for a while, was disinherited by his parents, and ended up working as a banker. Robert's client and her moronic boyfriend also became junkies. (Neither Robert nor I felt the faintest tug in that direction.) The last I heard of Claire she was living in France. I don't know what she is doing now but I assume it is grand, international and highly expensive. Jane was beginning to make a name for herself as an artist-photographer but then she got ME and her career stalled somewhat. After meeting again at a wedding, Bella and I got back together when I was in my late thirties. Her parents had just bought her a house in Brighton, where she lived with her daughter. She had become a posh, languid mum and had lost neither her looks nor her capacity to make me unhappy (she chucked me again after about six months). Robert – Robert the communist, the beat, the Buddhist, the friend who could always be relied on to fuck your girlfriend – is now a judge.

And me, I sit here at my desk, looking out of the window on 9th Street as I've sat at various desks in the long years since the events jotted down in the pages of that little diary. As I look back through it, I find myself thinking two things. First: *Wow! That was a lot of fun!* And second: *What an exemplary way to spend your early twenties!* But the thing that I'm most struck by, the thing I most love and of which I am really proud, is the way that the job hardly merited a mention, either in the original diary or in this annotated commentary. It meant nothing to me, that job. Compared to the books, the films, the parties, the drugs, the women, the sex, the laughing, the drinking, the clubs and the friends, that job – and the career of which, had I been unlucky, it might have formed a part – was insignificant. It merited the amount of time I devoted to it in my diary: about two lines.

It takes a bit of getting used to, the idea that spending 365 days a year doing exactly as you please might be a viable proposition. Getting sacked from that job was what allowed this notion – that the three years spent as a student could actually be extended indefinitely and rather profitably – to gain some kind of purchase on my adult consciousness. Since then I've done pretty much as I pleased, letting life find its own rhythm, working when I felt like it, not working when I didn't. I've not always been happy – far from it – but I've always felt responsible for my happiness and liable for my unhappiness. I've been free to waste my time as I please – and I *have* wasted tons of it, but at least it's been me doing the wasting; as such, it's not been wasted at all, not a moment of it.

2004

On the Roof

Although I've written quite a bit about photography and photographers, I don't own a camera and hardly ever take photos. Apart from a few sexually explicit Polaroids (Pornaroids?), the only personal pictures I have are ones taken by friends, all crammed haphazardly in a folder in my filing cabinet. If I rummage around in this image-compost, I'm never sure what I'm going to dredge up. Last week I became convinced that I needed to see a photo of the sky-blue Vauxhall Victor my dad used to drive and, in the course of looking for it (unsuccessfully), I came across this one, taken on the roof of a block of flats in Brixton, London, some time in the mid-'80s . . .

I looked at it for quite a while, trying to remember more exactly when it was taken. Then I saw that, on the back of another one from the same afternoon (the same series, as photographers say), I'd written: 'Taken on the day England got knocked out of the World Cup by Argentina – Summer '86.' This unprecedented inscription meant that I was able to date the picture with absolute precision: Sunday, 22 June 1986.

Back then my friends and I claimed to hate everything about England, including the football team, but I remember being pretty disappointed when Maradona single-handedly put an end to England's chances of making it to the semi-finals. Gutted, actually. Over the years this feeling – high hopes and nail-biting expectation culminating with the taste of ashes in the mouth – has become such a familiar part of watching England as to have taken on the quality of a national destiny. Not that anyone in the picture looks devastated or inconsolable. No, if it weren't for that strangely specific caption you'd think this was just another afternoon on the roof of Crownstone Court. Brixton was a lot rougher then than it is now but the roof was like a waterless lido above the city. I loved it up there.

A friend recently said that, for as long as he could remember, his dream of perfect happiness always centred on the idea of having a family (my idea of perfect misery). Perhaps I suffer from some kind of arrested development but my sense of perfect happiness has never progressed beyond a slightly archaic idea of bohemia. And it was in Brixton, in the '80s, that that dream first came true.

Many people leave university with only a vague idea of what they might do for a living but I knew exactly what I wanted to do: sign on the dole. At Oxford, undergraduates reading English rarely went to lectures. The only thing you *had* to do was see your tutor once a week (it might have been an obligation for the students but the tutor left you in no doubt that it was an unpardonable intrusion on his time). This set a precedent for the chore of signing-on, which, initially, also had to be done once a week. After a while, as the number of people out of work increased, so this dropped down to once a fortnight and, in Lambeth at least, to once a month. Thatcherism had ushered in an era of high unemployment but the safety net set up by the post-war commitment to the Welfare State was still just about intact. Housing Benefit paid your rent and Social Security gave you money to live on.

Mass unemployment might not be a desirable social or economic goal but it does mean that there are plenty of other people to hang out with in the afternoons. Before moving to Brixton I had lived briefly with a bunch of apprentice lawyers in a house in Balham. By nine in the morning they were all up and out and I was left on my own with nothing to do but lament my lot (i.e. my little). Then I moved into a house on Brixton Water Lane where only one of the six inhabitants was gainfully employed. The tables were abruptly turned: we felt sorry for her because she had to go to work. The rest of us did what we wanted all day. If Oxford had given me a taste for idleness, living on the dole in Brixton refined it still further. The difference was the quality of study – which, of course, was far higher in Brixton. Postgraduate work takes you down a path of greater and greater specialisation (culminating in the supreme pointlessness of a PhD). In Brixton I went in the opposite direction: I read whatever interested me, became interested in a wider and wider range of things.

It was an idyllic time and – such is the nature of idylls – it is now a vanished time. Students these days have to work part-time while they are studying and take out loans which oblige them to start earning serious money once they have graduated (or at least after a gap year of backpacking in South East Asia). From this radically altered vantage point I see now what a privileged historical niche I occupied for the first twenty-five or more years of my life. Free health care, free school, free tuition at university, a full maintenance grant and then – the icing on the cake – the dole!

I say 'free' but it was paid for, of course, by the sweat of my father's labour. My childhood memories of my dad involve him going to work and then coming home and working some more: on his allotment, on the garden, in his garage, on the house. Except for television (hour upon hour of it in winter) even hobbies like gardening had to take on the quality of an arduous chore if they were to be pursued with impunity. Work, like tidiness, was an absolute moral value. In common with many working-class parents mine hoped that after going to Oxford their only child might become middle-class but I went one better (i.e. worse) and became part of what Thorstein Veblen termed the leisure class. Well, the low-income dosser class at any rate. At Oxford I'd got used to doing pretty much as I pleased; on the dole I had even fewer claims on my time (signing on once a month soon came to seem a Herculean labour) and the situation has not changed significantly since then.

I'd been doling it up for years when this picture was taken, but I had also managed to pull myself a few rungs up the ladder of welfare dependency: I'd moved round the corner, out of the shared house on Brixton Water Lane and into a place of my own in Crownstone Court. The picture might well have been taken by one of the people who still lived back in the shared house, possibly by my friend P.J., the self-described 'dole wallah'.

It so happens that one of the people in this picture – Steve, the guy standing next to me – was not a doley (he was a solicitor, actually) but if it had been taken on a sunny weekday rather than a Sunday there would have been an equivalent group of people up there, all of whom were unemployed and living within a mile radius, many of them (like Nick, the guy with his back to the camera) in the block itself. The roof was a form of what I am tempted to call Restricted Access Public Space (RAPS) where you could turn up without ever quite knowing who was going to be there. You could sit quietly on your own (reading, yoga) or hang out with whoever else was around. There was almost always someone up there you had never met before, which meant that although, on any given day, the individuals might have changed the collective identity of the group remained more or less constant.

I say this and then, glancing through my diary for 1986, I see that the group ideal was already changing, dissolving, fragmenting. Steve's wife Sharon had left him and gone back to Chicago. The woman on his left was a new girlfriend, whom I barely knew, and she and Steve were together for only a few months. I was in the process of splitting up with Kate, who I'd been going out with, off and on, for the previous three years. Which means that all sorts of people – most, actually – who were an essential part of the time and world the picture depicts aren't actually in it.

Steve was one of my closest friends. Then, as happens, we drifted apart. Actually, that puts it too passively. I came actively to dislike him. This happened much later but by the time this picture was taken I'd already decided that I didn't like my old friend Robert – whom I'd known at school and university – any more either (he was always trying to sleep with my girlfriends) and by then he had certainly split up with Jessica (who I had tried to sleep with on several occasions). The more I look at this picture, in fact, the more conscious I become of the people who aren't in it. People like Jane (with whom I once had sex hours before having sex with Kate) and Nick's good friend Sally (who was probably downstairs having sex with Jane), both of whom lived in Crownstone.

To anyone looking at this picture it is probably hard to believe that someone with a physique (if we can dignify it with that word) like mine could ever have had sex with anyone. When I was fourteen my dad said I would thicken out when I got older and, at twenty-eight, when this picture was taken, I still hoped it might happen. Now I'm forty-four and realise it never will. Look at that leg. Have you ever seen anything like it outside of a famine-ravaged part of Africa? How does a leg like that function *as a leg*? How did it even keep me upright, let alone enable me to chase after these fit feminist chicks?

A clue is perhaps to be found on the ground, just behind the gnarled root of my right knee. I am referring, obviously, to my infamous homemade bong. Apart from my triumph at A-levels (three grade As!) that bong was and will remain my greatest achievement. There are more elegant bongs in the world but few are more efficacious. I'm no longer in contact with anyone in the photograph, but I still have my loyal old bong. I made it from a chillum, a length of tubing and a coffee jar. The chillum is sealed in the lid of the coffee jar with candle wax but you can unscrew the lid and fill the jar with ice so that you're totally unaware you're smoking (or would be if you didn't start coughing your lungs up ten seconds later). I'm so glad that bong is in the picture. It played a decisive role in many of the key events on that roof. Listening to Miles Davis' *Sketches of Spain*, seeing a display team of parachutists drift into nearby Brockwell Park, playing tennis-ball catch with people on the roof of the neighbouring block . . . Without the bong they'd have just been great moments; that bong made them sublime, transcendental, timeless.

I wanted to preserve some of these stoner spots of time in a book, a kind of photo album with words instead of pictures. That's something else this picture doesn't record: that the skeletal figure on the left was possessed of a considerable desire to be a writer. When this photograph was taken I had already written an unbelievably boring book about John Berger, but what I really wanted to write was a book about the life I was leading then, a book, in fact, about that roof. Some of my contemporaries from Oxford had gone on to pursue successful careers; they had become yuppies, had a stake in the property boom, were part of the world imaginatively recorded by Michael Bracewell in his novel *The Conclave*. The flipside of this was the grim

London of riots, unemployment and recession. That was the essential two-tone contrast of the Thatcher years. But there was also this in-between world of semi-creative idleness, of voluntary disenfranchisement. In some ways we had made a separate peace. It even seemed to me that there was a kind of aristocracy of welfare dependence, that a contemporary equivalent of the boundless leisure of the bright young things and the country-house novels of the 1930s or '40s or whenever it was could be found in the squats of Bonnington Square or Oval Mansions.

Most of the people in this scene harboured artistic hopes of one kind or another. Everyone wanted to be a writer, artist or film-maker or something. As Roland Gift told an American interviewer: in Britain the dole supported a whole generation of aspiring actors, dancers, writers. The dole was the equivalent of waiting tables in New York.

It is possible to have aspirations without having ambition – and vice versa. Whereas people coming out of university ten or fifteen years after me – Thatcher's children – combined the two, I had aspirations but was not ambitious. I liked the idea of writing because that was a way of not having a career. Those coming later saw writing *as* a career. And though many of my friends aspired to be artists, not many of them had the will, talent, luck or stamina to stick at it. Some of them were just too lazy. That is the inevitable weakness of dole 'n' dope culture. Not surprisingly, it was the dissolute models of Rimbaud or Kerouac (not Bukowski: we didn't sink *that* low) that appealed, especially the idea of a systematic derangement of the senses. A lot of people couldn't get beyond that phase of the artistic apprenticeship.

Let's suppose that instead of me looking at the photograph fifteen years after it was taken, the younger version of my scrawny self was able, instead of just gazing out across the roof in his shades, to look fifteen years into the future. What has happened in the interim to the people who are in the picture and the people who should have been in it but aren't?

The same things that happen to everyone: home-ownership, marriage, a kid or two, disappointment, divorce, cancer scares, worsening hangovers, death of a parent or two, qualified success, school fees, depression, sudden rejuvenation following the discovery of Ecstasy, holidays in India or Ibiza, telly-watching, coming out (as homosexuals), coming in (as heterosexuals), going to the gym, more telly-watching, new computers, bad knees, less squash, more tennis, re-writing (and downplaying) of earlier ambitions to diminish scale of disappointment, fatal breast cancer, less sleep, less beer, more wine, more cocaine, hardly any acid, frightening ketamine overdose, total breakdown, more money, discreet tattoos, baldness, stopping going to the gym, yoga, even more telly-watching . . .

Some permutation of the above pretty well covers everyone. Me included – except that whereas many people my age are starting to feel worn down by the burden of obligations, responsibilities and commitments, it's the *freedom* that's getting to me. On Fridays I sometimes find myself thinking almost enviously of all those people who are coming home from work and looking forward to putting their feet up and having a few days off. That's the problem with having a lifetime off – you can never take a few days off. Yes, all those years of doing just what I want have started subtly to take their toll. Or perhaps it's just the first glimpse of looming middle-age, the lure of television to which we all eventually succumb. But how could it have happened? How did I go from being interested in *everything* to not being that bothered about *anything*? When did the weather in the head cloud over like this? I am not only unsure how to describe this feeling, I am unsure exactly *what* I am describing. I certainly had no inkling of it – whatever *it* is – when this picture was taken, in 1986 . . . But looking at the picture and its inscription, I realise it *was* familiar to me back then, that the taste of ashes in the mouth was as much a generalised premonition as it was a particular reaction to a football result. Destiny, I think, is not what lies in store for you; it's what is already stored up inside you – and it's as patient as death.

2002

Reader's Block

'*Don't read much now.*'
Philip Larkin, 'A Study of Reading Habits'

Could I have become a symptom, or is this an entirely personal indisposition?

Either way, I find it increasingly difficult to read. This year I read fewer books than last year; last year I read fewer than the year before; the year before I read fewer than the year before that. The phenomenon of writer's block is well-known, but what I am suffering from is reader's block. The condition is creeping rather than chronic, manifesting itself in different ways in different circumstances. On a trip to the Bahamas recently I regularly *stopped* myself reading because, whereas I could read a book anywhere, this was the only time I was likely to see sea so turquoise, sand so pink. Somewhat grandly, I call this the Mir Syndrome after the cosmonaut who said that he didn't read a page of the book he'd taken to the space station because his spare moments were better spent gazing out of the window. Sometimes I'm too lazy to read, preferring to watch TV; more often I am too conscientious to read. Reading has never felt like work in the way that writing has, and so if I feel I should be working I feel I should be writing. Theoretically, if I am not writing then I am free to read but, actually, I always feel vaguely guilty and so, instead of writing (working) or reading (relaxing) I do neither: I potter around, rearranging my books, clearing up. Basically I do nothing – until it's time to catch a train, whereupon, like a busy commuter nibbling away at *War and Peace* in twenty-minute snatches, I plunge into a book thinking, *at last I've got a chance to read*. In no time, though, I'm like Pessoa in *The Book of Disquiet*, 'torn, in a futile anguished fashion, between my disinterest in the landscape and my disinterest in the book which could conceivably distract me'.

Back home there are plenty of books that I've not read and yet, gazing blankly at my shelves, all I can think is, *there's nothing left to read*. Hoping to lance the boil, to get to the heart of the matter in the course of a trans-Atlantic flight, I bought – but couldn't face reading – Bernhard Schlink's *The Reader* and Alberto Manguel's *A History of Reading*. Having resigned myself to not reading them (or any of the other books I'd bought for the flight), I scavenged around for *anything* to read: the in-flight magazine, the duty-free catalogue, the emergency evacuation procedure. And yet, at the same time that I am ready to read scraps like this, I am an over-discriminating reader. I am always not reading something in the name of something else. The opportunity cost of reading a given book is always too great. Some books, obviously, are a waste of one's eyes. To feel this about airport blockbusters is perfectly normal, but I feel it is beneath me to read Jeanette Winterson, for example, or Hanif Kureishi. In fact most so-called quality fiction that is story-driven seems a waste of time (time which, by the way, I have in abundance). This would be fine if I could transpose a reluctance to read James Hawes into a willingness to read Henry James, but I am unable to get beyond the first five paragraphs (i.e. four sentences) of *The Golden Bowl*.

The strange thing about this is that at twenty I imagined I would spend my middle-age reading books that I didn't have the patience to read when I was young. But now, at forty-one, I don't even have the patience to read the books I read when I was twenty. At that age I ploughed through everything in the Arnoldian belief that each volume somehow nudged me imperceptibly closer to the sweetness and light. I read *War and Peace*, *Anna Karenin*, *Ulysses*, *Moby Dick*. I got through *The Idiot* even though I hated practically every page of it. I didn't read *The Brothers Karamazov*: I'll leave it till I'm older,

I thought – and now that I *am* older I wish I'd read it when I was younger, when I was still capable of doing so.

Even at this late stage, however, some books *do* slip through the net and get read. I could make neither head nor tail of the first part of Jean Rhys' *Wide Sargasso Sea*; normally I would have abandoned it, but, since the book was short and the end in sight almost from the first page, I finished it and realised that it was indeed the master-piece everyone had claimed. Given that my faith in the canon remains relatively intact, why can't I do that over a longer distance?

To an extent I've become if not a child then an adult of soundbite culture, unable to concentrate on anything that does not offer imme-diate gratification. I have succumbed to what George Steiner in his essay 'The Uncommon Reader' calls 'the near-dyslexia of current reading habits'. (Just as I am often too discriminating to read, so my inability to read first manifested itself as a negative proof of my being, by Steiner's definition at least – 'a human being who has a pencil in his or her hand when reading a book' – an intellectual: I found I *couldn't* read without a pencil in my hand.) It is in this sense that I am symptomatic 'of the fate of reading in the digital age'. The phrase is Sven Birkerts', the sub-title – and all I've read – of his *Gutenberg Elegies*. Appropriately enough I look back elegiacally on my life as an obsessive reader, on my Bernhard phase, my Brodsky phase, my Camus phase, my DeLillo phase . . . I think of those sublime periods of lamp-lit solitude when, in Wallace Stevens' phrase, 'the reader became the book'. It can still happen, but it has something of the character of the occasional love-making of a long-married couple in that it reminds me of how things have changed, of how infrequently I am now consumed by a passion that was once routine. Losing myself in J.M. Coetzee's Booker-winning *Disgrace*, I remember how I used to pass from one book to another in a tranced relay of imag-ined worlds. Looking at André Kertész's photographs of readers sharing – however precariously perched – in the repose of the text, I find myself wondering and remembering.

Specifically, I remember two pieces in the American journal *The Hungry Mind Review*, which asked a number of writers to select a single book from this century that they would take with them into the next. Reflecting on the way he had gradually lost interest in fiction, Gerald Early asked if 'this is how one, by stages, loses the ability to read or the interest in reading altogether'. This in turn, he thought, might be part of a process whereby one loses 'slowly but inexorably the ability to feel deeply about anything'. For his part, Sven Birkerts chose Rilke's *Duino Elegies* because 'it is there we find the most potent possible distillation of subjective inwardness, our most endangered attribute'. Is this lack of 'subjective inwardness' the malady of which my – and Early's – declining ability to read is a symptom?

Perhaps not. In *And Our Faces, My Heart, Brief As Photos*, John Berger has speculated that the inability to remember might itself be a memory (of being a memory-less baby in the womb). In the same way, my declining ability to read is itself the product of having read a fair bit. If reading heightens your responses, shapes your idea of the world, gives you a sense of the purpose of life, then it is not surprising if, over time, reading should come to play a proportionately smaller role in the context of the myriad possibilities it has opened up. The more thoroughly we have absorbed its lessons the less frequently we need to refer to the user's manual. After a certain point subjective inward-ness becomes self- rather than textually generated. Of course there is more to learn, more to read, but whereas, as a teenager, each new book represented an almost overwhelming addition to what I knew and felt, each new book now adds a smaller increment to the sum of knowledge.

As an eighteen-year-old in Cheltenham, waiting to study English at Oxford, my experience was radically circumscribed. I'd never been abroad. Except for teachers I'd hardly met anyone who was not from pretty much the same working-class, non-reading milieu as my family. On the other hand, I was bursting with the limitless imaginings of Shakespeare, Wordsworth, Dickens, Lawrence. A life devoted entirely to the study of literature seemed the highest possible destiny. No longer. Reading, which *gave* me a life, is now just *part* of that life, at the moment rather a small part.

Books played a crucial part in determining how I became what I am. That slightly ungainly phrase is derived from the sub-title of

Ecce Homo in which Nietzsche delivers the pronouncement with which anyone who has learned anything from books – from his, at any rate – will agree: 'Early in the morning, at break of day, in all the freshness and dawn of one's strength, to read a *book* – I call that vicious!'

1999

My Life as a Gatecrasher

In the autumn of 1989 I served some time at the Institute of Jazz Studies at Rutgers University in New Jersey. I'd gone to New York to write a book about jazz and was browsing through the institute's archives. One of the librarians was more than a little curious about my unsystematic rummaging. He wanted to know if the book I was writing was a history. No, I said. A biography? No. Well, what kind of book was it going to be? I told him I had no idea. Having made little progress with this line of enquiry, he turned his attention from the book to its author. Was I a musician? No. A jazz critic? No. Was I this? Was I that? No, I was neither this, that nor anything else. Becoming a little frustrated, he asked, 'So what are your credentials for writing a book about jazz?'

'I don't have any,' I said. 'Except I like listening to it.'

It was an honest answer, simultaneously modest and confident. The Institute of Jazz Studies is a place of special interest and expertise and to that extent I had no right to be there. I didn't know much about jazz. Certainly not enough to write a book about it – that, precisely, was the motivation for doing so. I loved jazz but it was infinitely mysterious to me. If I'd known what I needed to know before writing the book I would have had no interest in doing so. Instead of being a journey of discovery writing the book would have been a tedious clerical task, a transcription of the known.

People doing dissertations spend a certain amount of time researching the subject and then, when they've done the knowledge, begin writing it up. As far as I was concerned writing the book would bring me to exactly the point at which I needed to be in order to be qualified to start writing it. But it's not what you know that's important; it's what your passion gives you the potential to discover.

If my answer was modest because I was in this haven of specialist expertise, it was slyly confident for exactly the same reason. In the presence of specialists I am always conscious of all the things they don't know and are not interested in, all the things that lie beyond their particular area of expertise. So I was pretty sure that this jazz buff would not have read Roland Barthes' book about photography, *Camera Lucida*, would not have known that Barthes constructed his great book around a few pictures that he liked looking at (particularly one of his mum, taken when she was five). E.M. Cioran's excellent suggestion – that 'we are enriched only by frequenting disciplines remote from our own' – is ignored by the very people who would gain most by heeding it.

The jazz book was the beginning of my life as a literary and scholarly gatecrasher, turning up uninvited at an area of expertise, making myself at home, having a high old time for a year or two, and then moving on elsewhere. This, it goes without saying, is no way to make a career (a word which, for anyone seriously committed to a life of writing, should never be spoken, only spat). The usual course of action is to map out an area of interest that you can call your own. My first book had been about John Berger, a writer profoundly opposed to any kind of specialism. It was a boring, timid, sub-academic thing, almost a textbook (and, as such, an unintended insult to its subject). As soon as I finished it my then-editor asked if I'd like to start a new one, on Raymond Williams! There stretched ahead of me the punishing vision of a life devoted to writing synoptic books about writers and thinkers. Something similar happened after *But Beautiful* came out and I sort of had a chance – though, to be honest, nobody actually *asked* – to become a jazz critic. But by then I was busy reinventing myself as a military historian. To be precise I was living in Paris, failing to write a novel that would in some ways be a version of *Tender is the Night*. In the footsteps of Fitzgerald's hero, Dick Diver, I took a train to Albert to visit the cemeteries of the Western Front. I went on a whim but when I got there it felt almost as if I had been summoned to a rendezvous. Standing in front of Sir Edwin Lutyens' memorial to The Missing of the Somme I knew I would write a book about the Great War. I spent the next several years doing just that.

I never quite made it as an orthodox military historian but, after the book came out, I did become enough of an authority on the Great War to be invited onto *Newsnight* to debate the quality of Haig's command with Correlli Barnett – who rolled over me like a tank.

Not that it mattered; by then I was writing some kind of half-assed book about D.H. Lawrence, someone who never let the fact that he was technically ill-qualified to write about something deter him from doing so. On the contrary, Rebecca West remembers him arriving in Florence and beginning an article about the place 'without knowing enough about it to make his views of real value'. Late in his life, when he became interested in the civilisation of the Etruscans, Lawrence wrote to thank a friend for sending a book by Roland Fell that he had hoped might help with his writing. Fell was 'very thorough in washing out once more the few rags of information we have concerning the Etruscans: but not a thing has he to say . . . I shall just have to start in and go ahead, and be damned to all authorities! . . . Must take the imaginative line.'

My most recent attempt at taking Lawrence at his word is a book about photography, a book that owes much – how could it not? – to Berger and Barthes. Photography seemed to lend itself particularly well to someone whose methodology was nicely formulated by Harold Rosenberg: 'loiter in the neighborhood of a problem. After a while a solution strolls by.' Arriving unannounced at this already crowded area of expertise conformed to a pattern established by turning up uninvited elsewhere. Some of those already safely ensconced are generous and hospitable from the outset; others are xenophobic, fearing that the outsider might piss in their jealously guarded pot. This suspicion – that you have not paid your dues, have not worked your way up through the ranks of scholarly specialism – tends to manifest itself in ferocious nitpicking. Then it is conceded that you were actually quite a nice guest, that an unfamiliar face livened up the place somewhat. If you have not already left and moved on elsewhere, you might even be asked to stick around and make yourself at home.

Being a gatecrasher is especially precarious if you don't have the support of any kind of institution to back you up. But independence from academic responsibility comes with its own freedoms and rewards. It might be comforting to be the Something Professor of Anything at the University of Whatever but the writer's self-sufficient – and therefore ideal – status is expressed with sad and beautiful pride by Lawrence: 'I am no more than a single human man wandering my lonely way across these years.'

Lawrence, needless to say, is not the only inspirational example of intellectual nomadism. An important influence on Lawrence, Nietzsche abandoned his university job as a philologist and became a vagabond and renegade, profoundly hostile to those who 'study and prowl around a single domain simply because it never occurs to them that other domains exist. Their industriousness possesses something of the tremendous stupidity of the force of gravity: which is why they often achieve a great deal.' He preferred the type 'who never penetrates into the depths of a problem, yet often notices things that the professional with his laborious poring over it never does'.

If Rebecca West was initially shocked by Lawrence's habit of issuing intuitive bulletins about the places in which he found himself, she came later to derive considerable confidence from his methods. In the course of writing *Black Lamb and Grey Falcon* West met a student interested in writing a thesis about her work.

> I explained that I was a writer wholly unsuitable for her purpose: that the bulk of my writing was scattered through American and English periodicals; that I had never used my writing to make a continuous disclosure of my own personality to others, but to discover for my own edification what I knew about various subjects which I found to be important to me; and that in consequence I had written a novel about London to find out why I loved it.

This is valuable not only as a statement of West's own practice and goals. It reminds us that, although great store is set by measuring incremental progress ('research', in academic parlance) in precisely demarcated areas of knowledge, significant advances are often made by people happy to muddle along within the splendidly vague job description advanced by Susan Sontag, whose 'idea of a writer [was] someone interested in "everything"'. Why, in all modesty, would anyone be interested in settling for less?

2005

Something Didn't Happen

In my first year as an undergraduate at Oxford – this was 1977–8 –
I lived on the ground floor of the Corpus Christi New Building, just
across the road from the venerable old college itself. During
Michaelmas term, at about two in the morning, I was woken up by
a gang of people singing Bob Dylan's 'Rainy Day Women' outside my
window. They kept going up and down the narrow lane, singing
'Everybody must get stoned.' It went on for ages and eventually I got
dressed and went out to confront them. As I did so I met my friend
Paul, an American who lived along the corridor. We were both furious.
Seeing each other like this meant our fury turned into bravado and
made us more furiously brave.

'Let's get those guys,' he said. On the way out of the New Building
we armed ourselves with empty milk bottles from the crate inside
the gate. By the time we got outside into the lane the stoners were
gone but we could still hear them, more faintly now. We followed
the sound, crossed over to the college. From a first-floor window we
could hear them singing the same chorus, the same song. If we had
been back in our rooms we would not have heard them and could
have slept soundly but we were outside on the street, wide awake,
furious and excited. Paul looked at me and said, 'Shall we?'

Without another word we threw our four milk bottles through
the window. The crash of glass was unbelievable. We tore back into the
New Building. As we separated, Paul shouted 'Night, Geoff!' as though
we had just done something exciting and mischievous.

As soon as I got back to my room the awful gravity of what we had done came crashing in on me. Four bottles exploding through a window: what physical harm would this have done to a room full of people?

In the morning, after an almost entirely sleepless night, I went out to look at the scene of the crime. The glass had all been cleared up. The windows were unbroken. Miraculously all four bottles had shattered either against the walls or the metal diamonds framing the small windows. Not a single bottle had made it through. It was like a nightmare where you dream that you have done something terrible and then wake up, bathed in sweat, relieved to find that you have not done it in real life.

In the autumn of 1997 I went to Durham, North Carolina, to write about the photographer William Gedney, whose archive had ended up at Duke University. Durham itself is tiny, part of the Triangle Area that also comprises Raleigh and Chapel Hill. In the course of my two-month stay I regularly drove fifteen or twenty miles to go to a cinema in the suburbs of one of these affiliated towns. I say suburbs but, at night, it felt like driving in the open country, along deserted roads in complete darkness. I rarely drive in England so the problem of driving on the 'wrong' side of the road never came up. Then, on my way back from seeing *The Ice Storm*, I did exactly that: drove up a totally dark lane on the wrong side of the road. I had no idea I was doing this until a car screamed towards me and, at the last moment, swerved past. There wasn't even time for the driver to sound the horn. The car swerved around me and was gone and I was unscathed.

Two years later I travelled to the Bahamas with my then girlfriend to write a piece for an American magazine. We had to change in Miami, entering the US before boarding the connecting flight to Nassau and taking a boat to Harbour Island.

After a few days on Harbour Island we started sniffing around, trying to buy grass. The Bahamas is not like Jamaica, where every few minutes someone is asking – to put it mildly – if you would like to buy sensei. There were quite a few dreadlocked young guys with whom we exchanged glances but we never quite approached anyone.

Bahamians are big drinkers but Harbour Island didn't seem like a stoner scene and my policy, in these matters, is to be cautious to the point of paranoia.

We had been on the island three days. As I was putting on a pair of trousers – cargo pants, to use the correct sartorial term – I had not worn since the flight I felt something bulky in my pocket: a large bag of skunk complete with pipe. Accidentally I had taken this through what is probably the most drug-alert airport in the world – Miami. There were sniffer dogs everywhere. I had walked though emigration in the UK, sauntered through immigration in the US, strolled through US emigration, boarded a plane to Nassau and entered the Bahamas. And nothing had happened.

This occurred during a phase when I was smoking a lot of the skunk that was in the process of gaining complete market domination in the UK. The immediate cause for my unwitting bit of smuggling was that on the Saturday night before flying out I had worn these trousers to a Return to the Source party.

My girlfriend was understandably furious. How could I have been so stupid, forgetful? Because I was smoking lots of skunk. It was doing to me what it is apparently doing to teenagers up and down the country: rotting the brain. Her anger was understandable and not entirely convincing. My forgetfulness meant that we now had exactly what we wanted: grass. We could get stoned. In fact we *had* to get stoned because I did not want to repeat, in reverse order, the process of smuggling, especially now that I would be doing so consciously (i.e. conspicuously).

What would have been the consequences of each of these episodes turning out not as they did but as, in all probability, they *should* have done?

In the case of the Oxford incident, apart from the injuries I might have caused, I would almost certainly have been caught owing to Paul's calling out my name. (In the morning the woman who cleaned my room – a scout, in Oxford parlance – said that whoever had thrown the bottles had run back into New Building.) I would have been sent down. If there had been injuries, presumably some kind of criminal prosecution would have followed. So I would have been sent down and I would have been in more trouble with the police (I had actually gone up to Oxford on bail, for criminal damage, but that is another story). Now, students get sent down from Oxford the whole time and go on to lead interesting lives. But if I had been sent down I would not have travelled abroad or done anything adventurous; I would have gone back to my home town and re-applied for the boring job in the Mercantile & General Reinsurance Company that I was doing during the nine months between school and university.

In North Carolina the consequences would have been much more straightforward. I would have been killed, paralysed, brain-damaged or injured. I might have killed, paralysed, brain-damaged or injured the other driver. I would have wrecked two cars. If I had survived I would, presumably, have faced some kind of massive law suit.

If I had been caught with that big bag of grass in Miami then, most immediately, we would not have had our trip in the Bahamas. I would not have been able to complete my assignment for a prestigious American magazine and so would have forsaken my fee. All small beer compared with what would, surely, have been the eventual outcome: being jailed in the US.

None of these things happened. I didn't get sent down from Oxford, I didn't die in North Carolina and I didn't go to jail in Florida. I completed my degree, as a result of which my life-options expanded to the extent that I ended up becoming a writer who was invited to Durham and sent for a luxurious, all-expenses-paid trip with my girlfriend to the Bahamas. Life turned out extremely nicely, thank you.

When he was considering promoting one of his soldiers Napoleon famously asked, 'And does he have luck?' I have got into the habit of thinking of myself as an extremely unlucky person. I could compile a huge list of all the ways in which my luck has been bad. I mean, how many times has it started raining within minutes of my beginning a tennis match? But these three incidents are examples, obviously, of *good* luck. They are incidents which you would expect to have quite terrible, life-shattering or life-ending consequences. It's not just that I was given a second chance, I was given a third and a fourth as well. If I were a cat, each of these incidents would have used up a life: three down, six to go.

As far as I can remember these are the three luckiest things that have ever happened to me – more exactly, the three luckiest things that have *not* happened to me. Thinking of any of them now fills me with retrospective dread. I have never done anything where the immediate and expected consequences could have been anything like as bad. I had a certain amount of random, unprotected heterosexual sex in the 1980s and '90s but the chances of getting AIDS was minimal compared with the chances of facing the consequences of these actions. Put it this way: given the limited extent of my sexual adventures I would have been extremely *un*lucky to have contracted HIV. These three incidents, on the other hand, would be the equivalent of having unprotected sex with a promiscuous homosexual, IV drug-user – the kind of thing, I guess, that might well befall someone who ends up in prison in Miami.

I would estimate that it was about ninety-nine per cent certain that I would pay the price for my actions. But I didn't. I got away with all three of them, scot free, without a scratch. Did I learn anything from them? I don't think I did. Or at least I didn't learn anything that I didn't already know: not to throw bottles through people's windows, not to drive on the wrong side of the road, not to carry smelly, illegal drugs into the US; in sum, *not to be stupid*.

So I ask myself the Dirty Harry question: Do I feel lucky? 'Well do ya, punk?' Not particularly, no.

And what about fate? Or destiny? Can one draw a larger conclusion? Only that most people reading this could put together their own list of three similar episodes. There are a few others who, even by cat standards, have been super-lucky, have not used up even one of their nine lives. And there are some who are not reading this precisely because they could not put a similar list together, because they did not have my kind of luck. Irrespective of whether these things had anything to do with my volition they have turned out to be my three enduring achievements.

2009

Otherwise Known as the Human Condition (with particular reference to Donut Plant donuts)

For many years I lived in various flats either on or just off Brixton Water Lane. So I was always walking, cycling or taking a bus down Effra Road. How many times did I walk down Effra Road? How many hours did I spend walking down Effra Road? If I was going to Brixton Rec to play squash, or to Franco's for a pizza or a cappuccino (this was before I acquired the refinement of taste in cappuccini that, in the years since then, has invariably been a source of torment and frustration rather than enhanced satisfaction) or to the aptly named Effra to meet friends for drinks, or just to take the Tube to some other part of London, I always had to trudge or cycle down Effra Road. Wherever I was going the journey began and ended on Effra Road. One of the reasons I moved away from Brixton was because I could not face trudging, cycling or taking the bus down Effra Road again. Effra Road was so deeply lodged in my muscle memory that I could have made my way home blind or after some kind of seizure or stroke had completely wiped out part of my brain. Assuming I was able to walk I could have made my way down Effra Road when I was no longer capable of going anywhere – or doing anything – else.

The route never varied but, in small and large ways, the experience changed over time. In the mid-'80s, when a lot of my friends lived in the area, the fact that I was always bumping into someone

I knew as we made our respective ways up and down Effra Road added to the cosy sense that this was exactly where I most wanted to be in the world. Over time, the road itself changed also. The disused Cool Tan plant was co-opted for various alternative ventures: pre-rave-type parties, a sensory-deprivation flotation tank. My friend Heather Ackroyd grew the first of her grass sculptures there in the 1980s. Then it became the European Business Centre or something like that. Then branches of Halfords and Currys opened (very handy for the one time I needed to buy a fridge). What struck me about this was how completely each new development obliterated the previous one. At first you would notice that the Cool Tan plant had been knocked down, that something was being built in its stead. But once that new thing was completed it was as though the previous thing had never been there. It was the opposite of the model of the unconscious offered by Freud: a version of Rome in which all successive stages of construction are preserved simultaneously. I struggle to remember the Cool Tan factory. To all intents and purposes Currys and Halfords have been there for ever, even if they are no longer there. I don't know. I haven't been to check, haven't walked down Effra Road for ages (thank God) and hope I never have to do so again.

I say Effra Road but it could be any road. We are always taking the same routes through cities. The Tube forces us to do this, and so – less claustrophobically – do buses. Even on a bike, when we can take any route, we allow ourselves to get funnelled along familiar paths, preferring the often slightly longer but nicer cycle lanes because they are ostensibly safer even though they can actually be more dangerous because one is in a state of less-than-heightened alert. As pedestrians, too, we not only stick to the same routes, but prefer to cling to the same side of the road (north side of Effra Road going into Brixton, south side coming home, in the same direction as the traffic). This tendency to the habitual expresses in linear terms the way that, in a vast city like London, we avail ourselves of only a fraction of the numerous other opportunities – all those concerts, films and lectures listed in *Time Out*, a magazine which I stopped buying years ago – and alternative routes open to us. As the routes prescribed by habit grow more and more familiar so we become increasingly oblivious to them. Alex, the protagonist of Alan Hollinghurst's *The Spell*, lives in Hammersmith but he speaks for all of us when his immediate environment gets reduced to 'a block or two worn half-invisible by use'.

We tend always to approach a given place from the same direction, via the same route. I am always surprised how thoroughly disorienting it is if I arrange to meet someone at a café I know well but, for whatever reason – an earlier appointment somewhere else – end up approaching it from an unusual direction. It's completely bewildering, as if the place we are supposed to be meeting at has disappeared. What's happened to it? Where did it go? Psychologically, the location of a place is not fixed. It is determined not by *where* it is but how we get to it.

Even though I was unhappy and lonely for much of my time there, I always think of the period when I lived on rue Boulle in the 11*eme* arrondissement of Paris as an idyllic phase of my life. Partly this was because I liked the *quartier* so much, partly it was because I was able to leave and approach my apartment in such a multiplicity of ways. Depending on where in the city I was going, I could use one of three Metro stops served by three different lines. I could get buses at the Bastille. If I was walking somewhere I could set off in all sorts of directions. Now, obviously, your home is always the hub from which you branch out but when I lived off or on Brixton Water Lane, ninety per cent of the time I would be heading east, into Brixton, along the Effra Road. Whereas when I lived on rue Boulle, my routes were divided equally between the ten options that were available. All points of the compass were equally alluring. There was always some reason to go in a new direction. Having said that, being a creature of habit, I did tend to go to the same place every morning for my coffee and croissant – a café on rue de la Roquette – and I always took the same route there, just as I always took the same route to the same café – the Croissant D'Or – when I lived on Esplanade in New Orleans, or as I did when I trudged down Effra Road for a cappuccino in Franco's (or Franca Manca as it has now become).

I am like Michael Hofmann in his poem 'Guanajuato Two Times':

> I could keep returning to the same few places
> till I turned blue, till I turned into
> José José
> on the sleeve of his new record album
> "What is love?"

I like to go back to the same few places all the time – then, as soon as I break free of the prison of routine, I am left wondering why I kept going to a place I had stopped enjoying years earlier. For many years, whenever I had errands to run or meetings to attend in Soho, I would have a cappuccino at the Cappuccetto. Then, for reasons I can no longer remember, I started going to Patisserie Valerie's a hundred yards down the road, on Old Compton Street, and wondered why I'd wasted so many years in the Cappuccetto, which, by comparison, was a dismal and unatmospheric place. I kept going to Patisserie Valerie's for years after it had stopped being any good, for years after it had become a source of constant and terrible disappointment, for years after the nice Spanish waitress, Maria (who worked there for years, who always flirted a bit with my friend Chris and me), had left so that instead of this nice, unchanging waitress–customer relationship we were faced with such a rapid turnover of staff as to suggest that Valerie's might not be an entirely happy ship. The pastries got bigger and bigger, I no longer liked the coffee, and the staff, though rapidly changing, seemed always to be drawn from the same ex-Soviet republic where the idea of service or charm was anathema. On the larger stage, meanwhile, Valerie's began opening new branches across London, thereby undermining the idea that you were at a unique quasi-bohemian hang-out and creating the feeling that you were part of a mini empire, a Starbucks in the process of formation. But I kept going anyway, even though I ranted on to anyone who would listen about how terrible the service, coffees and pastries had become. Nietzsche loved what he called 'brief habits' but so hated 'enduring habits' that he was grateful even to the bouts of sickness or misfortune that caused him to break free of the chains of enduring habit (though most intolerable of all, he went on, would be 'a life entirely devoid of habits, a life that would demand perpetual improvisation. That would be my exile and my Siberia.'). Unlike Nietzsche I succumb all too easily to enduring habits. Programmed by habit, I kept going to Patisserie Valerie's until I met the woman who became my wife. She persuaded me to meet her in the Monmouth Street coffee shop or, later, at Fernandez and Wells on Beak Street, one of the new wave of antipodean cafés that is revolutionising the coffee scene in Soho. Once I had taken my custom to Fernandez and Wells or to Flat White (on Berwick Street), I never thought of Patisserie Valerie's again except with regret for all the years I had loyally wasted there. I would like to claim I am now in a state of bliss, but the truth is that the pastries at Fernandez and Wells and Flat White could be a lot better, are actually a bit on the dismal side.

Which brings me to the thing I really want to talk about: namely the donuts of New York.

In September 2004 I rented a studio apartment on 37th Street, between Park and Lex, in Manhattan. It was a very busy period for me; all sorts of things had to be sorted out with some urgency, but although there were other, ostensibly more serious, things to sort out, nothing was more urgent than the need to find a local café I could go to every day for my elevenses.

Given that so many conditions had to be met, this was easier said than done. First, the coffee had to be exactly as I liked it although I would have been hard pressed to define exactly how this was. Second, the pastry had to be exactly as I liked it. By pastry I mean a croissant or donut – I don't like those American staples, muffins or bagels. Third, I would never drink my coffee out of a paper cup; the coffee had to be served in a proper china cup. This is not as easy as you might think. There are plenty of places in Manhattan where, although the coffee is good, it is only served in a paper or Styrofoam cup. Fourth, when I said cup I meant cup (i.e. cup not mug) and, fifth, it had to be the right size cup. This question of size is not simply a matter of size; I have never ever had a nice cappuccino in a place where they serve them in those jumbo-size cups; all you get is a great bucket of foam.

In the excited hope that it might be possible to fulfil these conditions I began to explore the neighbourhood, which turned out to be far more promising than I'd initially thought, especially if you walked east a couple of blocks to Third Avenue. I went into a place called Delectica on the corner of Third and 38th. It looked like the kind of place where people had a quick lunch or picked up a coffee on the way to work – but they did at least have proper cups. It wasn't atmospheric but I saw that, as well as proper cups, they had a wide selection of pastries. I ordered a cappuccino and it was OK – a bit too frothy but it came in a cup the right size. I also ordered a croissant. It wasn't up to much but great croissants are quite rare in Manhattan (and, increasingly, in Paris too). When I'd stayed for a few weeks on Prince Street, near Mott, I went to Gitane's, an amazing café, but the croissants, as is so often the case, were just a species of bun. I once commented on this to the dreadlocked waitress, who said, in explanation, that they came from Balthazar, as though the fact that they hailed from this swish restaurant transformed them from soggy buns into something crisp and fluffy.

I went back to Delectica the following day and ordered another cappuccino and a donut. The donut I ordered that day was a ring donut and it was an amazing donut. This was a major turning point in my New York life. As such it will feature prominently in my forthcoming book: *Great Pastries of the World: A Personal View*. It will be autobiography, odyssey and testament. It will be a tale of epic disappointments and giddy successes, one of which, undoubtedly, is the discovery of the donut in Delectica. It had a slight glaze of icing – but not too much – and this icing wasn't too sweet. And the texture . . . What can I say about the texture except what I said to myself on that fateful morning: 'Wow-ee,' I said, 'this is really something, this is a *major donut experience* I'm having here.' The donut experience was perfectly complemented by the cappuccino experience, which had been quite nice the day before but which today was right on the money. It wasn't a coffee with a scum of foam floating on the top; no, the foam was *integrated* with the coffee. Foam and coffee were one. It had been made by a different person and she had made it perfectly. I had not made any specific requests but this waitress, quite by chance, had made my cappuccino exactly as I liked it and had, in the process, made something much more than that – namely my day. And not just *that* day because, from then on, if I was in the queue and the other waitress offered to serve me I would say I was still making up my mind – even though I had exactly the same thing every day – and wait until the waitress who made my cappuccino exactly as I liked it was free.

It's funny, even though I ended up going there every day for six weeks I never achieved any great rapport with this waitress, who brought me so much happiness each day. We never chatted or flirted in the way that I had eagerly flirted with the dreadlocked waitress in Gitane's as she brought me my soggy – frankly soul-destroying – crois- sant each day; in fact after a very short time the waitress in Delectica would prepare my cappuccino and serve my donut without my saying a word, but in its austere, functional way it was a perfect relation- ship. Part of the reason for this silence – at least on my part – was that the stakes were so high. Every day – except Mondays, when they didn't have any donuts so I had, as they say, to take my custom else- where – the coffee and donut were perfect. Anything less than perfec- tion would have been disappointing and disappointment would, in this context, have been devastating. It's quite possible that disap- pointment could have made me go completely to pieces or completely berserk. I could have ended up throwing the coffee in her face and then breaking down in tears of self-pity. But it never happened – each day this standard of unparalleled excellence was maintained.

And so my life fell into the unvarying routine I crave and need. I would wake up, have my muesli at home, work for a bit and then go to Delectica for my elevenses. I say 'unvarying' but gradually, as my eagerness to go to Delectica increased, I found it impossible to concentrate on my work because all I could think about was my donut and coffee and so I started having my elevenses earlier and earlier until I ended up skipping breakfast and having my elevenses at nine. At the latest. I went to bed at night looking forward to my nineses and then, as soon as I woke up, I stumbled out of bed, dressed and went to Delectica before I was even properly awake. I got dressed in a hurry, I hurried down there, and then although I loved them and should have savoured them, I started gobbling my donut and drinking my coffee in a hurry, gobbling and slurping them down in such a frenzy that I barely tasted a thing. Before I knew it this, the highpoint of my day, was over with. It was only 8.45 and there was nothing to look forward to. I also found it increasingly difficult to keep my rapture to myself. One morning, as I gobbled my donut and slurped my coffee, thinking to myself, 'What a fantastic donut, what an amazing coffee', I realised that I had not just thought this but was actually saying aloud, 'What a fantastic donut!', 'What a totally fantastic experience!', and that this was attracting the attention of the other customers, one of whom turned to me and said,

'You like the donuts, huh?'

'And the coffee!' I said. 'The donut would be nothing without the coffee – and vice versa.'

'Where you from?' he said.

'England.'

'Don't they have donuts like that in England?'

'Not like this, they don't,' I said. 'I've spent twenty years searching for just such a donut. Now that I've found it I can go to my grave a happy man. I've achieved everything I wanted from life.'

'Well, enjoy,' he said, as though I had been making a joke.

'Sure will,' I said and resumed my chewing.

The problem of going to Delectica earlier and earlier for my elevenses was eventually resolved in a very simple way – by going there for lunch as well. It turned out that they made very nice roasted-vegetable sandwiches, but I don't intend dwelling on these sandwiches because what's important in this parable is me and my state of mind, otherwise known as the human condition. I'd moved into what I thought was a non-neighbourhood in quite desperate circumstances in a thoroughly distraught frame of mind. Basically I was on the brink of total nervous collapse but gradually, largely through the discovery of Delectica, my state of mind improved and I regained my appetite for life of which my appetite for donuts might best be seen as a metaphor or symbol.

Time passed. I was only subletting this apartment for six weeks. I arranged to sublet another place, for another six weeks, in the heart of the East Village, on Ninth Street between First and A. As the time for moving grew close I realised that I had actually come to love my apartment and my neighbourhood and that I was blissfully happy there. No sooner had I realised this than I realised I was in countdown mode, that I only had five mornings left to take my coffee and donut in Delectica. Then I had just four, then three . . . It wasn't just the thought of leaving that was terrible; it was the knowledge that as soon as I moved into my new place I'd have to start over again. Eventually I had no more days left. I moved into my new place and once again began rolling the stone up the steep hill of consumer choice. The problem here was almost the opposite of the one I'd faced on 37th Street – there were too many cafés. I hardly knew where to start so I sought guidance from my friend Jaime, who lived a couple of blocks away and who explained that the donuts I loved at Delectica came from a place called the Donut Plant and that the aptly named Donut Plant distributed their donuts to quite a few places, one of which was on the corner of Third and A, opposite 2 Boots, the Cajun pizza place that I had been completely obsessed by and utterly dependent on when I lived in New York in the late 1980s. They did have the donuts at this place on the corner of 3rd and A but the coffee came in a mug and wasn't so nice. It was too frothy and rather bland. After a while I discovered that I could get Donut Plant donuts even closer to home, on my street, on the corner of Ninth and A but the coffee there was really not up to much so I preferred to go down to Third and A. Well, it was OK and I trudged down there every day but with nothing like the spring in my step that had characterised my trips to Delectica. In every other respect this was a perfect neighbourhood, it was full of cool people, there were tons of cheap places to eat and the St. Marks bookstore was only a five-minute walk away . . . Yes, it was a great neighbourhood but in my cups I often fell to thinking about Delectica and although I never walked up there just for coffee, if I had any excuse to go up that way, however flimsy, I would stop off at Delectica. Delectica had been my base, it was the point from which my sense of familiar and localised happiness had spread. It was the epicentre of my well-being, what Marx, in a non-pastry-related context, termed the heart of a heartless world. I've always been dependent on places like this wherever I've lived. In New Orleans it was the Croissant D'Or, in Rome it was the bar San Calisto in Trastevere, in Brixton it was Franco's. Even if I am only in a place for a short while I quickly build up a routine: I want not just to visit a city but to in*habit* it as rapidly as possible. A few years ago I was in Turin for a conference. I was only there three days but, in a classic instance of the Nietzschean 'brief habit', I came to love having my coffee and cornetto in the café across the road from my hotel. (Turin, of course, is where Nietzsche suffered his final breakdown – a desperately successful attempt to break free of the habit of sanity?) If I were in Turin tomorrow I would return to that same café immediately and it would be a completely satisfactory experience, but when you've had an ongoing relationship with a place, when you've built your life around it as I had built mine around Delectica, there is no going back. Sometimes this is literally the case: places close or change hands, the disused Cool Tan factory where Heather grew her grass sculptures turns into a branch of Halfords; the lease runs out or the management changes or a new chef comes along and where previously you found delight now there only lurks the grim spectre of the kind of disappointment that haunted my last years at Patisserie Valerie's when I kept going back there even though I knew, in my heart, that it was time to move on. But even if nothing changes, even if the place and the food and the staff remain unchanged, there is still no going back even though, of course, one does exactly that: one goes back. When we went to New Orleans for a wedding earlier this year, I took my wife to see my old apartment on Esplanade (I could not find it exactly, was not sure that the building that seemed in roughly the location was actually my building or was a new building that had been built on the same site) and then we took exactly the walk that I used to take to the Croissant D'Or. It was still there and we ordered cappuccinos and croissants and the croissant, while just about tolerable, was nowhere near as good as I remembered and the coffee was pretty terrible (too milky and the foam was all bubbly and although it seemed OK at first by the halfway stage I decided it was totally revolting). That was nothing, though, compared to the disappointment of my return to Delectica about a year and a half after first discovering it.

I was staying at a hotel on 48th Street and Seventh Avenue but such is my compulsion to repeat experiences that I trudged across town and went to Delectica. It took about forty minutes to get there. They still had the donuts but I recognised none of the staff. I ordered a cappuccino. When it was prepared I looked in horror: it was like a Knickerbocker Glory or something, with foam piled high like cream in a tall glass.

'What on *earth* is that?' I demanded.

'A cappuccino,' she said proudly.

'Well, that's where you're wrong,' I said. 'It's not a cappuccino. It's an abominaccino! If you knew how much this place meant to me . . .' I couldn't go on. I felt so angry and so sorry for myself that I stormed out of the door and into the street, where I began asking people, randomly, if they knew any cafés where they stocked Donut Plant donuts, getting myself into more and more of a frenzy as I did so. Obviously most people had not heard of Donut Plant donuts and the few who had heard of them did not know of a café that stocked them but eventually someone said that they thought Orin's Daily Roast stocked Donut Plant donuts and he thought that there was a branch of Orin's in Grand Central Station. And so, like a commuter hurrying for a train, I made my way to Grand Central Station. Finding Grand Central Station was easy enough, but finding Orin's Daily Roast within the vast station complex was extremely difficult. Eventually I found it, saw it, saw a line of people queuing up, saw that although it was essentially just a stall, they did indeed stock Donut Plant donuts but that only one vanilla donut remained. I joined the queue. If anyone had taken the last donut I would have pleaded with them and put my case – 'If you knew what I have been through this morning . . .' If, after pleading with them to take something else, they had refused, I would have snatched the donut from their hand and started chewing on it frantically, but no one wanted this last donut and so I ordered it together with a cappuccino and although I had to drink my cappuccino out of a paper cup, standing, like a commuter who has missed the train he had been hurrying for, I was grateful, in the circumstances, to have got a coffee and a donut at all.

Thereafter, whenever I was in New York, I checked online at the Donut Plant website to find a Donut Plant outlet close to wherever I was staying. When I was staying at the Maritime in Chelsea for a week the best bet seemed Joe's Art of Coffee on Waverly Place. A fifteen-minute walk, often in terrible weather, but it was well worth it. The coffee was amazing, they had the donuts, though it was often touch and go whether they had *enough* donuts. On two occasions there was only one donut left and, as had happened at Orin's Daily Roast, I found myself in a state of great tension, waiting to see if someone would take the last donut, girding my loins to say, 'Excuse me, sir/madam, but I wonder if there is anything else that takes your fancy because, frankly, I *must* have that donut.' It never came to that; miraculously, there was always at least one donut left for me, and the combination of donut and excellent coffee was bliss, even better, in a way, than Delectica, because unlike Delectica this was a cool and atmospheric place in a fun neighbourhood. I went there so often in the course of my week-long stay that I took out a loyalty card and, on my last morning, my loyalty was rewarded with a free coffee: a perfect example of Nietzsche's ideal of the brief habit.

My last trip to New York was nothing like as happy. I was staying at a hotel on 55th Street and Broadway, very near the N and R subway lines, so I took the train down to Joe's Art of Coffee on 13th Street near Union Square. They had Donut Plant donuts all right but not the ones I like, only the more exotic flavours and so, thinking quickly – I had a hectic schedule, was pressed for time, should not really have been schlepping down all this way just for a coffee and a donut – I decided to walk back to the Waverly Place branch. I got there and it was the same story except it was even worse than the same story because in addition to not having the donuts I wanted the coffee was too milky and the donut I opted for – coconut glaze, filled with coconut cream – was actually a bit horrible and as I sat there chewing I found it hard to fathom what could lead anyone to abandon the basic donut, the default donut from which all others are derived, in favour of the more elaborate versions which may appeal to some tastes. To be honest, I made my way to the subway with my tail between my legs, wishing, at some level, that I was not forced to live this way, was not compelled to seek out things I have decided I like in the face of terrible odds. Sitting on the clanging subway car as it clanged and hurtled back to midtown I reflected on the way that wherever we live we are always compelled to repeat the same thing over and over, that at some level, perhaps every level, all we ever do is trudge up and down Effra Road and that whatever we are talking about, whether it is something pleasurable (like finding the supreme donut) or something onerous (like taking the subway or Tube) when we talk about life we might just as well talk about trudging up and down Effra Road, irrespective of where we are in the world.

The story could have ended there – I intended ending it there – on a note of glum resignation, but to present a truly global picture of how things stand mention must be made of a recent trip to Tokyo. It seems to me that we are always trying to re-create our particular ideal of a city in whichever actual city we happen to find ourselves. Before going to Tokyo I remembered reading, on the Donut Plant website, that they had opened a branch in Tokyo, not a concession in the sense of a place where Donut Plant donuts cooked in New York were available for purchase in Tokyo but an actual donut-producing Donut Plant. As in New York these donuts were available at a number of locations throughout the sprawling megalopolis that is Tokyo. We were staying at the Peninsula in Marunouchi and by studying the Donut Plant website carefully we saw that the nearest location was a branch of Dean & DeLuca, a mere fifteen minutes' walk away. There were other reasons for going to Japan, of course. There were ancient temples and carp ponds, there were geishas and cherry blossom, there were incredible feats of retail architecture and there was the sci-fi neon of Shinjuku, but at the back of my mind, in contrast to the untranslatable otherness of Japan, was the familiar prospect of Donut Plant donuts, which, far from being reminders of home, were, for most of the year – the part of the year spent in London – site-specific New York treats, edible emblems of every-thing that New York was and London was not. So that what I was looking for was not *London*-in-Tokyo but *New York*-in-Tokyo. Ryszard Kapuściński claimed that whereas in the past an encounter with 'the Other' meant an encounter between a European (white) and an easterner (non-white), increasingly there would be contacts between these Others and *other* Others (Indians and South Americans, say, or Chinese and Africans). That, it seemed to me, was what we had here. The donut as Other (i.e. not England) being consumed in Dean & DeLuca (the quintessential upmarket New York deli) in a part of Tokyo (the quintessential urban Other) that looked incredibly like downtown Chicago. I am not quite sure what I mean by this, am worried slightly that I am using 'Other' in the sense of 'Same', but it doesn't matter because we went kind of insane in Tokyo. Because it was not New York (home of the donut), because it was a kind of double treat (a place where one did not expect to find donuts *where donuts were miraculously available*), my wife and I ordered two donuts each and two coffees each, each and every day. We would sit there with vanilla ice stuck to our faces and noses, smiling and chewing. In a sense this was everything that was bad about the homogenising effect of globalisation, an upmarket equivalent of finding a McDonald's in every city on earth, or a branch of Patisserie Valerie's in every area of London, but the thing is, the point I want to emphasise, is that I love donuts and I wouldn't mind if there were a Donut Plant outlet on every city block in London – the world would be a better place.

We arrived at Dean & DeLuca at ten on the dot every day. One day it wasn't open, would not be open until eleven, because, we discovered, this was a Japanese national holiday. We stood outside. There was nowhere to sit but there was a keen wind which made standing even more irksome. There was nothing to do but wait. We were in a pedestrian version of the London double-bind whereby if we walked back to the hotel – and we had already begun to find this walk onerous; in less than five days Naka Dori had taken on some of the qualities of Effra Road, stroll had turned to trudge – we would have had to set out again the moment we got back there. So we had pure dead time to kill. We were in this strange, strangely familiar city, and we stood there as time congealed around us on the nearly deserted, litter-less street. We stood and waited and it was like being one of the undead, because whatever we thought of doing, there was nothing to do and so we just stood there in the keen wind, wishing time would pass, wanting one thing and one thing only: for time to pass, to get out of the wind and into Dean & DeLuca so that we could order our donuts and coffees and sit down, eating and drinking them in this distant part of the world that, at this moment, at the moment which was not yet at hand but which was drawing closer at an agonisingly slow pace, contained everything that we wanted from a city, namely *donuts*. Eventually Dean & DeLuca opened, we scoffed our donuts and swilled our coffees and then, when we had finished scoffing and swilling, walked back to the hotel, noticing, as we had failed to on the way down (I was blind to everything except the prospect of donuts), the Japanese flag – the red circle on a field of white – flying from many buildings. It seemed that although there were many nice flags in the world none was nicer than the Japanese flag even though, when I was growing up, reading about Japanese atrocities in the Pacific War, it had seemed a symbol of pure evil. It did not seem like that at all now; now it became a symbol of the healing potential of the donut, of a world community of donut-lovers living in peace and harmony, bound together by the vision and ambition of a Czech immigrant who went to New York, opened his Donut Plant and then forged a donut empire, extending from New York to Tokyo while regrettably bypassing London, where we still have to make do with croissants that are like stale buns, so that at times the whole of the London seems like nothing else so much as an interminable extension of Effra Road.

2009

Of Course

I'd only known my girlfriend for a fortnight when I popped the question. I say 'girlfriend' but that puts it too strongly; we could have been in the midst of a series of brief encounters. For the sake of complete accuracy, then, I told Rebecca, the woman that I had recently started sleeping with, that I had a *very important* – in fact a *life-determining* – question to ask her.

'So can I ask you?' I said.

'Yes.'

'OK. Ready?'

'Yes.'

'Do you want to go to Burning Man with me?'

This was in June 2000. Burning Man, the annual freak-out in the Black Rock Desert, takes place in the week leading up to the Labor Day weekend but because we would be coming from England and because Rebecca, at that time, had a senior job in publishing and because going to Burning Man is a huge palaver and involves months of planning and commitment, we needed to get on the case immediately. She didn't hesitate.

'Of course,' she said. It was one of the great *of courses* of all time because although I had talked about Burning Man pretty well non-stop from the moment we met, although I always turned every other topic of conversation round to Burning Man and was interested in almost nothing *but* Burning Man, Rebecca, prior to meeting me, had not been part of any of the scenes that bring Europeans within the gravitational tug of Black Rock City. She'd never been a raver, wasn't part of the trance scene, and wasn't even into night-clubbing in London.

The very short version of what resulted from that 'of course' is as follows: we went to Burning Man and, within a few days of getting back, arranged to get married as soon as bureaucratically possible (12 October 2000).

We didn't want to wait and I'm glad we didn't because I hate waiting. I am temperamentally incapable of waiting. Waiting for me is torture. I've spent too much of my life waiting and I can't wait another second for *anything*, but in this context – the context of the narrative of how we couldn't and didn't wait to get married – it's necessary, well, not to *wait* exactly but at least go right back to the beginning, to the night we met.

It was at a party thrown by the art magazine *Modern Painters*, at the Lisson Gallery, for the launch of the new issue to which I had contributed an evangelical piece about the art of Burning Man. It was a nice party with a very relaxed vibe. By this I mean that, in addition to the expected bottles of red and white wine there was a huge and varied quantity of beer. There was such an endless flow of beer that thirsty guests could relax in the knowledge that it was not going to run out. I was also relaxed because I wasn't looking for a girlfriend. I wasn't dating anyone at the time but I wasn't exuding the off-putting air of celibate desperation that has often sabotaged my attempts to get a girlfriend and which, in turn, has made me even more desperate to get one. I was, as they say in the submarine world, at periscope depth. Although I wasn't looking for a girlfriend, I had a look around to reassure myself that there really were no gorgeous women here and that I could concentrate on doing what I had come to do, which was to drink a lot of beer. But then, as I scanned the room, beer in hand, already looking forward to following up that first beer with a second, third and probably an eighth and ninth, I realised that there *was* a gorgeous woman in the room. She had long dark hair, eyes like the Madonna; she was tall, thin, and was not smoking cigarettes. If she had been smoking cigarettes the spell would have been broken and I would have concentrated on swilling huge quantities of beer, drinking up a storm and going home. But this very beautiful woman with long hair and eyes like the Madonna was not smoking. She was wearing stylish London clothes. I don't really know about these things. Especially back then, before I married the woman wearing them, I didn't. At that stage it was funky trance-wear that caught my eye, but she still looked nice in her modest and expensive-looking London anti-trance wear. I established all of this on a number of sweeps through the room but there was never any chance to speak with her because she was always speaking with someone else and although I was introduced to many people in the early stages of the evening and often hovered in her vicinity, hoping to be introduced by virtue of geographical proximity, it never quite happened. During one of these protracted hovers she did glance over at me, though, and this was all the enticement and incitement I needed to speak to her even though we had not been introduced.

'Have we met before?' I said.

'No, but I know who you are,' she replied, very courteously.

To which I replied, in my mock-pompous way, 'Geoff Dyer, of course.'

'Rebecca Wilson,' she said. We shook hands. She was there with a bespectacled guy called Mark, who didn't know I was doing my mock-pompous thing. He thought I was just doing my pompous thing. As a result, I learned subsequently, he thought I was 'somewhat of an asshole'. I also learned that, as I had been hovering and generally waiting for a chance to speak to her, Rebecca had said to Mark that she had fancied me. To which Mark, who is gay and from Maryland, said, 'You don't want to bother with a skinny, grey-haired old thing like that!'

It was a fine example of the myriad blessings of heterosexuality. From this admittedly small sample we conclude that I had reached the age where I was no longer attractive to men (if I ever had been) but was still attractive to women. It's even possible that although I was in undoubted physical decline I was more attractive to women than I used to be because I was no longer giving off the desperate air that had been a feature of life throughout my twenties and, if we are being utterly frank, much of my thirties. The lack of desperation manifested itself in my being comfortable about an inability, as we say in England, to 'chat up' women. I had never been able to do this but I had only recently given up trying to and even if I was, at some level, trying to do exactly that, it didn't feel like *chatting up* a beautiful woman with eyes like the Madonna; it felt like chatting to a very nice clever person who happened to be beautiful. I slightly worry about this in retrospect. Rebecca has a tendency to get cornered by bores at parties. People blah on at her because she is such a good listener. I wonder if I blahed on. And if I did blah on, what did I blah on about? Myself, probably, and Burning Man. It is also possible that an over-eagerness to appear intelligent manifested itself in a tendency to express vehement opinions, of a generally negative bent. In practice this meant I *denounced* people, especially internationally successful authors with high and, in my view, undeserved reputations. To compensate I exaggerated the achievements of under-rated writers whose work deserved a far larger audience. We could easily have become deadlocked in this, but I happened to mention a terrific novel I had just read, published by the company Rebecca worked for, called *Reservation Road* by John Burnham Schwartz. And it turned out not only that Rebecca shared my high opinion of this book, but that she was actually John's editor. She had *acquired* the book. Yippee! We were in agreement and we were chatting away like mad, having a good old chat, creating positive vibrations and everything, and although I didn't know that Mark was gay, I was starting to sense that he was just a friend rather than a boyfriend and that he was no longer thinking I was *somewhat of an asshole*. I was right about this: by the end of the evening, Rebecca told me later, he thought I was a *total* asshole.

Although we had been having a good old chat Rebecca said she had to be leaving. There was no need to ask for her phone number. I knew she worked for Weidenfeld & Nicolson.

'Perhaps,' I said, 'perhaps I could call you there.'

'You know where I am,' she said. In a way I was relieved that she left when she did because although I had enjoyed speaking with her I had been somewhat on my best behaviour, and now that she had gone I could start drinking up a storm and having the skinful that I had refrained from having in the course of our stimulating chat.

* * *

I called her on Tuesday – which, she later told me, was exactly when she thought I would call if I was going to call (which she knew I would). I was forty-two at the time and in some ways I was quite wise, wise enough to know that it is no good trying to set up a romantic encounter with someone in publishing in the guise of a semi-professional meeting (a lunch, say, to talk about forthcoming books). So I phrased my question very carefully.

'I'd love to see you one evening,' I said, emphasising but not quite italicising the 'love'. 'If that's possible,' I added after a telling pause.

'Yes,' she said, and then, after an equally telling pause, 'that's possible.' The reply was every bit as clever as my question and similarly encoded. By saying 'That's possible' she was also intimating that *anything* was possible. There then followed the part of the conversation I had been dreading, so totally dreading, in fact, that I'd eventually phoned without even being sure how to address it. This was the problem of what to do on our first date. The worst thing you can do on a first date is to do what people nearly always do on a first date: go out to dinner. I couldn't face that, couldn't face any aspect of it. I couldn't face the tacit compatibility check of the whole evening and I couldn't face the look of disappointment on her face when I suggested – as I knew I shouldn't, as I was determined not to, but as I knew I would – either that we split the bill or that she pick up the tab and claim it back on expenses. Anything was better than that, than going out to dinner and running through the list of who likes what, but I wasn't sure what to do instead. One possibility, one which I hesitated broaching, was that she came down to visit me at my flat in Brighton on the south coast. Although I kept on a room in a flat in London I mainly lived in Brighton, in the greatest apartment I will ever own. It was on the fourth and fifth floors of a building on First Avenue, I said. The top floor was one big chill-out room. One whole wall of this room was a window with doors leading out onto the epic terrace. If it was sunny the distinction between indoors and outdoors dissolved, I said. We discussed various possibilities about what to do but since Rebecca was busy until Saturday, and since people from London always like to visit Brighton, and since

I had talked up my flat so much, I said, 'How about coming down to Brighton on Saturday?'

And she said yes.

Saturday was grey and cold, but did I care? Yes, I cared. I was pissed off. I was really pissed off. I had foreseen a day out on my terrace with the sun beating down, drinking fresh fruit juices and hanging out as though we were in South Beach or LA. Instead, I was looking out at the greyness pressing against the window. Then the phone rang. It was Rebecca. As soon as I heard her voice I knew she had got cold feet and was calling to cancel but no, it was just that she had missed her train, and was going to be late.

I went to the station to meet her. Her hair was long and dark. She was wearing a loose-fitting Japanese shirt and, in keeping with this oriental touch, we greeted each other by pressing the palms of our hands together and bowing – something I'd been affecting since going to Thailand earlier in the year and which she had picked up from spending time in India. It was a nice beginning, ironic and genuine in equal measure without being genuine – or ironic – at all.

'I'm so sorry I'm late,' she said, looking and sounding really quite mortified.

'That's OK,' I said.

'I hate being late.'

'Me too,' I said. 'I mean, it doesn't matter that you were late today but in general I deplore lateness.'

'Me too!' she said.

'I love punctuality so much. I'm not meaning to reproach you but I do love it.'

'I love it too!' she insisted.

'Then why were you late?' I pleaded.

'Have I spoiled everything?'

'Yes. The day is ruined.'

'Shall I just go straight back to London?'

'Shall we have a coffee and talk about it?' I said. 'See if we can salvage something from a day that has already been comprehensively ruined?'

'I'd like to try,' she said.

This conversation pretty much set the tone for our entire subsequent relationship. We've spent hundreds of evenings since then, talking nonsense like this about one thing or another, but, at the same time, we were being quite honest: the fact that we are both so uptight about punctuality makes us feel totally relaxed together.

From the station we went to a café, where we ordered two cappuccinos '*without* chocolate on the top' and sent them back because they arrived *with* chocolate on the top. Even when they were re-made, minus the offending chocolate, the cappuccinos weren't up to much and we had a frank discussion about cappuccinos in general and I blahed on about the cappuccino situation in Brighton in particular. With our cappuccinos we each had a croissant. I say 'croissant' but really they were just dreary croissant-shaped buns. I put raspberry jam on mine, to liven it up a bit. After that we walked down to the depressing seafront. Brighton is a depressing place. It's especially depressing if the weather's bad and it's even more depressing if it's grey in June when it's meant to be sunny and blue and you have just drunk the kind of scalding bucket of foam that passes for a cappuccino in these parts. We walked along the promenade and looked out at the sea.

'*Oed' und leer das Meer*,' I said, and then, after a pause: 'Wagner. *Tristan und Isolde*, of course. Quoted by T.S. Eliot in *The Waste Land*.'

'You really *are* an asshole, aren't you?' said Rebecca. 'It's that "of course" that I really hate.'

'I was sort of joking,' I said. 'Of course.'

'I wasn't,' she said, slipping her arm into mine.

It started drizzling soon after this and then, as happens, the drizzle became rain. There was nothing to do except go back to my amazing flat. Rebecca said how much she loved my chill-out room with its lilac walls, UV lights, incense, statues of the Buddha and its pervasive *I've just got back from Thailand where I did nothing but get stoned for a month* look. Later she said it was like a cross between a vegetarian café at a festival and a night club, but that was only after we were married (but before the divergences in our tastes in interior decoration had resulted in some quite brutal arguments). I made risotto –

the one thing I know how to cook well. We ate the risotto upstairs
in this huge chill-out room, one wall of which was entirely composed
of windows against which the rain lashed relentlessly.

It was late afternoon. If it had been sunny the sun, at this time of
day, would have been pouring into the room, flooding everything
with gold light. Instead, as Rebecca said, it was 'like being on a trawler
in the North Sea'. It was still fun, though, especially after we'd had
a couple of bong hits. This was a slight gamble: we could have got
all weirded out, both by the fact that we were up here in my flat in
Brighton and hardly knew each other and by the way the weather
was so bad on a day when I had so wanted it to be good. As it
happened the grass made us feel even more relaxed and I stopped
getting bummed out about the rain and the lashing wind. We were
sitting on the sofa together, listening to Hariprasad Chaurasia play
the Raga Puriya Kalyan ('Strictly speaking, it is of course an early-
evening raga,' I said).

When I was younger I regularly used to try to sleep with women
before I really wanted to. I would make passes at them not because
I wanted to but because I felt I ought to. If Rebecca and I had gone
out to dinner we would either have had to say goodbye after dinner
and drinks or we could have agreed prematurely to go home together.
As it was, like this, we could just listen to music and chat about
cappuccinos or me or Burning Man until gradually, without any
nudging or coaxing, our hands touched and we were kissing.

Rebecca stayed that night and the next. On Monday she had to
go to work. I remained in Brighton for the whole of that week and
on Friday she came down again.

'You're even more beautiful than I remembered,' I said as I opened
the door and saw her again.

We didn't actually go on a date until the week after that, when we
went to the launch party for Will Self's new novel in London. It was
in Rebecca's flat in London, later that night, that I asked her about
Burning Man and she said, 'Of course.'

I knew we would have a good time there and I also knew that
Burning Man is a parable and test. The previous year I had gone with
my then-girlfriend and we had known within days that we would

split up. I'd kept wishing I was there alone, partly because of all the sexual opportunities that weren't coming my way, but mainly because of the issue of responsibility. I was left doing everything, taking care of our camp, making sure things didn't get blown away, while my girlfriend went running around the *playa* and generally going as crazy as a kid in a sweet shop. We both became total Burning Man converts but we also knew we'd split up. We duly did so the following January, a few days after going to see a film called *Lies* at the ICA. At the time I did not attach any significance to this. That was just the way it happened.

Rebecca and I flew to San Francisco on Friday, 25 August. We hired a van, bought a couple of cheap bikes and tons of food and water. There was so much to take care of and sort out in those few days prior to going to Burning Man that what we mainly looked forward to doing once we got there was sleeping.

There was a slightly strange light in the sky as Rebecca and I headed north from Reno towards Gerlach late on Tuesday afternoon, the day after the festival had started. It wasn't as bright as it should have been and I had to grip the wheel tight because our van was being thumped by strong winds. We arrived in Black Rock City after dark and couldn't find the Canadian friends we had arranged to camp with – but we did find some friends from San Francisco. We spent the first night at their camp, sleeping in the back of our van, and the next morning decided to stay put. We also decided not to bother pitching our tent: it was so cold and windy that we were better off continuing to sleep in our van. A good decision, it turned out, since 2000 will be remembered by everyone who went as the year Black Rock City was assailed by terrible winds and dust storms. We spent a lot of time just hunkered down in our friends' yurt or cowering in the back of our van, feeling it buffeted by these gale-force dust storms. We also spent a lot of time *rummaging* in our van. *A place for everything and everything in its place* – that was our motto even if we rarely managed to abide by it. We were always looking for things – a can opener or a pair of socks – which, I insisted in tones of absolute bewilderment, 'I had in my hand two seconds earlier.' We did other things, fun things, but it's the rummaging I mainly remember – the rummaging and the weather, which had conspired against us on our first day in Brighton and which was conspiring against us on our first time together at Burning Man. To be honest, although it was great being at Burning Man it was also disappointing. It was windy and dusty and cold. One night it even rained. Our bike tyres became so clogged with mud the wheels wouldn't go round and we had to drag them back to camp.

'It's like being at fucking Glastonbury,' I whined. The struggle to survive is part of the experience of Burning Man and I can see how, for people from sunny California, it *is* fun but, as I told anyone who would listen, we *came* from a rainy, windy place with poor visibility and I really didn't need to come all the way to Nevada – to the Nevada *Desert*, what's more – to experience more of the same. We had a great time but we could have had a better time, which meant we had a terrible time because I spent all my time thinking how much better it would have been if the weather had been better. I cannot make the best of a bad job, put a brave face on things or settle for second best. Anything less than the apotheosis of whatever it is I am hoping to experience will be a crushing disappointment. This is an item of faith with me and, although this attitude has been a terrible burden that has, in some ways, blighted my life by making imperfect situations twenty times worse, it has also – as we will shortly see – stood me in good stead in other respects.

From time to time Rebecca has outbreaks of something like herpes around her eyes. She gets these tiny ulcers on the inside of her eyelids and it is agony for her. One morning, soon after we had started sleeping together, she woke up with her left eye swollen shut like a boxer's. It was the saddest thing, especially since her eyes are so lovely. A week after getting back to London from Burning Man I fell ill. At first I had a sore throat and flu but within days I was iller than I had ever been in my life. My throat and tongue were covered in thirty or forty white ulcers. I couldn't eat, couldn't swallow, couldn't even get out of bed. My head felt like it was going to implode and explode at the same time. The doctor said that herpes was the most likely diagnosis. I moped around in Rebecca's flat all day, whimpering and waiting for her to come home with soothing treats – juices, books, CDs – in the evening.

Fortunately we had already done the paperwork for getting married. We were doing it as cheaply as possible. No expense had not been spared. Two days before our wedding I went to a literary prize-giving at the Reform Club, where I ate a lunch that looked like it had been sitting around since Graham Greene and Anthony Powell had dined there before the war. I'd just gotten over this herpes-type thing and now I had food-poisoning. As a result, on the day of our lack-lustre wedding, I looked like death warmed up. Rebecca looked gorgeous, of course. We didn't invite our parents, just two friends (one of whom was that asshole Mark). We went to the registry office on the bus and came back home on the bus after a lunch that Rebecca was persuaded – after some initial reluctance – to claim back on expenses. Although I still felt shitty from the food poisoning and the herpes it didn't matter because we had at least succeeded in getting married as quickly and cheaply as possible.

Aside from its amazing cheapness the only unusual thing about our wedding was an agreement we made – a private addendum to the regular vows – whereby I would be free to write anything I wanted about us and our relationship, irrespective of whether it was true.

Obviously we got married in great haste but were we *rash* as well as hasty? No, partly because a week at Burning Man is the equivalent of a year of normal life, and partly because this apparent hastiness was actually founded on a long patience. One of the most important qualities in life is to hold out for happiness. I've known plenty of people who were incapable of really holding out for their own happiness. They've made-do, settled for the next best thing, made the best of a less than perfect job. I'd had lots of girlfriends, had even, on occasions, been on the brink of making long-term commitments, but always at some point I was selfish enough to jump ship. Either I would find someone who could be everything to me – or I'd continue as I was, quite happily, on the serial monogamy treadmill with its interludes of loneliness, involuntary celibacy and total despair. In a world with however many millions of women in it, it didn't seem too much to hold out for someone who was beautiful, funny, sexy, clever, kind, punctual, with nice manners and good moral bearing. I mention beautiful first because, for me, that was essential if I were to make any kind of commitment or achieve any kind of relaxation. I *had to have* a beautiful girlfriend. Otherwise, if I went to a party, I'd always be wishing I was with someone more beautiful. Because of this obsession with beauty I'd often had girlfriends who, though beautiful, weren't friends at all. Now I had a beautiful *wife* who was my friend and who was clever and kind and everything else. So getting married actually felt like nothing else so much as a liberation. It didn't feel like settling down – which I've never had any urge to do – and it didn't feel like it required any conscious effort on the part of either Rebecca or I. We can't even remember who asked who. It was all like a continuation of that first afternoon when we were sitting on the sofa listening to an early-evening raga and the next minute we were kissing – and then we were married.

I've often noticed that certain things that happen in life – often the things that are most important – seem to occur without your conscious participation. It's almost as if you are oddly passive, that things just fall into place. Of course you are not completely passive but whereas life often feels like you're riding a bike with the brakes on – every attempt at progress is met with some kind of resistance – there are instances when you are scarcely aware of having to exert yourself. Destiny is not handed to you on a plate but sometimes the effort normally demanded by life is replaced by a feeling of ease and grace. You get it in tennis during those strange interludes when you find yourself making strokes in such a way that the distinction between what you have been trying to do and what you are actually doing evaporates and you are just . . . *playing tennis*. It happens in writing when the words, which have been coming only grudgingly and haltingly, begin to flow. In both circumstances you know that you are doing it right even though you can't say exactly what it is that you're doing differently. This is how getting married felt – like doing something right without being sure why. For me, this was confirmed by a little incident that occurred when we'd been married for a couple of months.

Six months before meeting Rebecca I was in the lingerie department of Fenwick's on Bond Street in London with my then-girlfriend (with whom I'd first gone to Burning Man). While she was in the changing room, trying on underwear, a woman came into the shop. Tall; beautiful eyes, long hair. I couldn't take my eyes off her. It wasn't just that she was beautiful, she transfixed me totally. My heart went out to her. There was a smouldering of desire – what kind of underwear was she buying? – but mainly I felt the familiar melancholy of longing. I sort of fell in love with her then and there but knew I would never see her again. She seemed to be in a hurry. I watched her pay and leave. She didn't see me. End of story.

Time passed. A million other things happened, most of them forgotten. I broke up with my girlfriend around this time and then, six months later, met, fell in love with and married Rebecca. And then one morning I woke up and realised, immediately and with absolute certainty, that the woman lying next to me, Rebecca, my wife, was the woman I had seen that day in Fenwick's.

After leaving Fenwick's my girlfriend and I had gone to see a Korean S&M film at the ICA . . . I couldn't remember the name of the film but, yes, there it was in my diary for 22 January: 'Saw *Lies* @ ICA.' We'd walked down to Pall Mall in bright afternoon sunlight that ricocheted off the windows of buses and cars. The branches of trees were stark against the blue sky. We arrived at the film with several minutes to spare and killed time in the bookshop. All of which means we must have been in Fenwick's between two and two-thirty. Rebecca checked *her* diary. Yes, she had been in Fenwick's that day, at about that time – and she *was* in a rush, her car was parked on a yellow – buying underwear because, later that day, she was flying off to see her lover in New York.

So it was true: I'd completely forgotten that first glimpse of her – but I had never quite forgotten it. The memory developed as I slept, its colours becoming deeper, more distinct: the ghost of a dream, but permanent, lovely.

2005

Sources and Acknowledgements

'Jacques Henri Lartigue and The Discovery of India': a very different version was broadcast on *Night Waves*, BBC Radio 3, in 2004.

'Ruth Orkin's "VE Day"' and 'Lorrie Moore: *A Gate at the Stairs*' first appeared in the *Observer*. Thanks to Robert Yates and William Skidelsky.

'Richard Avedon' was first published in *Richard Avedon: Photographs 1946–2004*, edited by Michael Juul Holm (Louisiana Museum of Modern Art, Humlebaek, 2007).

'Larry Burrows', 'Joel Sternfeld's Utopian Visions', 'Miroslav Tichý', 'Idris Khan', 'Richard Ford: *The Lay of the Land*', 'Denis Johnson: *Tree of Smoke*', 'Ian McEwan: *Atonement*', 'Ryszard Kapuściński's African Life', 'The 2004 Olympics', 'What Will Survive of Us . . .', 'Reader's Block', a version of 'The Moral Art of War' and 'My Life as a Gatecrasher' all first appeared in the *Guardian*. Thanks to Lisa Allardice, Claire Armistead, Paul Laity and Katharine Viner.

'Enrique Metinides' combines the foreword to *Enrique Metinides*, (Ridinghouse/The Photographers Gallery, London, 2003) and a piece first published in the *Daily Telegraph*. Thanks to Thomas Dane and Kate Bush.

'Jacob Holdt's America' was published in *Faith, Hope & Love: Jacob Holdt's America*, edited by Michael Juul Holm and Mette Marcus (Louisiana Museum of Modern Art, Humlebaek, 2009).

'Martin Parr's *Small World*' was first published as the introduction to the revised edition of *Small World* (Dewi Lewis Publishing, Stockport, 2007).

'Alec Soth: Rivverrun' was first published in the catalogue *Deutsche*

Borse Photography Prize 2006 (The Photographers Gallery, London, 2006). Thanks to Stefanie Braun.

'Michael Ackerman' was first published in *ArtReview*.

'Trent Parke' was first published in *Tank*. Thanks to Emily Moore.

A short version of 'Saving Grace: Todd Hido' first appeared in *OjodePez* 13; the version reprinted here was published as the introduction to *Ram's Motel* (Nazraeli Press, Portland, Oregon, 2010). Thanks to Aaron Schuman.

'The American Sublime' was first published in *Prospect*. Thanks to David Goodhart.

'The Awakening of Stones: Rodin' was first published in *Apropos. Rodin*, with photographs by Jennifer Gough-Cooper (Thames & Hudson, London, 2006). Thanks to Thomas Neurath.

'Turner and Memory' was first published in *Tate Etc*. Thanks to Simon Grant.

'D.H. Lawrence: *Sons and Lovers*' was first published as the introduction to the Modern Library edition (New York, 1999).

'D.H. Lawrence: *Lady Chatterley's Lover*' was first published as the introduction to the Signet Classic edition (New York, 2003). Thanks to Tracy Bernstein.

'F. Scott Fitzgerald: *The Beautiful and Damned*' was first published as the introduction to the Penguin Modern Classics edition (London, 2004). Thanks to Simon Winder.

'F. Scott Fitzgerald: *Tender is the Night*' was first published in *The American Scholar*, Spring 2001. Thanks to Anne Fadiman and Natasha Wimmer.

'James Salter: *The Hunters* and *Light Years*' was originally posted on the penguin.com website. Thanks to Maria Teresa Boffo.

'Alan Hollinghurst: *The Line of Beauty*' was first published in the *Daily Telegraph*.

'Tobias Wolff: *Old School*' and a much shorter version of 'W.G. Sebald, Bombing and Thomas Bernhard' first appeared in the *L.A. Weekly*. Thanks to Tom Christie.

A longer version of 'W.G. Sebald, Bombing and Thomas Bernhard' was published in *Pretext 9*, Spring/Summer 2004. Thanks to Jon Cook and Katri Skala.

'Don DeLillo: *Point Omega*' was first published in the *New York Times Book Review*. Thanks to Gregory Cowles.

'The Goncourt Journals' was first published as a foreword to Edmond and Jules de Goncourt, *Pages from the Goncourt Journals* (NYRB Classics, New York, 2007). Thanks to Edwin Frank.

'Rebeccca West: *Black Lamb and Grey Falcon*' was first published as the introduction to *Black Lamb and Grey Falcon* (Canongate, Edinburgh, 2006). Thanks to Jamie Byng.

'John Cheever: *The Journals*' was first published as the introduction to the Vintage Classics edition (London, 2009). Thanks to Liz Foley.

Parts of 'Is Jazz Dead?' were originally published in *The Independent Magazine*, the *Observer* and the *Guardian*. This version first appeared, in Italian, in a magazine whose title now escapes me.

'Editions of Contemporary Me' was first published in *Horizons Touched: The Music of ECM*, edited by Steve Lake and Paul Griffiths (Granta, London, 2007).

'Fabulous Clothes' was first published in *Vogue*. Thanks to Alexandra Shulman and Jo Craven.

'Sex and Hotels' was originally posted on the nerve.com website. Thanks to Susan Dominus.

'On the Roof' was first published in *Granta*. Thanks to Liz Jobey.

'Something Didn't Happen' was first published in the *Fire* volume of *Ox-Tales*, edited by Mark Ellingham (Oxfam/Profile, London, 2009).

'Otherwise Known as the Human Condition' was published in slightly different form as 'Inhabiting' in the anthology *Restless Cities*, edited by Matthew Beaumont and Gregory Dart (Verso, London, 2010). Thanks to Tom Penn.

'Of Course' was first published in the anthology *Committed*, edited by Chris Knutsen and David Kuhn (Bloomsbury, New York, 2005).

'Regarding the Achievement of Others', 'Sacked' and 'On Being an Only Child' are previously unpublished.

I would like to thank my agent, Victoria Hobbs, and Francis Bickmore, Jamie Byng, Lorraine McCann and Norah Perkins at Canongate, for their help in turning this collection into a book. Special thanks, as always, to my wife, Rebecca.

The author and publisher are grateful for the permission to reproduce the following works:

Adonis. 'The Funeral of New York', from *The Pages of Day and Night* (translated by Samuel Hazo), The Marlboro Press/Northwestern University Press, 1994. Reprinted with the permission of Northwestern University Press.

Auden, W.H. 'I Am Not a Camera', from *The Collected Poems*, Faber & Faber, 1991. Reprinted with the permission of Faber & Faber.

Auden, W.H. 'In Time of War', from *The English Auden*, Faber & Faber, 1977. Reprinted with the permission of Faber & Faber.

Doty, Mark. 'Couture', from *Atlantis*, Jonathan Cape, 1996. Reprinted with the permission of The Random House Group Ltd.

Hofmann, Michael. 'Guanajato Two Times', from *Approximately Nowhere*, Faber & Faber, 1999. Reprinted with the permission of Faber & Faber.

Larkin, Philip. 'Going, Going' from *Collected Poems*, Faber & Faber, 2003. Reprinted with the permission of Faber & Faber.

Paterson, Don. Extract from *The Blind Eye*, Faber & Faber, 2007. Reprinted with the permission of Faber & Faber.

Stevens, Wallace. 'American Sublime' and 'Like Decorations in a Nigger Cemetery', from *Collected Poems*, Faber & Faber, 2006. Reprinted with the permission of Faber & Faber.

Index

CANON▌▌GATE.tv

CHANNELLING GREAT CONTENT

WATCH
INTERVIEWS, TRAILERS, ANIMATIONS, READINGS, GIGS

LISTEN
AUDIO BOOKS, PODCASTS, MUSIC, PLAYLISTS

READ
CHAPTERS, EXCERPTS, SNEAK PEEKS, RECOMMENDATIONS

DISCOVER
BLOGS, EVENTS, NEWS, CREATIVE PARTNERS

SHOP
LIMITED EDITIONS, BUNDLES, SECRET SALES